The Traffic in Hierarchy

The Traffic in Hierarchy

Masculinity and Its Others in Buddhist Burma

Ward Keeler

University of Hawai'i Press
Honolulu

Publication of this book has been assisted by a grant from the President's
Office of the University of Texas at Austin.

© 2017 University of Hawai'i Press
All rights reserved
Printed in the United States of America

22 21 20 19 18 17   6 5 4 3 2 1

Library of Congress Cataloging-in-Publication Data

Names: Keeler, Ward, author.
Title: The traffic in hierarchy : masculinity and its others in
Buddhist Burma / Ward Keeler.
Description: Honolulu : University of Hawai'i Press, [2017] |
Includes bibliographical references and index.
Identifiers: LCCN 2016058306 | ISBN 9780824865948 (cloth ; alk. paper)
Subjects: LCSH: Social status—Burma. | Buddhism—Social aspects—Burma. |
Masculinity—Social aspects—Burma. | Burma—Social life and customs.
Classification: LCC HM821 .K44 2017 | DDC 305—dc23
LC record available at https://lccn.loc.gov/2016058306

University of Hawai'i Press books are printed on acid-free
paper and meet the guidelines for permanence and durability
of the Council on Library Resources.

Contents

Preface — vii
Acknowledgments — xv

Introduction. Hierarchy in Traffic — 1

Chapter One. Everyday Forms of Hierarchical Observance — 5

Chapter Two. A Description of the Shweigyin Monastery — 33

Chapter Three. Discretionary Attachments: Monks and Their Social Relations — 93

Chapter Four. Taking Dumont to Southeast Asia — 110

Chapter Five. Hierarchical Habits — 134

Chapter Six. Gaining Access to Power — 152

Chapter Seven. Meditation — 184

Chapter Eight. Masculinity — 212

Chapter Nine. Masculinity's Others: Women, Nuns, and Trans Women — 233

Chapter Ten. Taking Autonomy and Attachment
    Further Afield   266

Notes   287
References   313
Index   325

Preface

Readers opening a book about Burma published at this point in the country's troubled, but suddenly brighter, history, will expect to find answers as to how the country took such an unexpectedly isolationist and repressive turn in the 1960s, and how it finally escaped the military's iron grip close to fifty years later. Taking caution as the better part of intellectual valor, however, I do not try in this book to explain how it is that Burma's citizenry tolerated, however unwillingly, such oppressive military rule. The question is a worthy and important one, but I am reluctant to try to explain Burmese history by reference to patterns I have discerned in Burmans' social relations because I do not want to fall prey to accusations of reductively "culturalist" explanations of complex historical phenomena. I leave it to readers to speculate as to how such notions as the workings of hierarchy or the location of power "above one's head" encouraged Burmans to submit to their repression, or how, perhaps more pointedly, such ideas encouraged members of the former regime to impose control over the nation's populace with such ferocious complacency. My own concerns are more everyday and immediate, even perhaps, as the opening pages of this book suggest, pedestrian. Monks and laypeople in Mandalay live on the ground, not for the most part in the realm of national politics, perceived as both distant and treacherous, and it is to matters closer to the ground that I wish to direct readers' gaze.

Although I no doubt disappoint some readers in my reluctance to pronounce upon Burma's late twentieth and early twenty-first-century history, I owe it to readers to recount both the history of my research in Burma and, even if only very summarily, the country's recent political history, particularly for those readers who may know little beyond news about its ongoing "democratization." I weave these two stories together in what follows, since the larger story about Burma's political evolution has indeed affected the course of my research there.

Just before I was due to begin my first extended period of research in Burma, in September 1987, news came that the government had demonetized all bills over ten kyats (a sum of about US$1.40 at the then-official exchange rate, although closer to US$.25 at the more realistic unofficial one). General Ne Win had once again startled the nation, which he had ruled according to his own xenophobic and irascible temperament since staging a military coup in 1962, by means of this sudden move. Somewhat selfishly, I worried that this new twist in Burma's unpredictable history would introduce yet another delay in my efforts to conduct research in the country. Trying to get a research permit and a visa had already disrupted my life and career for three years at that point. Fortunately, the Burmese embassy in Jakarta issued my visa on schedule—I was living in Indonesia at the time—and I was able to travel without incident.

Once in Rangoon, I was told that people waited for news of how they could exchange their now-worthless bills for legal tender at government-owned banks, as had happened when the government had taken bills out of circulation once before. (All banks in Burma had long since been nationalized in accordance with a vaguely conceived, incoherent, and corruption-prone "Burmese way to socialism.") This time, no such announcement ever came. Official channels claimed that the demonetization was intended to eliminate the ill-gotten gains of smugglers and drug dealers. It was certainly true that smuggling had become rife, since official policy had driven the Burmese economy into disarray, and virtually no consumer goods were available except through unofficial trade networks, mostly overland from neighboring Thailand. (In later years, smuggled goods from China started flooding in, but Burma's border with China was still too dangerous in the 1980s for large-scale trade to develop.) Still, a great many people, distrustful of banks and not privileged enough to be able to move their money overseas, found that what money they kept in cash at home was now totally without value. This body blow to people's finances was further cause for rage among the nation's citizenry, especially among the vestiges of an educated middle class that could recall better days but had lived under Ne Win's autarchy at that point for twenty-five years.

Anyone aware of the cataclysms that had befallen much of the rest of Southeast Asia in the 1960s and 1970s—the unspeakable and unfathomable brutality the United States wreaked on Vietnam, Cambodia, and Laos; the massacres the Indonesian government sponsored among its own people after Sukarno's fall, starting in late 1965; the horrors the Khmer Rouge visited on its own population in 1975 through 1979; even the explosive but extremely unjustly distributed growth Thailand experienced during and following its intimate relationship with the US military during the latter's wars on Southeast Asia—had to look on Burma's radical isolation during those years with mixed feelings. Compared with what took place very nearby during those decades, Ne Win's policies assuring the country's stasis and isolation—although frustrating for many people in Burma, and certainly so for foreign business people hoping to get access to the country's riches—had to arouse a certain degree of respect, however grudging.

For that matter, Ne Win had replaced the legally elected, if hapless, Prime Minister Nu in 1962, on the grounds that ethnic and political divisions risked making the whole country fall apart and only the military could hold it together. Such a claim, repeated ceaselessly by military leaders over the ensuing decades for opportunistic and self-serving reasons, could nevertheless not be dismissed out of hand.

Burma's integrity as a nation-state had always been shaky. The charismatic General Aung San, leader of the forces that fought with the Japanese against the British, and then against the Japanese with the British, during World War II, and then against the British after it ended, brokered a deal with the British government assuring Burma's independence, set to be attained in 1948. Tragically, he and a group of able colleagues were gunned down by agents of a political rival in Rangoon's imposing ministerial building in July 1947, so he did not have a chance to help guide the new nation.

Aung San had proved his political skills not only in his encounters with the British but also with leaders of the colony's many ethnic groups. The ethnic Burmans, of which he was one, make up about two-thirds of the population of the area the British colonized as Burma; a great many other groups, speaking an array of other languages, make up the remaining one-third. Aung San had convinced leaders of the most important of those ethnic minority groups, the Chin, Kachin, Karen, and Shan, that they should cast their lot in with the ethnic Burmans in their bid to form an independent nation, rather than remain loyal to the British. This move required that they overcome long-held suspicions toward Burmans, whose rulers had often tried to exert undesired control over those ethnic groups. The agreement Aung San was able to formulate granted those groups the right to opt out of the proposed "Union of Burma" in ten years' time, should they choose to do so.

Politics during the first few years of the newly independent Burma were fractious, and the ethnic Karen, in particular, were soon engaged in warfare against the national government and its military. During the 1950s, matters improved enough for the economy to appear poised for steady growth. But by the later 1950s, dissension among Burmans, on the one hand and, on the other, not only the Karen but other ethnic groups as well—who resented Burman efforts to profit from the considerable natural resources, such as forest products and gems, that were found mostly in areas the ethnic minorities controlled—put the nation in a state of great tension. Prime Minister Nu invited General Ne Win, as the head of the military, to take charge of the state in 1958 for a limited period. Ne Win did so, and then relinquished power back into the hands of civilian politicians, once again led by Prime Minister Nu. Ne Win grew alarmed at the continued squabbling among politicians, however, and in 1962 staged a coup, summarily dismissing the government and taking all power into his own hands.

Ne Win tolerated no dissent of any sort. Nor did he tolerate subordinates who might proffer opinions he did not find acceptable, or advice phrased with reference to policies enacted in other countries. In keeping with his xenophobia, he restricted tourist visas to twenty-four hours at the start of his rule. (He eventually relaxed this to a seven-day period so that a small number of tourists got glimpses of the country; I was one of them, spending a week in the country, en route to Indonesia, in December 1970.) But the country was for all intents and purposes closed. A tiny elite ruled the nation from Rangoon, at least in name: government control was ineffective in much of the country, where insurgents waged warfare at varying levels of intensity for decades. By 1987, impatience with Ne Win's autocratic ways was pervasive. Demonetization in September of that year added one more infuriating cause for resentment.

I moved from Rangoon to Mandalay in December 1987, and had little further contact with people in Rangoon. I was largely unaware of a series of increasingly violent incidents taking place there. However, I was aware that a former colleague of Ne Win, "Cake General" Aung Kyi (so called because after falling out with Ne Win he had opened a cake shop in Rangoon), had written an open letter to Ne Win detailing the many ways the regime, one in which he had participated importantly early on, had abused the Burmese people. The letter was not really "open": it was not circulated publicly, because Ne Win tolerated no public political discourse. But its existence was known to the educated few, and it worked in tandem with student unrest to put unprecedented pressure on the regime. In late July 1988, Ne Win went on national television to announce his imminent resignation and to say that a vote would be held on whether his political party, the only legal one, should remain in control, or whether a return to multiparty democracy should be implemented. People I spoke to at the time discounted the significance of this announcement. They knew better than to trust anything the "Old Man" said. (Name avoidance is common in Burmese conversation, especially in reference to the powerful or feared.) It was, everyone seemed to agree, simply another one of his tricks, of which they had seen a great number.

The authorities, which is to say, people Ne Win had permitted to make careers for themselves in the government and military, responded by accepting Ne Win's resignation while dismissing any thought of holding a referendum on political reform. Instead, they named another general, Sein Lwin, in his place. On August 8, 1988 (8/8/88 or "Four Eights," as the date is referred to in Burmese), Rangoon exploded as the military opened fire on peaceful demonstrators in the streets. Thousands of people (the figure usually cited is three thousand) died before the military retreated to its barracks a few days later. For the next several weeks, people demonstrated throughout downtown Rangoon and in other cities in the country, venting in verbal tirades the fury they had had to hold in during so many years of economic and political hopelessness, a time during which many of them both suffered under and had had little choice but collaborate in corruption at all levels of the system.

Quite fortuitously, just a few months before this outbreak of public rage, in March 1988, General Aung San's daughter, Daw Aung San Suu Kyi, had returned to Rangoon after many years overseas to tend to her ailing mother. She had married an English historian, Michael Aris, with whom she had two sons, but she had come back to Burma alone. Horrified by what she witnessed in August of that year while caring for her mother in Rangoon's public hospital, she found herself pulled into political activity, and was immediately seized upon by a public in search of a leader to contest the military's hold on power. Her physical resemblance to her beloved father, her unaffected speaking style, and her quiet dignity contrasted dramatically, and winningly, with the bombast and arrogance of Ne Win, as well as of most other Burmese people in positions of authority. She aroused enormous enthusiasm as she spoke to great crowds of Burmese wishing to see the end of military rule. However, she, along with everyone else, was forced to curb her demands for change when the military reasserted their control, killing at least another thousand people in Rangoon, on September 18, 1988.

To everyone's dismay, and eventual despair, the standoff between the military regime, led by General Saw Maung and, later, by General Than Shwe, on the one hand, and the political opposition headed by Daw Aung San Suu Kyi, on the other, lasted from August 1988, until August 2011. Daw Aung San Suu Kyi's National League for Democracy won an overwhelming victory in elections held in 1990, but the results were abrogated by the military regime, which was so out of touch with popular sentiment as to be completely unprepared for those results' crushing rejection of their rule.

Following that cancelled election, there followed a long period, during much of which Daw Aung San Suu Kyi was held under house arrest, marked by half-measures of economic liberalization, ongoing civil wars with the ethnic minorities, political stalemate, and a thoroughgoing sense of generalized stagnation. Particularly shocking to the Burmese public, as well as the world at large, was the government's iron-fisted response in 2007 to protests staged by Buddhist monks against the lifting of subsidies on basic commodities. Just as appalling were the regime's efforts, once the extent of the devastation caused by Cyclone Nargis over one awful night in May 2008 became clear, to conceal its complete inability to respond effectively by refusing permission to enter the delta region to both foreign and domestic agencies offering to provide help. Such extraordinary heartlessness, apparently intended to save the regime from shame-inducing revelations of incompetence, served to dramatize its leaders' inability to understand their role as anything more than the right to make themselves rich and feared.

For reasons that remain unexplained, an election in late 2010 led to a transfer of power from the military to a civilian government in March 2011. The newly elected President Thein Sein, along with most of the other high-ranking officials, had been military personnel until just before the election, and people held little hope of real change. But then in August 2011, Thein Sein met with Daw Aung San Suu Kyi publicly and officially, and was even photographed with her standing in front of a portrait of her father. The moment indicated a real change in the political atmosphere. During the many years the regime had engaged in publishing the most vicious and almost comically mean-spirited slurs against Daw Aung San Suu Kyi, her father's image and memory had been eliminated from all government communications, and the rigidly controlled press was forbidden to allude to him.

By a fortunate coincidence, I arrived in Burma in July 2011, to begin a second stint of extended fieldwork. (I had returned for a number of short research trips in the years after 1988, but never for more than a few weeks.) So I was in a position to watch the increasingly encouraging signs of political liberalization in situ. It was a very exciting time, and I discussed events as they transpired with Burmese friends. I have also watched with mixed emotions, as must anyone who cares about the country and its people, the ongoing series of achievements and missteps that have made the path away from dictatorship exciting and unnerving by turns. At the time of this writing, following Daw Aung San Suu Kyi's National League for Democracy's sweeping electoral victory in 2015, much hangs in the balance, and the challenges in any case remain many and immense.

Yet my research interests have never been focused on politics. I recognize, as must anyone familiar with the works of Foucault, that matters of power infuse all domains of life, and that there is a politics to any social phenomenon to which I might turn my attention. Still, it is important to recognize that many people live their lives without thinking of politics, in the strict sense, all that often, particularly if thinking about politics can only induce feelings of discouragement or rage, as was the case in Burma for just shy of fifty years. Many contemporary academics seem to forget that fact, even though they themselves may think about politics without actually engaging in political action of any meaningful sort and, in that respect, resemble the people whose political passivity they decry.

Note on transliteration: I have modeled transliteration of Burmese words that appear in the text on the *Myanmar–English Dictionary* published by the Myanmar Language Commission of the Ministry of Education (1998).

Acknowledgments

A faculty research assignment from the University of Texas made it possible for me to carry out the research in Mandalay, in 2011 and 2012, on which this book is largely based. I gratefully acknowledge the assistance of the Sitagu Sayadaw, U Nyanissara, in my obtaining a visa for the period of this research. I am particularly indebted to the abbots and other monks resident at the three monasteries in Mandalay where I have lived, although they must remain anonymous. Lay friends in Mandalay, in particular Dr. Soe Tint, and Dr. Kyaw Kyaw Win and Daw Ah Mar Kyi (now living in the United States), have been sources of invaluable support and information over many years.

I was fortunate to receive residencies at three institutions, the Asia Research Institute of the National University of Singapore, the International Institute for Asian Studies in Leiden, and the Department of Anthropology, Stockholm University, in 2013–2014, during which time I wrote the first draft of this book. Revision and preparation for publication were made possible by an additional residence, at the Institut d'Études Avancées in Nantes, in 2015–2016. I am deeply grateful to the administrators of all of these institutions for the opportunities for sustained reflection and writing that these residencies made possible.

I had the opportunity to present some of the materials that appear in this book at a number of different institutions, among them the Université du Mirail, Toulouse; the École Nationale d'Extrême Orient, Paris; the Australian National University; Monash University; Sydney University; the University of Texas; the Asia Research Institute; the National University of Singapore; the University of Freiburg; the University of Leiden; the University of Heidelberg; the Christian Michelsen Institute, Bergen; the University of Michigan; and the University of Wisconsin; as well as at the Annual Meeting of the Asian Studies Association and the Burma Studies Conference, held jointly by the Northern Illinois University Center for Burma Studies and the Institute for Southeast Asian Studies in Singapore.

I also wish to thank the two scholars who read the manuscript for the University of Hawai'i Press and who provided many helpful suggestions for how to improve it. I gratefully acknowledge a grant from the President's Office of the University of Texas at Austin that assisted in making publication of this book possible. Finally, I thank Pamela Kelley and Debra Tang of the University of Hawai'i Press for the honor of seeing this book added to a distinguished list of publications about Burma and Southeast Asia.

INTRODUCTION
Hierarchy in Traffic

When I arrived as a Fulbright fellow in Rangoon[1] in 1987, I was given a copy of a pamphlet the US embassy distributed to new members of their staff containing tips about living in the city. One point stood out: it concerned the astonishingly risky behavior of pedestrians on the city's streets. Indeed. Although I had lived several years in Indonesia and had stayed on occasion in some of the region's biggest cities—Bangkok, Jakarta, and Singapore—I had never seen pedestrians engage in such death-defying practices. Jaywalking was the rule; traffic lights counted for nothing; stepping out in front of oncoming traffic, whether on the part of brash young men or matronly ladies or parents grasping the hands of young children, was very much the norm.

The pamphlet's author suggested that this extremely dangerous behavior could be explained by reference to the fact that few Burmese had any experience driving a motorized vehicle and therefore had no appreciation of how difficult it is to stop a vehicle traveling at speed. It is true that by the late 1980s the Burmese economy had been in bad straits for some time and there were very few cars on the road. An American friend, John Badgeley, told me that there had been more traffic on Rangoon's streets when he did research there in the 1950s than in 1987. So getting behind the wheel of a car or truck was something very few people ever did. Yet in later years, as the amount of traffic in the city increased precipitously—and as recently as 2012, when I completed another longish stay (ten months) in the country—pedestrians continued to engage in behavior that looks, to an outsider, little short of suicidal. By this time, at least a few of those pedestrians must have sometimes also been drivers, and in any case, they had had a fair bit of time to reconceive their relationship with the far greater number of cars on the road. They had not done so. I have myself gone native enough to take on street-crossing habits, when I'm in Burma, that would horrify people elsewhere who care about me were they to see me at it.

The key to understanding what pedestrians are doing when they set off across a broad avenue in Rangoon, one on which there may be a number of private cars, taxis, buses, and trucks[2] coming straight at them, is to see that they are entering into an overall system, one in which they occupy the lowest rung but do still have a place. Like virtually all elements of Burmese society, that system is fundamentally hierarchical: it is characterized by the principle of relative standing, not rights.

I open this introduction, and this monograph, with an account of people's behavior on streets because, although it may appear puzzling and even irrational, it turns out to make sense within the terms of the hierarchical system in which it is embedded. I continue my discussion of pedestrians in traffic in chapter 1, "Everyday Forms of Hierarchical Observance," followed by brief accounts of two other commonplace scenes in contemporary Burman life: Buddhist sermons, called "*dhamma* talks," delivered by monks to public audiences;[3] and the interaction among customers and the young men and boys who serve them at tea shops. What I wish to show by reference to these common practices—and it is the burden of this book to develop the point more amply—is that we can better understand Burmans' everyday lives if we appreciate that hierarchical understandings condition everything.

"Hierarchy" is taken by most English-speakers to refer to simple differences in power, wealth, or status among people. My first example, traffic on the roads, requires little beyond such a basic understanding of differences to see what guides the ways participants interact. Even in this case, however, it is important to note that people are indeed interacting: however much each actor appears to act without regard for anyone's interests except his or her own, the fact remains that they must constantly gauge their position relative to everyone else's and adjust their behavior accordingly. Differences in power, measured in this case in horsepower, appear to grant much greater privileges to some players than to others. Yet even the most powerful are hardly free to do as they please. They are still constrained in various ways, and in ways that vary according to ever-shifting circumstances.

The constraints of relative position within a hierarchical system are precisely what make such a system appear, prima facie, unjust and indeed unacceptable to many people in the world today, particularly as it affects those people consigned to subordinate positions. Yet Buddhist sermons, which are occasions in which many people make willing and even enthusiastic display of their subordinate status, are becoming increasingly popular in Burma. To those people who think subordination implies humiliation, such displays are necessarily puzzling. The French anthropologist Louis Dumont, however, suggested that hierarchical relations are just that, relationships, in which both privileges and obligations, although diverse, are incumbent on all parties. He helps us in this way to see why subordination need not be experienced as demeaning—although it may very well be experienced as such at times.[4]

Precisely because superiors, too, find themselves to one degree or another constrained when they enter into hierarchical relationships, they are likely to take pleasure in situations in which they can enjoy the privileges implicit in superordinate status without finding themselves in any way beholden to subordinates. Tea shops, I contend, wherein interactions among customers and servers take on consistent and specific patterns, illustrate such idealized circumstances. Indeed, they illustrate, at however minimal a scale, those principles of free-market exchange—wherein people with money can satisfy their wants without any implication of entangling relationships—of which both Marx and Polanyi made us aware.[5]

I put aside the theoretical issues briefly discussed in chapter 1 to provide in chapter 2 ethnographic material about one of the three monasteries in which I have lived in Mandalay. Titled "A Description of the Shweigyin Monastery," the chapter opens with an account of the daily recitations monks and novices perform before the monastery's principal Buddha image, which constitutes the core site of the entire complex. Thereafter, structuring my account spatially, I describe what is to be found along the outer circumference of the grounds, and then move inside the monastery's gates to describe the various structures standing within its walls, as well as the activities that go on inside those buildings. In chapter 3, "Discretionary Attachments: Monks and Their Social Relations," I look more specifically at the tenor of interactions that take place inside the monastery.

I intend chapter 4, "Taking Dumont to Southeast Asia," as a bridge between the preceding, largely descriptive, chapters and the later, more analytic, ones. I first embark on a more extensive discussion of Dumont's writing on the subject of hierarchy, developing points only briefly mentioned in chapter 1. I go on to explain that I find it useful to complement Dumont's ideas with those of Benedict Anderson and Marina Warner. Anderson's early and illuminating essay about power in Java helps us understand how hierarchical thinking inflects ideas and behavior in Southeast Asia more generally (Anderson 1972). Warner analyzes fairy tales to illustrate the way that women's relatively weak structural position in virtually all societies in history, certainly in the West, has obliged them to subordinate themselves to men (Warner 1995).

In chapter 5, "Hierarchical Habits," I describe the many ways hierarchical considerations inform all social interaction among Burmans, and I propose that people's constant attention to the status implications of face-to-face encounter makes interaction always appear fraught. I suggest in chapter 6, "Gaining Access to Power," that precisely because so much rides on what happens in interaction, means must be found to counter its potential ill-effects, either by tapping into concentrations of power outside oneself or, better, developing one's own resistance to it. Means for doing either include practices surrounding tattoos, esoteric formulas, and various cults. The allure of meditation, the focus of chapter 7, "Meditation," must lie in part in the possibility it offers, at least conceptually, of avoiding encounter, and indeed, all social relations, in favor of radical autonomy.

Turning, in chapter 8, "Masculinity," to idealized versions of masculinity, I suggest that masculinity in Burman gender ideology can be idealized in apparently opposite ways, most notably in the form of the productive lay male, or the ascetic monk. Yet in either case, masculinity is characterized by autonomy, as discussed in the preceding chapters. In chapter 9, "Masculinity's Others: Women, Nuns, and Trans Women," I argue that femininity and nonnormative masculinity are thought characterized by attachment, which is seen as the less-valued but still essential counter and complement to autonomy. In a concluding tenth chapter, "Taking Autonomy and Attachment Further Afield," I discuss how the issues I have addressed with reference to Burma—hierarchy, autonomy, and attachment—link up to larger questions with which social scientists have long concerned themselves. Finally, I look at the realms of popular culture and market exchange for the ways they offer fantasized, but necessarily contradictory, resolutions to the existential conflict between our wishes to feel bonded to others and at the same time to remain unbound, or "free."

Chapter One

EVERYDAY FORMS OF HIERARCHICAL OBSERVANCE

Time to get back out onto the streets. I have mentioned that Burmese traffic must, like all Burman social relations, be understood as ordered by a concern with hierarchy, and so with relative standing. Relative standing can incorporate complicated, sometimes crosscutting, sometimes ambiguous, often contestable features of a person's identity or role. We will get to that when looking at other forms of interaction in Burmese society. In the anonymous realm of street traffic, however, things are quite simple. In a phrase, size matters. Larger, heavier, faster vehicles take precedence over smaller, lighter, or slower ones. Trucks and buses enjoy a preeminence comparable to that of elephants: smaller beasts know better than to defy them and scurry out of the way as they approach. No one, however, is obliged to look back—many drivers have no rearview mirror—because vehicles in front have precedence, both literally and figuratively, over those behind them. At the same time, since larger vehicles enjoy precedence by virtue of their size, they can always pass lesser vehicles: they can take precedence at whim. As soon as the driver of the passing vehicle gets beyond the driver of the vehicle being passed, the latter becomes irrelevant—in effect, invisible.

In Mandalay, where motorcycles and bicycles are ubiquitous, their riders behave in ways that car drivers cannot easily emulate. Motorcyclists starting up at the side of the road do not look back before they enter traffic. To do so would undermine the impression of their intention to enter the game. Only once they are in motion do they begin to gauge the possibility of moving out into the stream of traffic. That implies glancing to the side rather more than to the rear. Motorcyclists and bicyclists alike, should they wish to move into the lane of traffic on the far side of the road, will, if no break in traffic presents itself, start moving against traffic near the sidewalk, waiting for a chance to cross over but not remaining in place till that chance arises. When such cyclists meet up with others coming toward them on the side of the road, no rule applies as to which side either of them will take to pass. It must be negotiated separately, on the move, as it were, in each case.

In Rangoon, drivers are forbidden to use their horns, a remarkable form of social control. Everywhere else in Burma, horns enable drivers to indicate that they are approaching, and lesser vehicles must yield. Traffic lights are usually observed, but when streets cross in the absence of a light (as is the rule in Mandalay), vehicles do not stop but only slow down, while drivers sound their horns. Drivers slow down less if their size empowers them to assume control of the road. Horns are graduated in their sound to indicate the relative size of the vehicles to which they are attached. Some cheating takes place here: a few motorcyclists attach car horns to deceive other drivers ahead of them, and owners of some small vehicles put in horns appropriate for trucks. But for the most part, horns provide accurate indices as to the size and therefore standing of the vehicles whose approach they announce.

The order of traffic is, therefore, perfectly clear: trucks and buses take precedence over cars and minivans, which take precedence over motorcycles and scooters (if present), which take precedence over bicyclists and, finally, pedestrians. At the same time, conditions allow for considerable wiggle room. Smaller vehicles are, after all, capable of getting into spaces larger vehicles cannot enter. This means that when traffic halts at a traffic light, motorbikes and bicycles surge forward to place themselves around, between, and ahead of larger vehicles. When traffic starts up, the smaller vehicles will lose the bit of advantage they momentarily enjoyed, but that is no reason not to pursue it when the chance arises. All players spend all their time pursuing whatever chances for precedence they might happen upon.

That includes pedestrians. Anyone who stands by the side of the road waiting to cross might just as well not exist. Only once they start moving—into traffic—do pedestrians enter into the game and so start the delicate dance of daring, negotiation, and assertion that will result in their reaching the other side. One particularly risky ploy is simply to refuse all eye contact and stride across the road: drivers confronted with such behavior have no choice but to cede to the reckless assertiveness of such players. But it is very much the high-stakes option and not one that many pedestrians opt for. Much more frequent is a maneuver by which a pedestrian indicates the intention to cross by looking into incoming traffic and gauging the speed and distance of the closest vehicles. Pedestrians may decide to run for it; they may decide they can simply walk; they may decide to hold out where they are, which can be at any point between the sidewalk they have left behind and the one they are approaching. Drivers do not display the anxious dread of coming close to pedestrians that Western drivers often evince: Burmese drivers show complete equanimity passing extremely close to pedestrians, often at fairly high speed.

Little thought is given, for that matter, to what might make things convenient for pedestrians. Sidewalks are often extremely high. Their height raises them above the water that floods the roads, often to great depth, during monsoon rains (because of the inadequate street drainage[1]), and it benefits pedestrians at such times. But that height also means that walking is at all times hard work: every driveway that puts a break in the sidewalk requires that pedestrians make a big step down and a big step up if they are going to remain on the sidewalk. In Burma (indeed in Southeast Asia generally), making conditions easier for people too poor and insignificant to have access to any vehicle is no one's remit.

Understanding Traffic

My point is not to decry the uncivilized or untutored ways of the natives but rather to demonstrate that the behavior of drivers, cyclists, and pedestrians on Burmese streets turns out to conform to principles obtaining in many areas of Burmese society. Granted, I am too much schooled in the traffic rules of Western cities to find Burmese approaches to traffic advisable, or to deny its terrifying risks. But I experience such fear more in thinking about crossing the street in Burma than I do when actually crossing one. In the moment, I am too busy negotiating my moves to worry about the overall nature of the situation.

By the same token, I am too much schooled in a good many Western, middle-class assumptions about social relations to find Burmese approaches to social life obvious or compatible with my own social expectations. As Dumont would predict, my egalitarian commitments make me impatient of much that strikes me as unfair or unjust, because patently anti-egalitarian, in Burmese social relations. What I would underline, however, is that Burmese approaches to interaction among people, whether in traffic or in other areas of social life, are not unfathomable, nor, for that matter, unjustifiable. Certain core understandings about such matters as selves, gender, and standing, turn out to be internally consistent, and if we can get a grasp on those assumptions, we can not only make sense of much that happens in Burmese society, we can also, in what seems to me the most valuable use to which anthropological research lends itself, come to greater understanding of ourselves.

No one, as noted earlier, enters Burmese traffic with any assumptions about fundamental rights. Pedestrians, certainly, enjoy no "right of way." No one, by the same token, is ever excluded from the game as long as they remain in motion. What everyone must do at all times is enter into negotiation with all other players, and do so cognizant of what the characteristics that they bring to the specific context impose on or afford them. Drivers are not "thoughtless" or "mindless" or even "rude." Truck drivers, in a kind of transportational noblesse oblige, will often use their turn signals to indicate to other large vehicles behind them, when going up hills, say, when they have a chance to pass. What drivers, pedestrians, cyclists, and the like all have in common is a ceaseless alertness to chances, ones that their principal characteristics (size, weight, speed) will allow them to take up or will preclude them from acting on.

It would be possible, even fashionable, to see (after the manner of de Certeau) in the behavior of riders of smaller vehicles, such as motorcyclists or bicyclists, and of pedestrians, as they make their way in Burma's increasingly tight traffic, so many forms of minor resistance (de Certeau 1984). It would also be silly. Resistance has come to mean many things in recent anthropological and cultural studies literature, but surely it should imply some rejection of the circumstances to which one is subject: as its etymology suggests, it should imply pushing back against something. That is not what anyone is doing on Burma's streets.

Hierarchical arrangements give rise to reactions or responses shaped by the nature of the hierarchy that they counter. I use the word "counter" advisedly, because it strikes me as a more fitting label for such ideas and practices than "resistance." The latter term too often introduces a romanticizing celebration of those who fight back from positions of relative weakness—a celebration that progressive academics as well as fans of pop culture are partial to but that misconstrues more often than it illuminates actual behavior (cf. Keeler 2009). People who live in a society in which hierarchy pervades all relationships do not try to imagine relationships in which it falls away but rather relationships in which they will find themselves better positioned, especially if they find themselves disadvantaged in the way things now stand.

Small fry on Burmese streets are not pushing back; they are pushing ahead, worming their way through tiny openings without arriving at any critique of the overall system. To claim that they are doing so, that they understand the nature of the system and the way that it disadvantages them, and its vulnerabilities to their tiny yet real attacks, falsifies the nature of their enterprise. It also implies (to the degree that the observer who attributes resistance to their behavior idealizes them for doing so) that they deserve our attention only in so far as they fulfill our romanticization of them and their behavior. That is, we right-thinking progressives prize those subalterns of this world who share our disdain for hierarchy. But what of those who do not? What of those subalterns who simply size up the situation in which they find themselves and proceed from there?

People in Burma are opportunists. So are people everywhere: the differences turn on what principles and preferences shape the way people understand and act on what they take to be opportunities that arise. James Scott is right that on occasion people find escaping to the hills an attractive opportunity and take it (2009). But more often, people find that moving closer to power, rather than away from it, offers more interesting, indeed attractive, opportunities, and so they act on that impulse instead. This readiness to subordinate oneself to power appeals less to our taste for stories in which the relatively weak take up whatever weapons come to hand to oppose the strong. But most people realize, whether or not they have read de La Fontaine, that "*la raison du plus fort est toujours la meilleur,*" or to put it another way, that life really is not a movie.[2]

Burma is undergoing important and much-anticipated change. Debate as to the appropriate foundations on which Burmese society should be based has finally been initiated in earnest. But we must not be complacent about our own assumptions, or dismissive of Burmese ones, if we are to appreciate the tenor of how things are now. One type of complacency we should be particularly alert to, as Dumont noted, is an easy Western idealization of egalitarianism's virtues and its corollary, the denigration of hierarchy's shortcomings or disadvantages. Real life always turns out to confound such straightforward simplicities.

Any discourse of "rights" presumes at least some degree of equality, some degree of sameness, among a number of parties. Individuals enjoy similar rights in some respect, without regard to whatever differences may distinguish them otherwise. In such contexts, pedestrians to whom traffic rules in some societies give the "right of way" are undifferentiated in their right to precedence vis-à-vis cars. If that right is contravened, if a car driver fails to respect a pedestrian's right of way, the pedestrian is liable to voice much righteous indignation, and bystanders and the law are both likely to side with the pedestrian. Road rage, a ubiquitous feature of the current American landscape, stems from conflicting claims as to who has seen his or her rights compromised, and who has seized a precedence to which they had no right.

In Burma, by contrast, road rage is almost nonexistent. If you get ahead, you were right to try. If you don't, you were right to yield. What's to argue or get enraged about? At the same time, what looks to the unaccustomed eye like chaos always verging on disaster turns out to give rise to far fewer accidents than one might anticipate. Since no one has rights, everyone must pay close attention—constantly—gauging degrees of precedence and staying on the lookout for chance opportunities. Hierarchical assumptions grant some people precedence, but if in practice they fail to or choose not to take it, or for whatever reason are prevented from doing so, others are always ready to take the opportunity. Righteous indignation flourishes in many Burmese contexts, but it flourishes not when people fail to observe others' rights but rather when they fail to know their place, relative of course to other people's.

The idea of order in American traffic (and I believe this applies to traffic in most Western societies north of the Alps) builds on like participants travelling at like speed in shared (or if need be, imposed) respect for uniform rules. So on American freeways there are minimum as well as maximum speed limits, and roadway participants likely to move at very different speeds are usually enjoined to remain in lanes designated for their ilk. Witness the (very welcome) growth of bike lanes in European and American cities. The idea of order in Burmese traffic is based on the notion that differences generate different capacities and opportunities. People act on both as they will. Knowing one's place does not preclude someone making a daring move, should they be in the right place at the right time, in an effort to get ahead. The outcome—they get ahead, they fall behind, they suffer grievous injury—reveals the accuracy of their estimation of the situation and their place in it, whether or not, in other words, it was the right place or the right time for them to do what they did.[3]

Traffic is impersonal, which is why the only criteria for distinguishing among participants consist of such matters as size and speed. Relationships do not obtain: encounters are, obviously, brief. The basic rule that applies to all interaction, that it reflects and enacts hierarchical differences, applies here, but hierarchy takes a very basic, elemental form, consisting only of a ranked order of relative standing. And like any hierarchical dispensation, it does not really force people to keep their place, which is one reason it is not necessarily experienced as oppressive. It encourages people not only to know their place but also to act to their own advantage by virtue of the degree of precedence they can try to gain for themselves. They do so by playing on the chances that their (always relative) place affords them at any given moment.

I have said above that the notion of rights does not pertain to Burmese traffic. There is much talk these days of "human rights" in the Burmese press and, to some degree, even in casual conversation. Yet it is worth noting that the Burmese translation of the phrase *lu. ahk-win. ayei:*—and it feels like a translation rather more than a phrase of long standing—actually means "people's opportunities." This rendering is telling. Hierarchical arrangements are based on the idea that people are different and relate to each other on the basis of those differences, which grant them diverse opportunities. Rights pertain to egalitarian understandings wherein differences are irrelevant. The idea that everyone should enjoy the same treatment is hard to put across in Burma because it runs counter to fundamental assumptions about how social relations function. How can women and men be said to have "equal rights"—read, "equal opportunities"—when everything about them differs: their qualities, their aptitudes, and their desires? To Burmese men, especially, but to many Burmese women as well, the idea makes no sense.

It is a mainstay of American political rhetoric to state that everyone should enjoy equal opportunities. For example, young people should have access to equally effective education. Everyone knows that nothing about the American educational system comes anywhere close to such a condition, and that the system of local control and financing we have come up with guarantees that it never will. But the phrasing is comforting: it waves away the obvious fact that social inequality is both rampant and increasing in American society, sustaining our fantasy that "if you work hard, you'll get ahead." "Opportunities" in the American context is a fig leaf for the glaring contradiction between the egalitarian ideals we espouse and the fiercely unequal arrangements whose intensification we accept and do nothing to counter. In Burmese, "opportunities" is the closest people can come to the idea that everybody could be "the same," and that that could be a good thing. It is hard to see just how such an understanding will come to be widespread in Burmese society. Indeed, much about American society implies that it has yet to be fully embraced by large segments of that country's populace, however "egalitarian" their rhetoric.[4]

Embracing Hierarchy: *Dhamma* Talks

Westerners and others who see in egalitarian principles a more just and more effective framework on which to base social relations and political structure tend to think in terms of a simple binary: between hierarchy, on the one hand, and egalitarianism, on the other. Interestingly, in a collection of essays in which a number of anthropologists address the subject of hierarchy, Tcherkézoff suggests that in a place like Samoa, the fundamental contrast is between hierarchy, on the one hand, and inequality or stratification, on the other (2009). Situations in which hierarchy obtains, he tells us, are thought to be marked by orderly relations among people who are aware of and acknowledge each other's place. Situations in which hierarchy does not obtain set people loose to compete with each other according to their animal nature. Westerners note inequality in both circumstances without realizing that, to Samoans, the contrast is fundamental. In hierarchy, participants are oriented to a whole that binds them to one another; in inequality, they relate to each other only as individuals in conflict, in a simple contest for power.

Ideologically, at least, hierarchy imposes obligations on all parties: superordinates have responsibilities to their subordinates just as much as the reverse, although of course the nature of those responsibilities differs. For this very reason, hierarchy should be understood not as the imposition of a static and unjust inequality on people, but rather as a system of exchanges. In Burma, furthermore, as in many places, superordinates often manage redistributive systems wherein material goods ascend to persons of greater authority or holiness, and are then spread about (or rather, down) among other religious or lay recipients. Just as importantly, subordinates receive immaterial benefits, such as merit, which is essential to their well-being and standing in future existences, and emotional satisfaction.

Particularly difficult for many adherents of modern, egalitarian ideology to grasp, the satisfactions gained through subordination are nevertheless real and meaningful to many Burmans. This point is made vividly clear at the increasingly popular "*dhamma* talks" (*dama. pwe:*), the public sermons monks are invited to present to lay audiences, which have proliferated in recent years in Burma.[5]

When a monk arrives at a place where he is to give an evening *dhamma* talk, he is received with terrific pomp. He will have been brought to the site in a car driven by members of the sponsoring organization—a township, a local Buddhist community hall, a charitable organization, or the like—and accompanied by his own acolytes and other representatives of the sponsors: important figures should always be attended to and surrounded by a number of individuals ready to look after their needs. On arriving at the site, more representatives of the sponsors meet him as he gets out of the car and a parasol (evocative of Burma's erstwhile royalty) is held over him as he makes his way either to some area where leaders of the sponsoring outfit greet him and offer him sweet drinks and snacks a monk is permitted to have after noon, or directly to the stage on which he will be seated to give his sermon. It is evening, and so the parasol serves not to protect him from the sun but rather to demonstrate his impressive standing. A crowd of pious spectators will already have found places sitting on mats in front of the stage but leaving a clear path to it so that he and the entourage can pass by unimpeded once he is about to start his talk. As he approaches the stage, walking deliberately, members of the audience hold up their hands, palms touching, perhaps raised above their bowed heads, or they prostrate themselves three times, to show him their great respect. He in no way acknowledges their obeisance, or even their presence.

The stage is festooned with an enormous array of flowers. There may well be strings of flashing colored lights. There are certainly a number of baskets (resembling American Easter baskets) containing a collection of gifts appropriate for monks: sweet drinks, snacks, boxes of tea bags, packets of coffee powder mixed with powdered dairy creamer and sugar, tooth paste, razors, combs, shampoo, and on and on, the whole array wrapped in cellophane. In the center of the stage is a huge chair, painted a uniform gold color. Often the seat—given its size, it might better be called a platform—is so high off the ground that steps have to be placed in front of it to enable the monk to reach it. There may be a cushion on the seat, but one of the precepts a monk is obliged to observe forbids him using luxurious furnishings, so often the seat lacks any kind of cushion or pillow. Once he has made his way onto the chair, he sits down, folds his legs, and arranges his robe. In light of the importance of the occasion, he has put on his robe in the most formal manner, with his arms tightly bound in layer after layer of cloth, greatly restricting his movement. A number of microphones are arranged in front of him so that his remarks can be amplified through a great many loudspeakers pointed toward the audience and beyond, to the surroundings in all directions. At least one, sometimes more, cameras on tripods set up among the spectators video-record the proceedings. If it is a very large crowd, attracted by one of Burma's most famous sermonizing monks, there will be TV monitors and other screens set up so that spectators far from the stage or in areas without any view of it at all can still observe him as he speaks.

Once the monk is seated and starts to speak, the contrast between the enormously rich and luxurious setting and the plainly dressed, usually older, man at its center is striking. His head is shaven, his robe is monochrome, his body almost motionless. For an hour to an hour and a half or two hours, or on some occasions, still longer, he sits and he speaks. Whatever the contents of his sermon, the worldly domain of pomp, wealth, and beauty that surrounds the monk makes a sharp contrast with the ascetic realm of simplicity, which is to say, of the ascetically spiritual, that his plain appearance, dress, and demeanor all illustrate. The audience, made up largely of women unless the monk is one of a very few, immensely famous ones who attract a certain number of men, sits quietly throughout, rarely engaging in the side conversations that almost always start up in the course of public events in any other Burmese context. Few members of the audience leave before it is over, despite the fact that entering and leaving any public event in Burma is otherwise so routine as to arouse no notice whatsoever. Some audience members sit with their hands in a gesture of respect throughout the entire sermon, an unusually great display of reverence.

When the sermon is over, the monk may be presented with gifts on the part of lay donors who have contributed large sums to sponsor the event. Photographs are taken as they hand him gifts. A cluster of males then rushes to the seat to help him down off the chair and the stage, and then accompany him, once again carrying a parasol above his head, back through the audience to the car that will transport him back to his monastery. The audience sings a song expressing wishes for his good health and longevity as he makes his way along the path, demonstrating once again their obeisance as he passes by. He pays them no more heed at the conclusion of the event than he did at its opening.

When I lived in Mandalay in 1987 and 1988, I came across a few such events. In 2011 and 2012, I was astonished at their frequency. In most cases, the sermon any given monk declaims is only one in a series of such sermons given nightly over a number of days. Many pagodas and townships in Mandalay no longer sponsor the *za'pwe:* (nightlong stage performances), put on over a number of days, as were long popular in the city and elsewhere in Burman areas. They have switched to holding a series of sermons instead. Such events are announced in a series of identical panels, set up in a row along the street, each one showing an image of the monk scheduled to speak, a list of his titles, and the date of his talk (usually given in the Burmese lunar calendar). If the series is to consist of, say, ten sermons scheduled over as many consecutive nights, the progression of speakers follows an informal rank order, in an ascending degree of fame. The last speaker is the most famous, and probably the one to whom the largest fee has to be paid. In 2011 and 2012, the monk generally thought of as possessing the most immense star power was the Sitagu Sayadaw. He invariably drew the largest crowds, and he always came last in a series.

Giving a sermon represents yet another means by which a Buddhist monk can acquire merit. In doing so, he is "spreading the *dhamma*," which it behooves him as a member of the sangha to do. Listening to a sermon, by the same token, represents yet another means by which a Buddhist layperson can acquire merit. Demonstrating respect for the monk, in all the gestures of ritual subordination and respectful attention a listener makes, represents yet another means for a Buddhist layperson to show that he or she "takes refuge in the sangha," as well as in the Buddha and the *dhamma,* which is something all Buddhists must do.

Yet taking note of these benefits, although they are real and figure in people's motivation for engaging in the undertaking, does not suffice to explain its particular appeal. There are many ways in which laypeople can support the sangha and acquire merit. So the fact that attending a sermon generates merit does not explain why people should attend these events in such large numbers. I suggest that the particular allure of attending a sermon, for laypeople, lies in the opportunity it gives them to enact a subordinate role and, in doing so, to reap the benefits that subordinating yourself should—but can in only certain cases, like this one, be counted on to—assure someone.

It is clear from even the most elementary reading about Theravada Buddhism that relations between monks and laypeople are symbiotic. When laypeople give material support and respect to monks, they accrue merit, provided that the recipients of their donations observe the precepts incumbent on monks and so constitute valid "fields of merit" on which donors can cast their donations as seeds of future merit. When monks accept such gifts, thereby making it possible for laypeople to obtain merit, they, too, acquire merit in turn. The ascetic regimen that monks are obliged to take on means they are, in principle at least, poor in material goods. Indeed, they are forbidden to raise or cook food; they are dependent on lay supporters to take up these labors on their behalf. But they are rich in spiritual prestige. Thus not only do they enter into relations of exchange with laypeople, relations in which each party is necessary because each party differs in fundamental ways from the other, but monks also enjoy higher standing: once again, they are rich in prestige. The exchange between monks and laypeople is one wherein material goods and obeisance are given up (or rather, raised up—the appropriate verb in Burmese for giving something to a monk means "to raise above one's head") in return for immaterial instruction and merit, bestowed by monks on their lay supporters.

The exchange is looked on by lay Burman Buddhists as both valuable and fair. Monks who are revealed to contravene the precepts in serious ways arouse terrific outrage, since with that news comes the realization that donations made to them were of no karmic benefit to the donors. If supposed monks fail to observe the precepts, or at least the major ones, they are not monks but rather "men in monks' robes," and the donations they receive generate no merit for the donors, who have cast their gifts on "barren fields." But monks are rarely looked on with suspicion. The prestige of the sangha is such as to assure most people's confidence in the probity of monks until incontrovertible counterevidence proves that faith to be misplaced.

Making donations and showing obeisance to monks accords with a clearly rational effort to increase the store of one's merit. This is believed to affect both one chances at being reborn in human or higher form in the next life and also good outcomes in the present one. (The latter notion enjoys less doctrinal support, but the idea is nevertheless widely held.) Such behavior brings affective rewards as well. Subordinating oneself to an appropriate other fulfills a desire, a felt need; otherwise an occasion such as a *dhamma* talk at which people show their deep respect for monks would hardly draw such crowds. Attending a sermon affords people an opportunity to enact the worthy, and satisfying, action of "taking refuge" not just in Buddhism's relatively remote "Three Jewels" (the Buddha; the *dhamma,* the doctrine that he promulgated; and the sangha, the community of monks, those who follow that doctrine most assiduously), but in a charismatic and present individual, a prestigious and authoritative monk.[6]

People voice their opinions of a speaker after the event, and they are not invariably positive. A very few monks speak in a deeply serious manner that makes few concessions to an audience's desire for entertainment. I attended a sermon during a visit to Lashio given by an eminent abbot from Mandalay. I found it very hard to follow: he often turned away from the microphone in a way that made it hard to hear him, and in any case, he spoke in a little-inflected voice that suggested seriousness but a certain inaccessibility. When friends who had not attended asked me about it the next day and I reported my difficulties, they told me that a neighbor had reported similar trouble in getting much out of it.

A lively and entertaining sermon, on the other hand, arouses enthusiastic comment, and many monks blend into their sermons lighter moments. These may consist of jokes, of sly and oblique political references, or of stories, whether from the Pali canon or from the monk's own experience. Particularly frequent is the use of a device that might be called aural/oral fill-in-the-blanks. A monk often poses a question to his audience to which they can be relied on to know and voice the answer. Or he may use a device that I recognize from Indonesia as well as other, secular, contexts in Burma: a speaker makes remarks on some matter and finishes up by stating the first syllable of a word or phrase with a rising intonation that invites his listener then to say the rest of the word. The required completion is invariably so obvious that no one hesitates in guessing what it is. In no instance does a monk giving a sermon seek to challenge or puzzle his listeners. He expects and can rely on his listeners to say precisely what he anticipates them to say.

For example, a monk often states that Buddhists take refuge in the "Three Jewels:" the Buddha, the *dhamma,* and the sangha. Having stated this fact, he may at a certain point put the question to his listeners, "Respected listeners, Buddhists take refuge in how many jewels?" To which the only possible answer is of course, "Three." What listeners say, loudly and with great enthusiasm, is "Three Jewels, Venerable Lord!" often raising their hands, palms touching as they do so in a show of fulsome and enthusiastic deference.

Needless to say, the fact that Buddhists take refuge in the Three Jewels, consisting of the Buddha, the *dhamma,* and the sangha, is news to no one. Nor for that matter is much else that a monk is likely to say in the course of a sermon. Granted, if he chooses to relate something out of his own experience, he may relay information that is new to his listeners. The Sitagu Sayadaw always makes reference in his sermons to his many trips abroad and the many extremely important figures he meets with on those travels (the pope, the Dalai Lama, other religious leaders, political leaders, and so on), to the clear interest as well as entertainment of his listeners. A monk in Mandalay who was particularly generous and helpful to me, U Dhammananda, is much called-upon to give sermons: he is a famous sermon-giver in Mandalay and beyond. He likes to allude to Einstein's comments on Buddhism, and to other information he has culled from his reading. Nevertheless, much, and indeed most, of every sermon I heard him deliver, as well as those given by other monks, consisted of a review of basic tenets of Buddhism that anyone growing up in Buddhist Burma would know full well.

When I asked Burmese acquaintances why sermons had become so terrifically popular in recent years, they answered variously. One reason some people mentioned was that such events draw a much more trustworthy and disciplined crowd than other kinds of public events, particularly *za'pwe::* no drinking, no carousing, no loud noise into the wee hours. (The fact that young men attend *za'pwe:* in great numbers but few go to Buddhist sermons helps explain the contrast, of course.) Elders in a neighborhood find this much more to their liking than events that lead too easily to fighting and disorderliness.[7] But the most frequent response people made, at least among those people who actually attended such events, was that they enjoyed sermons because sermons enabled them to learn more about Buddhism: what the Buddha said, what was contained in Pali texts, what responsibilities were incumbent on Buddhists, and so on.

These remarks puzzled me, since when I attended sermons I found myself, much less knowledgeable about Buddhism than my interlocutors, learning very little about Buddhism that I did not already know.

Doctrinal differences do show up in Buddhist circles. Yet these are not the stuff of public discourse, and not the stuff of most sermons. Sermons consist of highly familiar, agreed-upon tenets of Buddhist learning and practice, as stated by a learned and respected monk. If the audience is lucky, he is also lively and entertaining, but that is not always the case.[8]

More important, I believe, than learning about Buddhism when attending a Buddhist sermon is enacting a properly Buddhist role as a layperson.[9] In the many displays of respect that audience members make—and the word "display" is particularly apt, since there is an ostentatiousness about the whole endeavor that betrays no insincerity but rather a deeply felt reverence in which the spectator takes pride—one senses a gratifying opportunity to subordinate oneself to an eminently trustworthy and admirable figure. The enthusiasm with which people respond to the questions the sermon-giver puts to them seem genuine: the alacrity with which people respond, as well as the volume at which they voice their response, leaves little doubt as to how much pleasure participating in the exchange gives them. They are doing precisely what they are being urged and invited to do, and it appears to make everyone very happy—everyone among the laypeople, that is. The monk may or may not evince any such pleasurable feeling. U Dhammananda may be particularly favored as a sermon-giver because he clearly enjoys himself so much in entertaining an audience. Yet other monks opt for a more serious demeanor throughout and register little by way of a reaction when they engage in the fill-in-the-blanks device I have described above.

Women take up the opportunity to attend *dhamma* talks in much greater numbers than males because doing so conforms with women's role in social relations more easily than it does with men's. Women are expected to look to powerful others on whom they can depend: they should attach themselves to others by providing service and respect, in return for their superiors' beneficent regard.[10] The fact that they can do so in relating to monks without risking any inappropriate sexual inferences being made about the relationships they enter into, since these are relationships with monks, who are fundamentally asexual beings, makes their subordinating themselves to monks much more attractive, because less equivocal and so less fraught, than most alternatives.

Males can, and often do, engage in similar behavior vis-à-vis powerful others, but less frequently or obviously, particularly when it comes to the sangha. Lay males are praised for aiding monks in material ways and showing them deference. They see benefit and reassurance in attaching themselves to a powerful political leader or wealthy businessman or other individual (almost always male) of great power, whether material or spiritual. Yet they may well show a certain ambivalence in doing so. Particularly as they grow older, subordinate males become restive at the lack of autonomy they enjoy in such relationships: to be without autonomy reflects poorly on their standing, threatening to keep them always in a kind of social immaturity. Better that they become the superordinate party in as many of their relationships as possible, or failing that, then that they withdraw as much as possible into their own sphere.

Or that they become monks, which is in many ways the same thing. A monk's ascetic practice implies control not so much over resources and other people (although in the case of powerful and famous monks, such control is real) as control over the self.[11] However, a certain irony inheres in a monk's efforts to attain such control. The more he can be seen to have progressed in the spiritual advance toward triumph over his own desires, the more fervently others (especially women, but if he grows truly famous, many males as well) wish to attach themselves to him. The plainer his existence, the more Spartan his practices, then the more extravagant the gifts laypeople want to give him. Lay supporters take great joy, should they be possessed of sufficient means, in offering up to him gifts of terrific luxury. The size and pomposity of the buildings they build for him or the Buddha images they can present to him evoke, but in more permanent form, the extravagant proportions of the chair on which he is seated to give a sermon, and the cascade of flowers that surround it. A monk's rising spiritual power raises the standing of all supporters attached to him, and those supporters take real satisfaction in glorifying the evidence of his charisma, which is to say, in collaborating with him to generate it.[12]

Nevertheless, the demands that a monk can place on his subordinates are, evidently, circumscribed. Unlike powerful secular figures, he cannot send them (if male) into battle. (In fact, he may employ inflammatory rhetoric that can result in lay males committing violence, but the link between his words and their action must not be direct.) He cannot use them (if female) as a source of sexual pleasure or providers of offspring. He cannot (whatever their sex) exploit their labor to benefit himself in any straightforward manner. (He can, it is true, list tasks he wishes to see accomplished and, if he is powerful and important enough, assume that they will be.) Furthermore, he cannot make explicit demands on their wealth. (In actual practice, I have observed monks making fairly bald requests for expensive gifts, despite strictures against a monk expressing material wants.)

In sum, the exchange relations laypeople and monks enter into with each other impose constraints (sometimes stretched), while apportioning benefits, on all parties. Monks give up many material and physical comforts and pleasure, while laypeople cede all explicit claims to their own social standing when they make a great show of offering deference to them. How attractive acting on these options is for individual Burmans varies. But the advantages, while they vary according to the specific traits of the parties involved, are compelling to a great many people.

We see in these relationships all the features Dumont identified as being at play in hierarchical arrangements. Monks and laypeople, especially laywomen, enter into relations in which each party's specific qualities and abilities—monks' spiritual superiority, laypeople's capacity to provide material support—make them dependent on the other for the satisfaction of important needs. Lastingly bound to each other, they take advantage of their differences to ensure the durability of their connection and the mutuality of their benefits. At the same time, there exists a clearly ranked order of prestige. Monks enjoy great respect for their ascetic ways and their knowledge of Pali scriptures. Laypeople enjoy some measure of respect in proportion to their material wealth and power in lay society. Yet they must nevertheless acknowledge at every turn their inferior standing vis-à-vis monks. I was quite surprised, when I first lived in Rangoon in 1987 and was taken by a military officer of fairly high rank to visit a monastery, to see him prostrate himself on the floor when we met the monastery's abbot, and yet again when we took our leave.

In the largely anonymous encounters that take place outside on the roads, inequality reigns and differences entail a ceaseless competition for preeminence among those with the wherewithal to make a bid for it. At a *dhamma* talk, or even in the ordinary encounter of a monk with laypeople at a monastery, by way of contrast, hierarchical understandings come fully into play. Scenes informed by Buddhist roles are ones in which people know their place, and people are happy, for the most part, to take their place. It is true that people of similar standing may compete quite resolutely: lay sponsors may find themselves locked in arguments with each other. But encounters among unlike participants, such as among monks and laypeople, are expected to proceed smoothly, to the benefit and satisfaction of all concerned. They instantiate all that Burmans idealize about appropriate, which is to say, hierarchically ordered, relationships.

Few Burmans are very familiar with egalitarian ideology, and for most Burmans, hierarchy, and so inequality, which differences necessarily generate, is in the nature of things. There is simply no other show in town. But to say that does not mean that inequality admits of no argument, or of no variation. Hierarchical relations, as an organized form of inequality, are marked by enormous degrees of variation and manipulation, with people playing constantly on the constraints and opportunities that any given situation presents them with.

I insist on this point because readers may incorrectly infer that I believe Burmans quiescently accept the roles they find themselves in, thus that I deny them the agency I would attribute to more self-reflexive members of an egalitarian society. On the contrary. To state that most Burmans accept the hierarchical nature of social relations does not mean that they accept the specific distribution of roles, prestige, and prominence that they encounter in any given instance. In traffic, as in all other contexts, everyone remains alert to opportunities to raise their standing, as well as sensitive to the degree of deference others grant them. Agreeing on hierarchical principles implies only that the terms on which competition takes place are largely agreed on, not the circumstances, or distribution of power and prestige, that obtain in any given instance.

Loosely Structured Tea Shops

The justification for hierarchical arrangements, as Dumont explains in *Homo Hierarchicus* (1980), is that they bind people together in strong and lasting ways. Therein lies such arrangements' effectiveness as well as their burdensomeness. The advantage to gaining superior status in hierarchical situations is that it grants someone greater room to maneuver. But in principle, at least, it also brings people greater responsibilities for others'—their dependents'—welfare. A fantasized ideal, but one very difficult to attain (given its logical similarity to the notion that one hand could clap), would be to enjoy the freedom of superordinate status and the security that comes with having many people ready and available to do your will, without the obligations that such status usually entails. This ideal finds illustration in the practices characterizing a ubiquitous Burmese institution: the tea shop.

Tea shops were found everywhere during my more recent fieldwork in Burma. When I lived in Mandalay in 1987 and 1988, there were a certain number. By 2011, their numbers were vastly greater. Their rapid spread reflected, paradoxically, both greater prosperity—more people had the means to set up such establishments—and at the same time, the apparently endless stagnation of the Burmese economy: more people, or at least more males, had nothing better to do with their time than sit in tea shops, whiling away the hours in conversation, or smoking, or watching TV.

The largest crowds come to tea shops when an important soccer match is being broadcast live on satellite TV. If the match is being held in Europe, this can be very late at night Burmese time, but some tea shops at least stay open for the event and can count on drawing a great many customers, virtually all men, for the duration. At other times of day, crowds are greatest at meal times, but a fair number of customers appear throughout the course of the day. Most tea shops open about six in the morning. Many shut at six in the evening, but a certain number stay open through the evening, and there are even a very few open twenty-four hours a day.

What gets served at a tea shop is, first and foremost, tea, or actually, two kinds of tea, black and green, with a great many further distinctions among the ways black tea is prepared. (The model for this is black tea as served up in India.) Very fine black tea leaves, fannings, leaves of very poor quality, are boiled a long time in water (not infused in water that has been brought to a boil and then removed from the heat, as better grades of tea are treated elsewhere) to produce an intensely strong brew. Some of this brew is poured into a cup, to which is then added sweetened condensed milk and, sometimes, sugar. (Despite the bland wording of my description, making tea is quite a dramatic performance that requires pouring liquids in cascading ribbons from one container into another and finally into one of the tiny teacups in which it is served.) How much of each ingredient is added determines the degree of sweetness and intensity of the taste: every tea drinker has his preferred blend, which he names when he orders it. I drink it "lightly sweetened" (literally, "sweetness light"), which is still intensely sweet by Western standards but less so than how most Burmese drink it. Sweetened condensed milk comes in two varieties: domestic and foreign. The latter is considered smoother, richer, and better. Many tea shops offer it as an option, in which case a waiter asks those customers who look rich enough to indulge themselves in this way whether they want their tea *shè* (for the Burmese pronunciation of the English word, "special"), for which an extra charge is levied.

Green tea is not called "tea" at all in Burmese. It is instead referred to as "plain warm water," and a thermos of it is placed on every table at a tea shop, along with a number of tiny mugs set in a bowl full of water. Once someone has finished drinking the cup of black tea he has ordered, he takes one of the mugs out of the water.[13] Many men clean the mug by sloshing a bit of green tea in it (usually trying to hit most parts of the rim) and pouring that on the ground, then filling it with more green tea to drink.[14] The green tea in the thermos is free to anyone sitting at the table, whether or not they order black tea, or a different drink, or food. The thermoses are constantly refilled; if one is empty, or its contents have gone cold, a customer waves it in the air to have someone come refill it. Cartoonists make fun of losers who spend their days drinking free green tea at a tea shop without consuming anything they have to pay for.

Worth noting in all this is the procedure by which customers and waiters interact. Every tea shop employs a number, sometimes a large number, of young men and boys as waiters.[15] When a customer enters a tea shop, he finds an empty table or, if the place is crowded, an empty chair at a table where other people are already seated, and tells any one of the waiters what he wants to drink and, if relevant, what he wants to eat. The waiter yells the drink order, full voice, to the man making tea to the side of the seating area. Similarly, the waiter yells any food order to the kitchen. He returns shortly after with the order and puts it down. If the customer wants to order more of anything, he tells any of the waiters—it doesn't matter which one, and there is little probability it will be the same waiter he interacted with earlier—what else he wants, whether another cup of tea, or other drink, or snacks, or the like. No order gets written down. Instead, the size and variety of cups, plates, bowls, and other utensils sitting on the table provide a record of what the customer has ordered. (It would be clear whether a customer ordered his tea "special" because tea is served in differently shaped cups according to whether it is prepared with domestic or foreign condensed milk.) No cups or glasses or dishes are removed for the duration of a customer's stay. If he and others with him order a lot of drinks and food, the table may get crowded. But in that case the dishes are simply stacked and shoved aside, not removed.

When a customer is ready to leave, he says, "Clear accounts!" or "Money!" and any one of the waiters counts up how much the customer owes, based on the cups, plates, and other items remaining on the table. The waiter then takes cash from the customer and delivers it to the cashier. A tea shop has one seat, often raised and often in a square enclosure, where the cashier sits. The owner or a representative of the owner (often a relative) acts as the cashier, making change. The waiter tells the cashier how much the customer owes, takes the change, and returns it to the customer. There is no tipping in Burma. The nature of the system precludes any such practice.

These arrangements enable a customer to engage with any waiter at any time. After placing an initial order, should a customer develop a new need, he engages with any waiter who happens to be within hailing distance. He does not try to reengage with the same waiter he has had dealings with earlier. There would be no point. What matters is getting a waiter's, any waiter's, attention, whenever a customer has some want, whether to order or to pay. No bond is established between a customer and a specific waiter that lasts beyond the time, usually brief, from when a customer states his order to when the waiter brings it to him.

The relationship, which barely qualifies as one, between customers and waiters at a tea shop may seem inconsequential. It is of course fleeting, although not quite as fleeting as the brief encounters among vehicles and pedestrians on the roads. Yet it is telling. The difference in standing of the two roles, customer and waiter, is patent. A customer does not greet a waiter; he simply states an order, usually brusquely. Bourgeois manners have little currency in Burma, so people rarely say "thank you" in everyday interaction. (A monk mused to me once, "We didn't used to say 'Thank you' much. It's only since you foreigners showed up saying it a lot that we've started saying it.") If he needs to attract a waiter's attention, a customer can shout a phrase, one that translates literally as "Hey, beast!" or another one meaning, "Hey, little guy [kid]!" Or he can make a particular sound with his lips, one that to a Westerner brings to mind kissing, although it has no such associations in Burma. These methods do not strike Burmese as rude, simply unadorned. They reflect the obvious fact that a customer is of considerably higher standing than a waiter. Since the waiter is usually young—boys as young as eight or nine sometimes work in tea shops, although a majority are probably in their teens—and uneducated, and very likely of rural origin, no customer needs to show any form of deference toward a waiter. Many waiters live above or behind the tea shop at which they work, sometimes following older brothers or cousins who have started working there before them. They work long hours, often from dawn till dusk. They do not attend school. They are, as they are called and as they are interpolated (in both the literal as well as the sociological sense), "little people."

A tip is an artifact (one might say, optimistically if one has egalitarian commitments, a vestige) of hierarchical arrangements. It adds a supplement to the superordinate's payment to the subordinate, now taking the form of a gift, indicating the superordinate's awareness of the obligations his status imposes on him while at the same time shoring up his claims to that status as demonstrated by virtue of his magnanimity and economic power. Australians' more thoroughgoing egalitarianism relative to that of Americans shows in their refusal to engage in this clearly feudalistic practice. In Southeast Asia, by way of contrast, most payments are thought of in terms Westerners would label "tips" rather than "payments," because any payment tends to be tangled up in relationships, obligations, and expectations in the complicated ways that Mauss, Polanyi, and Bourdieu, among others, have analyzed (Mauss 1990; Polanyi [1944] 1957; Bourdieu 1990).

The fact that arrangements in a Burmese tea shop preclude the possibility of tips, that they so rigorously restrict the exchange among customers and waiters to that of individual acts of service and a single, impersonalized payment, shows how radically these brief, little-contextualized encounters differ from the norm of hierarchically ordered relationships otherwise common in Burman society. What might be called "tea shop rules" maintain clear-cut, in no way euphemized indications of inequality, with none of the inconveniences of obligation that hierarchical exchanges usually entail. In this way, they epitomize the seductive allure of market exchange: a chance to satisfy one's wants without having to interact in any meaningful way with another person or persons to do so. More immediately, in the Burman case, they indicate the appeal of what I will label autonomy: the capacity, largely although not categorically reserved for males, to act on one's own, in a social context that is only very loosely binding on its more privileged participants.

THE FLAP OVER LOOSE STRUCTURE

In terming the way tea shops work as "loosely structured," I invoke a phrase made famous with reference to Thailand by the American anthropologist John Embree in an article entitled "Thailand: A Loosely Structured Social System" that he published in 1950 (1950). A collection of essays edited by Hans-Dieter Evers, following on from a panel devoted to the subject at the Association for Asian Studies meetings in 1968, demonstrates both how fruitful and how controversial Embree's suggestion was, primarily although not exclusively among anthropologists specializing in Thailand (Evers 1969b). The critiques launched against Embree's essay are many, but much of the argument against it developed, rather unfairly, because people took Embree to mean that Thai society was without norms or organization, whereas what he appears to have intended was to note how many of Thai society's "rules," while real, nevertheless left individuals considerable room for maneuver.

Evers suggests in his introduction to the collection of essays why Embree's article aroused so much interest and argument when he, Evers, alludes to "the challenge posed by a society whose social structure seems to defy attempts at analysis within the normal categories of current anthropological and sociological theory" (1969a, 1). In other words, all those people who were used to looking at societies in Africa and East Asia characterized by unilinear kinship had not come up with tools with which to look analytically at a place like Thailand, where kinship is bilateral and most of the population consists (or did in the 1950s and 1960s) of farmers.[16]

Reading Embree's article today feels a bit like listening to a radio broadcast of FDR or Eleanor Roosevelt. Did people really sound like that then? Could a respectable anthropologist really write that way in 1950? Embree does not aim to denigrate Thai ways: he does not condemn Thai society in the ways that casual Westerner observers, such as tourists, may well do (to this day), even as he notes such unflattering facts as that theft among neighbors in villages is commonplace and that work arouses little by way of commitment. His essay does still have a very odd ring to it, such as when he refers to "the almost determined lack of regularity, discipline, and regimentation in Thai life" and illustrates the point by mentioning that when Thais walked together "there was no attempt to keep in step or to swing the arms in rhythm" (Embree 1950, 182). Outside military contexts or Indonesian civil servants' early morning calisthenics (which they learned from occupying Japanese soldiers during World War II), who in the world ever makes such an attempt? (Ah, the Japanese perhaps? See below.) Yet it seems too bad to throw the baby out with the bathwater. It may be exaggerated to see in a Thai habit of not walking in lockstep evidence of what Embree calls Thai individualism, yet that should not rule out thinking about Thai individuals' inclination to set their own priorities. Other points Embree makes—the flexibility about obligations to kin, the lack of enthusiasm for military discipline, the vagueness about a community's members' rights and obligations—support his claim more effectively and ring true, as Kirsch suggests, to many people with longer experience in Thai villages (Kirsch 1969).

Embree's views become more understandable when his real expertise and ethnographic experience are kept in mind. He specialized, after all, in Japan (and wrote a famous book about it: *Suye Mura: A Japanese Village*, 1939). In the heyday of structural-functionalism, the close adherence of many Japanese to the behavior Japanese society demanded of them was perhaps not surprising. Looking beyond Japan and Africa, however, Japanese habits can only strike outsiders as impressively consistent and conforming, sometimes, indeed, astonishingly so.[17] Embree stayed only very briefly in Thailand, but a brief stay was obviously sufficient to make clear to him how much unlike Japan it was. A brief stay in Japan would make it clear to people from almost anywhere how unusual Japan is.

Pointing out that Japan is something of an outlier does not make it otiose to ask whether Embree's characterization of Thai society is illuminating. Those, such as Niels Mulder, who dismissed it out of hand, tended to object to any label applied broadly to a society as a whole (1969). Those, like Herbert Phillips (1969) and Steven Piker (1969), who found more to appreciate in Embree's suggestion, took it as a useful way to describe the ties that bind—but only loosely—individuals in Thai families, in Thai villages, and in other group settings. Indeed, these and other scholars pointed out how few corporate groups were to be found in Thai society compared with many other societies in the world. At the same time, they emphasized how binding the constraints were on face-to-face encounter in Thai society, and how powerfully social standing impinged on people's thinking. They emphasized, in other words, the point that to speak of "loosely structured" elements of Thai social relations did not mean that nothing else was "tightly" regulated. Phillips made this point explicitly, when he protested, against Tambiah, that "in *Thai Peasant Personality* [Phillips's own book] it was clearly demonstrated that there were specific areas of Bang Chan that were 'tightly structured,' as contrasted with those that were 'loosely structured'" (Phillips 1969, 28).

Worth retaining from this now largely forgotten contretemps is the fact that in Thailand (and the same can be said of Burma), hierarchical understandings pervade all social relations and appreciating that fact clarifies much that goes on in Burmese society, just as in the Thai case; and that, at the same time, contrary to what some Westerners may assume mention of hierarchy implies, individuals within these societies act with varying, but in some cases considerable, degrees of autonomy. An unthinking Western understanding of hierarchy—really, it is often more a simple gut reaction to the word—takes it to suggest oppression, coercion, an unjust distribution of power and duties such that some people get to lord it over other people. As I have suggested above (and discuss at greater length in chapter 4), Dumont points out that these negative associations reflect a fundamental misunderstanding of what hierarchy is about, which is not necessarily power but rather values. For that matter, Embree's surprise at the way that Thais conducted themselves, a surprise predicated on the contrast he immediately noticed with Japan, should remind us that hierarchical arrangements are by no means uniform in the forms they take, the reasons adduced to justify them, or the effects they have on people. Thai and Japanese societies are both highly hierarchical in nature and highly disparate each one from the other. A point that I cannot develop here but nevertheless deserves mention is that we should start thinking in terms not only of "alternate modernities" (about which see Wagner 2007) but also of "alternate hierarchies."[18]

COMPARATIVE HIERARCHIES: TRAFFIC, SERMONS, AND TEA

Traffic, *dhamma* talks, and tea shops illustrate diverse ways in which disparities in power and hierarchical considerations manifest themselves in Burma.

Traffic on the roads throws people together only very briefly, with minimal communication taking place in momentary encounters. Traffic can be thought of as social relations at their most elementary because participants know nothing about each other except what can be inferred from the type of vehicle they are driving or riding in, or, in the case of people of little significance, not driving or riding in.[19] Hierarchy obtains only inasmuch as all parties have constantly to bear in mind the ways the weight, size, and power of the vehicle they control or, at the base of the order of prestige, the absence of any such vehicle at their disposal, establish the privileges and liabilities they bring to the encounter. Long-term relations of exchange do not in any way apply, and although people's behavior is clearly rule-bound, it is defined primarily by the simple fact of inequality. Or maybe it could be better called "size-bound," inasmuch as there is a definite order of precedence among participants who have to share the road. Still, as circumstances change, which they do constantly in traffic, relative size by no means precludes looking out for and acting on opportunities as they arise, opportunities available to different participants according to the respective features they bring to the competitive space they enter as soon as they start to move.

The world over, situations in which participants interact anonymously are likely to strip away the rules of deference and self-discipline most people would otherwise observe. There is an impression in such circumstances that cultural sanctions are in abeyance. Nevertheless, as I have tried to show, behavior on the streets of Rangoon or Mandalay, as elsewhere in Burma, follows a coherent set of rules, rules wherein actors pursue their advantage in accordance with their relative strengths, as these define their standing. Standing is always relative, however: how participants behave depends always on what other actors are also present.

Dhamma talks bring people and monks together in an elaborately organized performance of differentiated standing, privileges, and responsibilities. They provide a miniaturized version of relations among subordinates and their superiors that brings satisfactions both spiritual and affective to those who subordinate themselves, as well as to those, in this case monks, who enjoy superior standing. Males, ever ambivalent about forswearing too much of their autonomy, are likely to submit themselves only to the most famous and powerful monks. This is because they are likely to find an exchange in which they must defer to others somewhat compromising, unless the charisma of the sermon-giver is truly great and so warrants their submission. Thus many men simply give such occasions a miss. But women attend *dhamma* talks in great numbers, and when they do, they show great pleasure in having the opportunity to make dramatic display of their obeisance to respected figures of spiritual authority. Committed to attachment rather more than to autonomy, but of necessity wary of compromising impressions of their purity in displays of attachment, women appear to find subordinating themselves to charismatic sermon-givers deeply reassuring and highly satisfying.

In tea shops, interaction is face-to-face. But it is hardly any more sustained than in traffic. It allows maximum autonomy, which is the point, for the customers, whose position enables them to obtain service from any of a number of servers without the constraint of having to resume contact with a server on whom they have relied for service (and in this sense depended) earlier. This depersonalized, unequal arrangement provides a kind of model for one way that social relations may be idealized, at least for those in superordinate positions. It makes life easy for superordinates while maximizing their autonomy.

Long-term hierarchical relationships suggest obligations; the appeal of momentary relationships, for superordinate parties at least, is that they do not. Market economies appeal so much at least in part because they propose to make all encounters self-contained. Beyond the fleeting moment wherein objects or services are exchanged for money, no link remains, no tie continues to bind. Accounts are then, precisely as a customer at a tea shop calls out when he wishes to leave, "cleared." A tea shop offers a momentary instantiation of what superordinates can wish for but not always obtain: the privileges of superior standing without bothersome obligations.[20] It gives them a brief experience of what enjoys such popularity in much of the rest of the world among those who can assume that the superordinate role is theirs as a matter of course: a neoliberal dispensation that prizes market exchange over all other forms of interaction, at least in public.[21]

How people interact on the roads, at *dhamma* talks, and in tea shops reflects a simple but fundamental point about Burman social relations: behavior follows from relative standing among those present. No one who has spent time in Southeast Asia is likely to contest that assertion, or for that matter, find it surprising or perhaps even interesting. Yet the implications of that assumption, and related assumptions about hierarchy and difference, are sometimes too little attended to in outsiders' accounts of Southeast Asian social life (and by that phrase I mean to include political life). I propose to follow out those implications in a number of domains of contemporary Burmese life. Much of my focus concerns Buddhism and Buddhist monks, in large part because Buddhism was the topic people seemed most interested in discussing with me, whether inside or beyond monasteries' walls. In light of my own scholarly interests, and notwithstanding the fact that the monkhood is a largely homosocial environment, I take gender as key to my analysis of Burman society. The larger point, however, is that in analyzing attitudes and behaviors surrounding Buddhist beliefs and, more specifically, the institution of the monkhood, and in analyzing, more generally, issues surrounding gender that the institution of the monkhood implicates, we can see how Burmans have chosen to address the questions of how to handle difference and, furthermore, how to handle the conflicting wishes for solidarity and freedom, or attachment and autonomy, that people have to deal with everywhere.

Chapter Two

A Description of the Shweigyin Monastery

I have lived in three different monasteries in Mandalay. My longest stay was in one I have chosen to call the "Shweigyin Monastery"[1] and it is the one I return to whenever I spend time in the city.[2] To give readers some understanding of how life proceeds in and around a Burmese Buddhist monastery, I devote this chapter to a description of the monastery, its inhabitants, and their practices.

It is appropriate that I explain the way I have chosen to organize the material presented here, lest the meandering description appear unmotivated. Shelly Errington, a fellow specialist in Indonesia and a friend, once noted something about cookbooks that helps me think about ethnography. She said she had come to believe that there were two kinds of cookbooks: those that provide a compendium, as in *The 1,000 Recipe Chinese Cookbook,* and those clearly motivated by some overriding idea, with titles like *The Zen of Rutabagas.* Writing ethnography, it seems to me, presents an anthropologist with a similar choice. Do I want to relate all the information I learned about a Burmese Buddhist monastery, in the manner of thorough, responsible, and wearying monographs such as British social anthropology often produced in its glory years? Or do I want to present an analytic take of my own devising, supporting it by adducing, sparingly and strategically, information I choose to relay from my fieldwork? Like most of my contemporaries, I prefer to read a convincing analysis over a detailed and diffuse description. After all, we have learned that supposed exhaustiveness gives no more than the impression of objectivity, not its reality. Better that an ethnographer come to the point by making his or her argument clear, rather than burying it in an obscuring mountain of detail.

Nevertheless, in reading the literature about Buddhist Southeast Asia, I have often felt dissatisfied. Too often I have felt I was being given a partial, often interesting but highly abbreviated, description of a monastery, say, or of a meditation practice, or other elements of Buddhist religious behavior and institutions in Thailand, Burma, or elsewhere. Living a number of months in three monasteries in Mandalay, but not as a Buddhist, and without claiming to be one, I wanted to be able to fill in the record somewhat: to give readers a sense of what I myself was curious about, namely, the day-to-day activities and rhythms of a Buddhist monastery in Burma, and the tenor of the social relations monks entered into with each other and with lay people. Of course, social scientists have given up illusions about finding the perfectly representative token of any type. What I experienced was conditioned by the particular personalities, histories, and encounters that took place among the residents of particular monasteries at particular moments in time. The same goes for me: I brought a particular history and personality, as well as preoccupations, to the monasteries where I stayed.

So I have chosen in what follows to seek out a middle path. I first describe the monastery in which I lived longest, and I provide that description without a specific analytic agenda but rather with an eye to actual detail and, too, to those details' contextual circumstances. In later chapters, I make more analytic comments. Readers should be forewarned that I am not a scholar of Buddhism, properly speaking, and that my purpose, whether conducting fieldwork or reflecting and writing about it, has never been to take up the sorts of doctrinal matters that concern Buddhologists. Thus, for example, I do not discuss the particular texts whose study, discussed below, figures so importantly in the activities of many of the Shweigyin Monastery's residents, but rather the circumstances and methods whereby such study takes place. My interest in texts focuses on their uses rather more than on their meanings, which are sometimes nearly as esoteric to their learners as they are to me.

My hope is that in allowing myself the occasional excursus in the midst of a fairly detailed account of one monastery in this chapter, I will not try a reader's patience but rather provide relief from what might otherwise seem too microscopic a description of the institution itself. At the same time, I try to avoid judging the monastery's residents, on the one hand, or idealizing them, on the other, even though lay Buddhists concern themselves deeply with the degree to which monks and novices do or do not live up to the rules incumbent on them. Because I am not a Buddhist, and so do not believe that their behavior impinged on my chances of acquiring merit, I was free to look on monks, novices, and their lay supporters with relative detachment, just as Buddhist principles would enjoin me to do.

My description of the monastery begins with an account of the daily recitation in praise of the Buddha that brings all the monastery's residents together. I then describe the outer circumference of the grounds, and next move inside its gates to describe the various structures within its walls and the activities that go on inside those buildings.

Evening Recitation

Shortly before sunset every evening—so, sometime between 5:30 and a little after 6:00, according to the time of year—the slit gong sounds near the abbot's quarters at the Shweigyin Monastery in Mandalay. Slit gongs in Burma are struck with the same distinctive pattern that people use in many parts of Southeast Asia: a series of strokes, the first ones widely "spaced," but each one a little less so, till a series of very fast strokes is sounded, then gradually slowing again and finally stopping with one loud, final whack.

As soon as the sound can be heard, monks and novices start gathering on the pathway that runs through the middle of the monastery. They form two lines. One line, the longer one, is made up of novices; they line up according to their height, the tallest ones in the front of the line, the shortest ones at the back. (This tracks pretty closely with their age, which ranges from seven or so to nineteen, but not precisely.) A few feet to their left, monks form another line. They do so according to the consecutive number of "lenten seasons" they have worn the robe.[3] The monks tend to show up a little later than most of the novices, and they are a bit less diligent about attending evening recitation every day. Two of the monks, however, take special responsibility for keeping an eye on the novices. They hang back near the end of the novices' line, stopping them from cutting up too much.

Once the lines are formed, all the monks and novices raise their hands in a respectful gesture (in what looks to Westerners like a prayer position, although in Burma it is a general gesture of deference) and start to chant as they walk toward the *dhamma* hall, a very large space, about a hundred and fifty feet long and forty or so feet wide. At one end is a large image of a seated Buddha; facing it at the far end is a large gate and steps down to the ground level, under a porte cochere. High on the walls on either side of the hall are portraits of the monastery's earlier abbot (there have been only two in the monastery's history) and a few important donors. The floor is covered with large pieces of carpeting made out of some synthetic material: it is thin and fairly rough, of a bright green color.

The monks enter the hall first, followed by the novices, all forming a single line as they approach the building. They take off their slippers as they ascend the steps up to the *dhamma* hall. Each carries a square piece of cloth made out of the same material as their robes, a dark crimson or brown cotton. They put this down on the floor and then squat on it. Monks sit arrayed according to their status on a platform raised about six inches above the floor, close to the Buddha image. Beyond them, the novices sit in rows on the room's floor, grouped according to the hall in which they reside. The youngest ones, living in a hall presided over by an ethnic Palaung monk, sit in the back row.[4] Many of these younger novices know only the most basic of the material to be chanted and so sit silently through much of the recitation, although as the months pass, they get more phrases memorized and can participate more and more fully in the chanting.

The three highest-ranking members of the monastery's residents, the abbot (*hsayado*), the *tai'ou'*, and the *tai'kya'*, do not actually join the line entering the building. They enter the *dhamma* hall independently. The latter two monks sit on the platform on which the Buddha image itself rests, so about half a foot higher again than the platform on which the other monks sit. The abbot sits on a plastic chair placed at the rear of all the monks and novices. During my longer stay at the monastery, in 2011 and 2012, a layperson from Rangoon suffering from some sort of impairment (it may have been epilepsy), who lived behind the abbot's quarters, accompanied the abbot to the hall and then sat behind him, fanning him, during the proceedings. During a more recent stay, in 2013, that layperson had left, and a novice helped the abbot get up the stairs and get seated, although he then joined the other novices of his hall. The two monks in charge of the younger novices take places to the side and slightly behind the abbot.

At some point while the monks and novices arrange themselves in the hall, lights for the Buddha image are turned on. These consist of clear, bright lights directed at the image, and of colored lights that play about the Buddha's head. The latter, more evocative (to this American visitor, at least) of Times Square than anything more ethereal, create fast-changing patterns of circles, arrows, darts, and dots that expand, contract, go clockwise, go counter-clockwise, and so on, in blue, white, yellow, red, and green, in a series that takes about seven minutes to complete, whereupon it repeats without pause. It was explained to me that these lights (and those like them found at other Buddha images in Burma) represent the immense mental energy emanated by the Buddha at the moment of his enlightenment.

Once everyone is settled, one of the monks sitting at the rear of the hall starts the chanting. The abbot recites along with everyone else, but in a low voice and at his own pace. (I could usually hear him because, as the only layperson present, it behooved me to sit farther back than everyone else, and I chose to sit on the floor a bit behind the abbot.) The chanting consists of a series of formulas, said more or less in unison, lasting from twenty minutes to half an hour. After the first ten minutes or so, everyone changes from a squatting position to a seated one (aside from the abbot, seated throughout in a chair). The most respectful position in which to sit in Burma is not with legs crossed (as would be the case for males in many parts of Southeast Asia) but rather with legs to one side (as is considered most proper for women at all times). The monks and novices assume this position, with their legs to one side, and then continue chanting.

Mandalay is notorious for its mosquitoes, and early evening is a time when they are particularly bothersome. Monks and novices wave and swat away mosquitoes, and then within a few minutes start scratching the inevitable bites, every evening of the year. I learned to slather on mosquito repellent before going to join everyone outside the hall, but I never escaped an evening's recitation without bites.

I know no Pali (other than a few words taken into Burmese, in the same way that English has adopted a few Latin items) and so could not follow the contents of the chanting. I was informed that the chants consist of praises for the Buddha's virtues, as well as commitments to taking refuge in Buddhism's "three jewels" (once again, the Buddha; the *dhamma,* the legacy of the Buddha's teachings; and the sangha, the community of monks). But the chants vary, in principle at least, according to the day of the week. In 2011 and 2012, a senior monk told me, somewhat disdainfully, that monks did not alter the content of their chants appropriately, opting to stick to the chants intended only for Tuesday, which are the briefest and easiest. In 2013, some degree of variation did occur on different days. I knew this not only because on some evenings recitation lasted several minutes longer than other days but also because there was from time to time some confusion as to what chant came next. One of the two monks at the back of the room usually led off, chanting at the greatest volume, guiding the novices sitting in front of him. But sometimes, at a point of transition from one set of phrases to another, his chanting was overruled by one of the senior monks seated closer to the Buddha image, and then everyone followed suit, making the switch after a moment or two of confusion.

Shortly before the recitation ends, monks (but not novices) gather together in groups of three. Two of them recite a phrase; the third one then does so; they continue alternating in this way for a number of phrases. Then the monks go back to their original locations. The two monks seated behind the novices come over and crouch on either side of the abbot when this time in the proceedings comes, if the abbot is in attendance. This interaction, it was explained to me, is when monks "confess" to each other errors or missteps they have or may have committed. However, the whole exchange is scripted: no actual information is revealed, but rather generic references are made to "infractions, intentional or unintentional" any of them may have made. The interlocutor's response is similarly scripted: he urges the other or others to be mindful so as to avoid making the same error(s) again.

When the chanting ends, announcements pertaining to all the residents are made. For example, if lay donors are hosting the monks' and novices' first, early-morning meal the next day, the fact is made public at this point, with information as to whether it will take place here in the *dhamma* hall or off-site (in which case transportation is provided). The abbot may also choose to address the assembled monks and novices. He sometimes does so while seated in his chair. Other times, he makes his way forward, walking between novices along a pathway always left clear down the middle of their rows. Often he speaks simply to name different residence halls, granting them permission to leave. On occasion, he reads out the names of each of the monks and novices living at the monastery.[5] Every person whose name is called responds, in Burmese, "Present, Lord," and rises to leave. If he is not present, there is silence. The point is to note who has come and who has failed to come to recitation. If too many monks or novices have not appeared, the abbot rails against such fecklessness. Other days, he does not engage in this exercise but rather delivers brief "admonitions" as to proper behavior. He is particularly likely to do this on Sabbath days, the days that occur four times each lunar month at intervals of seven or eight days.[6] He never speaks above his usual, subdued volume, however, and when I asked one of the monks who sit near the front what the content of the abbot's remarks had been one Sabbath-day evening, the monk laughed and said he had no idea, adding that very few people could ever hear what the abbot was saying.

Often there are neither announcements nor admonitions, nor attendance checks. In any case, the event ends as the monks file out, in order of seniority, followed by novices, ordered by residence halls. The abbot exits separately, aided once again by the layman or novice who helped him come in. He is given the cane he used to steady himself on his way in and his slippers are positioned for him to put on as he starts down the steps.

As the monks and novices file out, one of the monks whose quarters are in the *dhamma* hall itself (there is a small room to either side of the Buddha image where a few monks are housed) turns off the fans and the overhead lights, and then closes the grating at the entrance everyone uses to enter and exit the hall. The monks and novices fan out in several directions to attend the various evening Pali classes or study halls, undertake other activities, or go back to their residence quarters.

The evening recitation is the moment of every day in which the "community" of monks and novices in this monastery comes closest to constituting something like a community, that is, a corporate group. Attendance is rarely, if ever, perfect. A few of the residents have permanently valid excuses: a team of monks cooks (and directs laypeople who join in the cooking) on evenings when lay donors have contributed funds for a meal the next day. They often start the process in the late afternoon and continue working till well after the recitation is over. Monks who have visitors stopping by their quarters do not interrupt their conversations to attend. And some monks and novices alike simply choose to cut class, as it were. Attendance falls particularly precipitously when the abbot is away. U Dhammananda, the monk who, as mentioned in the preceding chapter, was particularly kind to me, commented that it is like at a government office: when the bigwig isn't around, everyone slacks off.

U Dhammananda told me that at other monasteries, matters are not nearly so lax. For one thing, many monasteries hold recitation every morning, before dawn, as well as every evening. That used to happen at this monastery, too, but the abbot decided that it was simply too cold on winter mornings and, during one winter season, cancelled the practice. He never got around to starting it up again. The informant who told me this intimated that the abbot's own physical infirmity—he is in his eighties and clearly in somewhat delicate health—encourages him to let the morning cold justify cancelling early morning recitation.

Furthermore, although the abbot makes his unhappiness with monks and novices who fail to show clear, he does not impose any further sanctions. At other monasteries, miscreants suffer greater retribution, even if only in the form of public attendance-taking on a daily basis, rather than, as here, only from time to time. In his youth, U Dhammananda had stayed five years in a famously strict monastery in Pegu. He told me that there, at every recitation, the abbot read off every name of every resident, starting with his (the abbot's) own (to which he himself responded, "Present," but using the Pali word, not the Burmese word used at the Shweigyin Monastery). While he went down the list, another monk recorded the responses. Any monk who failed to attend was fined. At the Shweigyin Monastery, the youngest novices, shepherded about by their two teachers, are probably the most consistent attendees. Only as they grow older do they start setting their own agenda.

Loosely Structured Recitation

What I wish to underline about the practice of evening recitation is the degree to which it is and is not a collective undertaking: the degree to which even those who do attend the activity do so in the spirit of individual (or autonomous) versus collective (and in this respect, constrained as well as communal) action.

I should state at the outset that this take on evening recitation reflects my preoccupations more than theirs. Two monks, to whom I put the question of whether reciting such praises of the Buddha differed when done together or (as many people, both monks and lay, do remarkably often) individually, assured me that it did not. What matters about it, they both insisted, is that it is a way of concentrating one's attention. Whether you do this on your own or with others makes no difference.

U Dhammananda, however, did lament the fact that at this monastery, and throughout Burma, the chanting is so little disciplined. He contrasted this with what he had heard about the situation in Thailand, where, he is given to understand, one monk leads a group's chanting and does so in such a way that everyone starts each phrase and ends it together. He thought this admirable. But he added that it would take not only the abbot's insistence that the practice be taken on but also the use of a microphone and loudspeakers.

The fact remains, however, that little about the contents of the chants themselves encourages anything resembling chanting in unison. They display no rhyme scheme. They have no consistent rhythm: they are unmetered, and consecutive phrases differ considerably in length. Even these features of the chants do not rule out the possibility for some degree of collaborative performance. In other situations, monks sometimes use a patterned intonation when reciting two consecutive phrases. In the *Pahtan:* events many monasteries and pagodas undertake annually (see chapter 6)—the uninterrupted recitation of what is considered the most esoteric text in the canon, over the course of five, seven, or even ten days—for example, one phrase ends with a rising intonation, and the following one with a falling one. In evening recitation at the Shweigyin Monastery, however, this device is not used. Phrases are led off and concluded in a fairly repetitive but unremarkable intonation, with monks and novices joining in and finishing at approximately, but only approximately, the same time.

All the ways in which evening recitation could be made obviously pleasurable, therefore, were minimized: there is no singing, no meter, no choreographed movement aside from the transition from squatting to sitting, and no interaction except for the monks' scripted (and perfunctory) asking for forgiveness of one another. Group activity can be an occasion for shared attention, in itself an experience that can foster a sense of community. This sense could be further enhanced and made more aesthetically powerful by a number of modes (oral, aural, and physical). But in evening recitation, these options are not taken up.

This deliberate passing over of opportunities for group action—and with it, group solidarity—seems a consistent pattern at the monastery. The solidarity conceivable among its residents, a masculine solidarity that the environment might foster, certainly appears to obtain among some of them. Indeed, monks are social beings, like all the rest of us, and some degree of such solidarity exists for all of them. Yet it is neither recognized nor honed. A monk's pursuits are solitary. In principle, a community is irrelevant to an individual monk's efforts—except, of course, and this stands in contrast to what I have just described, inasmuch as he is completely dependent on laypeople for his basic needs. Yet the ideal, and this is true in Thailand and Burma alike, is the lone forest monk pursuing his spiritual improvement far from all human company. Solidarity, in fact sociability in any form, is precisely what this ideal figure stands firmly and dramatically against.

Indeed, the play between collective and individual action evident in the monastery's evening recitation, and the greater store set by the latter, shows in an array of features of monastic life, of Buddhist understandings, and of social life in Burman society more generally. It brings us back to the question of whether we can profitably resurrect the concept of a "loosely structured social system" when discussing Buddhist Burman society, no matter what conclusions Thai specialists may have reached, or failed to reach, on the topic (see chapter 1). I would like to suggest that the concept is indeed useful, that it need not be dismissed, provided we take it to refer not to a given, stable, condition of Burman (or Thai) society but rather to a set of options or choices that people must confront in any society, and that Burmans (and I think Southeast Asians more generally) are inclined to respond to in fairly consistent ways.

Those choices, as the following chapters are intended to demonstrate, turn on the degree to which any individual wishes to feel him- or herself closely bound to others. In respect to both the ideological preferences that Burmans express and the practices that Buddhism prescribes, Burmans display an inclination to prize autonomy, countering a contemporary Western psychological (and pop-psych) emphasis on intimacy. In either context, of course, Burman or Western, individual variability is great: I am not promoting a return to inflexible notions of "modal personality" or cognate concepts. Nevertheless, I am confident that communities everywhere have to address the matter of how people will connect to one another, and with what degree of intensity, and that different communities value some patterns and disvalue others in the forms such connections take. None of us are robots; none of us follow a memorized script called "culture," a point that critics of the concept of culture never tire of repeating. Yet social interaction poses questions we all have to address, and we address them on the basis of what we hear, observe, and intuit as members of communities—on the basis, that is, of our cultural experience, or what Bourdieu has taught us to call our habitus (1990).

The Monastery's Periphery

The Shweigyin Monastery occupies a rectangle of flat land in a relatively prosperous, although not truly wealthy, neighborhood in Mandalay. A solid brick and plaster wall surrounds the perimeter, interrupted by two gates large enough for cars to pass through on the west side and one of similar size on the east. A smaller gate, permitting only foot traffic, grants access to the street on the south side of the monastery. There are no openings in the wall along the north side, which runs parallel to a small canal.

When I stayed just one night in the monastery in 1987, all the gates were closed and padlocked at night. Lay students living there at the time told me that the gate along the east side could be used for sneaking back in after hours—or you could always hop the wall. When I stayed there in 2011 and 2012, the gates were no longer locked at all under normal circumstances. I was told, however, that during the Saffron Revolution, the period in September and October 2007, when monks in Rangoon and elsewhere in Burma demonstrated against the regime, the abbot of the monastery locked all the gates, refusing monks and novices permission to leave the grounds for any reason. He justified this move by saying that he didn't want any of the monks and novices under his supervision to endanger themselves by getting involved in political affairs. Some people suggested to me that he also wanted to make sure that residents did not, by getting involved in political affairs, endanger the good relations that he enjoyed with important military and political figures in the city.

A lot of garbage, especially plastic bags, blows into the area between the wall and the canal on the monastery's northern side. Other than that, nothing is found there except for some trees and bushes. A sign of changing times was the work I saw being done to clean up and stabilize the walls of the canal in September 2013. This project was undertaken by the city authorities, not the monastery. During the long years of military rule, very little by way of infrastructural projects was ever undertaken in Burma's cities. The sole exception was the colossal project of building the new capital of Naypyidaw (Lubeigt 2012).

At the northwest corner of the monastery, between the wall and the street, is a bathing and washing area with a steady supply of water available for public use. Poorer inhabitants of the city, even if not truly indigent, often have no indoor plumbing (although they usually have pit toilets in the backs of their houses or workshops) and so rely on these street-corner water sources for washing needs. Burmese always bathe fully clothed, with a cylinder of cloth wrapped around their bodies, so no one's physical modesty—much insisted upon—is ever compromised, and it is not considered inappropriate for males and females to bathe in close proximity to each other at such public sites.

There is nothing else along the western wall of the monastery other than the two large gates that provide access to the monastery for most visitors, plus a few large trees that provide shade. At the southwest corner, a number of men with motorcycles often stand about. They provide taxi services, cheaper than the fares for a regular taxi would cost. (There are very few taxis in Mandalay in any case; these motorcycle taxis are much more numerous and more easily found.) An elementary school across the street causes a traffic jam, made up mostly of motorcycles, plus a few cars and a few bicycles, in the morning when the school day is about to start, again at lunchtime, when parents or nannies bring the students their lunches, and at the end of the school day. Many parents eat lunch with their children and will spill through the two gates into the monastery looking for shade and places to sit when they do so. A monastery's grounds constitute a kind of public space (in a city where parks are almost nonexistent), and no one is surprised at this temporary occupation of benches, steps, and other convenient places to sit—some people bring along mats to spread on the ground for the purpose—during the lunch hour.

To the east of the monastery is a quiet residential street. The streets running along the monastery's western and southern walls, however, although not really main streets, are busy and the source of considerable noise. Mandalay's streets are crowded with an enormous number of motorcycles, most of them smuggled in from China. Young men often choose to ride them in such a way as to maximize the noise they make, or arrange, by fiddling with their engines or mufflers, to make them tremendously loud. Trucks and cars in disrepair are also very noisy. Late at night, even if traffic is light, the noise of watchmen making their rounds (which always includes striking metal against metal in the same pattern as used when the slit gong is struck to summon monks to evening recitation) precludes anything like silence. A monastery is conceived of as a place of refuge from the world, but not of quiet refuge.

The space between the southern wall of the monastery and the street, a strip of uneven ground about ten or twelve feet wide sloping up to the street, accommodates a number of informal businesses. Close to the southwest corner is a betel quid stand. Chewing betel is a pervasive habit among Burmese men. Statistics published during my stay in Mandalay indicated that the habit—actually, an addiction—is more pervasive among Burmese males than among any other population in Asia, higher (at something like 51 percent of Burmese men) even than among males in India. Although the combination of a certain type of leaf, a dab of lime, and the fruit of the betel has beneficial health effects on its own, virtually no Burmese takes it without also putting tobacco, and sometimes other ingredients, in their mouth at the same time. Tobacco consumed in this way is deleterious to people's health in a number of ways. Ironically, some men take up the habit to try to break their smoking habit, either because they cannot afford to smoke as many cigarettes as they desire or because they are aware that smoking is bad for their health. Too often, they end up addicted to cigarettes and betel both.[7]

A number of plastic strings suspended between the wooden betel stand and a nearby tree provide a way to hang issues of weekly journals and magazines available to buy from the same couple that run the betel quid stand. Passersby can see whether a new issue of a journal is out yet by glancing at this display. If they see something they want to buy, the sellers get a copy from stacks of them they keep behind the betel quid stand.

Burma's censorship laws prevented news of any interest from being published for decades. Weekly journals covering popular culture, sports, and a few other innocuous topics were the only fare available, apart from the government mouthpiece, the *New Light of Myanmar,* until quite recently. But by the time I started my more recent fieldwork, in August 2011, a few more interesting journals, published weekly, were testing the waters, publishing political news, both domestic and international, and seeing what the censors would tolerate. No one knew just what the change of government—from the military State Peace and Development Council's overlordship to the new, putatively civilian regime that took power in March 2011—meant with respect to journalistic freedom of expression. (I say "putatively civilian" because virtually all the new leaders had been high-ranking members of the military till shortly before parliamentary elections were held in November 2010.) But as mentioned in the preface, once

Daw Aung San Suu Kyi met with President Thein Sein, in August 2011, and at the end of their meeting the two of them posed for photographs beneath a portrait of her father, the slain revolutionary hero, General Aung San, at the presidential palace in the new capital of Naypyidaw, people knew that matters had certainly changed. For decades, the image and even the very mention of Daw Aung San Suu Kyi's father's name was anathema to the military rulers.[8] The fact that she could now be received by the president, and that they could both be seen standing below an image of her father, meant that a sea change had taken place in the authorities' relations with her, and so, implicitly, with a Burmese public for whom she stood as a symbol of resistance to the military's ironfisted rule. It remained the case until April 2013 that the government reserved to itself the right to publish a daily paper. But weekly journals were able to mix political commentary in their contents, making them interesting and readable in a way that they had not been for decades.

Further east along the wall, beyond the small gate allowing pedestrians entry to the monastery grounds, two food stalls started up during my stay in 2011 and 2012. The first, which opened late in the afternoon every day, was manned by a university student who was paying for his education and living expenses by serving up a mixed vegetable stew, *malahin,* originally Chinese, that has become popular recently in Mandalay. He had a large table with the various ingredients set out on it. To one side, he had a single burner, powered by propane, on which he cooked the vegetables in broth. If a customer wished to eat on the premises, a few tables, very low to the ground, with plastic chairs to match (common to all sorts of modest roadside places to eat or drink in Burma), were set between his work area and the monastery wall. More customers ordered food and then took it away. In that case, like other food sellers in Burma, he poured their food into cheap-quality plastic bags in bright colors—pink, green, blue, and so on. Before plastic bags became so ubiquitous, Burmese often brought metal containers with them for carrying food they bought from sellers. The practice has almost completely died out. Alarmingly, hot liquids are also transported in plastic bags, not metal containers. Tea shops dispense great quantities of the hot, sweet milk tea described in chapter 1 to customers in this way. This young man did not serve drinks other than green tea ("plain warm water") in thermoses on the little tables. If customers wanted to eat their vegetable stew with rice, he got a plate of it from the women who had opened a food stall next to him. The two stalls were separated, partially, by a cloth draped between them. When I returned to the monastery in 2013, the student had closed up shop. His neighbors did not know what had become of him but assumed he had finished his studies.

The two women who ran the stall next to his are nieces of the monastery's abbot. They live on the monastery grounds with their husbands and young children. The husband of the younger woman sometimes comes and helps out with the cooking and other chores that arise, including looking after their small child. A greater range of foods is available here: various Burmese curries and fried snacks. Customers can order Burmese salads (ginger, green mango, and the like) made up while they wait, to eat on the premises or to take away. Most customers show up on motorcycles and take the food away with them.

Lighting after dark here along the street that runs south of the monastery is poor, as it is in many places in Burma, because the power grid is highly unreliable. This is not necessarily cause for complaint. Monks are forbidden to eat after noon, according to the *vinaya,* the list of 227 rules guiding their behavior. Nevertheless, novices and younger monks do not always observe this rule scrupulously. A few of them sometimes appear on the other side of the wall, so still within the monastery's grounds, at the back of this stall and order food. It is convenient for them to be able to place their order and pick up the food relatively discreetly, hanging back in the shadows rather than having to come out and stand in front of the sellers' table. The abbot would not approve of this behavior. But in the evening, he could be assumed to be in his quarters, well away from this spot. His nieces, making a tiny profit on each order, are hardly likely to report the infractions.

Directly across the street from the two food stalls is a large tea shop. In addition to tea, prepared in the manner described in chapter 1, a full range of other hot drinks is served. Coffee, prepared from packets containing dried milk powder and sugar, has become popular in Burma in recent years. It is considered more cosmopolitan and prestigious to drink coffee than tea—it is also more expensive—but few foreign visitors to Burma would find it palatable if they were used to drinking coffee of even the most mediocre quality elsewhere. Cold soft drinks are also available. Fresh fruit drinks can be had as well, but only from about eight o'clock in the morning till about six o'clock in the evening. (This tea shop stays open from six o'clock in the morning till the wee hours, especially if a soccer match is being televised from Europe.) The fruit drinks are sold out of a different stand, not from the tea shop's kitchen, in a pattern characteristic of a number of food suppliers: noodles are available from another stand, rice and curries from yet another. These are actually distinct businesses, working semi-independently from the tea shop. Other foods, especially those associated specifically with tea shops (such as the Burmese version of the Indian bread *naan*, baked in clay ovens and served with small portions of curried chickpeas; *poori*; and Chinese crullers, although the latter only in the morning) are prepared in the tea shop's kitchen.

Dramatic illustration of how fast Burma is changing came in January 2012, when signs appeared in the tea shop that free Wi-Fi was now available. Very few customers possessed personal computers, but at any given time, two or three well-heeled customers could be seen using them. Connections tended to be slow, and some days service was shut down for whole regions of the country. Still, this was a spectacular advance from the recent past, when getting access to the Internet required going to an Internet café and relying on difficult connections.

Monks and novices come over to this tea shop often. Many of them watch soccer matches avidly. When no match is on, they sit and drink tea or soft drinks. They are unlikely to eat in so public a place after noon, but soft drinks are considered acceptable refreshment in the afternoon and evening for monks. These are, for the most part, younger monks, perhaps in their twenties or at most their thirties. Older monks, in their later thirties and older, tend to adhere a bit more closely to a general sense that monks should avoid places of public entertainment, whether tea shops or sporting events or theatrical performances. U Dhammananda told me that when he travels to other towns to give *dhamma* talks, he regrets the fact that once he has delivered a sermon in public, he no longer feels free to go to a tea shop, even in the morning when it would be perfectly licit for him to do so. Too many people would recognize him, he told me, and seeing him sitting there, their respect for him would be diminished. "You feel free," he said, addressing me directly, "to go to the tea shop across the way, but that's because you have no official position here in Mandalay. If you were to take a job teaching at Mandalay University, you would soon feel embarrassed to be seen at a tea shop. You would only be willing to go to fancy coffee shops, sitting behind glass windows. Otherwise, your standing would fall."

Another sign of changing times: the tea shop's manager told me in October 2013 that the establishment would be closing down at the end of that month. The land on which it stood was owned by a wealthy family. They had raised the rent repeatedly over the years, from manageable sums at first to a very substantial US$2,000 a month recently. Now the land was to be sold; there was no chance, the manager felt, that anyone would be able to operate a tea shop on the premises in light of what new owners would likely charge by way of rent. He was going to move to the northern part of the country and go to work in the jade business. His father lived in that region; his family would remain here in Mandalay but he would travel back and forth regularly.

The manager's predictions turned out to be wrong. A famous tea shop in downtown Mandalay was forced to move when the landlords there decided to use the land for a different purpose. The owners moved it to this location, where they built an impressive two-story structure. They charged higher prices than normal, to the dismay of many monks and novices at the Shweigyin Monastery. Yet they appeared, in 2014, to be doing a thriving business.

Farther east along the monastery's southern wall is another betel leaf and snack stand, and a little stall selling a few small items in daily use: laundry detergent, matches, charcoal for kitchen fires, and so on. These two stalls are run by a couple who live about a block away but spend all day every day in and around the monastery. The man spends most of the day manning the stalls. His wife is sometimes there, but she can often be seen doing minor chores on the monastery grounds. She and her husband have no children and doing good works seems to matter considerably to this woman. Shortly after sunrise, she often sweeps the area near the abbot's quarters. She also helps burn garbage when it piles up near one of the front gates. When I first moved into the monastery and asked how I might get my laundry done, a couple of monks informed the woman of my needs and she turned up early the next morning, saying she could take care of it for me. When later that day she gave me back my now laundered clothes and I asked how much to pay her, she demurred, saying she was looking for no payment. I gave her the equivalent of what I had been paying the Indian launderers I had taken my washing to elsewhere in the city when I lived at a different monastery. She accepted the money with some show of embarrassment, saying, as she continued to say whenever I pressed payment into her hands, that she would use it to make donations to the monastery.

INSIDE THE WALLS

Within the monastery compound are set a great variety of buildings. Virtually none of them date back more than about fifty or sixty years, and many are more recent than that. As Thant Myint-U notes in his book, *The River of Lost Footsteps,* old things—buildings, pagodas, furnishings—mean little to most Burmese (2006). Prestige surrounds what is new, not what is old. As a result, lay donors who wish to display their devotion provide materials and labor to build new structures on the sites of older ones that are torn down to make room for them. The fact that the Burmese economy fell into such disarray between Ne Win's takeover in 1962 and his (at least ostensibly) departure from the scene twenty-six years later means that a great many buildings in Burma, whether private homes, public offices, or buildings in monasteries, were built in the 1950s or 1960s, in a style that is familiar from other regions of Southeast Asia: boxy structures made of brick and plaster, with wire obstructions in front of windows (sometimes the wire is arranged in a decorative design) and flat roofs. Several of the buildings at the monastery are of this style. But the most prominent buildings are of more recent construction and in a somewhat grander, or at least flashier, style.

Probably the oldest buildings, out of thirty-six in the compound, are two wooden structures in the northeast corner. One is only one story, raised on stilts, with just a few rooms. This building was occupied, at the time of my longer stay, by a man in his twenties, ostensibly a university student but whose health prevented him from attending school. He hailed from the village that the abbot is from, and he said that he was related to the abbot, although I was not clear precisely how. (As another friend from a village said, "Eventually, everyone's related to everyone in a village, either by descent or through marriage. But you lose track of the exact ties except for the closest ones.") His mother was staying with him, cooking and doing his laundry and tending to his needs, although he was by no means helpless. A narrow porch along the front of the structure enabled the student to talk with people when they stopped by; as is common in Burma, host and guests were happy to sit on mats spread on the floor of this verandah.

A few yards west of this structure is a two-story one, with no verandah and only a few steps leading up to a door cut into the plaited bamboo walls. The walls are a blotchy dark brown because pitch has been applied to them to make them last longer and to keep out wind and rain. There are a few openings on the ground story and the second story: these pass for windows. The downstairs portion of the structure makes up the living quarters of a man in his late thirties, also a relative of the abbot from their native village, near Myinjan, a town several dozen miles southwest of Mandalay on the Irrawaddy River. This man lives alone. His furniture, which includes a large TV and a display case made of good hardwood, takes up only a small portion of the downstairs. So it seems as though more people could live there. But telling people where to live is the abbot's responsibility, and for some reason he has not told anyone to live here with this man. He works as the manager of a Chinese-owned motorcycle store a few blocks away. He has never married; he told me that a number of women would like to marry him, but he has yet to meet the woman he wishes to marry. (A monk told me disapprovingly that he is a playboy who has taken up with a number of women and then cast them aside.) He spends little time here. He works long days and then goes to the tea shop across the way—I saw him there quite often—to watch soccer on TV.

The second story of the structure is occupied by five younger men. Four are university students; the fifth, Ko Kyaw, moved here from the abbot's natal village seven years before my arrival to start his university studies and then, once he finished his studies, stayed on. He now works collecting monthly payments people make on motorcycles they have bought on credit. One evening when I met him at the tea shop and we wanted to continue our conversation elsewhere, I asked if I could come with him to where he lived, since I had never seen the upstairs or met the students resident there. He said that wouldn't work: there were no lights. Since the students do not study in the evening but only watch soccer on TV and play cards, the abbot did not allow the generator providing electricity to the structure to be turned on. Only in the weeks immediately preceding exam time, when the students might be expected finally to start looking at their books, are their quarters illuminated at night.

Another older, wooden structure near the students' quarters is used only for storage and is kept locked. Two rows of latrines, cement structures with wooden doors fronting individual cells with a squat toilet in each, are set near the northern edge of the compound, west of the two structures where students live. One short row of latrines appears to be for the use of the students and other lay visitors. The other, longer row of latrines has lettering over each door indicating whether it is for the use of monks or of novices. The most senior monks in the monastery have private latrines and bathing areas inside their respective residence halls, but most of the monks and all the novices use these or similar facilities located along the periphery of the monastery's grounds. South of this set of latrines is a bathing area. Many residents, although more novices than monks, enjoy playing soccer in this area in the afternoon, removing their outer robe and hitching their lower garment up around their loins. Playing sports is not actually permitted them, according to the *vinaya*. A senior monk told me that novices played soccer in this area because there were enough buildings between it and the abbot's quarters that they were pretty sure he wouldn't see them. Other people in Mandalay, both religious and lay, told me that playing sports is a new development in the sangha but one that is tolerated now as it has become more and more difficult to persuade boys and young men to take on the robe.

To the west of the bathing area is a two-story house originally built to house the abbot's mother. Since her death several years ago, it has housed the abbot's sister and her husband, along with their two daughters and those daughters' husbands and small children. The abbot's brother-in-law is a contractor; when a new building is constructed on the monastery grounds, something that happens quite often as older structures get replaced by newer ones, he takes charge of the project—to his considerable profit, one of the senior monks noted laconically.

Cooking and Eating

Next to the house of the abbot's kin is a kitchen area. This area is quite large, but little of it is now in use. The large, older installations for cooking great quantities of rice, consisting of a number of big cement hearths, have been made obsolete by the acquisition of two newer, compact rice steaming units wherein a great number of large pans can be stacked, saving both space and energy. West of this area is a large shed—a roof over a cement platform, without walls—in which curries, salads, and other dishes are prepared. Curries are cooked in large quantities in huge copper pans set over wood fires. A big, messy pile of wood of all shapes and sizes lies next to this cooking area; pieces of logs are pulled out from it as needed.

Cooking takes place when donors sponsor meals, often in connection with ceremonies they are holding in the monastery's large *dhamma* hall. Donors may have a meal catered by people outside the monastery. But more often, they arrange a date with the monk who takes charge of these matters, a monk from U Dhammananda's natal village, and ask the monks to prepare a meal for all of the residents of the monastery plus a specified number of guests. Certain months in the lunar calendar are considered particularly propitious for such events as weddings, and at those times the monks assigned to cooking duties may cook for many days in a row. They do not carry the curries to the *dhamma* hall, presumably because that would make too obvious the fact that monks as well as laypeople are not only cooking food but, still worse, they are cooking food for laypeople. Laypeople move the food from the cooking area to the *dhamma* hall where lay guests are seated at such times.

Other months, including the three months of the "lenten" season, are thought inauspicious and allow for no festive celebrations. During those months, the monks cook only when sponsors ask them to cook a meal in commemoration of a relative's death, some number of months or years before, or when the abbot has them buy food supplies so they can cook up curries to go with the rice the monastery's residents collect on alms rounds. No one wants to subsist on plain white rice.

It is not just the monks on the cooking crew who cook. Members of the abbot's family, such as his nieces, may join in cutting and chopping the great quantities of garlic, shallots, ginger, tomatoes, squash, meat, and the like that are the standard fare for these meals. (They or other members of their families often take tiffins of cooked food back to their house when the cooking is done.) In addition, lay visitors usually join in, people who have asked the abbot for permission to stay for a short period while they or their relatives seek medical treatment in Mandalay. These people cannot afford to pay for hotel accommodations. Provided they know someone who can vouch for them to the abbot, someone the abbot knows and trusts, they are unlikely to be turned down. Although most stay relatively briefly, everything hinges on how their treatment, or that of the relative they have accompanied, proceeds. In October 2013, I met a man in his sixties helping with the cooking who was spending several weeks at the monastery every few months. He and his wife lived in the Irrawaddy Delta area, very far from Mandalay. But when his wife was diagnosed with cancer, they were told that no facilities in Rangoon could treat her, because of long waiting lists, and they should seek treatment in Mandalay instead. So they went back and forth, the woman staying at the city's General Hospital while this man put up at the monastery, where he helped out with any chores he could tend to. He had had to stop working to care for his wife; their grown children paid for their transportation and their other needs. At the time, two other, younger lay men were staying in the same hall, south of the cooking area, while they put up temporarily at the monastery.

When laypeople are present to help with the cooking, monks on the cooking crew tend to sit on benches to one side and supervise the work, leaving the heavy lifting, especially, to the lay men. Lifting and moving the big vats of boiling curry require two men using large poles: it is something monks could do if they had to, but such work is more appropriate for younger, fitter, and lower-status lay men, if any are present.

South of the cooking area is a hall used solely to house laypeople putting up at the monastery. Laypeople who receive permission to stay at the monastery are assigned lodgings by the abbot. If they have particular connections with one of the monks, the abbot may tell them to stay in the hall where that monk lives. But such decisions as to where anyone stays, lay or religious, are the abbot's alone to make. U Dhammananda, from whom I had learned much in 2011 and 2012, seemed very pleased on seeing me reappear in September 2013. But the quarters where I had lived before were now occupied, he told me, so it was unclear where the abbot would choose to house me. U Dhammananda was happy when I expressed a desire to stay upstairs in the hall where he lived, since then I would be living among monks and novices, rather than in private quarters. (I thought that the loss of privacy would be outweighed by the greater opportunities to observe and talk with religious residents.) U Dhammananda coached me on how I should put the request to the abbot—and then sent me off to see how it went. He pointed out repeatedly that he could do nothing about this on my behalf, that the decision as to where I stayed was at the sole discretion of the abbot himself.

South of the cooking area and east of the hall where lay visitors put up is the hall in which the monastery's residents take their early morning and late morning meals.[9] Like all other structures on the monastery grounds, several steps lead up to the simple, rectangular room that makes up its entire interior. A number of round wooden tables are set on the floor, all the same size (with a diameter of about four feet), and all about a foot high. When the monks eat, senior monks sit at tables at the easternmost end of the hall, and monks and novices sit at greater distances from them, to the west, according to their status. East is generally a more prestigious direction than west in Burma. Buildings do not seem to be arranged relative to one another on the monastery grounds with reference to cardinal directions, but space within each hall is so distinguished. The large Buddha image in the *dhamma* hall is at the eastern end of the building; Buddha altars in all the other structures that possess them are invariably found along the eastern wall. The dining hall has no Buddha image. But on rare occasions, when the *dhamma* hall is being decorated or can for some other reason not be used for evening recitation, the monks and novices gather in this dining hall and face the eastern wall as though it did.

Monks and novices obtain their daily meals in a number of ways. At about dawn, or before, they are summoned to the dining hall for a light meal. Older monks often skip this meal; novices and younger monks do not. Then at about six in the morning, they form lines and, under the supervision of some of the middle-ranking monks, proceed through the monastery's gates in one of four directions to seek alms. They go barefoot at this time, members of residence halls going out together for the most part. Alms rounds take about an hour or so every morning. A monk leads the row, the monks and novices always walking single file and in silence, each of them carrying a black alms bowl suspended from the shoulder in a net bag. Laypeople, most of them women, standing by the side of the road with a container of cooked rice, spoon a small amount of it into each monk or novice's bowl in turn, the recipient standing still with his eyes downcast as laypeople do this. If the row of religious arrives at the home of laypeople who usually make food donations in the morning but are not in evidence, they halt and wait, silently, for a member of the household to appear. If no one does so, after a few minutes, they continue on their way.

Although rice is the primary form such donations of food take, laypeople may also give each mendicant some other small food item, such as one deep-fried fritter, or a small packet of coffee powder, or some food item other than rice. They put this on the cover of the alms bowl once the monk has set it back in place. Donations of curries, placed in larger containers, are carried by a few novices holding trays near the back of the line. As elsewhere in Theravada Buddhist societies, laypeople give monks and novices cooked food: cooking is proscribed for monks, who should have no part in growing or preparing their own food.[10] Although this rule against monks cooking is broken in practice, as mentioned above, it remains very present to everyone's thinking about proper religious behavior.

When these religious mendicants return to the monastery, they dispose of what they have been given in diverse ways. Most of the cooked rice in their alms bowls they dump unceremoniously into very large metal containers, retaining just a bit to eat as they please in the course of the morning. The large containers, placed at collection points near the east and west gates for the groups returning from different directions, get taken to the abbot's quarters, where they are stored until the residents are served their main meal between 10:30 and 11:00 in the morning. Whatever has been placed on top of the alms bowls is kept individually, to be consumed at leisure along with the small quantity of reserved rice. Rice that is collected from the mendicants but is left over, not eaten by the residents at their communal meal, gets dried and sold to merchants. The abbot's female kin take charge of this responsibility. The money they receive goes toward buying food during the lenten season. At that time, in the absence of lay-sponsored ceremonies in the *dhamma* hall, monks have little food coming in aside from what they collect on their rounds. The abbot then finances the purchase of food supplies (meat, fish, vegetables) for the cooking crew to cook and serve at the late-morning meal. Rice that monks and novices retain for themselves in their alms bowls does not always get consumed. What remains of it gets dumped, along with other garbage, near bathing areas where residents take their alms bowls later in the day to wash them. Laypeople often come around to gather up some of this discarded rice to feed animals they raise. Dogs also come by regularly to see what might be on offer.

During the weeks I lived with monks and novices in the hall above U Dhammananda's quarters, I noticed that the late-morning meal was actually consumed in two parts. The slit gong is struck to summon the monastery's residents to the dining hall, where they sit on the floor around the low round tables dispersed about the hall described above, and start their meal. But after a few minutes they get up and go back to their respective residence halls, where they resume their meal. A young monk explained to me that when they are sitting in the dining hall in the presence of their superiors, they feel inhibited. Only once they get back to their residence halls do they feel free to eat and talk in a relaxed fashion. Older monks, he went on, feel differently. They are happy to sit, eat, and talk in the dining hall long after the other, younger residents have retired to their respective living quarters.

Inhibitions surrounding eating in Burma take several, in some ways contradictory, forms. On the one hand, ascetic practices become the powerful: self-control demonstrates the discipline that characterizes, or should characterize, those who enjoy the right to exercise power. Both laypeople and monks often told me about monks of extraordinary potency who ate next to nothing during long periods, especially when they undertook meditation in the forest. More modestly, but closer to home (and to reality, I imagine), the fact that monks must not eat after noon convinces most Burmans that they are exceptional among humans: most laypeople say that they would find the practice of abstaining from eating from noon one day till dawn of the next very hard to sustain. Yet to say that refraining from eating is a way of demonstrating and enacting power fails to consider the social contexts in which eating takes place. To eat first, before others do, and to eat heartily, displays superior standing; it is those of lesser standing, and those particularly who feel it appropriate to display their awareness of their lesser standing, who eat little and hurriedly in the presence of their betters, like the younger monks living upstairs in U Dhammananda's hall.

Monks *must* eat in order to keep the system of exchange with their lay supporters going. The logic of the system is well-known: monks receive and consume cooked food from laypeople; laypeople receive in return the merit that accrues from donating food to the sangha. For monks to refuse to accept food from laypeople, as some monks have done at moments of great historical conflict in Burmese history, and as some did in 2007 during the so-called Saffron Revolution, packs such a wallop because they are excluding those laypeople from the chance to acquire merit in the most obvious and familiar way available to them. (Laypeople undertaking ascetic practices, especially meditation, for themselves short-circuits the system in another way, as discussed in chapter 7.) Acquiring merit is a real preoccupation among Burmans, as much (and with similar motivation, in some ways) as saving money toward one's retirement is for many Westerners. To find oneself blocked from being able to increase one's store of merit is as disturbing for many Burmans as learning that one's employer has stopped paying into one's pension fund would be for many Westerners.

Even though monks must eat food they receive from lay donors, both to keep themselves alive and to complete the exchange with laypeople, they should not concern themselves with what they eat, and they must not eat after noon. In principle, in accordance with the first point, a monk should let all the food he receives mix together in his alms bowl. In fact, that does not happen; it is an idea rather more than an actual practice, as my account of the Shweigyin Monastery's residents' alms rounds should make clear. The same can be said, for many monks, about the prohibition on eating after noon.

When U Dhammananda and I discussed the possibility of my staying in the upper story of the hall in which he lives on my return to the monastery in September 2013, he mentioned that the abbot might be reluctant to give me permission to do so. If I stayed downstairs, in the large room housing Buddha images and U Dhammananda's impressive collection of canonical texts, that would probably be fine. Upstairs, however, I would be privy to the compromising fact of monks and novices eating late in the day. This practice is not unknown to the abbot; in fact, it is common knowledge within the confines of the monastery (and of many others, as well). But for me, a layperson, to observe it would be unfortunate. I suggested that in asking the abbot permission I simply name the hall, without specifying on which floor I would sleep; U Dhammananda found this a fitting strategy. When I returned to the hall, having obtained the abbot's permission to stay there, U Dhammananda told the oldest monk staying upstairs (a monk in his late twenties) that I would be moving there but that the residents were not to alter their behavior in any way, that I was there to observe how they lived, not to judge their actions. I was impressed that U Dhammananda understood so well what I was about, and that he was so little concerned with keeping up appearances.

A monk's diet is often quite a rich one. Monks are proscribed by the *vinaya* from taking life, as well as from preparing their own food, so they must not, obviously, kill living beings to eat. But they are in no way prevented from accepting, indeed they would be failing to fulfill their own responsibilities to laypeople by refusing, cooked meat or fish when it is served to them. Thus Theravada monks are not vegetarians, any more than the Buddha was. (Indeed, he is said to have died from pork that had gone bad.)[11]

A meal served to monks by lay donors usually consists of a number of sweets, then an array of meat curries, vegetable curries, and salads, as well as rice, followed by another round of sweets, fruit, and tea or coffee, green tea, and pickled tea with the fried peanuts, fried garlic, and other condiments that go with it. Lay hosts who have invited monks to undertake a ceremony on their behalf, whether at their homes or at the monks' monastery, make sure that there is a great supply of bowls filled with these foods on the table; as the monks help themselves to some of each, the bowls are whisked away to get filled up again in a great display of devout hospitality. U Dhammananda commented to me wryly that monks' behavior is perfectly consistent: when their lay supporters are celebrating, monks eat; when their lay supporters are grieving, monks eat. Come what may, monks eat.

Monks' and Novices' Residences

Almost all the rest of the buildings to be found on the monastery's grounds, clustered along the eastern and southern edges of the compound, house at least one and in many instances a number of monks and/or novices. The abbot's quarters are in a one-story building. His bedroom is a small room off to one side, but the front room contains a set of large, new matching sofas and chairs, and a carpet, as well as desks and tables. No doubt important guests are invited to sit on the chairs, but I never saw anyone do so. Everyone else sits on the carpeted floor when they speak to the abbot; he either sits on a chair or stands before them, or walks about, tending to a number of matters at the same time. Many large sacks of rice donated by lay supporters are stored in a rear section of the room; they are kept there for safekeeping till the rice is to be cooked in the kitchen area. At the opposite end of the hall is a collection of Buddha images behind glass.

To the rear of the abbot's quarters is a room that was occupied during my earlier, longer stay by the man who accompanied the abbot to evening recitation, helping him to make his way up the steps, getting him seated, fanning him, and so on. This man had suffered some sort of medical or psychological difficulties and was said to be recovering in the calm surroundings of the monastery. On my return in 2013, I learned that he had gone back to his parents' home in Rangoon and the room was now occupied by the man who acted as driver for the abbot whenever he went out.

A number of vehicles are often parked on the monastery's grounds. In some cases, the identity of their owners is clear. For example, an old Land Rover was often parked in front of U Dhammananda's hall. He explained to me that it belonged to a Sino-Burmese woman who lived in Rangoon. She felt that the Chinese-language education available to her children in that city was inadequate, and so she had brought them here to Mandalay and enrolled them in a Chinese-run school, leaving her husband to continue working in Rangoon. She and her children lived nearby, but she found it difficult to park near where they lived and so often chose instead to park the Land Rover on the monastery grounds. I found this explanation a little thin: parking in this part of town was rarely difficult. But I never heard any fuller explanation of this woman's preference for parking her vehicle at the monastery.

The identity of other owners of vehicles is less clear, and is kept that way for good reason. The Burmese government has tried over many years to keep very close control over the flow of cars and trucks into the country. Anyone familiar with the horrific traffic of Bangkok, or worse, Jakarta, has to concede that unfettered access to cars brings nightmarish traffic congestion, pollution, and sprawl to Southeast Asian societies. It is as though traffic is a scourge as unstoppable as the Black Death. Only Singapore has managed to impose effective control over privately owned transportation (by means of draconian fees levied on car owners not just at the time of purchase but for the duration of a car's use), and the Singaporean government has complemented that control with the construction of an effective system of public transport. Burma has done the opposite: the government imposed hefty fees on the importing of cars but implemented the system in so corrupt a manner that ways could always be found to get around the regulations, while neglecting public transport (at least until very recently) to a scandalous degree. In recent years, the government has undertaken a number of initiatives to ameliorate matters. It has repeatedly made it easier to import vehicles from abroad (almost all of them used, as noted in the previous chapter), which pleases members of the new (if still small) middle class. It has exhorted owners to trade in older, inefficient vehicles (such as the formerly ubiquitous "four wheels," tiny little Chinese-made pickups used for decades as taxis) for newer ones. And it has made some effort to improve infrastructure and public transport. I sat in taxis in traffic jams in Rangoon for the first time in 2013, nothing like what I have experienced in other cities in Southeast Asia but still a clear sign of the plague of traffic that looms.

Through all the vagaries of official Burmese transportation policy, however, certain well-recognized exceptions to the labyrinthine rules have been made. Foreigners in Burma in the 1980s were often surprised to learn how many young men had started working on ships, no matter what their class origins. It often seemed a curious career choice for a college-educated son of elite parents. The explanation was simple: anyone working in that capacity had the right to import one vehicle a year into the country. This privilege brought a windfall, since the market in cars, reflecting myriad rules and the high cost of eluding them, allowed for a huge markup over what a (used) vehicle cost elsewhere. Another major exception, one that remains of interest to many, is for lay donors who wish to provide a vehicle for use to members of the sangha. In that case, in light of the laudable goal of assisting members of the sangha, many fees are waived, reducing the cost of a vehicle by half or more.

The "use" of a vehicle is, however, an ambiguous term. How much of the time would a vehicle need to be in the actual possession of a monk for it to be said to be in his use? What about when he did not need it? Might it then be borrowed back by the donors? Fine points, details: a monk cannot appropriately own a vehicle, since in principle a monk owns only a short list of items named in the *vinaya*. So some vehicles appear and disappear fairly regularly on the monastery's grounds. Asking whose cars or vans such vehicles are usually brings mumbled disclaimers about not knowing what the answer might be.

One car seemed to be a fixture outside one monk's hall. It was whispered to me that it belonged to the monk living in that hall and that he made money by renting it out, even though he himself could of course never be seen driving it. A widespread attention to what might be called, borrowing Buddhist phrasing, "right appearance" precluded my taking this matter up with the monk in question.

The most impressive of the residence halls, in outward appearance, is not the abbot's but rather that housing his younger brother, who is the second person in the monastery's hierarchy of offices, the *tai' ou'*. The building is very tall, with a large staircase in front. As is the case with important older buildings in Burma, the staircase makes the ground-level rooms appear insignificant, resembling the storage areas (and often domestic animal pens) to be found beneath farmers' houses, while magnifying the imposing impression made by the story above it. This building has three stories, decorated with a good deal of the gold-paint metalwork now popular in Burma that imitates the intricately carved woodwork of nineteenth-century monasteries and palaces. Lay visitors often stay in the ground-floor rooms. The abbot's younger brother lives alone in the upper floors. A few years younger than the abbot, this monk is physically stronger: his older brother would not be able to handle the many steps up to the higher stories. U Dhammananda assured me that on the abbot's passing it is obvious that this monk will succeed him as abbot of the monastery.

Several other residence halls also house only a single monk. One two-story hall is designated as the "Tipitaka Hall," the hall in which a copy of the entire Pali canon is stored. Its lower floor contains unused pieces of furniture—bookcases, chairs, bedframes, carpets—in some disarray. Upstairs, in a large room where the one resident monk lives, is to be found not only a large collection of identically bound books (there are many such collections in other halls) but also a printer and copier. The monk who lives there is responsible for making copies of texts required for courses being taught at the monastery. He is a friendly and talkative fellow in his later thirties, but I found him somewhat overbearing and avoided visiting him.

In 2013, a broken-down building that had gone largely unused during my earlier stay—except when lay visitors occasionally stayed in its cooler, lower space (cool because it is half dug into the ground), which they gained access to by crawling through a window at ground level—had been leveled, and in its place a new "Tipitaka Hall" had been built. This gleaming new hall will now house the computer and copying equipment, as well as the *Tipitaka*. With excellent air conditioning whenever the power is adequate (finally, in 2013, a fairly standard circumstance), its controlled temperature will no doubt help assure the technology's longevity. Not yet in use, though, for housing the computer, during my stay in 2013 it was occupied by a venerable monk from the abbot's home village who was in Mandalay for medical treatment.

Great piles of bricks seem to be permanent fixtures on the grounds of the monastery, kept ready for the many building projects, large and small, that are undertaken quite often. Donors are always looking for ways to show their support for the sangha, and fronting sums of money for construction, whether of large halls or simpler, smaller structures, is always an option. Indeed, every hall I have described, and every other structure on the monastery's grounds, as well as every image, article of furniture, fan, or virtually anything else, is carefully inscribed with the names of donors, plus in most cases the date on which it was donated. The lounge chair I was lent for my use in the private quarters in which I lived in 2011 and 2012, the nightstand next to my bedframe, and the water stands, were so inscribed, like everything that is in anyone's use at the monastery. In much the same way, inscribed donors' names cover entire surfaces of walls and structures. The naming of donors and recording the date of their gifts becomes a kind of elegant Buddhist graffiti. I came to think of lay support for the monastery as conspicuous donation.

Another hall occupied by just one monk is that nearest the southwest corner of the compound, thus near one of the two main gates facing the street running along the monastery's western edge. This hall is not particularly large, but it sees a good deal of activity. It is here that most public activities take place, other than the large ceremonies such as weddings or observances of the anniversary of relatives' deaths or other occasions that include feeding the monks. So if people gather to recite Pali formulas in groups (some women's groups do this regularly on the Buddhist Sabbath), or if a *dhamma* talk is being given by a monk who could be expected to draw only an average crowd, these events and other small-scale public events take place in this, the smaller *dhamma* hall. It has an altar at the eastern end and can probably house around eighty or so people comfortably.

The monk who resides in this hall has a small room to one side of the altar. He lived for a number of years on the ground floor of the hall in which U Dhammananda has his quarters. When he lived there, he slept on the bed frame in a corner next to the Buddha images, in the large room that takes up most of the ground floor. U Dhammananda, much more senior, has a private room off to one side of that room. At the time, the two monks shared the use of a cubicle with a toilet, and another one beside it for bathing, at the far end of the large room and on the other side of the building. By moving to this hall, the smaller *dhamma* hall, the younger monk lost access to private bathing facilities, so he must join others bathing at a tank near the compound's southern wall, but he gained access to a private room.

A monk's seniority can be tracked by the degree of privacy he enjoys. The most senior monks in the monastery have rooms of their own. With only a few exceptions, only the most senior monks have private bathing facilities and toilets. Some monks who have been residents of the monastery for many years but are not in the uppermost ranks share a room with one or two other monks. Such, for example, is the case for the monks who live to either side of the main Buddha image in the larger *dhamma* hall. One of those two rooms is shared by the monk who schedules the weddings and other events that take place in that hall, along with his younger brother, a much younger man; they are full brothers but from a family with many children.

A number of very small structures house individual monks, usually younger monks but ones who have been resident at the monastery for several years. However, a fairly unsubstantial structure, made out of wood rather than brick and plaster (the materials of which most structures in the compound are built), standing next to my quarters during my longer stay, housed a man in his seventies who is the abbot's cousin by marriage, a man who took on the robe after his retirement.[12] He is still legally married, and his wife stops in on occasion, mostly when she travels between their home village and Rangoon, where one of their grown children lives. It seemed clear from the man's remarks that she was not happy to see him leave domestic life for the sangha.

Another small structure houses an individual monk plus a large pump, for which he takes responsibility. Yet another structure, tiny but equipped with both a private bathroom and an air conditioner and located near the abbot's quarters, houses a monk, U Tharana, who is only about thirty but much favored by the abbot. They are from the same village, and the younger monk had already shown a fair aptitude in his Pali studies when I met him in 2011. He is also a generous and patient person whose friendship I valued. It is hard for me to do more than speculate that the abbot appreciated these qualities in the younger monk, since the abbot is at all times taciturn and remote. Yet it seems probable that the abbot is aware of U Tharana's virtues, particularly since when I first moved into the monastery the abbot advised me to turn to this younger monk for instruction in the most basic Pali chants. When I returned to the monastery in 2013, U Tharana's tiny quarters had been renovated and expanded: they were still very small but were no longer as cramped as they had been. And he himself had passed the third portion of the state-sponsored Buddhist Dhammasariya exams, a feat of some import, since many monks his age and even quite a bit older fail to win the Dhammasariya title that passing the three parts of the exam granted him.

Some rooms that house single monks consist of corners of larger rooms, cordoned off by means of makeshift walls of plywood or hard plastic, plus a door. In such cases, the monks who enjoy the privacy of their own space do so living on the same floor as younger monks and novices who sleep on bedding they put down every evening on the large open floor of the larger room. Space in Burmese structures, both religious and secular, used to almost always take the form of large rectangular rooms without any permanent dividers. No real privacy is afforded people beyond what a screen or just a mosquito net provides. When monks and novices share space in a large hall, they set off an area as their own by putting a stack of books and papers and a suitcase or box containing their other belongings along one wall. The mosquito net they set up in the evening before going to bed gets taken down again when they get up in the morning. They may leave mats on the floor, but only if the space is not also used during the day for other purposes, such as for Pali classes. In that case, mats are rolled up and everything is pushed up against the wall, to be rolled out again in the evening.

Some buildings on the grounds house only novices, no monks. The lack of adult supervision surprised me. I would have thought it ill-advised to allow a group of boys aged anywhere from about seven to nineteen to occupy a structure on their own. But novices' days are tightly regimented, and it must seem to the monks in charge that between the obligation to get up well before dawn to go on alms rounds and to stay up at night long enough to attend Pali classes, novices have little time to get in to mischief.

In the case of halls in which a senior monk has private space carved out of a larger room occupied by a number of younger monks and novices, the nature of the ties among them varies. The hall in the southeastern corner of the compound is two stories but is not particularly large. It houses one senior monk in a space separated from the rest with plywood walls on the upper floor. The rest of that room and the floor below house a large number of the youngest novices at the monastery. The senior monk is of Palaung ethnicity and comes from a village in Shan State. Every May he returns to his natal village and gathers up a number of Palaung and Shan boys from the area, some of them but not all novices at monasteries in villages already, and brings them down to Mandalay to continue their studies. Some he sends to other monasteries in the city; some he has stay with him in this hall or one of the halls nearby. Travel between the village and Mandalay is not easy. Getting to the village from Mandalay requires taking a bus toward Taunggyi, then a regional bus, and finally a motorcycle taxi, for a total of about thirty hours of travel.

Like other Palaung speakers, the senior monk speaks Palaung, Shan, and Burmese. (His Burmese is fluent but heavily accented.) The Palaung novices speak Palaung and Shan but know little or no Burmese when they get to Mandalay. The state schools in their villages no doubt include some instruction in Burmese, but pupils in the earlier grades of school will not have made much progress at it. Shan speakers, including the Shan novices, speak Shan and start studying Burmese in school, but not Palaung. The Palaung monk takes charge of the novices from his natal region, teaching them the basics of Pali as well as Burmese and getting them started on the novice's path. He is one of the two monks who sit at the rear of the main hall at evening recitation, surveying the behavior of the youngest novices (those sitting in the last rows, farthest from the Buddha image) and making sure that they sit still, even if they understand very little of the chanting that they are themselves just beginning to learn how to do.

In other halls, bonds between senior monks and more junior residents are not so close. The hall across from my first quarters is of medium size; at the eastern end of the building, it houses one senior monk upstairs and one downstairs. The monk whose quarters are upstairs hails from a village in the Burman area near the new capital of Naypyidaw. One or two other residents of his floor are from the same area. Otherwise, I saw no pattern in the places of origin of that floor's residents. The monk who lives downstairs takes great satisfaction in growing a considerable number of plants and bushes in the area surrounding the hall. One day he approached me to point out the great variety of medicinal uses many of those plants had. He showed me a photocopy of a book, dating from the early part of the twentieth century, that contained drawings and explanations of the medical uses of many of the species he grows in his garden. This is an activity he undertakes largely on his own. I once saw him directing novices to pick mangoes out of one tree to the side of the building, but I saw no other instance of cooperative labor applied to this hobby of his.

During the day, some residence halls double as classrooms, in which case, as mentioned, residents' possessions are pushed close to the wall, clearing space for students to put down their small squares of cloth to sit or lie on while they listen to their teachers' words or study on their own. Some halls are not needed for that purpose, in which case personal belongings can remain in place, extending a few feet out from the wall. Monks and novices alike wash their robes often. They wear their lower garments while bathing, then, changing into dry robes, wash both those garments and their outer robes in the buckets they use to draw water out of the wells where they bathe. They hang up their wet clothes on lines tied to structures near where they bathe to dry. Later, they move their robes inside, hanging them up once again on the cords running the length of the halls, cords to which the ends of their mosquito nets are tied when they sleep at night.

Most residence halls look much the same in the evening. Younger monks and novices roll out the mats that they sleep on and read or, more often, sit and talk among themselves, or most often, sit and watch videos or sometimes listen to pop music, in small groups of two or three, lying and sitting around devices that they have been given by donors, whether laptops or DVD or CD players or even just mobile phones.

One evening I went up to the second story of a hall in the southwest corner of the Shweigyin Monastery's grounds. Three young monks lay on their stomachs on the floor in the southwesternmost corner of the building, all looking at a screen. I have noted that in January of 2012 the tea shop across the street had installed Wi-Fi, and the monks living in this hall discovered that they could get on the Web if they got a computer as close as possible to the tea shop and turned it on. I made no indiscreet inquiries as to what they might be viewing. But I was a little frustrated at the time by how hard it was to get any resident's attention long enough to talk with me.

When monks and novices are ready to get to bed, they set up the mosquito nets they sleep inside of, tying strings attached to the corners of the nets on one end to handles on windows or window grates of the hall, and on the other, to a rope extending the length of the hall, a few feet out from the wall. Most of them go to sleep between ten and eleven o'clock at night, although this depends on how long the DVD they might be watching lasts. Some senior monks have television sets and DVD monitors in their private quarters and may stay up late watching them. Many monks and novices are, like a great many of their compatriots, avid spectators of soccer matches televised from around the world. If an important match, such as one including Manchester United, is being played in Europe, it might begin late at night and go on until the wee hours of the morning. Some monks and novices watch in the crowd that gathers at the tea shop across the way from the monastery, even if public opinion rather disapproves of such enthusiasm among monks for worldly activities like sporting events. Other monks watch such matches in the privacy of their own quarters.

Maintenance Duties and Pali Study

Two types of activity take up most of the monastery residents' time. These are daily tasks necessary for the upkeep and smooth running of the monastery and Pali study.

All work assignments are made by the abbot once a year. They are announced on a list posted outside the main hall and remain in effect until the following year. A few duties tend to continue year after year: the cooking crew shows little turnover; one monk takes charge of copying texts on the monastery's copier for years in succession; one monk is responsible for booking events for the main hall for a long stint. Most duties require less-specific skills and are rotated among monks and novices. Striking the slit gong, sweeping the grounds, serving food at meal-time, washing dishes: many such tasks can be taken on or passed along to others easily.

Jobs requiring technical skills, such as dealing with construction, water, or electricity, do not figure among these tasks. For those matters, the monastery turns to laypeople who are paid for their labor. But laypeople familiar to the abbot and other senior monks, people with whom the monastery has long-standing ties, are always the first in line to get these jobs.

For example, in anticipation of the hot season (March, April, and May, when the temperature in Mandalay exceeds one hundred degrees Fahrenheit for weeks at a stretch), I wanted to have an air conditioner installed in my quarters in 2012 and went to the abbot to request permission to have this done. The abbot replied that he had an extra air conditioner in his quarters and would simply have it moved. I found, however, that the power supply was so inconstant that the air conditioner was of no use. U Dhammananda explained that I needed a step-up transformer and sent me to the abbot's brother-in-law for assistance. This man put me in touch with another man, not a resident of the monastery but someone knowledgeable about such matters; when I spoke with him, he named the price of such a machine. U Dhammananda told me, when I checked, that of course that price reflected a bit of a markup, but I could trust the man not to cheat me, even though I was no doubt right that I had smelled a bit of alcohol on his breath. The man, it seemed clear, was known to the senior monks: they knew his skills and his foibles.[13]

If carrying out minor, daily tasks features in everyone's life—only the most senior monks do not share in these duties—the activity that truly matters is studying Pali texts in preparation for exams. Such study is indeed the major responsibility of almost every religious resident of the compound. With the exception of a few monks who have lost their motivation to seek more advanced titles, most of the monks participate either in teaching Pali texts or, if they are not yet advanced enough to teach, in their continuing study. All the novices are so occupied. The time and effort these endeavors take is impressive—indeed, to me, nothing short of astonishing.

Officially, classes are held in the morning from 7:30 till 8:30, in the afternoon from 1:00 till 2:00, and again from 4:00 till 5:00. In practice, all these times tend to slide later, but they do tend to last about an hour each time. In the evening there is another gathering of students following evening recitation in the *dhamma* hall, but while at some more advanced levels this is an actual class, at others it is a study hall. Studying is done aloud in Burma, usually very loud, so evenings at the monastery bring an enormous cacophony of monks and novices yelling Pali texts at the top of their lungs as they review passages they have learned in the course of the day.

I describe classes at two different levels, one for very young novices, the other for older novices and young monks, to illustrate the way that textual study takes place. I begin by describing a class for young novices held on the lower floor of the building housing the Palaung monk and his young charges from his native village in southern Shan State.

Several clumps of novices were already engaged in study when I arrived sometime after nine in the morning. One group of what appeared to be the smallest of them was sitting near a monk going over Burmese spelling books. The book consists of sections, each of which drills a feature of Burmese writing. For the diacritic *wa. hswei:*, for example, there is a series starting with the first element in the Burmese syllabary (*ka. kyi:*) and then the addition of other diacritics, ending with a word. Each novice seemed to be responsible for memorizing every series. But the novices I heard tended to have trouble remembering what came next in a series and needed prompting from the monk who was drilling them. He did this without evident emotion, displaying neither impatience nor sympathy. Sometimes a novice picked up the thread quickly and even did a bit in unison with the monk. Some boys did not speak Burmese, or spoke it very little. If a novice is an ethnic Burman but arrived at the monastery never having attended a state school, he too might need this training in the Burmese writing system.

The Palaung monk himself was seated on a platform that serves as a sitting area during the day and a place to sleep at night. Two rows of novices sat at his feet, each of them holding a small paper booklet with passages they were memorizing. They seemed to be at many different levels. The monk took the booklets from two of them in turn, and each of them started reciting. They sat on their haunches, their hands in the respectful gesture, at least at first. Some of them then covered their faces as they concentrated on trying to remember what they needed to recite. The monk sat there listening to them both at the same time, although they were reciting different passages. When one of them lost the thread, the monk prompted him. To a few of them, when they seemed particularly stumped, he showed the open booklet and had them look at what they were trying to recite. He then had them recite a bit of it while holding the booklet open. When they were done, he pointed out the passages they had to work on. Later he told me that he expected them to learn those passages by the evening of that same day, when he would test them again. With most, when they were done, he simply handed the booklet to them and took the booklets from the next two novices, without showing any reaction, positive or negative. He had a list of all their names in front of him, and for each of them he made some note about what they had done. In this respect, he kept much closer track of each student's progress than was the case in other classes I observed.

With only one student was the monk fairly stern. The student did not do well in his recitation. When he stood up, the monk told him that when it was time to sleep, he must sleep. (He told me later the student, who was about eleven or twelve, didn't go to bed when he should, preferring to play with his friends. Then he came to class and fell asleep, so he didn't learn anything.) He glared at the student; the student showed no reaction.

The monk also told me afterward that these students were reviewing material they had learned earlier. Their actual classes wouldn't start again until the beginning of Waso month, which was still a few months away. When I asked how students had done on their exams in March, he said only a few had passed. A lot of them have to repeat each grade several years over. It's hard, much harder, he seemed to say, to pass these Pali exams than for the state school exams (in which secular subjects are taught). In the latter, as long as you study, you can get it. Only in the tenth standard (the last year of public education) does it get a bit tough. Before that, it's easy. It's not like that for these novices, though, he assured me. They don't understand what they're learning. So it's much harder. I suggested that for novices whose first language was not Burmese it must be especially hard, but he said Burman novices fail just as often as other ones do.

He showed me two booklets. One was entirely in Pali; the other was a list of words and phrases in Pali, with Burmese translations and explanations. But the latter were in formal Burmese, so none-too-accessible to relatively little-educated people, even native speakers of Burmese. I understood him to say that novices memorize the translations and explanations, not just the words and phrases, so they are memorizing Burmese as well as Pali.

Another class I attended was at the "upper" level of the "first" course, that is, the third and last in a series of levels that novices and monks follow for each of the three "baskets" of the canon: the regulations governing monks' conduct; the sayings and stories of the Buddha; and the *Abhidhamma*. (The last are the more difficult, analytic texts that figure in the Pali canon.) This class treated material from the second basket. On the day I attended, students were memorizing one of the Jataka tales, the 550 stories that concern past lives of the Buddha. The class met in the early afternoon every day.

Before the class I attended began, fifteen students took up pieces of cloth, made out of the same brown or crimson material as their robes, and placed them under their feet. Then, walking back and forth the length of the room in which they were to have class, they cleaned the floor. Some of them chatted as they did this; others reviewed their textbooks, paperback ones made with poor quality paper. Eleven of the students were novices, although they appeared to be relatively close to the age of nineteen, when novices ordain to become monks. The other four were already monks, although probably only in their early twenties, so only recently ordained.

When the teacher joined them, they shook out the pieces of cloth they had used to clean the floor and laid them over the side of the balcony. Then they sat in rows on similar squares of cloth, ones they had brought with them, on the floor, with their books in front of them. It was hot but they wore their robes quite fully wrapped about their bodies as a gesture of respect toward the teacher. Their teacher read several lines of the tale aloud, then had them read the passage together with him, and then they read in unison a third time. All of it was in Pali, although there was a Burmese translation in the back of their books that they could consult when they wished. After the third reading in unison, the teacher left the room and the students started memorizing the lines individually. They did so by declaiming them, each on his own, in a very loud voice and at a very fast pace.

The novice sitting next to me looked at his book several times for the first ten minutes or so. After that, he closed the book and kept repeating the same lines, only opening the book once or twice to check something. At one point, he looked at the Burmese summary at the back of the book. At another point, he fell silent for a little bit. Then he did some more reciting but in a quieter voice. After about half an hour, the teacher came back, whereupon they all recited the passage together. Then each of them had to recite it on his own, starting with the monk closest to the teacher and proceeding through each monk and novice in each row in turn. (The teacher told me later they were just arranged according to diminishing size. But in other classes they can sit wherever they like.) Most of them did this with remarkably little trouble, although with varying kinds of intonation. One student had quite a bit more trouble than the others; the teacher prompted him and also corrected him a couple of times, neither angrily nor supportively. During each person's turn, the reciter sat on his haunches and held his palms together; once he was done he could sit as he liked. Finally, they all recited together, starting from the beginning of the Jataka tale they were studying, so starting from passages they had memorized in the preceding days. Occasionally they all faltered and had to be prompted by the teacher. But that was rare. At a few points some of them lost the thread but others were ready to keep it going and the others immediately joined in. Then they all paid obeisance to the teacher quickly, stood up, and started cleaning the floor once again. The teacher went back into his own room, and soon the students headed down the stairs and back to their own residence halls.

At their other classes on the same day, these students were memorizing passages from other books of the canon. They did this every day and every evening except for the eve of the (Buddhist) Sabbath and for the whole of the Sabbath (which falls every seven or eight days). On Sabbath days, they take practice exams. No other subjects are taught at this monastery. Some monastery schools, especially ones open to lay as well as monastic pupils, combine religious and secular subjects. This monastery does not. It is a purely Pali education consisting of memorizing an ever-increasing portion of the immense Pali canon.

The Purposes of Pali Study

What matters in all this immense activity surrounding Pali study is mastering the exact wording of the Pali text. Pali, an ancient language of South Asia, bears no resemblance whatever to Burmese, although a certain number of Pali words have been taken into Burmese over the centuries, and every Burman Buddhist acquires some command of frequently repeated Pali phrases, much as a Catholic will come to know a number of phrases in Latin, with or without precise knowledge of what each word means.

Pali is grammatically both complex and, to a Burmese speaker, totally foreign: the two languages belong to different language families. Burmese is a Sino-Tibetan language, whereas Pali is an Indo-European one. Pali (like Sanskrit) has an elaborate system of both verb tenses and noun cases, whereas Burmese has no trace of either. Burmese, furthermore, is a tonal language; Pali is, or was (more properly, since it has not been spoken outside religious contexts in millennia) not. Since most signs in the Burmese syllabary indicate tone, it is impossible to write Pali words using the Burmese syllabary without writing tones in, and Burmese speakers endow Pali words with tones when they chant them. ("Pali" for example has a low tone in the first syllable and a short, high tone, in the second, reversing the way an English speaker, putting stress on the first syllable, is inclined to pronounce it.) Conventions endow Pali consonants with Burmese equivalents (a certain Pali *s* becomes Burmese *th*, for example), although people can display their familiarity with Pali by choosing to use a sound they consider authentically Pali rather than its Burmese equivalent. For example, the Pali word *sura,* meaning "courageous," which is sometimes used as a man's name in Burma, is rendered in Burmese as *thuya,* because the first *s* goes to *th* and the *r* sound in Burmese was replaced in most versions of spoken Burmese by *y* long ago.[14] Monks and laypeople wishing to display their learning are likely to retain the *th* but pronounce the *r* as a flapped *r*.

Because of all the ways that Pali differs from Burmese (and from all the other indigenous languages of Burma), mastering passages from the Pali canon is a considerable endeavor. The notion of "mastery" is in itself a variable matter. The focus falls on being able to reproduce the text: to recite or write it without error. Understanding the content of the text figures less prominently. Shortly after I started living at the Shweigyin Monastery, in November 2011, I sat talking with U Tharana, the young monk the abbot had suggested I study with, and asked him about the progress that novices made once they arrived at the monastery. How far, for example, had those students gotten who had started their studies the previous June? (The academic year starts at the beginning of June in Burma, when the hot season should finally end with the coming of the monsoon rains.) U Tharana said they would have been proceeding through the first thin booklet of passages taken from various points in the canon. He was unsure where they would have gotten to at the time we were speaking, however, so he hailed a novice walking by: "Novice, what are you doing in U Kumara's class now?" The novice replied, "We have finished the first book. So now he is going back through it and telling us what it means." The novices had spent something like five months memorizing passages from the Pali canon without knowing the meaning of what they were reciting. Only now, with the work of memorizing complete, did their teacher find it appropriate to inform them of the meaning of what they had learned to recite.

Students do eventually come to acquire a steadily increasing Pali vocabulary, granting them a better grasp of what the texts they memorize mean. Indeed, many publications, readily available, contain lines of Pali text with interlinear Burmese translations of individual lexical items, written in bubbles above and below the original. Many vocabulary items recur often in the texts, and students can be assumed to come to know them without need of such cribs. However, U Dhammananda, who often bewailed the state of Pali learning among most younger Burmese monks, stated that knowing vocabulary does not suffice to attain real understanding of a text you encounter for the first time. Only if you have been thoroughly grounded in Pali grammar can you grasp how vocabulary, even familiar vocabulary, is to be understood in a text. Such a knowledge of Pali grammar had enabled him to achieve his impressive command of a large part of the canon; its lack is what prevents most younger monks from proceeding through the exam system to the higher titles reflecting deep knowledge of the texts.

Just how difficult memorizing becomes as a novice and then monk proceeds through the levels of a monastic education is particularly evident in light of what the Pali canon contains. Students agreed when I asked whether learning material from the second basket, containing stories and sayings of the Buddha, was easier than learning material from the other baskets. Memorizing the *vinaya,* the list of the rules of conduct for monks, is harder, they assured me, and the *Abhidhamma* harder still. Characteristic of the latter portion especially, although evident throughout the canon, is a great penchant for lists. Even at the most elementary level, this feature of Buddhist habits of mind quickly becomes apparent: the fourth of the Four Noble Truths with which all Buddhist instruction begins turns out to be a reference to the Eightfold Path—and so it goes. A great many lists turn out to contain lists within lists in this way, like so many Russian dolls.

U Dhammananda, who is renowned for the impressive progress he made as a young monk in memorizing much of the canon, dismissed my expressions of amazement at the achievement. He insisted that if you start memorization work young, your mind acquires the skill easily. Furthermore, monks who proceed to advanced levels receive from their teachers instruction in mnemonic techniques that prove very helpful. He himself would not have been able to make the progress he did without such aide-memoire, he assured me. He demonstrated how some of this worked, linking vocabulary in lists to the thumbs, fingers, and joints of his hands. When a list contained a repeating term, this he linked to a thumb, and he reverted to it as he enumerated sub-terms that he connected to sections of his fingers. He did this all at great speed, and I cannot claim to have been able to follow the intricacies of the system. Nor was I persuaded by his claim that such feats of memory were ordinary, even pedestrian, accomplishments, as his tone suggested.

I did notice, however, how pervasive the penchant for lists turns out to be in Buddhist rhetoric and, by extension, Burmese scholarship generally. Books by Burmese authors tend to contain many lists, lists that appear and reappear in books on any topic. For example, books about Burmese theater reproduce lists of theatrical genres over and over. There is no concern for copyright, and reproducing such a list almost never includes any sort of citation. Lists appear to constitute authoritative knowledge by virtue of the form they take, without need for further support, acknowledgement of source, or development.

In conversation with U Dhammananda, I noticed that if we were discussing a topic concerning Buddhism and he wished to speak of a specific point, it often turned out that it figured in a list of points he wanted to proceed through systematically. Sometimes he lost sight of the next point in a series and had to take a moment to recall it. To do so, he switched from Burmese to Pali, worked through the list, speaking aloud, in Pali, and then, once he had retrieved the term, explained to me in Burmese what it meant.

U Dhammananda does not employ memorization as an approach only to materials written in Pali, however. He owns a copy of a book, written by U Saw Htun Hmat Win and published by the Burmese government's Ministry for Religious Affairs, containing basic teachings in English about Buddhism. U Dhammananda claims only a very limited knowledge of English. However, he has felt the need to be ready to converse with foreigners who might appear at the monastery. Indeed, several years prior to my visit, a couple from Canada had spent a brief period there. They spoke no Burmese, so any communication that was to take place had to be in English. U Dhammananda had done his best but felt that it was inadequate. He had therefore set about memorizing whole chapters from U Saw Htun Hmat Win's book. He could still recite many passages. Never having received formal instruction in English, his pronunciation was far from standard. Indeed, he often laughed when he asked me how to pronounce some English word he came across, since how I said it and how he expected it to sound diverged so considerably.[15] The point, however, is that it struck him as appropriate and effective to take a book in a language he had little knowledge of and to memorize long passages of it in order to have it ready should occasion arise.

Justifications for memorizing portions of the Pali text are both proximate and long term. The ultimate explanation, although not, in actual fact, the most salient one for most practitioners, is to learn what the Buddha taught and so be able to live in accordance with those teachings. Another justification is to enable a monk to draw on such knowledge in order to tend to the needs of laypeople. Laypeople need to have the Buddha's message conveyed and explained to them, in the view of both lay and religious gatekeepers, and familiarity with the Pali canon enables a monk to do this on their behalf.

This account of why monks and novices need to study the canon is often repeated. But in my experience the relationship between monks and laypeople is hardly so pastoral. It is true that in recent years a great fashion has arisen of inviting monks to give evening sermons in public, such as described in the preceding chapter, and in such circumstances a monk who can recite lines from the canon fluently and then discuss them entertainingly will be much appreciated. But this is new and does not involve all monks. (One evening I heard a young monk pacing back and forth outside his hall, declaiming a sermon he had written in a notebook. He told me that he was practicing this new genre—sermonizing—but it was hard work and it was going to take a lot of practice for him to develop the fluency that people look for.) For a monk to be able to "live according to the Buddha's teachings," for that matter, although of course desirable, would in this telling require that he understand everything he memorizes, something that most people do not really expect a monk to be able to do.

Pali Exams

The immediate goal in memorizing passages from the canon is rather to pass a series of exams. The Burmese government's Ministry for Religious Affairs gives these exams annually, as do some private religious organizations. There is a whole series of such exams, but the ones to which many monks devote their energies, usually for several years, are the Dhammasariya exams, likened by some to a BA degree in a secular university setting. These consist of three parts, which monks take in turn, often over a period of years. Only once they have passed all three parts, as U Tharana did by the time I returned to the monastery in 2013, can they claim the title, much as one might fulfill the various requirements to obtain a university degree. A monk who has acquired the Dhammasariya title has the right to teach others. Should he wish to, he can continue his studies and sit for exams attesting to his having achieved still greater knowledge. But most monks find the challenge of obtaining the Dhammasariya degree plenty challenge enough.

The government administers the Dhammasariya exams annually in each of the country's states. Monks sometimes travel to different states to sit for the exams, which last seven days, because they are said to be easier in some states than others. (I was told in 2012 that the exams would be standardized nationally in coming years.) Mandalay is notorious for the difficulty of its exams. Concern in Mandalay that the contents of the exams might leak out causes officials to print them out in some other city, not in Mandalay, and even then only one day before the exams are given. Indeed, corruption in the system is believed to be rife. (I report these allegations but am in no position to confirm or discount them.) Monks sitting for the exams are thought sometimes to bring electronic devices with them, concealed in their robes, enabling them to check passages they encounter in the exam questions on the Web. Officials responsible for announcing the results of the exams are thought ready to accept bribes to pass monks who have actually failed them.

Private, nonprofit Buddhist organizations also set exams for the Dhammasariya title, and monks who win their title from these organizations enjoy greater prestige than those who obtain the title by sitting for the government version of the exam. The reason for this is that standards among the private organizations are reputed to be more stringent in both the content of the exams that are set and in their grading. In Mandalay, there is a further gradation in prestige between the two most notable organizations that sponsor Dhammasariya exams. Every difference, as per Dumont, necessarily implies a difference in value.

There is yet another means to obtaining the Dhammasariya title. The government has established a Buddhist university in Rangoon, and another one in Mandalay. Students who complete a BA at either of these institutions are granted the Dhammasariya title. But many monks are disdainful of this practice, saying that a degree obtained by coursework alone is unworthy of the name.

The Dhammasariya exams the government gives, even if easier than some other versions, certainly present many monks with considerable difficulty. Several monks at the Shweigyin Monastery had taken the exams year after year without success. Several others had simply given up trying. Even the lower-level exams monks and novices take as they approach the Dhammasariya title can pose real problems. In 2012, when the results were in from the three grades of the first level exams, disappointment was considerable: only one out of twelve students had passed in the second ("middle") of the three grades, and the same number, one, had met success in the third ("big") grade. Only in the first ("little") class had things turned out relatively well: nine students of eighteen had passed. It is not uncommon for students to spend two or three years studying in each of the three grades.

If a novice or monk fails to pass an exam, he repeats the same grade the following year in hope of doing better. His teachers will try to pitch their teaching at the appropriate level. But it is hard to foresee what any given exam will include, so they simply choose passages in the canon that they think might show up on the year-end exams. I have heard it said that the difficulty of the exams varies widely: if one year a goodly proportion of candidates pass their exams, the following year standards will be raised sharply, bringing the success rate down considerably. And the reverse. Success rates are said to vary widely because of this inconsistency in the exams' difficulty from year to year.

U Dhammananda ventured a number of opinions about why students were faring so badly on their exams. At the level of the sort of studies they were pursuing, he saw the way younger novices were being trained as inadequate: they were not being schooled sufficiently rigorously in Pali grammar to be able to get a good grasp of what they were learning. But more fundamentally, he saw novices and young monks as far too preoccupied with other matters to study with the kinds of dedication the work required. When he was a young monk, he pointed out, there were no smart phones, no Internet, no CDs, no DVDs, no soccer matches to watch on TV: in short, as a monk, he devoted himself to memorizing Pali texts many hours a day, whereas such is not the case for young monks today. Lay donors, he lamented, give the monks they support these devices without thinking what the consequences for the monks' practice will be.

It is true that discipline becomes difficult to enforce, especially as novices enter their later teen years and once they become monks. The abbot at the Shweigyin Monastery was, as noted, in poor health and moved about the monastery grounds only with some difficulty. I was startled therefore one afternoon in 2013, while sitting reading in the hall where I was staying, to see the abbot standing in the doorway. He had just come up the many steep stairs to this upper story, which cannot have been easy for him. He stood there glowering for a moment, then strode over to where a novice was napping under his mosquito net and started striking him vigorously with his cane, telling him to get up and get to class. He then went out onto the verandah and did the same to a monk, a man in his later twenties, who was sleeping under his net. I do not know what prompted the abbot to enact the role of truant officer on that day. But the fact is that attendance in class, although compulsory, is not terribly consistent, especially among monks. U Dhammananda noted that there were twenty or so monks at the monastery who were ostensibly studying for the Dhammasariya exams, but only three were attending his classes by late in the year of 2013, and he expected that even those three would stop showing up before the end of the academic year, which came in February.

Nevertheless, not all monks are so feckless, and some travel from monastery to monastery in search of good teachers. U Dhammananda did this as a young monk, and so did U Tharana. In 2012, U Tharana went to Rangoon for a six-week course in preparation for taking the third and final section of the Dhammasariya exams. I visited him at the monastery where the course was being held, and I was impressed at the very large number of monks and nuns who had registered for the course—and at the way they lived very tightly packed together in halls that seemed barely able to accommodate them all. U Tharana suggested I come along to a class to see the monk who teaches these intensive courses in action. I understood nothing of the esoteric content of the teaching (which concerned the third basket, the *Abhidhamma*), but I noticed that, as with so many effective teachers the world over, the monk displayed a high level of energy and much enthusiasm for the task at hand. The course served its purpose for U Tharana, since he went on to pass his exams the next time they were given, in 2013.

Certain monasteries, not just individual teachers, are renowned centers at which monks can prepare to take exams. In Mandalay, the Ma Soe Yein Tai' monasteries ("Don't Worry Monasteries," consisting of the "Old" and "New" divisions) are famous centers for exam preparation, and many monks either live at them to devote themselves to their studies, or go there from the monasteries where they live, attending classes as day students. U Wirathu, who has made himself controversial in Burma by virtue of his vitriolic anti-Muslim rhetoric (and has become notorious overseas—it is his face that appeared on the June 1, 2013, *Time in Asia* cover with the caption, "The Face of Buddhist Terror"), lives and teaches at the New Ma Soe Yein Monastery in Mandalay. He is considered a highly learned monk and is greatly respected for his textual knowledge, quite apart from all the anti-Muslim rabble-rousing he gets up to.

Some monks who sit for exams and fail them feel humiliated. Several monks told me that after the exam results are posted each year, a certain number of monks at any monastery, and they included the Shweigyin Monastery among such, simply disappear. They do not explain whether they are going to a different monastery where they hope to get better teaching or are instead going to disrobe. Most, I was told, probably remain monks but feel dissatisfied with the teaching they have received and wish to try their hand elsewhere. But there is no way to know what becomes of such monks, since they rarely stay in contact with monks they have left behind.

To what degree monks are expected to continue to try for titles varies from monastery to monastery. A monastery I stayed at during an earlier period of fieldwork in Mandalay, in 1987 and 1988, is probably typical. The abbot of that monastery, who is himself an avid student of Burmese history, told me that he did not insist that monks residing at the monastery be diligent about study. Whether they choose to study and take exams is up to them, he told me. His concern is only that they live according to the precepts and not disturb anyone.

Apart from sitting for exams or taking a university degree, an altogether different means to obtaining titles attesting to one's command of the canon is by receipt of honorary degrees. The abbot of the Shweigyin Monastery is highly respected for his textual knowledge. He often serves on exam committees, whether to set the contents of exams or to grade the results. Indeed, he is invited to travel the country for the purpose. The military government, and its now-civilian successor, has strived to burnish the government's image by conferring on such eminent religious figures a great array of honorary degrees, and the abbot of the Shweigyin Monastery has accrued virtually all that are available. A few extremely high titles he lacked could only be obtained by examination by his peers. That is, he would have to submit to examination, at the hands of other, still more learned, monks, of his knowledge of great swathes of the canon, not something a monk in his ninth decade would be expected to do.

Some monks evince ambivalent attitudes toward these honorary degrees. As obvious indicators of close relations between monks and the military regime, they impress some laypeople and some monks. But others, monks especially, look on them as a kind of bribe, a way for an irresponsible and corrupt secular authority to co-opt monks and borrow some of their glory. Sometimes both views, positive and negative, coexist in the same individual. The abbot of another, smaller monastery, whom I have known for many years and whose clear-eyed take on many matters has always impressed me, confused me in this regard. When I first met him in 1988, he often expressed disdain for the willingness with which his peers danced to the government's tune. Nevertheless, he is anxious to get whatever titles he can by virtue of connections he has to important political figures, and when he does so, he goes to some length to bring to the attention of many people the fact of his receiving honorary titles. He is not, in other words, oblivious to the allure of such titles, which bring prestige to him personally and the likelihood of continued, or even augmented, lay support to his monastery—which has seen a good deal of construction over the twenty-five years I have had occasion to visit it. One of his lay supporters told me that she knew other monks whose respect for this abbot had fallen considerably in light of his too-friendly relations with government authorities.

Rank and Prestige

One simple point about all of this Pali study needs to be kept in mind amid all the complexity of the texts that have to be memorized, the range of exams to take, and the diversity of authorities who set and grade them. The exams make it possible to rank monks and novices in an ordered series. As my description of evening recitation at the beginning of this chapter should make evident, the existence of such an ordered series is fundamental to the entire conception of the sangha's organization.

How much does a resident's place in this rank ordering matter? To what extent does a monk's standing inflect the relations he enters into with others? As a practical matter, or at least as far as daily practice is concerned, the answer is that a monk's relative standing comes into focus only at certain points, such as when monks file into the *dhamma* hall for evening recitation, or when they arrange themselves around tables in the refectory for the late-morning meal. Other than that, monks tend to associate among themselves quite casually, if they are friends, or to go their own ways, if they are not. (I come back to this point in the next chapter.) Nevertheless, relative standing matters a good deal.

First, there is a single line of succession among monks at a monastery. At times of momentous change, such as when an abbot dies or is incapacitated and a new abbot must be selected, only the top positions matter, since the abbot necessarily comes from among the top figures. U Dhammananda made it clear that the current abbot's younger brother is the only conceivable successor to the position upon his older brother's death or retirement from office. Even though he is third in line, U Dhammananda dismissed the possibility that he would ever succeed to the office, at least as long as the second-in-charge is still alive.

In other monasteries, succession might not be so straightforward. Indeed, the jockeying for position grows intense among the set of monks immediately below (and often physically surrounding) an important abbot, one whose prominence draws great donations to the monastery over which he presides. This is all the more true in that, aside from any ordering based on uninterrupted membership in the sangha and on titles attained (whether by examination or honorary conferral), an abbot's clear favor can prove crucial in swaying lay supporters' opinion following an abbot's passing. These lay supporters, in particular those who sit on a monastery's governing board, will matter importantly in determining who the next abbot will be.

Second, even if the number of lenten seasons a monk has worn the robe is ostensibly the single, simple determinant of relative standing among any given set of monks, in actual fact, formal titles and informal power both introduce important complicating factors in the politics of a monastery's workings. Some abbots confer constantly with their immediate juniors; some confer with them occasionally. At the Shweigyin Monastery, the abbot tends to keep his own counsel on matters of administration, only very rarely calling any meeting among the other higher members of the monastery's religious population. This is his prerogative. Yet even he is likely to be addressed at times on matters of administration by other monks at the monastery, and the degree to which he attends to such comments no doubt follows at least in part from their standing.

Even if relative standing matters at only a few points in the course of the day, and even if it implies exercising any important role at the monastery only on rare occasions, it matters to everyone quite intensely. That is to say, any way in which monks differ among themselves as to relative prestige arouses people's interest. An apparently insignificant but telling illustration of the point came during an annual celebration sponsored by the lay donors to the monastery on behalf of the monks and novices.

One day shortly after I moved into the monastery, a desk and a few chairs were set up between the two gates at the western border of the monastery grounds, with a canopy to protect the area from the sun. A loudspeaker was hooked up to a CD player, and a banner was hung from the canopy announcing an upcoming day of celebration to take place a couple of weeks later. Over that period, with recorded music playing constantly over the sound system, lay men sat manning the desk all day every day, collecting funds for the planned event. Anyone passing by could stop to make a monetary donation on behalf of the monks and novices resident at the monastery. The minimum contribution was K5,000, a considerable sum (about US$5 at the time). A donor could choose to make further contributions and receive such things as a picture of some religious nature, or a model of an alms bowl, and so on; each such extra cost an additional K1,700. Each contributor received a card listing the amount of his or her donation and a number, plus a small white slip stapled to the card. Donors could, if they so chose, give the white slip to a particular monk or novice to whom they wished to give their donation. Many, however, did not do so, preferring to add the white slip to a large pool of them.

When the appointed day came, all the monks and novices filed past the desk. Each of them took a white slip out of a container and handed it to a lay man who checked the number on the slip against a list and then announced on the loudspeaker the monk's or novice's title and the amount he had "won," along with the name of the lay donor. Some monks had, indeed, already been given white slips by lay donors; if they received many such slips, they put at least some of them into the pool rather than keep them for themselves, so sharing the wealth and earning merit in doing so. In the course of drawing a white slip, however, monks and novices submitted themselves entirely to chance. A crowd of laypeople gathered on the street to watch the proceedings, in addition to the monastery's residents, and there were many exclamations when particularly large sums were announced.

What is interesting about the entire exercise, which amounts to a monastic lottery, is that it contravenes the normal hierarchical ordering of the monastery's residents, but does so by instituting another, aleatory ordering. Granted, many recipients received the standard, minimal amount of K5,000, or something close to it. But a few lucky ones received a great deal more. I asked U Dhammananda if it would not make sense to pool all the contributions and then divide the money up evenly among all the residents. He laughed at the idea, noting that in that case, everything would be the same. "People here like things to be different. They don't like things to be the same," he explained, unknowingly confirming a Dumontian point. He told me, in answer to my questions, that a similar practice whereby monks and novices get varying cash prizes by drawing slips out of a pool of them takes place at many monasteries in Mandalay; it is not unique to this monastery by any means.

Do people lay much store by who it is among the monks and novices that wins large amounts? U Dhammananda said no: it makes a big impression at the moment; it gets talked about during the rest of the day; and then people forget about it. Yet I make much of what is, in itself, a fairly inconsequential practice because it illustrates so neatly a Burmese preference for difference over sameness, precisely as U Dhammananda said. It reflects a habit of mind very much in keeping with hierarchical difference. Since it is difference that binds people together (as I discuss further in chapter 4), whereas sameness obviates the needs for such bonds, difference is what draws and holds people's attention.

The Sociology of the Shweigyin Monastery

The monastery's residents can be sorted into a number of groups. A major distinction, obviously, is that between lay residents and religious ones. As I have noted, a number of students (all male) from rural areas live there while they pursue their studies. There are also a few former students who have finished their degrees but go on living there because they do not have families of their own and it is an inexpensive and convenient living arrangement. Almost all these students, current or former, come from villages that the abbot and his younger brother, or U Dhammananda, hail from. In a few cases, lay students are brothers of monks or novices also living at the monastery.

Another contingent of lay residents consists of the abbot's and his younger brother's close relatives: their younger sister, her husband, their daughters, their sons-in-law, and their grandchildren. These people form a web of kin-based ties. The monastery has become for them a kind of mini-village, but one subsidized by lay donors whose largesse assures a fairly steady supply of food and amenities. Members of the abbot's lay kin participate in food preparation, and, as noted, his brother-in-law takes on a major role as contractor for building projects. They form, in other words, part of an entourage in which, as is pervasive in Southeast Asia, privileges and obligations are not all that clearly specified but generally understood and accepted, whether by the residents themselves or lay outsiders.

A steady flow of laypeople also come and stay at the monastery while they or their kin seek medical treatment in Mandalay, and also a few other laypeople, such as long-haul bus drivers, who need a place to sleep on an occasional basis and have some connection to one or more monks at the monastery willing to take responsibility for their good character.

Among the religious residents of the monastery, further distinctions are apparent. Reflecting a critical difference running throughout Burmese society, there are Burman monks and novices, on the one hand, and non-Burman ones, on the other. A considerable majority of the non-Burman religious come from Shan State. This stems in part from the fact that Shan State's population, no matter what people's specific ethnic identity, is for the most part Buddhist, whereas other non-Burman ethnic groups in Burma (such as Karen, Kachin, and Chin) are at least partially, in some cases largely, Christian.

During my stay there in 2011 and 2012, only four monks at the monastery came from Shan State. Of them, three were native speakers of Palaung, and one was a native speaker of Shan. But in 2012 there were thirty-eight novices, eighteen of them native speakers of Palaung, five speakers of Wa, four of Shan, and four of the Danu dialect of Burmese.[16]

The reason for the considerable number of novices from Shan State is the one monk, mentioned above, who takes it upon himself to bring a number of boys to the monastery each year from his and surrounding villages in Shan State.

Among the Burman monks and novices, a further distinction can be made between those who come, on the one hand, from the same village as the abbot and his brother, or from villages and one town nearby, and, on the other, those who come from other Burman areas. Among the residents in 2012, eleven monks and eighteen novices came from the abbot's native region. Neighbors and kin (Burmans' bilateral kinship makes the distinction relatively vague), these constituted another kind of entourage. Twelve monks and three novices came from other Burman areas. Most of them had come to the monastery as novices, invited by monks already resident there. Some of the monks who had invited the current residents had since moved elsewhere, or died, but a resident who is of good behavior does not depend on the presence of a sponsor to retain his place at the monastery. There is a general expectation that, whether a novice or a monk, he will pursue Pali study while living there. But that expectation is not enforced. A fair number of residents have pretty much given up on that front but do not risk expulsion.

No universal generalizations, in sum, can be made about the monastery's residents: they come from diverse regions, speak a number of languages as their native one, and have been invited to become residents there by virtue of connections to a number of different individuals. A considerable proportion of its population comes from the abbot's native village or its surroundings, it is true. But as is so often the case in lowland Southeast Asia, the "community" is a loosely organized, shifting, amorphous collection of individuals. On occasion, most of the religious residents gather together, such as for morning alms rounds or evening recitation. But attendance is expected, rather than policed, or is only inconsistently policed. The monastery is, in other words, both clearly hierarchically ordered and quite loosely structured.

Who Becomes a Monk, and Why?

A question that runs through much writing on the Buddhist sangha turns on what motivates individuals to take on the robe, and whether they are likely to have primarily social or spiritual goals in view. The question can only be answered with reference, obviously, to specific individuals, if even then. After all, individuals are prone to having a mix of reasons for undertaking any major step in their lives. I later discuss what I see as social psychological implications of Buddhist practices and what allure they might hold for men in Burmese society who decide to become monks, as well as for laypeople who decide to support their endeavors. Yet certain basic sociological factors need to be taken into account, social standing especially, because the sangha represents a social institution that greatly enhances its members' prestige.

Aside from gender (treated separately in chapters 8 and 9), three types of identity markers condition fundamentally the prominence individuals enjoy in Burman society: language, rural versus urban origins, and lay versus religious identity.

Since, as per Dumont, every difference in a hierarchical society carries a difference in value, languages necessarily differ in prestige. Regional languages are inferior to national languages or more important regional ones, just as national languages are trumped by international ones. The Palaung-speaking boys who come every year to start studying as Buddhist novices live in a village surrounded by the more numerous and often better-off Shan. So they speak both Palaung and Shan. (The two languages belong to two different language families and are utterly unlike.) As noted above, Shan novices at the monastery know Shan, but none of them knows Palaung. All these boys must set about learning Burmese as soon as they get to the Shweigyin Monastery; indeed, learning Burmese (which belongs to yet another language family) is a major motivation for their moving so far from home.[17] Some senior Burman monks at the Shweigyin Monastery remarked, somewhat tartly, that these novices from Shan State only came to the monastery long enough to learn Burmese, then left both this monastery and the sangha. U Kalyana, the Palaung monk who draws these boys to the monastery, contests this view, saying that novices may move to a different monastery in Mandalay, or move to a monastery back in Shan State, but that they stay in the sangha. I have no way of confirming either view. The point is that learning Burmese is an important skill for these boys to acquire if they are going to get ahead, whether as members of the sangha or as laypeople.

Approximately 70 percent of Burma's population was rural at the time of my fieldwork. The allure of the cities was real, but economic activity had stagnated for so long that cities could not support the great influx of migrants from rural areas that other cities in Southeast Asia, for better or worse, have long seen. Rangoon and Mandalay were both growing, and economic liberalization, more anticipated than real at the time but certainly in the works, was clearly going to bring about more vigorous commercial activity and faster urbanization. Nevertheless, finding a way to make one's way from a village to town still poses a challenge. Monasteries represent an effective path for making the move.

Any society in which people are aware of and concerned with differences in relative position, and this applies to all but a very few societies in the world at present, looks like a game of chutes and ladders. The Shweigyin Monastery, like many urban monasteries in Burma, constitutes a ladder: it provides a pathway "up" from the village to the city.[18] Of course, an alternate prestige structure surrounds the logical opposite of an urban monastery: a remote monastery, far from the madding crowd, located "in the jungle," where a monk can pursue his spiritual advancement in isolation. But that is an outlier in figurative as well as literal ways, more imagined than actual in most monks' experience. A village monastery is looked on as a paler, humbler, duller version of an urban one. Indeed, although I know of no reliable statistics, I was impressed in the villages I visited at how consistently monks spoke of the fact that village monasteries were becoming depopulated.[19]

When I went with the Shweigyin Monastery's abbot to his natal village near Myingyan, we went for a walk and passed by the monastery where he had been a novice in his childhood, over seventy years earlier. The monastery was of teak when he lived there as a novice. Now there was a quite large building made of brick, constructed relatively recently. Another, smaller building was under construction next to it. There was also a smaller, new-looking building to one side. Despite the new construction, the place looked broken down. There were pieces of old wood, remnants of the older building, lying about. Nothing looked well-tended.

The abbot told me that only a couple of monks were living there now. When he was young, it was much livelier: about forty novices were living there. The reason things were now so different was, he said, (1) because the weather had gotten much worse, making farmers poorer and so less able to support the monastery; and (2) state schools in the village used to provide schooling up to only the fourth standard, so many boys came to the monastery for their studies. Now the state schools went up through the tenth standard (all the way through secondary school), so boys no longer went to monastery schools much.

I should not paint too desolate a view of village monasteries, however. This monastery was one of twelve in the village (quite a large one); others were in much better estate. We were staying in a newly built, and quite spiffy, hall in another monastery in the village. Its construction had been arranged by the abbot but financed by a wealthy lay supporter of the abbot who lived in Rangoon. As the hall's condition illustrated, how a village monastery fares now depends on how well-connected it is to urban patrons, whether lay or religious. The point became all the clearer as we proceeded on our way to yet another monastery in the village, one supported by an internationally known abbot, the Wa Kye' Sayadaw. This abbot had become known among foreigners, including many Westerners, for meditation retreats he sponsored in Sagaing. He happened to be present in the village at the time of our visit, of which he, too, was a native, along with a small team of Western and Burmese acupuncturists that he had invited to join him there. They were coming to the end of a weeklong clinic they had set up to provide local people with basic care. This monastery clearly benefitted from the Wa Kye' Sayadaw's largesse: it included a number of handsomely appointed buildings, all of them apparently of recent construction.

U Dhammananda, too, funneled money to a monastery in his natal village, just as the Wa Kye' Sayadaw must have done. Indeed, the most respectful way to name or address him is by the use not of his monk's name (actually called a "title," *bwe.* in Burmese) but rather by the use of the name of that village monastery followed by the word for "abbot" (*hsayado*), as I have done for the Wa Kye' Sayadaw. To be the abbot of a monastery is the jewel in the crown for any monk. U Dhammananda spends no more than a few days out of every year in "his" monastery in the village, the one of which he is the abbot. Most of the time, he resides in a hall at the Shweigyin Monastery in Mandalay. But the latter hall's upkeep means little to him. It is simply where he lives, not the place on which his reputation rests: the condition of the Shweigyin Monastery reflects on the prestige and acumen of its abbot, not that of U Dhammananda. U Dhammananda is of course invested in the monastery's good name, but beyond that he is not much concerned, particularly since the Shweigyin Sayadaw chose for the most part to keep his own counsel. The monastery U Dhammananda supports in his natal village, however, matters deeply to him.

He spends much of the money he receives for delivering sermons on the construction and expansion of that monastery. He takes great pride in telling me the considerable sums of money he has dispensed not only for its construction but also for its upkeep. During my stay in Mandalay in 2012, for example, he paid for the entire hall to be repainted inside and out—this in a society where mold and dirt on walls are so familiar as to go almost unnoticed. Such work not only reflects well on him, of course; it also enables people in the village to augment their incomes through paid labor.

The fact that funds flow from town "down" to village monasteries constitutes an obvious corollary to the point that for an individual novice or monk to move in the opposite direction is a move up. To say that Buddhist monks are supposed to avoid, rather than flock to, populous, lively, and temptation-laden locales would be to state the obvious—and make the speaker look both stodgy and naïve. More to the point is the fact that moving from a village monastery to an urban one, much like moving from the status of a layperson to that of a novice or monk, means choosing one option for enhancing one's standing in Burman society, a goal that few people, lay or religious, would dismiss as without value. Overall, it means moving closer to concentrations of power of many sorts: spiritual (such as the sites of great sacredness, including the Mahamuni Pagoda in Mandalay, where an extremely important Buddha image is housed), political, or financial. It also means living among the bright lights of the city, something that has, after all, drawn young people to cities for centuries.

As in many societies in which most people live on the land, Burmans both idealize and demonize village life and villagers. Villagers are pure, selfless, sociable, and unaffected, in the positive rendering. Some monks told me that it is easier to be a monk in a village because there is nothing to look at but trees and fields, so what would get you thinking about material desires? Yet a novice or monk who makes the transition from a village monastery to an urban one moves closer to sites of serious study. Learning, including Buddhist learning, is to be found only in town: villages, in the negative rendering, are generally looked on as the scene of ignorance, superstition, and intellectual stagnation. The prestige that follows from racking up titles in the Buddhist examination system, or from obtaining a degree from one of the Buddhist universities, is available only to the monk who has made it to town.

Furthermore, truly wealthy lay donors are much more likely to be encountered in town than in a village, and it is by becoming the recipient of a wealthy donor's largesse that a monk can best raise his standing. Gaining residence at a wealthy, that is to say, well-regarded and, so, well-funded monastery may also grant a novice or monk access to opportunities for study, and/or for participation in activities that will augment his prominence and prestige. Especially recently, making one's name in the sermon-preaching circuit brings the potential for great fame: a poster with one's title, maybe even a photograph of one's face, as well as the date of one's performance, will be placed in a prominent spot for all to see for an extended period before the date, and when that date comes, with any luck, a crowd numbering dozens, or even hundreds—for truly famous sermonizers, thousands—of people will sit on the ground listening to what one says.

As I became aware of how many residents of the monastery were of rural origin but had been able, through their kinship and/or territorial links to the abbot and other higher status monks, to remake themselves as residents of Mandalay, I came to think of the monastery not simply as a ladder but as a kind of escalator that raised individuals up as it moved them across space. Or maybe even a rabbit hole that enabled individuals to pop their heads out of the ground in the middle of Mandalay. Fortifying that impression was the absence of residents whose origins were urban.

The simple fact is that the Burman middle class, or indeed, urbanites of any standing, are little likely to give their sons to the sangha. Temporary residence as a novice, usually a week at most, more often only a few days, remains the rule for young Burman boys. The ritual wherein they are first dressed in finery, in imitation of the Prince Siddharta, and paraded about, and then dressed in robes, shorn of their hair, and initiated into the sangha, in imitation of the Buddha upon his departure from the palace in which he was raised, is well-described in the literature about Burma, and indeed other areas of Southeast Asia (e.g., Nash 1965; Bunnag 1973). Girls are also granted some of this attention and excitement. When a group of boys has been assembled, among kin or within a neighborhood, to hold a *shin byu* (novice initiation) ceremony, then girls are similarly dressed for the occasion; for them, it is the occasion of their having their ears pierced. But they are not necessarily then transformed into nuns as the boys are transformed into novices.

The *shin byu* ritual provides the occasion for extravagant displays of wealth and prominence on the part of those children's parents who can muster great means. From time to time, during auspicious months, traffic in Mandalay can be tied up for long periods when a procession of pickup trucks carrying prepubescent boys and girls plus parasol-bearing assistants takes them to important sites around the city linked to the Buddha and to spirits. This procession takes place in the first part of the rites.

Boys who remain as novices for longer periods in town are likely to be poor. Their parents need no longer worry about feeding them as long as they are living at a monastery, and they will obtain some form of education. (Whether that education is purely religious, in the form of Pali study as I have described above, or some combination of Pali and secular subjects, depends on what the particular monastery where they stay provides in its curriculum.) Living in a neighborhood on the outskirts of Mandalay in 1988, I noticed that the quite impoverished family next door relied on a nearby monastery to feed one of its sons, while it kept daughters and other sons (I was never clear how many) at home.

Not only at the Shweigyin Monastery, but at all the monasteries I visited in Mandalay, few were the monks who had grown up in town. Urban families are not less religious than rural ones. But young men in town usually envision other ways of making their way in the world than by becoming monks.

I have provided in this chapter a panoramic image of the monastery where I stayed in 2011 and 2012 in Mandalay, after the fashion of a photograph that wraps around to encompass a 360-degree overview. With the physical structures, the tenor of activities, and the sociology of the establishment now accounted for, I describe more specifically in the next chapter the kinds of interaction that take place among its residents, and among them and their visitors.

Chapter Three

DISCRETIONARY ATTACHMENTS
Monks and Their Social Relations

Ko Min, a man in his thirties who worked as the driver at a Buddhist academy where I stayed for three months in 2011, summed up an attitude that seemed to come up often among Burmans, whether lay, as in his case, or religious, when explaining why they lived at monasteries. He told me that he was not married and had no intention of marrying. A wife would insist that he take her here, take her there. It would be a lot of trouble. He preferred to live at the monastery. Living there enabled him to have a "cool mind" (*sei' nyein de*), that is, to be calm and untroubled. The phrase was one many residents of monasteries, both lay and religious (and for that matter, those laypeople who took on the robe for short stays) repeated frequently to describe the appeal of staying there. I did not point out to Ko Min what seemed obvious: that in light of his job as driver for a monastery, it fell to him to take the abbot here, to take him there, as well as to run errands all over the city. What he avoided by choosing to be a lay resident at a monastery and working as its driver was not so much being at someone else's beck and call. Rather, he avoided having demands placed on him for the kinds of intimacy—for compromises of his autonomy in favor of attachments—that marriage would presumably imply.

Any man who chooses to spend time as a monk, at least if he does so for more than a week or so at the time of Buddhist New Year, opts for relationships that allow for, but by no means assume or require, frequent contact with his peers and with laypeople. Although how importantly sociability figures in a monk's life varies according to individual personality and proclivities, it seems an ideal environment for those males who prefer to keep themselves at a certain remove from the demands of intense interpersonal relationships.

Relationships that obtain at a monastery are of three sorts: relations among monks and their kin; relations among monks and novices; and relations among monks and laypeople who may or may not be kin. All these relationships lend themselves to a range of degrees of intensity. For the most part, however, what I observed was relationships whose intensity was of a fairly moderate degree. The fact that sexual activity in all forms is expressly prohibited to monks, and not only that, the fact that it is one of the few precepts whose infraction appears to be taken extremely seriously by all concerned (unlike the many "minor" faults, such as eating after noon, that monks deem somewhat shameful but less egregious), means that the type of relationship that does not necessarily but certainly may imply particularly close bonds—a particularly intimate attachment—namely, that between sexual partners, is expressly ruled out.

I should emphasize here that my intention in making this observation is not to pathologize Burman monks or other residents of monasteries. If it is something of a commonplace in contemporary American public discourse to favor deep, emotionally intense, and long-term relationships—to favor, that is, attachments over autonomy—we must recognize this as a historically and culturally inflected preference, one that cannot be deemed "correct" or "normal" or "preferable" with respect to other inclinations in interaction. What determines degrees of satisfaction depends, obviously, on where someone expects to find satisfaction, and on how satisfaction is defined. The satisfactions that many Burman males find in residence at a monastery follow both from their religious convictions and from the preferences they tend to exhibit in the tenor of their relations with others. I analyze these understandings in greater detail in later chapters. In this chapter, I relate some of the conversations I had with monks and people in Mandalay and observations I made while living at monasteries there, on which my analysis is based.

Monks and Their Kin

As my description of the Shweigyin Monastery in the preceding chapter should make clear, kin ties link many of its residents, both lay and religious, to one another. The abbot's mother lived at the monastery for many years prior to her death. Two of his younger brothers lived there for decades. One of them eventually disrobed and married, but the other not only continues to live there but also holds the post of second-in-command at the monastery. As mentioned, it is assumed that he will succeed his brother as abbot on the latter's death. One of the abbot's sisters and her husband, and their two grown daughters and their husbands and children, all live on the monastery's grounds. Two of his other sisters live in their natal village but are frequent visitors to the monastery. Still other relatives, both religious and lay, not quite so closely related but kin nevertheless, also live at the Shweigyin Monastery. The man in his seventies who took on the robe at the age of sixty, mentioned in the preceding chapter, was the husband of one of the abbot's cousins, and that man's son, who has not married, is also a monk residing at the monastery. Some people hail from the same village and can be assumed to be related in some way to the abbot and his kin even if the ties are not completely clear. As noted earlier, kinship and territorial proximity tend to meld together in rural Burma, providing a general net of bonds that can prove useful, especially if someone wishes to make the move from the country to town.

Kawanami documents in her study of Burmese nuns (discussed in chapter 9) the way that, in the case of nunneries, kinship ties turn out to generate conflict, particularly at times of transition, such as on the death of a nunnery's abbess (2013, 213–231). Such is not generally the case for monasteries, because lay relatives do not try to pull their religious male kin back into a kin network (as Kawanami shows nuns' kin doing) so much as try to include themselves among the beneficiaries of the access to resources that monks gain for themselves and for the institution to which they belong (and, if they become the abbot, control). This is what the Shweigyin Monastery abbot's kin have obviously managed to do. Of course, monks' kin can well get into fights, and there is certainly evidence of dissension in the Shweigyin Monastery's past. But the idea that the sangha constitutes an institution whose integrity and continuity command respect insulates it from the sort of privatizing tendencies Kawanami reports in nunneries, where donated property accrues not to the institution but rather to individual nuns (and most often the abbess, which is why her passing is often so fraught).

Bonds among kin anywhere can be close and meaningful or not so. The nature of the relationships that people enter into with their relatives, neighbors, peers, and others depends in part on their particular temperaments. The abbot of the Shweigyin Monastery evinces an ascetic and learned reserve, not expansiveness or warmth. I do not have the impression that he spends much time among his many lay relatives living on the monastery's grounds, or that they are frequent visitors at his quarters. But he is a taciturn person in general; no doubt abbots at other monasteries may choose to spend more time among kin.

Relations among monks and their female kin are sometimes very cordial. U Dhammananda's mother was in her nineties at the time of my stay at the Shweigyin Monastery. Each year, U Dhammananda celebrates her birthday with much pomp, both in the village where she lives with his lay siblings and, if she is strong enough to travel (she was in remarkably good health during most of my stay in 2011 and 2012), at his hall in the monastery in Mandalay.

As Keyes has reported for the Thai case (1984), mothers reap particularly great stores of merit—more, the impression seems to be, than fathers—when a son enters the monkhood. They are thought to be giving up much on such an occasion, since a son who enters the sangha forswears, at least for the time being, any chance at marrying and bearing her grandchildren, something that mothers are assumed to desire especially strongly. A young monk I knew in the monastery where I lived in Mandalay in 1988 told me that his mother wept when he ordained as a monk for just that reason. "And if you decide to return to lay life?" I asked, having heard him say that was a possibility he hadn't ruled out. "She will weep," he said, smiling. She would weep because her son, and she, too, by the same token, would lose the cachet that accrues from having a member of the family pursue the monk's vocation.

As a matter of fact, U Dhammananda attributes to his mother's intervention his having succeeded in remaining a monk when he was on the verge of disrobing. As a monk of about thirty, when he was living at a very prestigious and wealthy—indeed, in his telling, luxurious—monastery in Rangoon and was just beginning to become famous for his *dhamma* talks, which laypeople as well as religious residents of the monastery were free to attend, he noticed an attractive and very attentive woman in regular attendance. Before long he found himself smitten and was seriously considering giving up his vocation to marry her. Suddenly, his mother appeared at the monastery, having travelled all the way from their village in central Burma. She had done so because for a few nights running she had had dreams of her son disrobing. Disturbed by the recurrence of the dream, which she interpreted as a significant sign, she had made her way, not without difficulty, to Rangoon to put the question to him whether he was indeed intending to disrobe. "No, of course not!" U Dhammananda quotes himself as replying, although of course he very definitely was. He expresses gratitude to his mother, retrospectively, for having "reminded" him that he must remain a monk. Although incidents later in his life suggest other kinds of emotional difficulties he encountered as an ascetic, he asserts that that one incident was the only time he was seriously tempted to disrobe.

Monks may also be particularly close to their sisters. The abbot of the monastery where I lived in 1987 and 1988 came from a village north of the city. His sister still lived there, but each of them travelled fairly frequently between village and city. She donated basic foodstuffs to him quite often, and he would send her gifts of goods lay supporters had given him that would be hard for her to get in rural areas.

But monks do not necessarily interact frequently with their lay kin, even if they live close by. A very personable monk at the Buddhist academy where I stayed a few months had a number of guests in his quarters one day. These turned out to be kin. Among them was a young cousin whose birthday it was: in a common pattern, they had come to donate food to the monk in observance of that event. (In this way, they earned merit for themselves, especially for the boy whose birthday was being observed.) They only stayed about twenty minutes, however, and later the monk told me that, although he was happy to receive them as guests at the monastery, he never visited them at their homes.

Monks' Relations among Themselves

It seems clear that, even apart from considerations of individual temperament, a consistent pattern characterizes monks' relationships with each other. As novices, they live in constant physical proximity; they are virtually never alone. Memorizing Pali texts, as I have described, is an individual activity much of the time, but it is by no means a solitary one. Groups of novices and young monks attend classes together and then sit together in a room, each one loudly declaiming lines of the canon at his own pace till he has it down: at such times their attention is divided but they are joined together in space and in the nature of their activity. For the rest, they go on alms rounds together, they eat together, they attend evening recitation together, they bathe in clumps (during the hottest months, they may do this at all hours of the day and night), they may play a bit of soccer together, they watch

DVDs or listen to the radio together, and they sleep near each other (although under separate mosquito nets) at night. Every minute of every day is spent in the presence of their peers. And through much of it, among novices, there is teasing and playful physical sparring.

As monks grow older, this constant interaction steadily diminishes. They come to spend more time on their own, whether studying or (more often) watching television, in their own quarters if they have them, or across the street at the tea shop if they do not. If they are senior enough to have their own quarters, they would find it compromising to be seen spending much time at tea shops, especially in the evening. Younger monks with less prestige to concern themselves with are more likely to engage in this practice, but they, too, may well think it little befitting their dignity. The most senior monks at the Shweigyin Monastery meet together to discuss institutional matters. Otherwise, they virtually never spend time together other than when they sit together for the late-morning meal. I do not want to suggest that they do not get on well with each other. Sitting together over their meal, they converse easily, at least so it appeared to me.[1] But they tend not to socialize among themselves at other times.

U Dhammananda cannot be more different than the taciturn and serious abbot of the Shweigyin Monastery. He takes evident pleasure in conversation with other monks and with lay visitors (including me). Nevertheless, he, too, usually chooses to spend his evenings, and when he isn't teaching, much of his days, alone in his quarters. A few other monks with whom he is particularly close may come by for a few moments of conversation. But many evenings go by without any such visits occurring. Unless he was out giving a *dhamma* talk or on a trip back to his native village, I could assume that if I went knocking on the door of his quarters, I was likely to find him there alone.

More common, it seems, than interaction among peers—among monks of similar age and seniority—is interaction among monks of a considerable age difference, or among monks and novices. If I saw another monk resident at the monastery at U Dhammananda's hall, it was most often U Kumara, a monk about fifteen or so years his junior who came over to visit from the building where he lived alone. Or if U Dhammananda was not in his hall but was on the monastery's grounds, he was likely to be found in that monk's quarters having a chat or watching TV or a DVD. Granted, U Kumara told me that he and U Dhammananda spent time together because they were both senior monks: they had longer experience and so greater understanding than younger monks, with whom they had little in common. Nevertheless, the difference in their standing was clear. U Dhammananda could, for example, tease U Kumara in a way that I never saw reversed. One evening when U Dhammananda was telling me about how a monk from the ages of about twenty-five or thirty to about forty or fifty was bothered by two sorts of desires—for material wealth and for women—U Kumara happened to pass through the hall where we were sitting on the way to the bathing area. U Dhammananda urged me to ask U Kumara if that wasn't the case, whether he was not still prey to feelings of lust. U Kumara simply smiled, and then continued on his way. U Dhammananda assured me that once a monk got to be, as he was, above the age of fifty, all he really cared about was remaining in good health.

As mentioned in the preceding chapter, a monk considerably younger than U Dhammananda lived for a number of years in the same hall with him. The younger monk did not share U Dhammananda's private quarters but rather lived in the large room that made up most of the downstairs portion of the building. That room houses a Buddha altar and U Dhammananda's impressive collection of books (the canon in a bookcase near the Buddha altar, the others on bookshelves at the other end of the room) and some bric-a-brac behind the bookshelves. The bed the younger monk used (the sort of simple wooden frame most Burmans sleep on) still stood to one side of the Buddha altar. When I asked U Dhammananda if he hadn't been sorry to see the younger monk move out after several years of co-residence, he said, on the contrary, that he had been pleased. With his customary frankness, he added, laughing, "If you live alone, you can do whatever you want. You can go ahead and fart and not worry about who else is around!"[2]

The warmest bonds that I observed among religious residents of the monastery were those between a monk and much younger monks or novices.[3] The Palaung monk mentioned in the previous chapter, who brought Palaung and Shan boys to the monastery before the start of every school year, seemed genuinely concerned for their welfare. Although there were always a fair number of them for him to look after—usually about thirty or so, I believe—he communicated a certain warmth and gentle humor that no doubt helped them deal with their having moved so far from home, with little chance of seeing their parents and other relatives again for at least a year at a stretch. A few other monks, aged, like the Palaung monk, in their forties, showed some similar degree of attachment to their younger colleagues, colored by a kind of avuncular benevolence. When I asked a monk whether young boys who moved far away from their families to come live at the monasteries didn't miss their families a great deal, he told me that, yes, it was hard for them at first. But eventually the older monks came to seem like their parents and the young novices no longer felt so homesick.[4]

Monks' Relations with Laypeople

As noted, relations among peers, that is, among monks of similar age and standing, seem less liable to be close than those among religious residents of disparate age and standing. But still easier, it seems, are interactions among monks and laypeople. In these situations, differences in role are so great (recall that the words for "person" and "monk" are mutually exclusive in Burmese) that questions of competition, challenge, or degrees of relative prestige fall away.

Typical, it seems to me, is the friendship between U Tharana, a monk in his late twenties or early thirties, and the slightly younger lay man, Ko Kyaw, who lives among university students in the northeast corner of the compound. As mentioned, Ko Kyaw continued to live at the monastery after completing his university studies. He does not make enough money, he feels, collecting monthly installments people make on motorcycles they have bought, to live on his own or to marry. He often spends time in the evening talking to U Tharana in the latter's tiny, freestanding quarters. U Tharana at such times sits or lies sprawled on his sleeping platform; Ko Kyaw sits, in a casual pose, on the floor in front of the monk. He is himself quite devout, a frequenter of the many *dhamma* talks given all over the city, especially during certain auspicious lunar months.[5] Sometimes U Tharana gets on the back of Ko Kyaw's motorbike and they go off to attend such events together.[6] If I stopped by U Tharana's quarters in the evening, I often found Ko Kyaw with the monk; they might be watching a DVD together on U Tharana's small laptop, or simply chatting, sometimes with other lay friends joining them. Thus their friendship seems real. But there is a good chance that it will fall victim to their very different likely trajectories. U Tharana told me that, once he had passed the Dhammasariya exams, he might well move and maybe even become the abbot of his own monastery. It was not clear that Ko Kyaw would move to whatever monastery that might be, should the eventuality arise. Monks, especially younger monks, do often move in groups from one monastery to another, but monks do so together with lay people less often.[7]

The most frequent visitors to U Dhammananda's quarters are laypeople who live outside the monastery. A Sino-Burman man is a particularly valued interlocutor: he brings along books translated into Burmese from Western languages for them to discuss. Business takes this man away from Mandalay often, for weeks or months at a time, so his visits are not regular. But in speaking with me, U Dhammananda often quoted exchanges they had had on a variety of topics. Another lay visitor was a man who travelled on business frequently between towns in the Shan States and Mandalay. He often stays in U Dhammananda's hall when he is in Mandalay. People from U Dhammananda's village who come to Mandalay for whatever reason often stop in, as well, sometimes, like the lay man just mentioned, sleeping on mats they spread out on the broad open space in the middle of the room. (If a monk spends the night in the hall, he sleeps on the bed platform to the side of the Buddha altar.) Many of those villagers come to Mandalay to seek medical treatment. One night when I was living with the monks and novices in the upstairs hall, I went downstairs in the wee hours to use the toilet and saw a man fanning his small, feverish child in the half-light.[8]

Particularly affecting to me, and representative of the sort of role that monks sometimes play in the lives of laypeople of their acquaintance, was a visit one evening of a middle-aged woman, her two grown sons, and the wife of one of the young men. They had come because it was the seventh anniversary of the death of the woman's husband. (I learned later that he had died aged only in his forties.) One of the sons presented U Dhammananda with a monk's robe. He accepted it with both hands, just as the young man offered it to him: this is the required gesture with which gifts change hands between laypeople and monks. U Dhammananda then started reciting a number of phrases in Burmese, which he had them repeat, line by line. This included several mentions of the husband's name. U Dhammananda explained to me later that what they were doing was sharing the merit with the late man, merit that they received by giving donations to him, a monk. It was not as though they could deliver the merit to him directly: they had to appeal to invisible beings (*na'*) to deliver it to the man on their behalf. Only people of great spiritual power (*dagou:*) would not need to go through intermediaries in this way. But such power was not within the reach of most people, so they had to rely on intermediaries, unseen, who acted as go-betweens. The dead man's relatives could not know whether he was now in one of the Buddhist heavens or elsewhere, that is, at what level of existence among the thirty-one such strata Buddhism posits. They could only hope that he was at some level among the heavens. No matter where he was, they hoped that by sharing merit with him, they could make sure that he received proper clothes, food, accommodation, and the like. In giving donations, they were relying upon the "energy of the *dhamma*" (*da̱ma. da'*) to gain the merit they sought to share with him, thereby assuring his well-being.

The reciting complete—it only lasted a few minutes—the woman then presented U Dhammananda with some cooked food in containers, which he had them transfer to the tin storage containers that he kept near the wall at the far end of the room. They all then chatted for a few minutes. The woman said that one of her sons had been taking drugs. U Dhammananda admonished him about this, telling him that he must stop doing so. The younger woman, his wife, said that for a long time she had not known he was doing this. He would tell her he was going to the market and she was unaware that what he was doing was going to get high with his friends.

When the conversation lulled, I intervened to ask how long the young man had been behaving in this way; about a year, was the response. U Dhammananda then remarked that the good thing was that he wasn't lying about it. It was still the beginning of his habit, so it was not too late for him to change. It used to be that people took drugs secretly, U Dhammananda and the young man's mother noted. Now they did it openly, in big groups! After a few more moments of conversation, the guests made obeisance to U Dhammananda and left.

U Dhammananda had known these people for over twenty years. They lived nearby. Recently, though, he hadn't seen them so often. He explained that this was because he was now an older monk. "In general, laypeople have more to do with younger monks. Laypeople go more often to the smaller *dhamma* hall [the building in the southwest corner of the monastery, where the younger monk moved to from U Dhammananda's hall], not here so much."

What informs this pattern is the fact that senior monks are looked on with respect bordering on awe: they are revered, which tends to preclude laypeople interacting with them casually or spontaneously. Indeed, laypeople freely admit the fact that in the presence of a powerful senior monk, they experience unmitigated fear. The driver at the Buddhist academy, Ko Min, did a hilarious imitation of himself bobbing his head and falling all over himself out of fear when he found himself in the presence of the head abbot of the chain of institutions of which the one we were sitting in was just one branch. Ko Min explained his behavior by saying that he "was afraid of" and "respected" that immensely famous and respected monk. Younger monks are more accessible, readier to collaborate with laypeople in whatever projects (such as fund-raising for the monastery, or organizing *dhamma* talks) they may undertake.

Some laypeople, perhaps especially monks' lay kin but non-kin lay donors as well, do, however, turn to monks they know to ask for advice about matters they face in their lives. One evening when I stopped by U Tharana's quarters, I found him talking with a young woman, perhaps in her late twenties. The woman was introduced to me as his "cousin," which is a broad category in Burmans' bilateral kinship reckoning but which was apparently sufficient to excuse his meeting with a woman alone in his quarters, something the *vinaya* normally forbids. She had come to ask him his opinion about employment she had been offered in China. The woman had a reasonably good job in Mandalay but she did not see the job leading to any advancement and she was interested in the job offer she was being made. She wanted to know what U Tharana would advise her to do. He seemed not to have strong opinions on the matter, although the woman appeared to find it useful to discuss it with him.

Kin are almost always a monk's first lay supporters, and they remain so through much of his existence as a monk if he does not distinguish himself in some capacity, such as by becoming famous for his textual learning or for his skills at giving *dhamma* talks. Only in that way does he stand much chance of gaining support from other, non-kin donors. Some monks are by no means shy about making requests (or demands) of their supporters, whether kin or not. One evening I visited a fairly senior monk at the Shweigyin Monastery and found that a young couple was visiting him in his quarters. The woman was a niece of the monk; she was paying a call on the monk following her recent wedding to the young man accompanying her. Both of them had good, white-collar jobs. The monk told me proudly that his niece had been sent to South Korea for professional training. She corrected him to say that it was Malaysia to which she had been sent; this would sound much less impressive to anyone in Burma, since Malaysia is thought of as relatively close and accessible, whereas South Korea is the rich, modern, and prestigious source of "Korean wave" TV serials and pop music. In any case, before long the monk was letting the couple know that he thought it would be appropriate for them to donate a computer to him. His niece demurred politely, saying they could not afford it, but the monk persisted in making clear just what sort of computer he wanted. It seemed to me unlikely that he would get his wish, but his niece and her husband seemed not to take it ill that he communicated the request.[9]

A young monk recently returned with a master's degree in Buddhist studies from an Indian university told me, when I thought to ask, that he had not been supported in his endeavor by the renowned and wealthy monastic organization of which he was a member but rather by his own lay supporters. He had approached them about supporting him in those studies and they had acceded to the request. (Yes, he responded to my query, they had been somewhat taken aback when he first brought it up.) Unfortunately, their fortunes were now less secure and they could not support him further. He wanted very much to return to India in pursuit of a PhD, but he would have to find alternate sources of funds to do so. He would certainly ask his kin to help, but his kin alone did not have the wherewithal to finance such a long-term and, for most Burmans, very expensive, undertaking.

When I asked monks about the whole matter of their relations with their lay supporters, I received, unsurprisingly, fairly diverse comments. For example, one young monk told me that when he went on alms rounds in the morning, he always followed the same route and visited the same households. He said that, over the years, he had come to know some of the families quite well and enjoyed hearing about how everyone was getting on. Yet another monk of about the same age (I would guess in his mid-twenties) said the opposite: he was careful *not* to learn about the affairs of his lay donors. To do so, he said quite emphatically, would be inappropriate to his role as a monk. It would prove distracting; he would get caught up in their worries and concerns, whereas his responsibility was to put all worldly affairs aside.

The way the first monk engaged with his lay donors probably resembled what I observed on an outing I made one morning with a young monk and the driver from the Buddhist academy. We got into the academy's van, drove to a fabric store in downtown Mandalay, and entered, carrying a considerable number of empty food containers. These were taken into the house that stood behind the shop, and while they were being filled with enough food for the academy's residents' midday meal, the shop's owners, the monk, the driver, and I sat and chatted amiably. The family provided this meal on a rotating basis once a week and had been doing so long enough for the family to know the monk and driver quite well.

I never saw the second of the monks I mentioned above, the one who ruled out the possibility of being an intimate friend of his donors, out on alms rounds, but I can imagine he acted much like a monk I happened to see stop by the home of middle-class friends of mine in Mandalay when I was visiting them one day. The monk came in the front door (left open, as front doors often are during the day) without fanfare, in silence, and simply sat down in the front room. A woman in the family took his alms bowl from him. He kept his eyes downcast as soon as he was seated and while awaiting the return of his alms bowl. When it was given back to him, he simply stood up and walked out the door. No words were exchanged. His demeanor demonstrated, indeed, dramatized, the fact that he was an ascetic being whose individual identity was irrelevant. The donors, the friends with whom I was visiting, told me afterward that they knew nothing about him. They had simply informed the abbot of a nearby monastery that they would be happy to provide alms regularly to any one resident of that monastery he directed their way.

Monks and novices in the Shweigyin Monastery did not enter people's houses individually in this way, instead forming lines and receiving alms in turn from people standing in front of their houses. Yet the pattern whereby food was given by laypeople to silent, impassive members of the sangha, who then simply moved on, was very much the same.

Long-term relationships between specific monasteries, particularly their abbots, and specific families, particularly their female heads of households, are common, particularly among more prominent or materially comfortable families in Mandalay. Once again, the affective valence of such relationships—how personalized they are, and how deeply the bonds are felt—depends in large part on individual temperaments.

There is, however, a certain tension or disparity in the bonds between lay supporters and the monks they sponsor, something that can put them somewhat at cross-purposes. Sponsors, especially women, often appear to seek out a level of intimacy that monks resist to one degree or another. One evening when I was visiting U Tharana, he spent a good deal of time talking on the phone with a female donor. He was a patient and generous individual, and he seemed quite willing to listen to her relate what I could only take to be quite long and involved stories. At several points, it sounded as though the conversation was drawing to a close—so I gathered from the tenor of U Tharana's remarks, which was all I could hear—but then the woman would, apparently, start in on another topic. U Tharana did smile at another lay guest and me a few times, but he did not roll his eyes. Not long after he hung up, in fact, she called again.

U Tharana said little about this woman, but it was easy to infer that she found satisfactions talking with him that she did not find talking with her husband. The pattern is not restricted to Buddhist societies, of course: laywomen in Western societies often find safe and real pleasure in their relations with members of the Catholic hierarchy, for example, pleasure that must make up for lacks in their relations with their husbands and other intimates. Outside religious contexts, women may find in gay male confidants satisfactions—sometimes the better word would be consolation—that they do not find in their relations with any heterosexual males. Some monks in Mandalay seem quite willing to take on the role of asexual male confidant, or at least interlocutor, in much the same way.

Yet some monks appear to push back against forms of attachment they find excessive. What U Kumara told me about his relations with his primary female sponsor (*dagama. kyi:*) struck me as particularly telling, if somewhat sad. U Kumara (the friend of U Dhammananda alluded to above) was a handsome, quite tall monk aged about forty. He explained that as a teenager, growing up along with five siblings in a village in Lower Burma, he had not wanted to become a novice. He enjoyed playing soccer and wanted to continue doing so. His parents prevailed on him to enter the sangha, however. He said he got used to the monastic life eventually; once he had taken on the robe as a youngster, he had never disrobed. He was a novice in his natal village for a year, then moved to another village monastery, then to a monastery in Amarapura, a former Burman capital located a few kilometers south of Mandalay. He was there for three years while still a novice. One morning when he went out on his rounds, a laywoman at one of the houses he passed by regularly asked him to come in. She was from Mandalay but, having never married, she often went to stay with her older sister in Amarapura, remaining ten days or longer at a time. She had seen him every day for a while when she spoke to him that morning. She asked him if he was already a monk or still a novice. When he said he was still a novice—he was still nineteen—she didn't believe him at first, since he was already quite tall. She then asked him if she could sponsor his ordination ceremony. He said he could not accept her offer to do so, because his parents were still his principal supporters and he knew they would want to be the sponsors for his ordination ceremony. But the woman went to speak to the abbot of the monastery where he was staying about her offer. The abbot thought it was a good idea. U Kumara explained again that his parents would not accept such an arrangement. But the abbot wrote to his parents and they did agree to it.

U Kumara was ordained at that monastery in Amarapura. But two months later he moved to the Shweigyin Monastery because the woman who had sponsored his ordination and was now his principal female supporter lived in Mandalay and, having long been close to the Shweigyin Monastery's abbot, wished him to live there. She told U Kumara that she had wanted to sponsor his ordination because, had she married and had a son, she was sure he would have resembled U Kumara.

I asked U Kumara how often he now saw this woman. He said he saw her from time to time. Unless he was sick (and so, presumably, in need of medicine), though, he didn't call her to the monastery. She might stop by once a month or so. But sometimes a year would go by between her visits. When he first lived here, U Kumara went on, she came often, twice a week or so, bringing him donations of various sorts: robes, or fish paste and other food. At that point he wasn't really settled here yet. But after ten years of residence at the monastery, he told her she "didn't have to come anymore," a polite way of saying that she should not. When I asked whether she was "disappointed," a polite way of saying "hurt" or "upset," at his saying that, he replied, "She just laughed," which is a polite way of registering any negative emotion in Burma. I couldn't help feeling sorry for the woman.

My conversations with U Dhammananda about his relations with his lay supporters were, if I am allowed the expression, fruitfully frustrating. They were frustrating because, whereas U Dhammananda was a patient and expansive commentator on a great range of subjects, my efforts to inquire about his lay supporters rarely generated much by way of comment. Over a number of conversations, I was able to piece together a certain amount of information. He had about twenty major donors, accumulated over decades. Yes, he had a list of them somewhere.... I did once prevail on him to find the list and start telling me about these donors. Yet we didn't get very far. "Some of these people are dead," he noted by way of introduction. "Some more of them probably are, I'm not really sure." "These people moved to Kachin State. I hardly ever see them anymore." And so it went. But only for a few more names: we never got very far down the list, despite my best efforts. The most recent entrant to the list of his major donors, and the one about whom he was most voluble, was the abbess at a large and important nunnery, whom he had taken me to visit one day. On the occasion of the dedication of the new building at her nunnery, to which she had invited one thousand monks and one thousand nuns, she had given each of them a donation of K20,000 in cash (about US$25 at the time). But to each of 108 special guests, U Dhammananda among them (108 being an auspicious number in Burmese Buddhist circles), she had donated the astonishing sum of K1,000,000 (about US$1,250).

Only very eventually did I discern what prevented me from learning much from U Dhammananda about his lay donors. I came to recognize a pattern: When I started asking about his lay donors, U Dhammananda soon started talking about his success as a giver of *dhamma* talks. The shift from the one topic to the other, I finally realized, was motivated by the fact that in accepting donations from laypeople, U Dhammananda was showing himself to be dependent on them. When giving *dhamma* talks, he won both prestige and monetary compensation as the result of his own skills, something he was much happier telling me about.

For a monk to act as a "field of merit" for his lay supporters is an entrenched and, for that matter honorable, merit-generating act. It fits into the long-term relations of exchange, as mentioned earlier, whereby laypeople offer up material sustenance and monks reciprocate with teaching, ritual action, and the opportunity for laypeople to obtain merit. Monks grant spiritual rewards in return for material goods. The whole exchange allows monks to remain as much as possible outside the realm of the worldly (*lo:ki*), focused instead on the realm of the otherworldly (*lo:kou'tara.*). Yet it seems clear that U Dhammananda still found the dependency implicit in his inclusion in such networks of exchange compromising. In stressing his success as a giver of Buddhist sermons, he emphasized his autonomy as an agent. The fact that he spoke relatively freely about winning material support from the famous abbess followed from her being a member of the religious community, first of all. Furthermore, she was a highly respected, famous, and, for that matter, well-connected one. To be in some way "dependent" on a very prominent individual means that one is linked to him or her. Entering into relations of exchange with such individuals can only redound to the prestige of the recipient of such largesse. To subordinate oneself is not intrinsically or irrevocably compromising: any implication of dependence it may carry with it can be more than outweighed provided the agent to which one is linked is of sufficient stature.

Conclusion

Exchange relations always play on suggestions of mutual dependency and entanglement; in this respect they stand in clear contrast to autonomy. I began this chapter by noting that males who choose to live at monasteries, whether as religious or laypeople, opt for residential arrangements that permit a flexible range in degrees of intimacy they enter into with others, but that those arrangements tend to attract males for whom a relatively modest degree of attachment appears preferable.

The great Tonle Sap, Cambodia's enormous lake, acts as a reservoir in such a way that when the Mekong River rises during heavy rains, the amount of water in Tonle Sap rises but the Mekong does not flood its delta, as the Red River to the north often does. Monasteries in Mandalay act in a similar fashion as a reservoir, a holding area, for males who, whether temporarily or permanently or intermittently, choose to take refuge in the Three Jewels, and in this way win relief from the demands of intense personal relationships. This affective dimension of the sangha's appeal is not the sole advantage it offers its members, as my discussion of the reasons many boys and men enter the Shweigyin Monastery shows. Yet it strikes me as a real concomitant of other, social and material, motivations novices and monks (and their families) may have. Neither social science nor Buddhist ideology should occasion us to judge such behavior as wanting. Indeed, Buddhism rather holds such detachment up as admirable, in keeping with the Buddhist ideal of "breaking attachments." In later chapters, I analyze the ways this inclination in interpersonal relations links to other patterns in Burman social relations. Before doing so, however, I undertake in the next chapter a theoretical excursus to lay the basis for the analyses of Burmese relationships that then follow.

Chapter Four

Taking Dumont to Southeast Asia

Louis Dumont wrote more extensively and more penetratingly about hierarchy than any recent anthropologist.[1] Among South Asianists, his work provoked enormous discussion, controversy, and then something verging on collective dismissal. Although his name is still invoked, certain key authors, particularly Arjun Appadurai (1984, 1988) and Nicholas Dirks (1987), voiced critiques that seemed to marginalize both the project Dumont set himself—analyzing a vast literature on the "caste system" in South Asia—and the account of it he came up with. Not a South Asianist, I am not in a position to evaluate Dumont's analysis of South Asian data, or the responses his work elicited from experts in the field of South Asian studies.[2] Nevertheless, key points he made about the logic of hierarchical thinking remain valuable and worth reviewing, at least as a stimulus for further thinking.[3] At the same time, since I want to apply his ideas to Southeast Asia, not South Asia, and (as he himself stated) the two regions differ in important ways, I note divergences between what he describes for India and what I want to suggest about Burma, and even about Southeast Asia more broadly. After all, the region used to be labeled, distortingly but not altogether unfruitfully, "Further India," or alternatively, the "Indianized states of Southeast Asia" (Coedès 1968).

Dumont's major claims can be summarized as follows. The caste system is predicated on a ranked ordering of prestige, not power, and degrees of prestige follow from degrees of relative purity. Differences in purity, like all differences, are both noted and evaluated: hierarchy always implies this dual endeavor of distinguishing elements according to some immediately given axis of difference and, at the same time, according to an axis of greater or lesser value. In Indian ideology, prestige (and its concomitant, status) matter more than power, which is always, according to ideology, of secondary importance. In actual fact, power must always be reckoned with: ideologically belittled, it is in practice never ignored. It is reintroduced "surreptitiously" because it is a crucial part of social life and so has to be dealt with (Dumont 1980, 77, 153). But only by virtue of the fact that power is put aside, or put down, ideologically can the hierarchical ordering based on degrees of purity appear so consistent and all-encompassing.[4]

Their clear advantage as to purity means that Brahman priests outrank Kshatriya rulers, whose relative lack of purity—they eat meat, spill blood, and indulge their sensual desires freely—precludes their carrying out essential religious functions, since the effectiveness of these depends on the purity of the people who implement them. At the same time, priests depend on rulers for their material sustenance and physical security. So a mutual interdependence binds them, priests and rulers, together, and in Dumont's view, that interdependence, based on fundamental differences, lies at the heart of all hierarchical arrangements. Hierarchical arrangements are always predicated on mutual interdependence through difference.

Dumont does not use this last phrase, "mutual interdependence through difference," but it provides a convenient shorthand with which to summarize much of what he means when he refers to "an orientation to the whole"—to the "holism" that hierarchy, in his view, necessarily implies. Taken alone, the phrase may suggest nothing beyond Durkheim's concept of organic solidarity, the kind of interdependence that the differentiation of roles in a complex society requires. But Dumont provides a different perspective on such interdependence. For one thing, he does not indulge in the vestigial evolutionary thinking characteristic of Durkheim's dichotomy between mechanical solidarity, which he associates with simple or small-scale societies, and organic solidarity, which he associates with complex and large-scale ones. The mutual interdependence in Dumont's representation of hierarchy follows not from the scale of the communities in question but from a fundamental take on how to bind people together. Should the differences among individuals and groups be ignored or, on the contrary, made use of for this purpose? Egalitarian thinking, which Dumont thinks is peculiar to modernity, would make difference (ideally, although in practice this turns out to be impossible) a matter of indifference—whereas hierarchical thinking, in contrast, makes difference the linchpin of the entire system. Furthermore, Dumont insists that difference always implies a difference in value, a point that Durkheim did not consider but one that has important consequences in the workings of any community.

In the case at hand, that of hierarchy in India, the differentiation of religious ("sacred") and secular ("politico-economic") functions, and their necessary complementarity, makes it possible to rank order two kinds of individuals, with reference to relative degrees of purity, yet assure that they remain bound to each other. Similar relations of interdependence bind other elements of Indian society to this preeminent nexus of priest and ruler. Concern—pervasive—for relative status gives rise, it is true, to many gestures that look fissiparous: groups of people in some subcastes refuse to enter into relations with certain other subcastes in order to maintain claims of greater purity. But this comes down to so much jockeying for position among groups who are bound to one another, if in no other way than in competition for greater purity and, so, prestige-ranking. Status, after all, exists only in light of difference: a subcaste can raise its standing only by appearing more pure than other subcastes, and such a difference must be maintained and noted if it is to be of any significance. Everyone therefore must always attend to how they fit into the larger whole: both how they stack up against others and, at the same time, how they rely on those unlike themselves to attain important ends. You may very well despise members of the sweeper caste; that doesn't mean you can do without their services.

Dumont believes that any hierarchical system takes one value as preeminent. It must do so, because hierarchy refers, in his view, to a series of encompassing values, an arrangement whereby values at a higher order of magnitude can incorporate while still dominating those more salient at lower orders of magnitude. For several values to be equally valid—that is, of equal value—would collapse the very principle of encompassment on which the system is based. For India, as mentioned above, Dumont identifies purity as the overarching value.

A concern for the larger whole, for the overarching context, is in the end the point Dumont most wants to stress about hierarchical principles: he states repeatedly that hierarchy is predicated on an orientation to the whole, or holism (1980, 232–233). This consistent attention to an overarching system connecting all constituent elements stands in contrast, Dumont insists, to Westerners' focus on individuals as providing the privileged level of explanation for all behavior. One thinks of Margaret Thatcher's famous remark about society, "There is no such thing!"[5]

Many critics have commented that the radical distinction between the two conceptual systems, what Dumont blithely labels "hierarchy" versus "egalitarianism," or "holism" versus "individualism," seems overdrawn, and I will echo that sentiment myself in later chapters. Indeed, Dumont suffered excoriation at the hands of many for making what his critics called simpleminded "the West vs. the rest" generalizations about hierarchical versus individualist ideologies.[6] Appadurai stated condescendingly that *Homo Hierarchicus* should be seen as the last manifestation of an outmoded intellectual project (1984).

Yet Dumont's approach can still be defended from charges of unthinking overgeneralizing, however much scholars may contest the conclusions he reached about India. He believed that understandings he called at times "egalitarian," "modern," or "individualist" are an aberration, an ideological take on social life that has gained immense purchase the world over but which must be subjected to critical analysis, in part because it so obviously distorts what actually obtains in contemporary societies, in or outside the West. In other words, the legacy of the Western Enlightenment has had real effects, both in the West and beyond, that it behooves us, as analysts of social life, to consider very closely. Yet we must be ready to recognize the contradictions and practical difficulties Western ideology generates. At the same time, Dumont's careful study of how German thinkers contrasted with French ones, from the time of the Enlightenment through the first half of the twentieth century, proves how alert he was to subtle differences even within a realm of ideas he labeled "Western" and "individualist" (1994). It is of course legitimate to argue with Dumont on the substance of his interpretations. To reject his project out of hand as too generalized, however, is to refuse to consider how useful it might be to ask questions at a very elevated order of magnitude, as he did over a number of decades in order to be able to gain better conceptual grasp of what he knew of India and of the West.

Dumont himself remarked, in his 1980 Radcliffe-Brown Lecture in Social Anthropology, on how much resistance his ideas had encountered, noting, "I have been trying in recent years to sell the profession the idea of hierarchy, with little success, I may add" (1986, 235). Some of Dumont's critics seem to find in him a defender of hierarchical values that they, right-thinking proponents of egalitarian ideals, fulsomely reject. Such a misreading demonstrates Dumont's point that egalitarian values so dominate our discourse as to make it hard for us to think clearly about any other take on social relations. Altogether relevant in this regard is Dumont's final point in *Homo Hierarchicus*'s introductory chapter, when he argues that to reject the validity of an inclination on the part of societies to establish hierarchies of value is an odd—if to us progressive members of a modern, educated elite, laudable—move, one that poses great and still unresolved challenges. Disclaiming any wish to undermine the egalitarian impulse in Western thought, Dumont nevertheless insists, "It is well to understand to what extent [the ideal of equality] runs contrary to the general tendencies of societies, and hence how far our society is exceptional, and how difficult it is to realize this ideal" (1980, 20).

I agree with Dumont that proponents of egalitarian thinking have not yet found a way to implement its principles effectively in any actual, existing society. In Burma, as my introductory sketches of traffic, *dhamma* talks, and tea shops in chapter 1 were intended to suggest, egalitarianism is indeed foreign to most Burmese thinking, whereas hierarchical thinking is very much the order of the day. Keeping hierarchical assumptions in mind, therefore, helps us understand much of what goes on in Burman society and should go some way to preventing us from imposing our own preoccupations on the people we observe. Such is the core understanding on which I wish to base the analyses of Burmese social relations I set out in the remaining chapters of this book.

Sameness and Difference

Dumont believes, as I have noted, that hierarchical arrangements rely on difference to bind people to each other. As a result, hierarchical ideology is inclusive and discriminating, indeed discriminatory in order to be inclusive: discrimination is the price to pay to assure inclusion. This matters especially to people whose claims on resources are tenuous. The example Dumont uses to illustrate the point concerns diet. In the hierarchical scheme, a group's acknowledged differentness, enabling it to be contrasted with other groups, becomes the very principle whereby it is integrated into society. "If you eat beef, you must accept being classed among the Untouchables, and on this condition your practice will be tolerated. It would only create a scandal were you to insist on your practice being recognized as indifferent" (1980, 192).

"Indifference" refers to a difference that is taken not to matter, written off as meaningless or inconsequential. In arrangements predicated on mutual interdependence through difference, such a claim is, Dumont implies, scandalous. A corollary is that similarity, if not scandalous, is at least of no help if people aim to establish ties to others. Complementarity predicated on difference is the key to solidarity in hierarchical thinking; similarity is the solvent that undoes or precludes it. Drifting apart is one evident outcome of similarity, as Tocqueville warned about the United States (Dumont 1980, 17–19). But if simply loosening bonds is not an option, then the need to establish differences among parties who appear (too) similar may generate competition, conflict, or even violence. So, scandalous or not, similarity may be dangerous. If two individuals do not differ vis-à-vis one another, what interest do they have in sticking together? If they do not differ, furthermore, they may both have a great interest in trying to instate a difference—one as simple, perhaps, as that between the living and the dead.

Southeast Asian history, to take an obvious example, is filled with murderous strife among royal half-brothers whose differential claims to status did not distinguish them enough to make it clear who should be superordinate and who subordinate, that is, who should rule. The last Burmese king, Thibaw, was responsible for the murder of between seventy and eighty of his half-brothers in the effort to establish his reign on a sure footing (Harvey 1967, 338). Members of Thailand's Chakri dynasty have fared better by having powerful half-brothers of kings take on the robe: introducing the distinction between monk and ruler enabled them to coexist peacefully. Mongkut, although born to his father's queen and so having the best genealogical claims to the throne when Rama II died in 1824, lacked the backing of powerful factions. He had the good sense to live twenty-seven years as a monk before ascending the throne as Rama IV on the death of his older half-brother in 1851 (Marshall 2014, 128). Throughout the reign of the recently deceased King Bhumipol IX, questions surrounded the circumstances of his older brother's death by gunshot wound, a death that brought about the younger prince's accession to the throne. Andrew Marshall claims that the Thai political scene's recent volatility stemmed from fierce disagreement within the Thai elite about who should succeed the king upon his passing (2014).

In egalitarian societies, according to Dumont, it is difference, rather than similarity, that generates problems. Do differences matter?

Can they be taken into account or do they need to be ignored? How can differences be made a matter of indifference? Dumont touches on these issues in an appendix to *Homo Hierarchicus* when he considers whether it is appropriate to equate the Indian caste system with American racism (1980, 247–266). His view is no: racism, by making people different in their bodies, compensates for—steps into the breach in the face of—an ideological rejection of the possibility of ordering people by status. In other words, differences, such as those that racial classification makes so much of, that would otherwise make some people superordinate and others subordinates, but by the same token bound to one another, now have to be taken as biologically given. This is dangerous. It encourages radical separation, rather than mutual interdependence, among groups of people based on their differences.

The challenge, as Dumont sees it (and here he anticipates a great deal of later efforts on the part of promoters of interethnic harmony in places like Australia and Europe, as well as the United States) is to acknowledge differences but strip them of evaluation:

> It is permissible to doubt whether, in the fight against racism in general, the mere recall of the egalitarian ideal, however solemn it may be, and even though accompanied by a scientific criticism of racist prejudices, will be really efficient. It would be better to prevent the passage from the moral principle of equality to the notion that all men are identical. One feels sure that equality can, in our day, be combined with the recognition of differences, so long as such differences are morally neutral. People must be provided with the means for conceptualizing differences. (1980, 265)

Gender provides an obvious, perhaps the fundamental, instance of difference, as a great deal of feminist scholarship makes clear. Men and women differ in their bodies. Hierarchical arrangements line up that physical difference with a whole series of other socially imposed differences: in responsibilities, in rights and obligations, in idealized and demonized behaviors, in everything that a particular society finds it important to note and treat of ideologically. Individuals and their behaviors with respect to gender will be differentially evaluated in hierarchically ordered societies, but none will be excluded.

Dumont cites gender difference both in Tocqueville's work and in his own experience, even if only in passing, to illustrate his general analysis of hierarchy as a system of encompassment, one in which relative values at one order of magnitude may flip at lower levels. He notes that in India,

> the same hierarchical principle that in some way subordinates one level to another at the same time introduces a multiplicity of levels, letting the situation reverse itself. The mother of the family (in an Indian family, for example), inferior though she may be made by her sex in some respects nonetheless dominates the relationships within the family. (1980, 241)

An egalitarian ideology cannot handle gender difference so assuredly. Dumont paraphrases Tocqueville's observations on the subject as follows: "If equality is conceived as rooted in man's very nature and denied only by an evil society, then, as there are no longer any rightful differences in condition or estate, or different sorts of men, they are all alike and even identical, as well as equal" (1980, 16).

Tocqueville, Dumont tells us, contrasts some Europeans, who believe that the sexes are not only equal but alike, with Americans, who see them as of equal value but having different roles. Approaching two hundred years on, I would regretfully say, pace Tocqueville, that many Americans have not yet figured out what it would mean for men and women to have equal value but different roles, or have even decided in their own minds whether that option would be best. Yet hierarchical understandings may actually allow for greater flexibility than egalitarian ones. As Dumont's comments about an Indian family suggest, if context trumps consistency, which is something that encompassment makes possible, then any set of ideas may allow a considerable degree of flexibility when applied at different orders of magnitude.

WHEN POWER COMES FROM ABOVE: BENEDICT ANDERSON

Dumont, in his initial glance, in *Homo Hierarchicus,* at the development of Western ideas about egalitarianism, makes the interesting aside that the rise of individualism as an ideology took place during the period, starting from the eighteenth century, when ever greater degrees of organic solidarity made individual autonomy in Western societies less and less attainable (1980, 11). Dumont says no more on this point in *Homo Hierarchicus,* but it seems well worth pursuing.

If, after the fashion of Foucault's attack on celebrations of the Enlightenment, we stop thinking of egalitarianism at least for the moment as the triumph of a brilliant new idea, we might instead see it, in the West, as an effort to compensate, maybe even somewhat desperately, for the insecurity that the loss of hierarchical arrangements gave rise to. Doing so enables us not only better to appreciate Dumont's remarks about egalitarianism and difference. It also provides a bridge to what Anderson (1991) writes in the illuminating opening pages of *Imagined Communities:* that hierarchy's hold on people's thinking and behavior declined in Europe in the centuries preceding the rise to prominence of the idea of the nation-state.[7] It seems obvious that these fundamental conceptions—hierarchical ideology, egalitarianism, and nationalism—about how people can and should relate to each other cannot help but be linked, and that they should be studied in tandem.

Let me, therefore, put Dumont aside for the moment to draw on Benedict Anderson's approach to hierarchy and ideas that came to supplant or compete with it. Anderson's argument about the rise and multivarious ("modular") adaptations of the idea of the nation-state are too well-known to need reviewing here (Anderson 1991). I want rather to invoke an earlier essay of his, well-known to Southeast Asianists but less so among other readers, in which he discussed the Javanese version of charisma. That essay, titled "The Idea of Power in Javanese Culture" (1972), is noteworthy not only for its brilliant account of much Indonesian political thinking but also, in retrospect, as the prequel to (and by way of contrast, elucidation of) his later analysis of the nation-state.

Anderson starts by summarizing Western assumptions about power: that it is abstract, derives from various sources (e.g., wealth, office, weapons, and so on), is indefinitely augmentable, and is in itself morally ambiguous. Javanese understandings of power (which Anderson distinguishes typographically from Western understandings by writing of "Power") illustrate a different take on the nature of power, seeing it as of a single sort, not open to moral evaluation in itself, but always at play in the efforts of individuals to claim some measure of it or, if they cannot hope to exercise it themselves, at least to position themselves appropriately in relation to it.

I find in Anderson's essay an insightful rendering of what it means to think hierarchically pretty much everywhere. Such thinking turns on the simple notion that power comes from above. In light of that fact, every individual must make it his or her business to find out where power lies—above their heads, as it were—and then find a way to connect themselves to it.

In the brief remarks with which he concludes the essay, moving beyond Java to meditate on the vagaries of charisma elsewhere in the modern world, Anderson contrasts the nature of the relationship that people enter into with such charismatic "Power," on the one hand, with one people enter into with "rational-legal authority," on the other (1972, 65). He refers to people subscribing to the former understanding as "believers" who "attach" themselves to "Power," as opposed to those who "submit" to power in accordance with the latter, rational understanding.

I do not think the distinction between attaching and submitting quite gets at the difference he is making. This turns rather on whether one sees oneself subordinating oneself to power that comes from above or, on the contrary, acceding, provisionally and indeed guardedly, to some degree of constraint in light of interests one shares with one's fellows, all of whom consent to yield up some measure of their own sovereignty in order to pool a certain quantity of power that they agree to place in a leader's hands for agreed-upon purposes. Recalling, then, Anderson's reference in *Imagined Communities* to "horizontal" versus "vertical" bonds, we can see the nation-state as a way, starting in the Americas in the eighteenth century, of founding communities on the idea that citizens of a territorially delimited unit are in some fundamental way similar to each other, and so can think of themselves as having shared interests. Other "communities" (to the extent, perhaps limited, to which the term applies) in which people seek to link themselves to centers of power, to which they must look up, are made up of individuals who think in terms of how they can prove themselves useful to those who are unlike themselves—those who are "above" them (with respect to status, wealth, authority, healing capacity, wisdom, and so on) but who, in light of that unlikeness, might have an interest in maintaining a bond with those "below" them, that is, in taking them on as their subordinates. In the nation-state, as per Anderson, solidarity stems from a sense of sameness. In Europe's older, hierarchical arrangements, it was based on difference, which is why, as Anderson notes, people found it perfectly sensible that a subject (subordinate) and his lord (superordinate) might have no language in common (1991, 19). Such interdependence through difference is where Anderson's and Dumont's understandings link up.

Anderson acknowledges a debt to Weber (Anderson 1972, 19, 46–47).[8] But Anderson focuses on that element of Weber's work that concerns power; he does not attend to Weber's separate treatment of status as distinguishable from power, a point that means much more to Dumont. Nevertheless, putting Dumont, particularly his later work on *Homo aequalis* (Dumont 1977, 1986), and Anderson together suggests that, in the West, the weakening of hierarchical arrangements not only coincided with but also fostered the rise of the emphasis on individuals. Thus, rather than take this individualism as a heady discovery of new and liberating powers, we might wish to follow Foucault, as suggested above, in changing the key in which we sing this song of the Enlightenment. If one could no longer count on bonds to others, especially bonds to people of superior standing to whom one could look for material and affective support, then reassuring oneself of one's own powers might help assuage the anxiety that the loss of connectedness generated at the very time that dependence on others—anonymous others—grew greater, and more obviously so.[9] At the same time, a Western preoccupation with "authenticity," hearkening back to Herder's attempt to cure Germans of their cultural cringe before the glories of the French and their Enlightenment (Wilson 1973), looks like a rearguard action to preserve some sense of stability in the face of hierarchical order's steady and patchy but real decline in modern European history.

As a matter of fact, the distinction between the various "forms of domination," to which Weber gives the labels "charismatic, traditional, and rational-legal" (1947, 324–369), reflects an Olympian perspective available only to those who do not feel themselves immediately dependent on any of those forms, those who, to adapt a phrase of Bourdieu, enjoy "freedom from political necessity." Such presumably was what the sons of the American colonial elite believed about themselves until they found their path blocked in the metropole—to their evident consternation, and, Anderson tells us, political radicalization.[10] Since that time, an educated elite looks ever more carefully, knowingly, and, in the progressive tradition at least, suspiciously, at what forms power takes. James Scott's work enunciates this perspective especially eloquently among today's Southeast Asianists (2009), but it characterizes a great proportion of contemporary writing in all the social sciences and the humanities. Where would cultural studies be without its demonization of the powerful and its celebration of those who resist?

Most people in the world, less assured in their material circumstances as well as less schooled in properly egalitarian convictions, look about for where power provides at least a toe-hold by which they can afford themselves some measure of security in a risk-filled world. They seek not to safeguard their liberties so much as to assure their basic material needs, their security, and their peace of mind. If they come to feel confident in their ability to sustain a threshold of security with respect to those basic needs, they may attend to the matter of where they stand in a larger social field, that is, to their social standing. But their first steps, at least, have to be that they figure out where power lies, and then make sure that they find points of access to such concentrations of power that lie within their reach. In other words, they need to find figures on whom they can depend. This means first of all that they need to identify people to whom they can usefully and effectively subordinate themselves: people with whom they can enter into long-term relations of unequal, yes, and sometimes demeaning, but nevertheless ongoing, exchange.

They must, in sum, try to address their vulnerabilities, which stem from inequalities of wealth, power, and status, and redress them by establishing hierarchical arrangements, in the Dumontian sense: arrangements in which their services are needed. More often than not, they must do so from below.

Women Who Know Their Place: Marina Warner

The always erudite and insightful Marina Warner provides, in her analysis of fairy tales, *From the Beast to the Blonde,* a clear demonstration of how women have had to negotiate for their welfare throughout history by looking to see where power lies, and then playing on difference to make sure that they are securely subordinate—attached by being subordinated—to their superiors, namely, their male kin and affines (1995).

The results are often anything but edifying: women, Warner points out, must often resort to denigrating their *semblables*—other women, individuals similar to themselves—to try to assure their own access to resources, both material and emotional. "In many fairy tales the tyrants are women and they struggle against their often younger rivals to retain the security that their husbands or their fathers afford them" (1995, 217). Women's most important and valuable difference from males, their capacity to bear and nurse children, does not, after all, last forever.

> Another set of conditions set women against women, and the misogyny of fairy tales reflects them from woman's point of view: rivalry for the

prince's love. The effect of these stories is to flatter the male hero: the position of the man as saviour and provider in these testimonies of female conflict is assumed, repeated and reinforced. (1995, 238–239)

As Warner explains, tales that play up an older woman's magical benevolence, or potential malevolence, or supernatural skills of whatever sort, all constitute bids for distinguishing such a woman not only from males but also from other females, so that, in a realm of limited means, the "old wives" telling the tales might not be cast aside as useless burdens (1995, 218–240).

If people of lesser power and standing choose not to subordinate themselves to others, they may look for other options, ones whereby they give up some opportunities for security (through subordination) in favor of greater autonomy. I will make this argument with reference to Burmese monks. But these are not challenges to hierarchy so much as forays, similar in some respects to what Dumont identifies as the renunciant's path in India (1980, 267–286), into marginal domains where the terms by which bonds among individuals are constructed take on exceptional form. These domains proffer certain niches in an overarching hierarchical structure. Within such niches, constraints are in some respects relaxed. They do not, however, offer an out from hierarchy in the ways that the chimera of Western thinking about "freedom," that Siren of adolescent desires (and not a few postadolescent scholars), implies.

Dumont beyond India: Hierarchy in Sri Lanka

The question to which I now turn is how useful Dumont's analysis of hierarchy's workings in India might prove when looking at how hierarchy works in Southeast Asia. Sri Lanka provides a useful stopping-off point when turning one's attention from India to Southeast Asia, since its dominant, Sinhalese population is Buddhist, not Hindu, but much about Sinhalese society is still similar to India. The distinguished ethnographer of Sri Lanka, Bruce Kapferer, has made explicit his intellectual debts to Dumont in his investigation of hierarchical and egalitarian thinking in Sri Lanka and Australia respectively (2012, 2010). I find his analysis of Australian egalitarianism particularly thought-provoking. But here I consider his work on Sri Lanka for the way he selectively applies Dumontian notions of hierarchy to the Sri Lankan case in order better to account for that country's recent, tragic history.

Kapferer says at several points that he does not rule out the importance of material interests in motivating many Sinhalese to provoke and/or participate in the island's recent ethnic violence. Nevertheless, he insists that a purely materialist account fails to explain the extremes to which the violence went. Stressing the ontological dimensions of the crisis as Sinhalese perceived it, Kapferer looks for deeper causes, more fundamental understandings of the nature of the world (or cosmos), and the risks that Tamil separatism posed to them, to explain the astonishing ferocity of the Sri Lankan civil war. He maintains that we can find such causes in deep-seated Sinhalese assumptions about proper hierarchical relationships and their abrogation.

Sinhalese cosmology, according to Kapferer, situates the "worlds of existence and social relations" within an all-embracing hierarchy whose poles are marked by the Buddha, reason, and unity, at the superior, encompassing apex, with the demonic, fragmented, and disorganizing pole at the base. Where beings get placed on that hierarchy depends on "the degree of their orientation to the Buddha or to the demonic" (2012, 11). These two poles, furthermore, the Buddha and the demonic, "define the boundaries of existence, the point of entry into nonexistence or extinction" (2012, 11).

Kapferer believes that Sinhalese judge political arrangements according to how they map on to this all-encompassing order: "The hierarchical principle of incorporation is vital to individual integrity and coherence. Outside the hierarchical order of society human beings can become weak and impotent or destructive of themselves and others" (2012,13).

Kapferer attributes the murderous ethnic violence that was already under way when he published his book *Legends of People, Myths of State* in 1988 (2012), and that continued all the more intensely and tragically thereafter, to the sense among Sinhalese that Tamil demands for some degree of political separateness constituted a fundamental attack on the unity of the state.

Kapferer appears to take "unity," for Sinhalese Buddhists, to constitute an overarching ideal, such as Dumont claims that any hierarchical ideology must have.[11] By virtue of their deep identification of the state with themselves as persons, such an attack was experienced by Sinhalese Buddhists as an ontological threat and required extreme responses. Introducing disorder into the unity of the nation, which is to say, throwing into question the hierarchical ordering of Sinhalese Buddhists, Tamil Hindus, and Muslims, suggested to Sinhalese Buddhists the collapse of order at all orders of magnitude. This explains how, in the latter part of the twentieth century, the Tamils became equated with the demons that have to be mastered and driven out if order is to be regained. Kapferer tells us that waging war on Tamils and Muslims came to resemble exorcistic rites long practiced by Sinhalese when they encountered domestic and local difficulties.

Hierarchy in Burma

Just as Kapferer has found leads in Dumont's writings for making sense of Sri Lankan events, I draw on Dumont (and Dumont's work as complemented and extended by that of Anderson and Warner) and Kapferer to better understand what I have observed in Burma.

In hierarchical arrangements, as long as different kinds of people have generally agreed-upon places within an all-embracing set that follows from their "orientation to the whole," there can be some measure of movement, or social mobility, even as competition is fairly well-contained. Or at least Dumont makes it appear that it was so contained in India in the past. More recently, agitation in favor of and on the part of the lowliest of India's groups, especially the Dalits, roiled the waters in the course of the twentieth century and continues to do so to this day.

India distinguishes among kinds of people with reference to kinship and caste in ways that outsiders have trouble fathoming and specialists of the region argue about at length. In the Sri Lankan case, ethnic, linguistic, and religious differences have come to constitute differences too radical to make any form of cooperation possible, and more recently, they have even come to rule out coexistence.[12] Do societies lacking the distinctions Dumont and Kapferer discuss in South Asia nonetheless deal with difference in similar ways? Or in any case, do Burmans?

With respect to their rulers, Burmans resemble Sinhalese: Kapferer notes that Sinhalese have always judged their kings according to how steadfastly they defended the Buddhist faith, and the same can be said about Burmans' estimations of their rulers. This was true in the days of Burmese royalty as far back as the kingdom of Pagan (Aung-Thwin 1985). It was for the same reason that Burma's State Law and Order Council made such frequent display of its piety in the 1990s and early 2000s (see Houtmann 1999; Jordt 2007; Schober 2011). The military regime was obviously illegitimate in the view of many citizens of Burma, who had witnessed its agents massacring thousands of people in the streets of Rangoon in 1988 (Keeler 1997) and then saw it abrogate elections held in 1990. The regime's leaders apparently believed that they could regain the people's respect through extravagant displays of material support for, and self-abnegating demonstrations of deference to, the sangha (Schober 2011). At the same time, the military's long-standing warfare against ethnic minorities could easily be seen as countering both political disorder and religious subversion, since so many of Burma's ethnic minorities are non-Buddhist.

If Burmans found secular authorities' support for their religious superiors laudable during the military dictatorship, despite the regime's egregious policies more generally, they resemble the Hindus Dumont describes in India as well as Sinhalese Buddhists. Yet were we to think of "the whole" sociologically rather than ideologically, it is difficult to see what an "orientation to the whole," as Dumont speaks of it, would look like in Burma. Dumont suggests (in a chapter of *Homo Hierarchicus* titled, "Comparison: Are There Castes among Non-Hindus and Outside India?") that elements of the caste system can be found in Southeast Asia and Sri Lanka but that the dissociation of prestige and power is not to be found in those places, and so one cannot really say that the caste system characterizes those regions (1980, 215). He appears therefore to state that, absent that dissociation, there can be no true, unambiguous ranking by status, no true hierarchy of values, and so no orientation to the whole.

It is true that Burman social organization offers very little that might qualify, sociologically, as a "whole" other than someone's natal and/or conjugal family, or village, or neighborhood. Individualism characterizes many Southeast Asian societies, and in this way it appears to differ from India quite radically. Along these lines, if at the risk of falling into kinship-based determinism, I would point to an inclination in much of Southeast Asia to make kinship highly flexible in both its structure and its implementation. Most lowland Southeast Asian societies exhibit bilateral kinship, in contrast to South Asia's pervasive unilineal (usually, but not invariably, patrilineal) descent. Bilateral kinship counters any impulse to form corporate groups based on kin relations: tracing kin equally on both your father's and your mother's side affords greater advantages for tapping into all your kin's resources and connections, but minimizes the chances of doing so on the basis of membership in a well-defined group. In a sense, bilateral kinship extends the range of people to whom you might be able to turn for support, but weakens the force of such an appeal in any given instance. Indeed, territoriality turns out to offer just as compelling grounds as kin ties on which to ally oneself with others. At the same time, in rural settings, bilateral kinship heightens the probability that people who live close by are also relatives. This matters a good deal in Burma where, in 2012, as I have mentioned, 70 percent of the population was estimated still to live on the land.

The high proportion of residents at the Shweigyin Monastery who were related to the abbot and his brother on either their father's or mother's side, and/or who hailed from the same village, or nearby villages, or the villages where their kin lived, attests to the fact that bilateral kinship encourages expanding networks of kin and neighbors. At the same time, it also makes it quite easy to do the opposite: to disengage from kin and neighbors, to disclaim responsibility for the welfare of those people who may try to place demands on you but can do so only in the name of a vaguely enunciated sense of "kinship" or "neighborliness" or simple fellow-feeling. Kinship and territoriality are available and optional; they offer opportunities for contact and the chance to try to make some claims on people, but with few obligations really incumbent on any party, whether the supplicant or those to whom supplicants appeal. These mildly effective strategies and lightly carried burdens account for much of what "loosely structured" social relations referred to (Evers 1969b).

Many Burmans emphasize the importance of filial piety, and for that reason would reject any characterization of them as "individualistic." Many of them do, indeed, display great solicitousness for their parents. I was impressed both by the greater rhetorical salience of this matter in Burma than in Java (let alone the United States)[13] and, in many cases, by the great efforts people made on behalf of their parents. Yet there is little to oblige people to compromise their own interests in favor of those even of their natal family. It is common for males to go off in pursuit of work opportunities in faraway places, separating them from all relatives for long periods of time. (Recently, this has come to include going overseas.) They may or may not send remittances back to parents or conjugal families during their absence.

People are of course very much concerned with their relations with others, however. That they are very much concerned with their standing relative to that of others is also true, and it is true to a degree that people thoroughly imbued with an egalitarian ideology may find surprising or even unappealing. Thus the form that hierarchical thinking takes in Burma does not shore up any so pervasive a set of social categories as Indian caste. But it does catch everyone up in a preoccupation with their place in a system of relative prominence and prestige, quantities that usually line up with the distribution of power and wealth but do also implicate a hierarchy of values, as Dumont suggests.

Difference and similarity, interdependence, its avoidance, or its dissimulation (what Bourdieu would call its "misrecognition") all figure crucially in the chapters that follow, because hierarchical thinking, which pervades Burmese social relations, is predicated on precisely these points. Let us take the difference between monks and laypeople as a simple but fundamental example. Everything about the bonds that tie any given monk and any given donor together stems from the fact that they are different. Monks must not raise food or cook for themselves; laypeople are enjoined to donate cooked food to monks. Monks must engage in no sexual activity of any kind; lay people are enjoined to marry and generate sons to give to the sangha. Monks generate merit in accepting food from donors; laypeople rely on monks to observe the discipline of the *vinaya* (the 227 rules of conduct to which they are subject) so that donations to them will generate merit for the donors, who are urged to follow only five of those rules. Several basic words in Burmese—pronominal usages, verbs for such activities as "to eat," "to sleep," and "to go"—take different forms according to whether they are applied to monks or to laypeople. Indeed, the words for "monk" and "layperson" are mutually exclusive in Burmese. One cannot refer to monks and "other" kinds of people, because "people" are a separate category from monks. A conversation between monks and laypeople draws constant attention to the line that divides them, since their speech will mark their difference with every utterance. And monks enjoy remarkable prestige in Burman society: very few are the lay Burmans who are willing to risk impugning the dignity of monks, whether in general or individually. A great deal of this basic arrangement defining the respective roles and interaction of monks and laypeople corresponds closely to Dumont's analysis of hierarchical relations as based on mutual interdependence through difference.

Autonomy as an Overarching Value

To follow Dumont's lead and identify a single, overarching value in any given society's ideology has, admittedly, a somewhat musty feel to it. Surely we have learned that claims to such consistency and conformity fail to take into account the irregular, unorganized, variable, and often contradictory nature of all things social and cultural. Not only do people in any given community disagree as to what values they hold most dear; any given individual may well hold contradictory positions from one moment to the next, or at the same time, as to what matters most to him or her (cf. Ewing 1990). Nevertheless, it does seem to me worthwhile to seek out a value that a particular community's discourse and institutions make it appear that people hold in particularly high regard.[14] In contrast to purity in India, or unity in Sri Lanka, I posit instead, for Burman Buddhists, the value of autonomy.

It strikes me as characteristic of any society that means must be found to reconcile people's desire for a sense of their own freedom of action and their desire for a sense of firm connection to others. These contrasting wishes could be labeled desires for autonomy and for attachment. What is striking in Burman ideology is that autonomy receives much greater validation than attachment, encompassing the latter as a necessary but less prestigious and worthy goal.

In Burman conceptualizations, the ultimate idealized figure among humans is that of the ascetic monk alone in the jungle, engaged in meditation. This figure is an emblem of autonomy beyond the reach of social relations; in this respect it resembles the renunciant Dumont sees as the only conceivable "individual" in Hindu society (1980, 234–235). Idealizing this figure means moving beyond unity to absolute detachment. Even the intake of food is said to be reduced almost to zero on the part of the truly accomplished meditator. (What food he does consume he finds in the forest; he no longer depends on lay supporters for sustenance.) Granted, such a monk may decide to rejoin human society. Indeed, important monks who are prominent in Burman society are always said to have (in most cases, they themselves make it well-known that they have) spent years in the forest engaged in meditative practice. The immensely influential Ledi Sayadaw did this in the nineteenth century (Braun 2013); the very powerful and highly respected Sitagu Sayadaw has done so more recently.[15]

The highly prized and overarching quantity, autonomy, stands opposed then to a necessary, but encompassed, quantity, which is attachment. The tension between hierarchical thinking, predicated on mutual interdependence through difference, and a hierarchical ordering that sets autonomy, denying interdependence, as its ultimate value, runs like a red thread through much of Burman beliefs and practices.

Indeed, the paradoxical nature of Burman Buddhism's validation of autonomy is thrown into stark relief by an odd rhyme, unremarked upon by Dumont, across a broad expanse of *Homo Hierarchicus*. Dumont sets out the contrast he wishes to make between hierarchical and egalitarian thinking at the start of the book by invoking Alexis de Tocqueville, who Dumont thinks perceived the nature and import of that contrast by virtue of his travels in the new, and egalitarian, United States, in the 1830s. Dumont quotes extensively from Tocqueville's magisterial *Democracy in America*. With reference to hierarchical arrangements, Tocqueville wrote, "As in aristocratic communities all the citizens occupy fixed positions, one above the other, the result is that each of them always sees a man above himself whose patronage is necessary to him, and below himself another man whose cooperation he may claim" (Tocqueville, cited in Dumont 1980, 18).

In "democratic nations," by way of contrast,

> As each class approximates to other classes, and intermingles with them, its members become indifferent and as strangers to one another. . . . They owe nothing to any man, they expect nothing from any man; they acquire the habit of always considering themselves as standing alone, and they are apt to imagine that their whole destiny is in their own hands. Thus not only does democracy make every man forget his ancestors, but it hides his descendants, and separates his contemporaries from him; it throws him back for ever upon himself alone, and threatens in the end to confine him entirely within the solitude of his own heart. (Tocqueville, cited in Dumont 1980, 18)

To read these beautiful phrases from the point of view of Southeast Asia is to experience a certain disorientation. In the first sentence I have quoted, we see Tocqueville anticipating Anderson's point that in Java and, by extension, in many societies, namely, those wherein hierarchy is seen as in the nature of things, power comes from above and is, in turn, exercised upon those below oneself. Tocqueville's choice of the word "cooperation" here suggests at once elegant euphemism and a hint of Tocqueville's own aristocratic origins. (His name, after all, was Alexis-Charles-Henri Clérel de Tocqueville. His father was Comte de Tocqueville; Alexis was born after the Revolution, so the title went by the boards, but not, one gets the impression, the Olympian attitude.) Dumont attributes the clarity of Tocqueville's understanding of what would transpire in a society such as that of the United States, predicated on equality, to the fact that he had a sincere interest in such a new dispensation while retaining his familiarity with, and place within, aristocratic society (1980, 16–17).

The longer quote, about egalitarian societies, conveys Tocqueville's insightful anticipation—a kind of pre-post-anomie-induced nostalgia, to adapt an indispensable concept ("pre-post-Christmas letdown") from Charles Schulz's *Peanuts*—concerning what Durkheim saw would come to plague Western societies: the sense of disconnectedness that comes from no longer being sure one has a place, let alone knowing one's place. Yet divested of its melancholic tone, the passage describes a state that Buddhism prescribes, that of the individual devoid of attachments. "Stand alone" is what the paragon of Buddhist practice, the monk alone in the jungle, does; confining himself to the solitude of his own heart could be rephrased to describe the way a meditating monk, or layperson, should confine his attention to the sensation of his breath as it enters and exits his nostrils, say, or to describe the studied indifference with which he experiences any and all sensory impressions. Even short of that idealized extreme, Buddhists should indeed understand that "their whole destiny is in their own hands," since each individual determines through his or her actions the store of merit and demerit affecting this and future existences. "Indifference," the word Tocqueville uses, and "lack of investment," as Buddhism urges on us all, carry different feeling-tones, but they are hard to distinguish in practice.

Many pages later in *Homo Hierarchicus,* Dumont writes of the renouncer in Indic traditions: "The renouncer leaves the world behind in order to devote himself to his own liberation. He submits himself to his own chosen master, or he may even enter a monastic community, but essentially he depends upon no one but himself, he is alone" (1980, 274).

It is remarkable how closely the last phrases resemble Tocqueville's words, even though Tocqueville is characterizing the individualism that comes from democracy, whereas Dumont is describing the renouncer in a society that he describes as completely oblivious to individualism. Yet that is, in a way, Dumont's point: that the renouncer is as close as Indian society comes to conceiving of "the individual" as a social reality. It can do so only by positing such an individual's existence outside the world. The notion must still cause renouncers themselves discomfort, Dumont goes on to say, since they devote their energies to attaining extinction (1980, 274–275).[16]

For the Burman Buddhist case, at least, I would not tie the effort to attain extinction to discomfort aroused by "individualism," but rather to discomfort aroused by interaction. Of course, as many scholars have noted about Buddhists' actual comments and behavior, nirvana may represent a notional goal usually displaced by more proximate ones: seeking comfort and prosperity in an anticipated rebirth. That deflection from Buddhist orthodoxy does not vitiate the interest in asking why any doctrine of "extinction" can enjoy such widespread idealization. One burden of the following chapters will be to consider nirvana's appeal.

Conclusion

Dumont could have made his endeavor more respectable, that is, he could have defended his project more effectively, had he phrased it not as a series of assertions about an all-encompassing contrast between India and the West but rather as a series of observations as to how a tension among contrasting inclinations in people's deeply held commitments—ones we might label a pull toward "individualism" and a pull toward "hierarchy" or "mutual interdependence through difference"—can be found everywhere, yet it gets played out differently in these two regions of the world. He could then have attended to how people try to reconcile conflicting wishes to commit themselves to others, on the one hand, and to maintain a sense of their individual agency, on the other. This tack would link directly to his analyses of Indian and Western responses to difference: in one case, that of hierarchy, emphasis falls on using differences (lay versus religious, male versus female, older versus younger, ethnicity A versus ethnicity B, and so on) to structure relationships; in the other case, that of individualism, emphasis falls on denying such differences any significance, in order to minimize their effects. Had he set out his ideas in this way, he could have drawn certain contrasts without laying himself open to easy accusations of stereotyping, because instead of drawing absolute contrasts, he would have pointed to degrees of relative emphasis.

Southeast Asia enables us to consider the possibility that hierarchical and egalitarian thinking, or holism and individualism, might not have to be taken as a single, clear-cut antinomy. We should be ready to accept, and here I part company with Dumont, that there exist alternative versions of hierarchical thinking. The many different forms that hierarchical arrangements take in such places as South

Asia, China, and Japan, as well as Southeast Asia, should support the impression that there exist "alternative hierarchies" just as much as there exist "alternative modernities" (for the latter, see Wagner 2007).

Thus rather than follow Dumont in taking hierarchy to consist of a monolithic and consistent approach to all matters social, I wish to take from him his many insights about how hierarchy works in principle, put aside elements (and disputes) that concern South Asia but hardly pertain to Southeast Asia, while bearing in mind the important point that it is not "they" who are exceptional or strange. Rather it is those contemporary thinkers (probably more numerous in the West, but by no means exclusively so) who fulsomely and somewhat cavalierly embrace egalitarian ideals who are atypical. And we continue to find it difficult to figure out how best to implement those ideals in real life.

As I have hinted earlier, the current preoccupation in the social sciences (particularly anthropology and cultural studies) with individuals' agency reflects egalitarian commitments that Dumont should have taught us to look upon with a certain wariness. As a reaction against earlier analytic perspectives (historical-materialist, psychoanalytic, structural-functionalist, structuralist) that implied (or could be mistaken to imply) that individuals were automata capable at best of groupthink, this new emphasis on agency provides a useful corrective. Yet it blatantly imposes our own idealizing expectations upon the people we are interested in. That is, we wish not to demonize others as our predecessors did. To describe them as not behaving as free agents would be, in our present view, to demean them. Therefore, we must be careful to insist that they are thinking beings who act in pursuit of their goals according to their own lights.

So far, well and good. The problem arises in the next step. Since we are suspicious of power, resentful of efforts on the part of the powerful to intervene in our lives, and aware of the ways that everyone is open to power's depredations, we can assume, or rather, we know for a fact, that everyone else shares these understandings. To suggest that they might not, that they might choose to accommodate themselves to power, to subordinate themselves to its manifestations or sources, that people might find it expedient or even satisfying to develop nuanced relations with power wherein their "agency" is to some degree diminished or compromised, to suggest, in other words, that others may fail to live up to the idealization we wish upon them, is highly suspect. But every idealization is a norm, a standard against which people can be judged. If people do not seek to maximize their own agency, they fail a test we have unwittingly imposed on them. Or better (which is to say, more academically acceptable), we may claim that the observer who has compromised their dignity by construing their actions in this way has no doubt misread the data.

But we must stop finding heroes, or rather, we should stop looking for them, in our others, just as our predecessors should have stopped looking for antiheroes. We must allow people to think differently from ourselves. Dumont has explained to us that people in South Asia think hierarchically, whereas contemporary Westerners (and some non-Westerners, many of them trained in our tradition) espouse egalitarian ideas. Once again, I would emend this to say that South Asians and Westerners think in complicated and sometimes contradictory ways about these matters, but that contrasting emphases do show up in one region and the other. Southeast Asians are inclined to think hierarchically, much like South Asians, although the criteria by which hierarchical orderings are established, and argued over, differ there from what obtains in South Asia. In any case, we must be ready to treat our own assumptions as forming one perspective, not the only or best one. In doing so, we fulfill the best impulse in anthropology, which is to gain greater understanding of—by attaining some irony toward—ourselves.

Chapter Five

Hierarchical Habits

Hierarchical arrangements in South Asia and East Asia, as well as in Southeast Asia, I suggested at the end of the preceding chapter, all differ from each other in important ways. Yet it appears that to think that power comes from above is an intuitively obvious impression, at least in any society in which sufficient power can be concentrated to get people thinking about where it lies or comes from.[1] To counter this perspective with assertions that power comes instead "from below" represents something of an oddity.[2] People living in small-scale societies in which resources are spread so thin on the ground that they must necessarily disperse themselves (people living at the furthest extremes of the planet's habitable environments come to mind) may not have to concern themselves with overbearing authorities, and recent writings about relatively "anarchic" societies in Southeast Asia suggest some groups in that region do make conscious decisions to prevent power accumulating in anyone's hands (Gibson and Sillander 2011, Scott 2009). But the Enlightenment thinkers' contention (and before them, John Locke's) that power might be thought of as originating in, or being available here among, "us," rather than up there, among "them," constitutes something of an historical anomaly. It is apt that so many of these thinkers should have lived in Paris, for centuries the belly of the beast among European power centers, although even France pales in comparison to imperial China in this respect, at least in terms of Chinese rulers' ambitions if not perhaps actual attainments.

Although thinking comparatively about hierarchy strikes me as an important project, it is not one I can undertake here. What I want to focus on in this chapter is how hierarchical thinking shapes the way people interact with each other in Burma, and how it induces certain kinds of strategies in how people engage with the world. It would appear from the ethnographic literature, as well as my own fieldwork experience in Indonesia, that much of what characterizes Burman social relations makes them resemble those of many other lowland Southeast Asians as well. Hierarchical thinking makes competing for superior standing highly salient in people's minds throughout the region. But how does such competition take place in the absence of groups, like China's patrilineages, South Asia's subcastes, or Japan's *ie*? In those societies, individual members of a lineage pool their resources and energies in the struggle to shut out their peers. In Southeast Asian societies, competition for superior standing instead focuses intense attention on individual comportment, while offering individuals options for making their own way, whether or not their kin join together with them in those efforts. The loose structure of kinship contrasts, as Phillips pointed out long ago for the Thai case, with very closely monitored face-to-face interaction (1965, 54–78; 1969). These points are not unrelated. In lowland Burma and Thailand, as in Java, a great deal rides on how any individual enters into interaction with others. Furthermore, in Theravada societies such as Burma and Thailand, the sangha offers something of an automatic "up." Not an out—there is no out from hierarchy's differentiated levels, at least not this side of nirvana—but an up. And nirvana, for that matter, is simply the ultimate up and out.

Showing You Know Your Place: Language and Gesture

Many scholars have noted the importance people in Southeast Asia place on the smooth flow of interaction. What they have not always appreciated is how intertwined this insistence is with hierarchical considerations, and that, therefore, how one behaves is always inflected according to one's relative place in any given encounter.[3] There may seem little need to belabor the point. Still it is worthwhile noting, especially for those more familiar with other regions of the world, but even for people schooled in Southeast Asian encounter who may need the reminder, a few of the many tiny gestures, both physical and linguistic, by which Burmans make evident their sensitivity to the importance of relative standing, and to what we might label, if a bit too loosely, the matter of respect. In focusing on these everyday verbal and bodily practices, I of course illustrate Bourdieu's point that sociological assumptions are deeply embedded in everyone's body and demonstrated in their comportment, a reference with which I intend the title of this chapter to resonate.

To start with language: Burmese has nothing so elaborate as the speech registers of Javanese and Balinese.[4] Nevertheless, as is the case for many Southeast Asian languages, people speaking Burmese indicate their take on their relations to their interlocutors in virtually every utterance they make. They do so, if in no other way, in the choices they make in their use of pronouns, or what they use in place of pronouns. So, for example, there are alternative versions of the first-person singular pronoun, "I," and of the second-person pronoun, "you." A person of lower standing demonstrates their awareness of that fact, when speaking to another layperson, by using a term, *kjundo,* derived from the former royal courts, meaning "royal servant."[5] Or by using, instead of a pronoun, a descriptor indicating inferior standing, such as "Daughter" or "Son" (meaning "your daughter" or "your son," thus placing the interlocutor in the superior position of a parent, while avoiding the second person possessive, "your," which would vitiate the strategy of avoiding use of the second person), or "Student." The different words for "you," meanwhile, might all be substituted for with a descriptor, such as "Teacher," or "Officer," or "Father." To use one of these terms indicates heightened respect, although a superior can also use such a term about him- or herself: in context, it may convey authority, and/or a kind of avuncular benevolence. Some basic verbs have different versions, aurally completely unlike each other, whose denotative meanings are identical but convey different overtones as to the degree of distance and/or formality among speakers. There is also a particle, *pa* that speakers can splice into the final portion of an utterance to give it a more respectful tone: it has no denotative meaning.

The significance of vocabulary choice increases when laypeople and monks address each other. Laypeople have then to indicate their deference to monks' superior spiritual accomplishments, and the superior standing those imply, by using a special set of pronouns, verbs (certain forms for such actions as speaking, eating, sleeping, and so on), and nouns (naming parts of their bodies, places of residence, what they eat, and the like). These lexical items are used only with reference to monks, whereas others are used, when speaking to monks, with reference to oneself and other laypeople.

When I was living in a monastery near the Mahamuni Pagoda in Mandalay in 1988, I once observed a conversation between the abbot there, who took a great interest in Burmese history, and a Burmese couple: a lay man who had earned a PhD in history from Cornell University, and his wife who was a historian and professor in her own right. The lay couple sat on the floor with their legs tucked to one side, as is incumbent on people when speaking to monks, while the abbot sat in a chair facing them. The lay man, a charming and lively person who later went on to become the director general of Religious Affairs in Rangoon, spoke in his customary speedy manner. At many points, he forgot himself and used the respectful first-person pronoun (*kjundo*) with which laypeople refer to themselves when speaking with other laypeople to whom they show some degree of deference, rather than the term, *tabi.do* "[your] disciple," with which laypeople refer to themselves when speaking to monks. Each time, his wife corrected him. Clearly, he meant no disrespect by this error; clearly, his wife thought it nevertheless important not to let it go by without repair.

As the way the abbot and his two lay visitors arranged themselves indicates, physical gestures are as salient as linguistic ones in demonstrating awareness of one's place. Degrees of honor are differentiated spatially: in general, higher is of greater honor than lower, east is of greater honor than west, and north greater than south. Buddha images are raised well above the floor. In a private home, a Buddha altar is set in a place of honor (usually with a Buddha image and a few marks of deference, such as flowers, fruit, a bit of money, and the like, set before it). Some wealthy Mandalay residents own houses several stories high, in which case the Buddha altar often takes up a considerable portion of the room in the easternmost or northernmost part of the top floor. Next to a Buddha altar, but necessarily lower down, although still above the floor, will be found some sign of deference to spirits (*nat*),[6] usually in the form of an unhusked coconut plus a few flowers and so on set on a platform. Showing deference to *nat* is considered somewhat déclassé, however, so fewer houses contained altars to spirits at the time of my recent fieldwork than had been the case in the late 1980s.

Lay visitors to monks' quarters are careful to keep their heads lower, or at least no higher, than those of any monks with whom they speak. When I went to visit monks in the various halls in the Shweigyin Monastery, I usually sat on the floor (with my legs tucked to one side, and my *longyi* covering my feet), while they sat on benches or chairs. On the many evenings in which I conversed with U Dhammananda in his hall at the Shweigyin Monastery, he insisted, in a generous gesture, that I sit on a chair, not on mats on the floor (as most of his guests did). However, he sat on a short, flat settee along the north wall of the front room (the Buddha altar was set against the east wall), and I sat on a plastic chair with a scooped seat. This meant that I sat comfortably but with my head still well lower than his. I addressed him as "Venerable Lord," as laypeople usually address older monks, although toward the end of my stay I inferred he might have preferred that I address him as "Venerable Abbot." (He was the abbot of the monastery in his home village that he supported financially, not of the monastery where we met, so it had not occurred to me that I should use the more honorific title of abbot when addressing him.) Younger monks are often addressed by the less deferential "*U:ba̱zin:*". I used this term, as instructed, when addressing the abbot at whose monastery I stayed in 1987 and 1988. On a return visit about fifteen years later, however, he told me that I should switch to using the term "Venerable Abbot" instead. U Dhammananda referred to himself in our conversations using a first person pronoun, *kjou'*, of moderate formality. For him to use the term meaning "royal servant" (*kjundo*) that laypeople use among themselves to indicate respect would have been senseless. I referred to myself as "[your] disciple."

Reaching above someone's head is inappropriate outside intimate circles. Someone who needs to do so excuses the gesture with a set phrase, *Ga̱do., ga̱do.*. Best translated as "Excuse me," the term actually refers to the gesture of placing the palms of one's hands together before the chest and touching one's forehead in a gesture of respect. The same phrase is repeated when showing, pointing to, or simply referring to a lower part of one's body. When a man with whom I was conversing mentioned having been burned on his thighs as a child, he said this phrase while standing up and lifting his *longyi* to show me the scars, still visible decades later. We had had several long conversations prior to that time and were on friendly terms; otherwise, he would not have presumed to make such a bold and potentially offensive gesture.

The possessions of people need to be treated with whatever degree of deference their owners deserve. In situations in which it was deemed appropriate for me, an adult male, a Westerner, and a highly educated person, therefore a person of considerable status, to sit on the floor, such as when in the presence of monks, there was no problem about my placing the shoulder bag I usually carried with me (somewhat quaintly—many Burmese have traded in their shoulder bags for Western-style backpacks) on the floor next to me. In situations in which I sat on a chair, however, such as when visiting lay friends in their homes, or conversing with U Dhammananda at his hall, if I dropped my shoulder bag unthinkingly on the floor next to my chair, it was invariably placed by my hosts on a chair or other surface raised above the floor.

It is important to bear in mind that although there is a rhetorical inclination to praise anyone who shows a consistently deferential demeanor, in actual practice such consistency would appear at best odd, sometimes silly, and at worst remote and cold. Inordinate deference can arouse smirks. In 1988, a young monk invited me to visit lay relatives of his living in a poor neighborhood on the outskirts of Mandalay. While walking along an unpaved lane in that neighborhood, we came upon a boy who immediately prostrated himself on the ground, out of deference to the monk's venerable status. When he got up and went on his way, the monk turned to me, smiled, and said, "Villager!" The boy's show of respect was uncalled-for, since he was not actually engaging with the monk; his prostrating himself in an anonymous context showed that he was not yet familiar with city ways. In town, prostrating yourself before every monk you came upon would lay waste to any plans you had—with so many monks about, you would end up spending a good part of your day prostrate on the ground—and cause monks some inconvenience, too, since they would be obliged to pause long enough for the process to be completed.

It is incumbent on superiors to speak and act as such: this shows, or should, that they are willing to take responsibility for how things are, to exert themselves on behalf of all, and/or to act authoritatively. Monks do not usually acknowledge the show of deference others make when they prostrate themselves on the floor before them. Part of the display of their superior standing consists in their looking on, or away, impassively, or engaging such a person in conversation, as though the elaborate procedure were not taking place. They, like laypeople in superior positions, are expected to take it upon themselves to instruct—the verb usually applied in such circumstances is best translated, "to admonish," but it has a positive valence, not a negative one—their juniors and subordinates as to appropriate and moral behavior. By the same token, it is in no way embarrassing or demeaning to show deference to one's superiors when it is due. Even high government officials, individuals not known for their humility, and indeed in whom excessive humility would undermine impressions of their authority, happily make a great show of their deference to important religious figures. I watched high-ranking military figures prostrate themselves before abbots of some, but by no means immense, note in 1987 in Rangoon. Such demonstrations of subordination to the deserving do not compromise the standing of the person showing obeisance but rather shore it up: such a person deserves respect because he knows where respect is due.

Not only does showing deference make evident one's own rectitude, which depends on knowing one's place; it may also provide real emotional satisfaction. Or so I read the displays of obeisance that mark many interactions, not only of laypeople with religious figures they respect but also, in some circumstances, among laypeople. A professor of English at Mandalay University, the late Daw Winnie, was a beloved teacher. One day at her office, a former student, a woman probably in her forties, stopped by and, when ready to take her leave, made a considerable show of prostrating herself on the floor before Daw Winnie. The gesture seemed both dramatic and heartfelt.

Neither taking a subordinate nor a superordinate role, then, should be seen as a feature of a person's individual character. It is rather a feature of a specific relationship. It is necessarily contextual, like pronominal usage. The important consideration turns on how well someone sizes up a situation and conducts him or herself therein.

For the most part, interaction goes off without a hitch. Individuals in Mandalay who are reasonably well socialized have no trouble assessing their standing relative to people they are with and so acting appropriately. Individual temperament also comes into play, of course: some people are inclined to a certain boisterous informality, others to a greater reticence, or gravity, or nervousness. Everyone understands that there is always room for individual variation.

Yet because impressions of one's standing do matter a great deal, it is hard to conceive of a time-out, a context in which one is not concerned with how one is comporting oneself—and how others are registering their sense of one's standing. It is true that among intimates, in the bosom of the family, say, or among close friends, one can relax one's guard. Patterns of interaction are of long standing in such contexts and are unlikely to require much attention. But you still have to choose pronouns, and you still have to consider any hierarchical ordering that applies. Young men in tea shops are notorious for the speed with which a friendly exchange, in which teasing banter, a mainstay of their interaction, proceeds apace, can suddenly turn hostile, or even violent, because one person present feels that another has treated him too lightly. It appears that the terrible violence in March 1988 in Rangoon had its immediate (although not, of course, deeply rooted) origin in a brawl in a tea shop among young men fighting over music getting played through loudspeakers (Lintner 1990).

"Shame" and Vulnerability in Interaction

People's sensitivity to how they are treated, which pairs with their concern to conduct themselves suitably, follows from the fact that social standing exists only insofar as it is elaborated in interaction. As Bourdieu notes in closing, at the end of his valedictory *Pascalian Meditations* (2000), it is the regard of others that motivates people's actions. I take him to be saying that materialism, idealism, and all the rest must be relegated to secondary significance before this fundamental feature of human behavior. In a deeply hierarchical society, others' regard focuses on people's relative standing, and competition for greater prestige preoccupies everyone. Perhaps particularly in societies in which corporate groups matter relatively little, the "surface" of encounter is the stage on which the drama of who receives honor, of what sort, to what degree and for what reason, takes place. Everyone, therefore, feels him- or herself "on stage" at all times.[7]

In an essay I wrote long ago with reference to Java, I took the term, labeled *isin/lingsem* in Javanese (the two lexical items correspond to two speech registers in that language), to refer not simply to "shame," as most outsiders translate that and cognate terms that are to be found throughout Southeast Asia (in Burmese, it is *a:nade*)—or, in Clifford Geertz's intriguing alternative rendering of the Balinese equivalent, *lek*, "stagefright" (1973, 398–404)—but rather to a generalized sense of an individual's vulnerability in interaction (Keeler 1983). It is clear that the emotion that English speakers refer to as "shame" is known to and experienced by people everywhere, as is the related emotion called "guilt" in English. Earlier efforts to distinguish among societies as characterized primarily by one or the other have long been discredited. An idea that should not, however, be dismissed along with that untenable approach is the point that triggers for these emotions may differ culturally, as well as individually. Furthermore, not only may some people prove given to either or both of these emotions more than others, but people in some societies may lay greater emphasis on one or the other of them than do people in other places.

As mentioned above, outside observers often remark on the importance Southeast Asians set on the smooth tenor of face-to-face encounter without always seeing how that emphasis fits in with hierarchical considerations.[8] Southeast Asians themselves often idealize their own interaction to distorting effect, depicting it as a graceful dance of mutual considerateness, without acknowledging the differential constraints and outcomes that follow for participants of disparate standing.

An article in the July 2011 edition of *Today,* an English-language Burmese magazine addressed to tourists and available for free in hotel rooms in Rangoon and Mandalay, encapsulated highly conventional representations Burmese like to make of their social relations when addressing outsiders. A certain U Tin U wrote the article, titled, "Some Endearing Aspects of Our Country." In it, he reiterated oft-repeated sentiments, describing "Myanmar culture" in largely Buddhist terms. He failed to consider those citizens of the country who are not Buddhist, claiming that the Four Noble Truths of Buddhist dogma have "sunk so deep into the hearts of the people that [they] can be considered as the core of our culture" (Tin U 2011, 43). Not atypically for Burmese of a certain age who were schooled in British and American schools, he chose to illustrate a point about the Buddhist notion of *dukkha* (Pali "suffering") with a quotation from Shelley. He went on to describe a Buddhist as serene in the face of both good fortune and bad. This led him to the subject of *a:nade,* to wit:

> The stoic outlook on life makes the Myanmar particularly conscious of other people's sensitivities. He is very reluctant to hurt the feelings of his fellow men whether they be his friends or total strangers. He would rather inconvenience himself than cause the slightest inconvenience to the other party. This sense of delicateness or solicitousness for the feeling of others is unique to the Myanmar. Perhaps a little incident I came across in an English village during my sojourn there some years ago might illustrate my point. I was staying with a family as a "P-G" (paying guest). The landlady was kindly. She complied with my wish to have rice and chicken curry for lunch. I thanked her for the care she had shown to me. And she said matter-of-factly, "Yes, but chicken is expen-

sive." It came to me with a bit of unexpectedness. She had no idea that her remark would cause any displeasure to me. Had she been a Myanmar lady she would never have made that remark, blameless though it was. To a Myanmar with that sense of delicacy about the other person's feelings—which we call "arr-nar-de"—such a remark is quite uncalled for. Yes, "arr-na-de" is a unique feature of our etiquette which finds no equivalent in any foreign tongue, simply because the very concept is unique to our people. (Tin U 2011, 44)

The passage has, clearly, a very old-fashioned ring to it. It reiterates long-standing Burmese assertions that must have been developed in response to the condescending treatment they received at the hands of colonizers and missionaries. In the face of such pejorative pronouncements, Burmese have long made claims to spiritual wisdom and social sensibilities superior to those of their Western interlocutors. Remarkable in this regard is the narrowness of the comparison: the Burman's "sense of delicacy" has no match in an English village and is therefore completely unique to Burmese culture, even though a moment's reflection on other societies in Southeast Asia should put paid to the assertion.

Intrinsic to the viability of the comparison, however, is the omission of all the contextual matters that would explain much of what happened in the English village and that would have to apply in a Burmese setting to prevent a similar bit of unpleasantness taking place there. That is, the "Myanmar lady" who would never make reference to the cost of chicken when having just served it to a guest would be a woman of some means. (Chicken is more expensive than pork, the meat for the masses, in Burma.) She would not in this case have been likely to have a paying guest in her home, or if she did, she would not be inviting him to dine with her and serving up a meal at his request unless straitened circumstances had made her take in boarders with whom she tried to maintain polite fictions to dissemble the commercial nature of their relations. We do not know enough about the English woman to understand just what induced her to cook a boarder a chicken curry. (How many English village women cook curries for lunch, and did so, especially, "some years ago"?) But we can probably infer that if she was taking in boarders at all, she was, at best, a member of the lower-middle class.

Sociological considerations, that is, such as class and residence (urban versus rural), necessarily pertain to what good form means and how much it applies in any given situation. What U Tin U calls "delicacy of feeling" is better labeled "sensitivity to status." Speaking with a bit of vinegar in one's tone, such as the English woman appears to have done—one doesn't have to be Burmese to catch a hint of an edge in her remark—happens frequently in Burma. It's just that it does so only on the part of superiors speaking to their subordinates, or among status equals who are "teasing." (Very rude remarks are often made under the cover of "teasing.") To represent all Burmese as acting in accordance with a cultural ideal of "solicitousness" requires that one strip away such qualifiers as relative standing, and all contextual circumstances, such as who is present in a particular place at a particular time, in favor of an idealized, generalized, and mythic national character. What the English lady's error consisted in was failing to appreciate the status of a Burmese man who was of sufficient stature and means to have made it to that English village in the first place. But then, she was a villager.

My claim is that people in Southeast Asian societies in which status considerations pervade interaction are acutely aware of how much the ways they conduct themselves in social settings matter to their social standing, and that, in light of how much social standing matters to everyone, they are therefore particularly sensitive to the obligation of showing their correct assessment of their "place." They are highly conscious of the need to show that they understand the nature of their relations to others present in any encounter. Behavior, whether one's own or that of one's interlocutors, that contravenes this principle generates the feeling—*isin/lingsem* in Javanese, *malu* in Indonesian and Malay, *lek* in Balinese, *a:nade* in Burmese, and so on—that Southeast Asians make much of. Behaving appropriately, and fearing the very disturbing feelings that follow from anyone's failure to do so, do not mean that people are forever hiding their feelings, or playing a part, or behaving insincerely. It means that they are constantly modulating their actions, words, and sentiments—their expressed thoughts and their bodily comportment—in order to keep themselves attuned to, and to demonstrate that they are so attuned to, the specific social context in which they find themselves.

The drawback to using the metaphor of being "on stage" (as I noted about Geertz's use of "stagefright") to describe this alertness to the implications of behavior for one's relative standing is that it suggests that there is also an "off stage," that there exists an individual apart from his or her place in interaction. As I suggest below, Buddhism offers something of a counter to the vulnerability people feel in interaction, but it does so in ways quite unlike any Westerner's intuitive understanding of a unique, "off-stage" self. Because social standing is always, necessarily, contextual, there is no invariant self who stands apart from interaction; there is no "real" self who escapes the exchange of signs of deference and superiority, subordination and superordination, that gives form to all social life. Certainly, there are distinguishing, ongoing features of any individual's place: gender, wealth, degree of education, and all the forms of capital Bourdieu has taught us to look for and label. Yet however compelling such markers may be, individuals are at all times responsible for their own comportment and, specifically, for demonstrating that they know their place. Once again, despite the contemporary, disparaging overtones of this phrase in English, it should not be taken to imply servility in Burma. Superiors, as noted above, have to act as such to show that they know their place and will therefore act accordingly: assertively, perhaps aggressively, but also responsibly, that is, showing their willingness to take responsibility for others' well-being, or for their rough handling, if that is what their behavior calls for.

One fear people have to deal with—this is what Geertz conveys vividly—is that they will fail to show that they know their place if their own impulses and desires get the better of them. Yet at the same time, people are also subject to the implications of whatever treatment they receive from others. Paradoxically, even though individuals are unable truly to control others' behavior, they are still held accountable at least to some degree for the behavior they elicit from them. Particularly if people lay claim to superior standing in a specific encounter, their standing is expected to be of such an imposing nature as to impose itself, precisely, on their interlocutors' awareness and demeanor. Should would-be superiors fail to exercise such influence over others, people who act inappropriately may well come in for censure. But the putatively superior person sees impressions of his or her own standing compromised.

Interestingly, Kawanami, in her study of Burmese nuns, suggests as one translation for the Burmese term *a:nade* (which she renders in its formal variant, *ānar-thi*), "'I don't want to become obligated to you'" (2013, 137). She goes on to summarize her understanding of the expression as one "of hesitation or even refusal to become forced into a kind of patron-client relationship with another social group to whom the recipient (client) will subsequently become subordinated"

(137). This rendering touches on an important point about relations between monastics and laypeople: it is in that context that Kawanami's discussion of *a:nade* comes up, and I return to her account of those relations when I discuss nuns in chapter 9. For the moment, I note that the reluctance Kawanami points to figures as one of a number of unwanted consequences people feel exposed to in interaction, thus as one of a number of ways in which interaction makes them feel vulnerable.

Kawanami's point, however, while well-taken, should be complemented by observing that someone can feel *a:nade* for being shown too much as well as too little respect. So people may, in many situations, express a fear of being made subordinate to others. But they may also fear being made superordinate to others: obligated by someone else's impulse to bind them in a relationship in which they are expected to take on the patron's responsibilities to a client. *A:nade,* I contend therefore, expresses a fear of the consequences of interaction, not only (as makes intuitive sense to many people) of being put down, but also of being put "up." Someone becomes *a:nade* when someone's behavior, whether their own or other people's, fails to conform with their sense of their own place relative to that of others in a given situation.

In hierarchical arrangements, to be put down or put up implies being drawn into relationships that may be experienced as burdensome. Yet at the same time, the desire to be respected and admired is deeply felt. Ideally, hierarchical arrangements should bind people together in light of their differences and complementary capacities. Actually, what proves most salient is people's effort to distinguish themselves as superior, but often without wanting to become responsible for others in the ways that superordinate status implies. Efforts to look good then preoccupy people, not to do good. The tension never really gets resolved.

The competition for greater prominence means that what matters about a self is his or her standing, and standing exists only insofar as it is reflected in encounter. No self exists, in any important sense, outside interaction. Yet selves, once again, are always vulnerable—in some sense, at risk—in interaction. Like pedestrians not yet embarked upon the project of crossing the street, until they enter into interaction individuals are of no significance. And like pedestrians once again, individuals who enter into interaction necessarily put themselves in danger. Yet there is no alternative means for them to make their way.

Self-Fashioning and Non-Self

It may appear contradictory to claim that no self exists outside interaction in lowland Southeast Asian societies such as Burma and Java, when a number of anthropologists have written persuasively that "self-fashioning" matters so much in the region. Fenella Cannell (1995, 1999) and Mark Johnson (1997) have both written particularly acutely with reference to this facet of Filipino social life, and Tom Boellstorff (2005, 2007) has done so for Indonesia. The fact that the phrase originates with a Shakespeare scholar, Stephen Greenblatt, thus someone whose work deals with theatrical representations deriving from an era in which hierarchy's claims were coming into critical consideration, is hardly accidental.[9] If individuals enjoy relatively great leeway in constructing the self they present to the world, in part because ascribed statuses count for relatively little, or less than they had until shortly before, then much depends on how they enact that presentation—down to the last pronoun choice or decision as to where and how to sit. But the self that gets fashioned in this way is a self that lays claim to prestige, the regard of others: a place in a social context, so in others' eyes.

A moment's reflection as to what Westerners usually prize about the "self," such as a constellation of laudable (or at least remarkable) personality traits, originality, a distinctive personal history, a unique "voice," should point to the contrast between what anthropologists discover Southeast Asians trying to hone, to "fashion," about themselves, and what Westerners are likely to want to foster as they go about fashioning their selves. The difference is one of degree. Yet Westerners seek distinction by asserting their "unique" selves, whereas Burmans and other Southeast Asians seek it by insisting not upon their uniqueness but rather upon their prominence, a prominence more likely to stem from overcoming what is individualizing, unusual, or unique.

Perhaps a sign of how hierarchical thinking, competition, and self-fashioning combine can be seen in the way that education takes place in Burma today. Everything in the secular education system is driven by tests with quantifiable results. Doing well on tests depends on memorizing scripts, never on formulating new ones. How well a student does this is immediately clear, because students sit in classrooms in the order in which their test results compare with those of all the other students present. Trying to reach the first desk is taken to be an incentive for everyone. That shame would induce students who are having difficulties to work harder, and that glory would constitute a reward for any one of them, never comes into question. Learning is a zero-sum game in which one student's advancement necessarily implies another one's demotion.[10]

Unfortunately, the state school system is hugely overextended. Virtually no parents I talked to in urban areas believed that their children could receive an adequate education during the daytime school hours. Indeed, there is a widespread assumption not only that teachers have far too many pupils to be able to teach them effectively, but also that teachers deliberately withhold important elements of the knowledge students need to do well on their exams.[11] Teachers are said to do this in order to make sure that they have plenty of students attending the private "tuition" classes they hold before and after school hours, often from 6:30 till 8:30 in the morning and in the evening from 6:00 or so till 9:00 or 10:00. Parents have to pay for this private tutoring, of course; teachers rely on these fees because their salaries are ludicrously inadequate. How early in their schooling children start such tutoring depends in large part on their parents' wealth. During the last two years of secondary schooling, and the last year especially, tuition is likely to keep students in class for most hours of the day, not only during the week but also on weekends. A middle-class family I know in Mandalay decided to send their daughter to board at a tuition center a few blocks from their home for her tenth standard year to maximize the girl's time spent cramming for the school-leaving exam at the end of the academic year.

The score students receive establishes whether they can attend medical school (requiring the highest score), engineering (somewhat lower), English (lower still), or Burmese literature (very undistinguished), and so on down a single, graduated series of majors. Majors, like students, therefore, can be plotted along a single, all-encompassing order of prestige. If students remain in school till the tenth standard, they face the national school-leaving exams that will determine to what faculty they will be admitted in university. Students can, if they so choose, go down the scale of majors, but the expectation is that they will opt for the most prestigious major they can pursue, rather than choosing on the basis of any affinity they might feel toward a particular field.

Performance in school and on exams generates inequality, not mutual interdependence through difference. In that respect, to label it "hierarchical" is somewhat imprecise. In an environment such as the educational system, an area in which a limited number of places is available to a growing number of applicants, it is unsurprising that an overtly competitive system should arise. Yet it is worth noting that hierarchical thinking encourages bonds among those of differential capacities even as it fosters competition among those whose relative places are not yet established. If students at school jockey ceaselessly for superior ranking (or are given incentives to do so by their teachers, whether or not they rise to the challenge, or bait), the bonds between a figure looked upon as particularly potent and his followers can be intense. The cults that Guillaume Rozenberg tracks so acutely in his work on Burmese Buddhism demonstrate the extraordinary devotion that some Burman Buddhist "saints" arouse (2010). At the same time, relations among their disciples may indicate intense competition, as when they fight over what to do about a saint's bodily remains following his death (2011). The *dhamma* talks I described in chapter 1 are a more modest but still real illustration of the enthusiasm with which some people subordinate themselves to figures they find worthy. Women do this more readily than men, but men are by no means always diffident about submitting to superiors. If truly convinced that spiritual power and prestige are concentrated in a particular person (or object), many males show a great willingness to demonstrate their respect, and to provide whatever labor they can in support of such personages.

If self-satisfied Burmese remarks like those of U Tin U cited above can be both quaint and instructive, and displays of great reverence, sometimes to the point of self-abnegation, look familiar from many religious contexts in Asia, the dark side to a preoccupation with relative standing, and the competition it fosters, must nevertheless not be overlooked or minimized. Competition among rivals is familiar everywhere. Television serials in the West, both comic and serious, provide hours of entertainment tracing the machinations of high-flying lawyers, single women, detectives, medical personnel, and the like as they vie with one another to get ahead, however that is defined. Yet in Southeast Asia such competitive impulses combine with hierarchical understandings, and the attendant obligation to withhold negative feelings from direct expression when in the presence of superiors, to particularly disruptive effect.

I have alluded to the violence that accompanied Thibaw's accession to the throne in Mandalay in the nineteenth century. Southeast

Asian history is filled with factionalism, violent conflict, and destruction, much of it predicated on competition for political control, certainly, but much of it, too, predicated on competition for greater glory. As Geertz maintained in his analysis of Balinese kingship in the nineteenth century, we cannot take the desire for political control to be more meaningful or real than the desire for glory. Geertz's critics are probably right to assert that power and pomp cannot be so easily disaggregated in Balinese royal ritual. Yet no one can deny that Balinese society exhibited then, and exhibits to this day, ongoing, vehement, and disruptive strife over such matters as who owes deferential language to whom.[12]

If events of great historical import, whether in Thibaw's palace or on Bali's battlefields and cremation grounds, seem too distant from the ordinary experience of most people to tell us much about their lives, I would nevertheless maintain that the sense that relative standing is on the line pervades daily life in Mandalay (just as it does among today's Balinese villagers), and that this preoccupation generates ongoing tension and sometimes dangerous conflict. Discretion prevents me from relating a particularly shocking series of incidents at one of the monasteries where I stayed that took place a few years before my residence there. Suffice it to say that conflict among senior monks generated great passions, and that the ill-effects of that conflict befell, as they often do, their subordinates, those individuals, whether lay or religious, who attach themselves to important people as dependents. In this particular incident, the result was one relatively junior monk's death at the hands of some of his peers. The victim was not actually the monk on whom revenge was intended but rather that monk's trusted subordinate. Fear of both mundane and supernatural consequences often protect the powerful from attack; such fears do not extend to their subordinates, who then suffer vindictive attack in their stead. Murder is no doubt rare. Yet every monastery with any resources confronts such issues of competition and hostility, particularly at moments of transition, for example, when an abbot dies or becomes disabled and a decision has to be made about who will replace him. Even from day to day, resentment arises over differential degrees of favor shown by an abbot to one monk rather than another. Similarly, lay supporters compete among themselves, and also get caught up in competition among monks they ally themselves with.

I have traced in this chapter the ways that Burmans act on their understanding of social relations. Specifically, I have illustrated the ways that people make their behavior conform with the hierarchical principles that shape those social relations. I suggest that a pervasive concern with relative standing places intense focus on face-to-face interaction as the stage on which people make clear their sensitivity to matters of relative prestige. I have also indicated the sense of vulnerability that such focus, and the concern for relative standing that it reflects, generates around social interaction. In the following chapter, I analyze the strategies with which people respond to that vulnerability.

Chapter Six

GAINING ACCESS TO POWER

When speakers address an audience in Mandalay, no matter what the occasion, at one or several points they usually express the hope that their listeners may be *kjan:ma chan:mja. ba zei,* that is, they may be "healthy [and] cool." When I asked people why they undertook meditation, they usually responded that it was so that they would feel *chan:,* "cold." It may not be surprising that in a place that gets as intensely hot as Mandalay, to feel cool or cold should constitute a desirable end, whether for oneself or for one's addressees. Or that to say that one's mind feels "hot" (*sei' pude*) means that one feels anxious.[1] But the emphasis on "coolness" refers to more than just the absence of heat or stress. It refers more generally to a lack of strong emotion, to a condition of well-being that stems from being unaffected by strong emotion. The best way to attain such imperviousness, which might also be called (by an outsider) a kind of invulnerability, is to be without investments: to be detached.

The burden of the preceding chapter was to show that an intense focus on face-to-face encounter follows from the view that all important, long-term relationships are hierarchical in nature, and that hierarchy is reflected, and at the same time constructed, in encounter. A consequence of the concern with hierarchy, and that concern's expression in a focus on face-to-face encounter is that in many situations competition for prominence becomes intense. This necessarily generates a sense that much is at stake, and at risk, in interaction. In fact, a sense of risk follows from a more general perception: that power is abroad in the world, and that one must find ways either to amass power for oneself or at least find ways to protect oneself from its use in attacks on one's person or fate.

Burmese use a number of terms to label concepts I translate as "power." The most important distinction falls between, on the one hand, *ana,* which describes brute force, the kind of power the military exercised over Burmese society for close to fifty years, and, on the other, forms of moral authority, which imply greater degrees of legitimacy. *O:za* best labels authority in the Weberian sense of publicly acknowledged control over people and resources, vested in officeholders, and it is usually assumed to be more or less legitimately sanctioned. *Dagou:* corresponds more closely to Weber's "charisma": a persuasive claim to other people's respect and allegiance. This and another, similar, word, *hpoun:,* both suggest that people who can rightfully make claims do so because of their great stores of merit, with the proviso that the latter term, *hpoun:,* is associated primarily with males (lay or religious), not females. A senior monk is most frequently referred to as a *hpoun: gyi:* thus someone possessed of great *hpoun:.* A common (if now somewhat down-home-sounding) way of addressing a monk is *Hpoun: Hpoun:.* U Dhammananda said of a very famous abbess to whom he introduced me that, despite his much greater textual knowledge, her *dagou:* was clearly much greater than his, given that she was able to finance the construction of an enormous nunnery. One would not, however, speak of her possessing *hpoun:.*

The words *hpoun:* and *dagou:* both correspond to what Anderson describes as the "Javanese idea of Power" (1990).[2] Like that conceptualization of power, both *hpoun:* and *dagou:* are thought to be accumulated through forms of moral restraint. Yet they endow individuals with power whose exercise may be baleful or positive: in this sense, they counter any purely moralizing claim that karmic notions assure good behavior. Ne Win was assumed to have had great stores of *hpoun:,* since he managed to rule Burma for such a long period despite the increasing unhappiness of the populace with his rule. Only once he fell from power did it appear that those stores of *hpoun:* had finally been depleted, diminished in the long years of his autocratic and unpredictable dictatorship.

Instantiating Power versus Subordinating Oneself to It

Despite the existence of various lexical items available to name "power" in Burmese, I do not distinguish among them in what follows because I do not think Burmese usually concern themselves with any difference other than that between secular and lay versions of power. Often even that distinction seems little salient in their thinking. What matters is whether anyone, self or other, or any object, of any sort, exercises influence, beneficent or malevolent, in the world. In other words, what matters is how effective any particular person or object is in affecting the world and one's place within it. Individuals who feel themselves endowed, for whatever reason, with little such influence must pursue what options they find available to them to make up for that lack.

The impression that one's circumstances are precarious and, furthermore, that the play of power is in itself unpredictable, means that everyone is to one degree or another at risk. Such a sense helps incline Burmans to idealize conditions in which any and all risks can be minimized. Often, particularly for males, withdrawing from interaction—opting for the autonomy end of a spectrum that runs between there and attachment—promises respite or, as Burmans speak of their relation to the Three Jewels, "refuge." In other words, the logic of the system of hierarchy and the psychological concomitants of its tenets as they play out in social life help generate a general sense of danger abroad in the world. The combined result of all this is to encourage people to idealize autonomy or, to use the Buddhist idiom once again, to encourage them to break their attachments.[3] Nirvana, which as Collins has shown is a necessary term to anchor the entire edifice of Buddhist doctrine (1998, 124), is the ultimate expression of autonomy, and its perfect manifestation, because it constitutes the ultimate break with all attachments.

But nirvana is a long way off.[4] So the question arises as to what practical action people can undertake if not to attain at least to move toward the few, readily identifiable, and much more accessible, ends they are liable to seek. At the most immediate and mundane level, these ends are easily named: good health and material security, thus safety from setback of any sort, or better yet, increasing wealth, rising social standing, and all the good things that come with these widely desired goals. In the longer term, people seek to assure their spiritual progress, understood to be a precondition for obtaining the ends just named in future lives: rebirth as a human, ideally as a male, and as someone capable of becoming and remaining a monk, meaning that they will be in a position to assure a still better subsequent rebirth, as a monk or even a god.

To become a god means coming to enjoy great luxury and pleasure. But in the view of many, only humans can become monks, and entering nirvana is much more likely for a monk than for others, including gods. So desiring to become a monk, or even just a male, rather than a god in one of the Buddhist heavens, might be called more soteriologically correct.

Access to any of these ends—more clearly that of reaching nirvana, which can only be obtained over the long term, but in popular thinking the former, more material ones, as well—hinges on how great the store of an individual's merit is, as compared with their store of demerit. So the short answer as to what practical action one can undertake in pursuit of one's goals is to maximize one's merit.

How most Theravadin Buddhists set about doing this has already been noted: laypeople should donate to the sangha; any male who has the strength (believed to depend, in large part, on how much merit he has already accrued in previous lives) should become a monk; monks should devote themselves to the study and propagation of Buddhist texts; monks and laypeople alike should engage as much as possible in the practice of meditation.

In addition to these straightforward and orthodox means for maximizing merit, a number of other options are available to individuals who wish to protect, better, and/or enrich themselves. These various practices, very widespread although less uniformly approved of, by which people try to protect themselves from harm, to seek healing or wealth, or to obtain other manifestations of success constitute the subject of this chapter, except for the practice of meditation, which deserves consideration in its own right and constitutes the subject of chapter 7.

What I want to point out in this range of possible actions is that it parallels or instantiates the continuum I have posited between engaging with others and disengaging from them, between fostering attachments and favoring autonomy. At the same time, the range of options, while paralleling the spectrum running from attachment to autonomy, also lines up with the continuum that hierarchical understandings necessarily imply, which runs from subordination to superordination.

Elective Subordination

The most common and, at the same time, most important means by which lay Burman Buddhists gain access to spiritual power is by making donations to the sangha. This practice is well-described in the literature for Southeast Asia and need not detain us long. I will simply review a few basic points that are noteworthy for my purposes.

First of all, however much monks may look the same—and the requirement that they shave their heads before every Sabbath day and wear simple, similarly colored robes helps assure that they do—they are believed to differ by degrees of spiritual potency, a fact that has direct bearing on how laypeople look on and distinguish among them. Donations to the sangha constitute ways of planting the seeds of one's own merit; only casting such seeds onto a "field of merit" that will enable them to flourish will bring the donor any karmic harvest. So laypeople must be attentive to signs as to the spiritual condition of a monk to whom they are considering donating cooked food, money, or any other material good, as well as obeisance. Is he strict enough in his observance of the precepts to assure that donations made to him will bear fruit? A monk's own bearing will matter to people's estimation of his purity and potency, certainly. So will other laypeople's treatment of him. Do many people appear drawn to him? Does he already attract considerable donations? The ability to draw respectful attention and impressive donations implies considerable spiritual advancement. Both of these indicators give charisma material form—and induce more laypeople to pile on with their own donations, thereby enhancing impressions of a monk's spiritual power.

It is very much in the interest of donors to feel that they are placing themselves, as well as their donations, in good hands. The exchange they enter into—their offers of material support and displays of deference in return for a monk's rectitude, which guarantees the fruitfulness of the donors' investment—is curious only in the sense that the "return" takes no obvious form. No one, however, doubts that the return is real, provided the monk is indeed ascetic and, so, spiritually powerful. Of course, monks also give returns of a more obvious sort, in their occasional participation in lay donors' lives: at life-passage rituals, or when delivering themselves of short homilies after being fed a meal, for whatever reason, at donors' homes, and so on. But the principal return donors hope for is the karmic fruit, in the form of merit, that their donations should yield. The pattern illustrates perfectly the principle of mutual interdependence through difference. Difference, in this case, consists of the disparity in degrees of spiritual advancement characteristic of laypeople vis-à-vis monks.

Yet paradoxically, donors feel more confident in the potency of the monks they enter into exchange relations with the more extravagant the signs accumulate of his command over material, as well as spiritual, resources. As I sought to show in my description of a *dhamma* talk in chapter 1, laypeople strive to magnify the impression of luxury and power surrounding a monk. To this outsider, the effect of the immense dimensions of the chair on which a monk sits is diminishing, since it makes the monk in the middle of it appear Lilliputian by contrast. Yet the intent clearly is to dramatize the immense respect with which lay supporters look on him, and the implicit suggestion therefore of the monk's immense spiritual accomplishments, which is what makes him capable of arousing such respect.

Of course, monks who wish to marshal resources for whatever purposes are not unaware of how much impression management matters to their ability to win laypeople's support. The most influential monks in Burma dress, like all of their colleagues, in plain robes. But they travel in very fancy cars. They may actually have a fleet of them at their disposal. And they speak a good deal of the powerful laypeople with whom they meet and the material resources that they control. Laypeople do not as a general rule hear in these accounts evidence of worldly interests or investments, or even braggadocio, but rather evidence of such monks' spiritual accomplishments in this and previous lives. Renowned monks' control of material resources and power in the world does not undermine impressions of their charisma but only provides evidence of its greatness—evidence, that is, of the extraordinary degree of their detachment.

That luxury can shore up impressions of an ascetic's charisma points to an important and generative paradox running through Burman ideas about how to relate to power. People who wish to subordinate themselves to concentrations of power, in cases in which these take human form, are drawn to those figures that best constitute the ideal of the perfectly detached individual. Such individuals are, in principle, the most remote, the least accessible, the least liable to be available and interested in engaging with laypeople who wish to depend on them.

Principle and practice do not, of course, always line up. Monks who become influential and powerful engage tirelessly with "the world": with other monks and with laypeople, particularly with wealthy and/or powerful secular authorities. Such monks take on the role of the superordinate ready to enter into long-term relations with an array of subordinates, whom they support materially, spiritually, and maybe emotionally, much as any powerful lay figure does. An important monk enters into more complex relationships with truly powerful secular authorities: he is materially dependent on them, in many cases, while at the same time enjoying greater prestige because of their spiritual dependence on him. In either case, whether entering into relationships with laypeople of only moderate resources and authority, or with the truly powerful, such monks must be careful to maintain impressions of detachment, at least in some forms. Above all, they must display evidence of their imperviousness to desire, most importantly with reference to sex and, to some degree, with respect to food consumed after noon. Such monks' prestige, in other words, still depends at least in part on the impressions of detachment they evince in their relations with the world.

The fact that people wish to subordinate themselves to those very individuals who are, in principle, least accessible to them manifests itself most familiarly in the contrast between town monks and forest monks (Smith 1978). A kind of karmic revolving door means that those monks who have been off in the forest, disdaining the secular world in favor of study and meditation, enjoy great prestige. Disengagement from the world wins them that prestige, making them attractive to a new ruling faction. Should the occasion arise, they are ready to be summoned to centers of political power to replace the too-worldly, and so, corrupt, faction of monks, their stores of merit now sorely compromised, who were allied with a prior, now displaced secular regime. But enjoying the favor of a new regime soon lays the forest monks who have accepted a secular regime's largesse open to charges of engaging too fulsomely with the world, and so losing all claims to prestige, or even minimal respect. That is, once ensconced near the seat of worldly power, these monks who have come in from the forest of course become worldly and corrupt in turn—or are so represented, if a new secular faction later comes to power.

This feature of Theravadin societies should be integrated analytically into a wider pattern of approach and withdrawal, whereby those figures who most effectively withdraw from the world attract in great numbers people anxious to approach them, people who want to avail themselves of the power that their withdrawal grants them. Thus enactments of autonomy attract parties interested in attaching themselves to and/or co-opting the figures who display this capacity for detachment. Rozenberg's *Renunciation and Power* provides dramatic illustration of this effort on the part of laypeople to avail themselves of the power of renowned monks, indeed to make use of it during those monks' lives and to materialize it (and so both prove its reality and keep it available) after their deaths (2010).

Minimizing Risks

Many commonplace practices on the part of laypeople, apart from subordinating themselves to monks, show a similar concern for availing oneself of the power that is known to exist, like so many air pockets, invisible but clearly sensed, in the world. In what follows, I first consider seeking amulets and chanting formulas and important Pali texts. I then turn to two cults, each of which plays variations on the prospect of exchanging submission to powerful others in return for their intercession on one's own behalf: the *nat* cult and the *wei'za* cult. Finally, in chapter 7, I take up an alternative strategy, that of instantiating on one's own the role of the powerful, when I discuss the discourse surrounding, as well as the practice of, meditation.

I draw on my own and others' ethnographic data to consider these various techniques. I want to show how, as per my discussion so far, they can be plotted on a continuum that proceeds, at one end, from submitting to the ministrations of a powerful other, to, at the other, enacting in one's own person ever greater degrees of withdrawal from the world. In looking at phenomena in this way, we can make sense not just of specific practices but also of repeating patterns in Burmese relationships with power, relationships predicated, once again, on the assumption that power comes from above.[5]

Aside from subordinating oneself to powerful monks, as mentioned above a number of other strategies present themselves to Burman Buddhists as means to assure their well-being and safety. My claim that Burmans (like many other Southeast Asians) feel vulnerable in interaction helps explain a widespread preoccupation among many people in the region, especially among males, with invulnerability magic. Indeed, the obverse is also true: this preoccupation supports the impression that their social relations make people in the region feel exposed.

A salient manifestation of this interest focuses on amulets. Stanley Tambiah wrote famously on the topic of Thai amulets (1984); more recently, both Justin McDaniel (2011) and Pattana Kitiarsa (Pattana 2011) have provided further ethnographic evidence for this abiding interest among Thais in small objects that are posited to protect from harm the people who carry them on their persons. Even a tourist in the precincts near the Grand Palace in Bangkok can only be impressed by the thousands of amulets for sale at little stands along the sidewalk. In Burma, I have come across less fervid interest in amulets than that among Thais. But similar phenomena—various means to make some powerful figure's protective capacity material, and so both cognitively and physically tenable—are certainly widespread.

Harm may take the form of physical attack, or some more magical or supernatural influence that will cause people to come to grief. Such distinctions do not, actually, much matter to Southeast Asians of my acquaintance, who concern themselves not with the nature of what visible or invisible entity or force threatens them or what particular threat it might hold but rather with the means with which to keep such threats at bay. An amulet may sometimes be thought to have positive benefits as well: it may help its possessor to attain wanted goals. Yet the greater emphasis seems always to fall on its prophylactic power, its capacity to neutralize danger. An obvious, if unstated, corollary to this preoccupation is that such danger is omnipresent.

At the most mundane and commonplace level, people in Burma often carry with them photographs of some very famous and powerful monk they particularly esteem. They may carry a tiny photo in their wallet, and/or put one on a Buddha altar in their home. A great many drivers suspend such an image from the rearview mirror in their car or place one on the dashboard. Such photographs are particularly prized if they have been received as gifts from the monk himself, or from one of his acolytes.[6]

Tattoos are another particularly prevalent means drawn on to protect people, especially males, from baleful influence, although the nature of that protection is variable, and it is not usually monks but rather laypeople who do the actual tattooing. Once I asked a language tutor with whom I was studying, a man in his thirties, about the tattoos that could be seen on his hands and arms, as they can be seen on the torsos and extremities of many Burman men. He disclaimed setting any store by them, stating that he had gotten them when he was young. He was among his friends when one of them challenged him to subject himself to the painful procedure. He quoted himself as saying, "Hey, I'm no faggot. I'll do it."[7] For him, therefore, getting tattoos was as much a matter of protecting impressions of his manhood among his peers as protecting himself from mystical attack. Still, the ostensible rationale in getting a tattoo is such protection.

During my second meditation retreat, in Rangoon, a fellow "*dhamma* worker" (individuals who sign up for a retreat to assure the ease and well-being of the full-time meditators, while themselves engaging in a minimum of three hours of meditation each day) had long lines of tattooed writing running the length of each of his arms. He said he was unaware of what the writing's contents were. But he had been told by the man who did the tattooing, his *hsaya* (teacher), that they would protect him from the ill-effects of snake bites. (His teacher was the disciple, in turn, of a Shan teacher. Shan, living in the highlands of eastern Burma, are often thought to possess particularly powerful techniques for dealing with spirits and other dangers abroad in the world.[8]) It is worth noting that, in his telling, the tattoos would not prevent snakes from biting him, but rather that, should one bite him, its venom would have no effect. The tattoos on his body did not impose an effect on the world but rather on him, granting his body imperviousness to the world. So it was not a matter of granting him effective, instrumental power but rather invulnerability, properly speaking.[9]

Similar to amulets but particularly hard to obtain and particularly valuable are what are termed *da'do*. These are tiny solid objects said to be found among the cremated remains of very spiritually advanced monks. Small and stone-like, they are thought to constitute the physical manifestation of a deceased monk's powers: they are a kind of concentrated, materialized vestige of his immense stores of merit. Followers comb carefully through the ashes of a monk's cremated body to find them. Anyone in possession of such objects is believed to enjoy great advantages, not least among them protection from attack.[10] A paperback book I have containing teachings attributed to a famous and powerful Burmese monk, the Mogok Sayadaw, has in its front matter full-color photographs of little stones, said to have been found among the great monk's ashes when he was cremated.

Amulets are usually conveyed to, and *da'do* discovered by, followers of great monks. They imply that those followers are privileged recipients of the monks' powers. As elsewhere in Southeast Asia, recipients must prove themselves up to the challenge of receiving and retaining such powerful objects. Trying to retain possession of an object whose power greatly exceeds one's own is dangerous. In Burma (as in Java and Bali), I have been told about people experiencing everything from petty annoyance to very grim consequences, including madness, from trying to keep in their possession objects whose potency was beyond what they were themselves capable of sustaining.

If small material objects can materialize and thereby make accessible stores of potency, greater objects can do so all the more substantially. Buddha images are the most obvious and important such objects.[11] I think the reason that they elicit great veneration is clear: each image constitutes a specific concentration of power. No image of the Buddha can be thought completely lacking in such power. All must for that reason be shown a certain degree of deference. But each image has its own store, and this store is not the same as that of other images. So certain Buddha images and certain pagodas are immensely powerful: in Burma, extraordinary concentrations of power inhere in the Shwedagon Pagoda in Rangoon above all, and, second to it, the Mahamuni Buddha image in Mandalay.[12]

Particularly intriguing in this respect is the image of the Reluctant Buddha housed in a grandiose new structure just outside Pyin Oo Lwin (the colonial hot-season capital, formerly known as Maymyo). This very large and imposing Buddha image was one of many produced recently in Mandalay for the Chinese market. It was being transported along the road from that city to southwestern China when an accident made the truck transporting it roll over, dumping the image out on the ground. People interpreted the event to mean that the image wanted, for reasons of patriotism, to remain on Burmese soil. So funds were raised and the imposing pagoda in which it is now housed was constructed.[13]

Amulets, *da'do,* photographs, tattoos, images: all these material artifacts are believed to give potency material form. They are charged with the spiritual energy either of the people who are their source or of the potent figure they represent. In each case, they have been obtained in the course of some form of exchange, and this exchange may be ongoing: the recipient has provided, and may continue to provide, the powerful other who constitutes the source of the object's effectiveness gifts of money, foodstuffs, service, and/or obeisance. What they afford the recipient is protection, invulnerability in the face of the constant threat that merely existing in the world, and entering into interaction, necessarily implies.[14]

An individual who has been able to win him- or herself some measure of invulnerability by drawing on another person's or entity's power has made some progress toward constituting a self that is impervious, both to baleful influence (mystical attack, snake venom, violence, and the like) and to interaction. Invulnerability in any of these forms does little more than start constructing a barrier between the self and the world. It builds a fence around an entity that, with discipline and dedication, can go on to concentrate power, becoming not just impervious but autonomous. Attachments to concentrations of power can be forsworn, like kicking the ladder away, when a new level has been reached. But till that point is reached, subordination to powerful entities makes perfect sense.

Assuring Protection through Sound

I recounted in chapter 2 the enormous efforts novices and monks make to memorize large portions of the Pali canon, and I noted that gaining comprehension of the text's meaning was not, in general, as salient in people's intentions as acquiring perfect mastery of the Pali words themselves. The relationship that this assiduous attention to acquiring (rather than understanding) the text implies is one of subordination and reception, effacing the self as an independent cognitive agent in order to obtain some measure of the text's power. That power is beyond question, and no one presumes to question or to interrogate, let alone to contest, the contents of the texts. People seek rather to draw into themselves some portion, however slight, of the power that the Pali canon exercises in and on the world. Or perhaps better, as I suggest below, they wish to make of themselves conduits through whom that power can pass. I believe this fundamental attitude helps explain many practices Burman Buddhists engage in with respect to powerful words.

Buddha images move many people to recite formulas, whether in Pali or Burmese or both, and this practice should be seen as yet another way in which Burman Buddhists channel the flow of power toward themselves, and do so particularly in order to afford themselves protection from destructive influences or agents. Burman Buddhists rely on voicing Pali and Burmese words (whether familiar formulas they can recite from memory or longer texts that they read) to protect themselves and their immediate surroundings. I have described evening recitation at the Shweigyin Monastery. A couple of other examples—one, daily recitation on the part of individuals of the Buddha's virtues, very widespread if seemingly minor, the other an event of greater magnitude, the collective reading of the *Pahtan:* text, actually practiced less frequently but probably of increasingly common occurrence and in any case of great public salience—further attest to the importance of vocalizing language in order to gain protection.

During the meditation retreat in which I acted as a *dhamma* volunteer in 2014, one of my fellows, Ko Htut Htun, was particularly committed to reciting formulas in praise of the Buddha's virtues and spreading loving-kindness. He told me that he usually spent an hour every morning chanting in this way and meditating. Over a number of days, I overheard him several times as he tore through a lot of memorized formulas at a terrific rate for as long as half an hour without a break. Evenings, he did the same for a much shorter period of time, maybe ten to fifteen minutes. The other volunteers I roomed with engaged in much the same activity at various times (always individually), although much more briefly. In fact, I have met a great many Burmans who engage in this kind of activity, reciting formulas in Pali or Burmese, or a mix of both languages, every day. Asked why they do so, they respond that it is in order to feel "cool," and to feel "safe."

A fellow meditator at the course I undertook in Maymyo and whom I met on later occasions in Mandalay told me that he, too, recited formulas in the morning and evening every day. In the evening, he did so for about an hour, and included about half an hour's recitation of portions of a section of the Pali canon called the *Pahtan:* (in Pali *paṭṭhāna*). This same text lies at the heart of a much more elaborate and highly structured event in which a text is intoned: when a group of monks takes turns reading this particularly obscure portion (one out of seven) of the *Abhidhamma*,[15] the most abstruse of the books making up the Pali canon.[16] It is said that after the Buddha attained enlightenment, he remained for seven days near the bodhi tree under which he was sitting when the great breakthrough had come. During this time, he meditated, light playing about his head throughout: this was a reflection of the intensity of his mental exercise. But when he turned to planning out the *Pahtan:,* the light grew considerably brighter.[17] Soon thereafter, when the Buddha had begun his long preaching career, many were the beings in the cosmos that wished to be made privy to the knowledge he had attained. He revealed the most difficult, and the most crucial, of his teachings only when he ascended to the heavens and presented the words now recorded in this text to its residents, sure that humans would never be able to grasp their meaning.

Burmans, who read the *Abhidhamma* more resolutely than most of their fellow Theravadin,[18] believe it very auspicious to invite monks to recite the text in its entirety, and continuously, over a period usually lasting five days and nights, although this reading is sometimes extended to seven or even ten days. It is my impression that the practice was becoming more widespread between my stay in 1987 and 1988 and that in 2011 and 2012. In any case, urban neighborhoods, monasteries, and organizations are all potential sponsors of such events, and most sponsoring establishments hold such recitations once a year. Monks take on the task of reciting the text in groups of at least two, usually three, sometimes still more monks and novices seated in front of a microphone, which they hand off to one another as they take turns reading the lines of Pali individually in a prosodically repetitious two-line pattern, the first phrase ending with a rising intonation, the second with a falling one. Loudspeakers outside whatever structure the monks sit in relay their reading at stentorian volume to the surrounding area.

The enormous volume is very much to the point. When I asked people why a *Pahtan:* recitation was done, they explained that reading the text was a way to make an area—the area in which the sound was audible—safe from dangers of any kind. Since I myself found the practice excruciating but was aware that that was my own, idiosyncratic reaction, I posed the question to people in Mandalay how they felt about it in as neutral a manner as I could manage. I detected in a few cases some impatience, and U Dhammananda assured me that many people found it bothersome but would not dare to say so. Still, a man in the outskirts of Mandalay in whose neighborhood a *Pahtan:* recitation had just ended told me, it seemed to me quite sincerely, that it brought him comfort, that it made him feel "cool," because it meant that the neighborhood would now be safe for the coming year. U Dhammananda, who remarked after the annual *Pahtan:* recitation at the Shweigyin Monastery ended that he wished they would turn the loudspeakers down after nine o'clock at night, said nonetheless that it was because of the frequent *Pahtan:* readings that Burma suffered so few natural disasters. With the exception of Cyclone Nargis, the horrific storm that ravaged the Irrawaddy Delta in 2008, he said, most storms brewing in the Bay of Bengal threatened the Burmese coast but then pivoted and turned toward Bangladesh and India. He attributed this pattern to the fact that Burmese protected their region from danger by means of *Pahtan:* readings.[19]

The extraordinary prophylactic power of the *Pahtan:* is explained in a number of ways. For one thing, its importance fits into the larger, very widely believed notion that the Buddhist teachings are fated to disappear at the end of five thousand years—this according to the prediction of the Gautama Buddha himself. Burmans believe that the first manifestation of such decline will consist in the loss of the canonical teachings, and they assume that the most difficult texts will be the first to go. The *Pahtan:*, in light of its extremely abstruse nature, is thought likely to be lost first. But as long as monks continue to read it, people assume that the threat of its disappearance can be forestalled, and if this, the most arcane of the canon's texts, can be so preserved, they reckon the rest of it will remain available as well. Both the inaccessibility of the text's contents and the mere fact that it is in Pali, of course, mean that few people if any within earshot can make out the sense of what they hear. That does not matter. Intelligibility clearly has little importance for the text's effectiveness as a means to clear a space of harmful influence.

I am inclined to think, actually, that the very hermetic character of the text, the fact that it is so difficult for its sense to be registered by anyone, even those well-versed in Pali learning, enhances convictions of its potency. In my earlier work in Java, I inferred that unintelligible vestiges of Old Javanese poetry were believed to be especially conducive to channeling power *because* they were unintelligible: that the words' and formulas' power, since it was not dissipated in mere meaning, was for that reason more effective (Keeler 1987, 139). It is as though, by virtue of the fact that people cannot understand their sense, the voicing of the words entails less energy loss, much the way that engineers seek to reduce such loss when, say, capturing the energy of flowing water in a hydroelectric project. It is hard to find ways to talk with people about such ideas, so I can only offer this interpretation as a hunch, rather more than a finding. Still, I believe much the same obtains among Burmans who deal with esoteric texts: inscrutable texts suggest more powerful charges than accessible ones whose instrumental effectiveness is diminished if listeners can easily absorb their meaning.

I was also told that since the *Pahtan:* was first delivered to *nats* living in one of the many Buddhist heavens, these celestial beings are particularly pleased to hear it recited again. This time they hear it recited not by the Buddha but by monks. Honored by the invocation of that earlier event—we can infer from this story that they, like the rest of us, are invested in being accorded signs of deference—they are particularly likely to look out for the welfare of those humans involved in such a latter-day recitation, since it flatters them by recalling the respect once shown them by the Buddha. One monk told me that reciting it at night is especially effective because, at times of such quiet, the *nats* are more likely to notice the sound and look down, benevolently, on the reciters and their sponsors.

Some monks at the Shweigyin Monastery told me, when asked, that whether you recited the text of the *Paḥtan:* from memory, because you knew it that well, or chose instead to read it, to make sure that you made no errors, made no difference. In either case, it was like meditating: it focused your mind on the Buddha's teachings and should keep your mind from wandering off. However, despite the beneficial effects for anyone participating in its recitation that this comment implies, it remains the case that the duty of doing the reciting falls to younger monks and novices, not senior monks. U Dhammananda told me that "everyone" participated in the annual reading of the *Paḥtan:* at the Shweigyin Monastery. But when I asked whether that included him, he laughed and said no, senior monks organized such events but left it to younger residents to carry them out.

Reading the *Paḥtan:* is the most formidable such recitation I encountered in Mandalay. Still, the Shweigyin Monastery supplemented its annual *Paḥtan:* recitation, held in April, with another, similar reading, this time of the *Vinaya* text (the first book of the canon) in October each year. The event took place over only three days, not five, and went on during the day only, not at night. (But these were monastic days: it started at four in the morning and stopped at ten at night.) Still, it was another occasion in which portions of the Pali canon were broadcast at great volume through the surrounding area. The loudspeakers through which the sound was piped were moved to point in different directions in the course of the day, whether to spread the beneficial effects fairly to all corners, or to provide people directly in the line of fire relief, or both, I was unable to determine.

Giving voice to Buddhist texts and related formulaic phrases that people either read aloud or recite from memory provides people with a sense of safety and serenity. It makes people feel "cool" and reassures them that either they have done what they can to stave off danger, or that it has been done by others on their behalf. I see in this practice people seeking not so much to become agents capable of amassing power as vessels through whom it can be channeled. Powerful language flows through them; they become entities we can only with difficulty call agents, if we mean by that term individuals who take action under their own steam. Yet they are, clearly, acting on their own behalf, as well as that of others. Neither quite possessors of power nor quite agents, any more than they are simply passive, they are instruments through which power passes, subordinating themselves to powerful language while becoming the means through which its effectiveness can be activated and directed.

My remarks concerning Burmans' attitudes toward the *Pahtan:* and its recitation can be applied to the more ordinary textual study I described in chapter 2. If it surprises outsiders that grasping the meaning of Pali texts matters less than memorizing their contents, we should appreciate that engaging cognitively with such texts in order to formulate or deepen one's understanding is not the primary aim. Pali texts' value lies in their prophylactic and instrumental rather more than in their intellectual power. Burmans certainly accept and honor the knowledge to be found in them. But the texts' most significant value does not lie there but rather in their effectiveness. By the same token, individuals who seek to gain by their study aim for protection, prestige, and effectiveness in the world, as well as eventual progress toward a better rebirth. These goals are not attained through understanding but rather through assimilation or incorporation. (An apt image, although the association is mine, not an indigenous one, might be of transfusion, as the texts' power enters the body of the person who "masters" it, or rather, submits to it.) Such individuals are not "selves" who consider it their duty or right to grasp, reflect upon, question, and compare what they read with other texts or ideas they may encounter. Such an attitude would be both arrogant and risk-filled. They are not elaborating a unique cognitive position but rather taking on quanta of power. They subordinate themselves to texts and hope thereby to become conduits to their power.

POWERFUL ACTORS TO WHOM ONE CAN TURN: THE *NAT* AND *WEI'ZA* CULTS

Two more dramatic, and more controversial, instances of how power can be channeled through the use of a person's voice are found in the *nat* cult and the *wei'za* cult. If we have learned anything from the debates that have raged among anthropologists and other observers of the forms interaction with the supernatural takes in Theravadin societies of Southeast Asia, it is that all such phenomena need to be considered with reference to each other. Spiro's claim that the Burmese *nat* cult constituted a sphere distinct from orthodox Buddhism (1978) came in for considerable criticism at the hands of such scholars as Leach (1968), Tambiah (1984), and Lehmann (1998), who insisted that such distinctions were externally imposed rather than reflecting indigenous understandings. More recently, Justin McDaniel has dismissed out of hand all attempts to distinguish among proper and improper, or orthodox and heterodox, versions of Buddhist practice in Thailand, saying that what Thais do—in all its diversity and in all its divergences from what text-based understandings of Buddhism might imply—is what Buddhism is in that society (2011).

I am certainly inclined toward this embrace of all understandings and practices to which people who call themselves Buddhist are given. Drawing categorical lines among kinds of activities strikes me as unfruitful. Nevertheless, we need to note how people in Burma and Thailand themselves draw such lines, which they certainly now do, and how they make invidious comparisons on the basis of them. The reformist impulse, with its attendant distinctions among degrees of correctness and prestige, resonates powerfully in Burma, and the tolerance an outsider might wish to espouse when approaching people's ideas and practices should not distract us from a rhetoric of intolerance, or at least relative degrees of approval and disapproval, when we are confronted with such attitudes among the people we observe.

I preface my remarks about the *nat* and *wei'za* cults with these cautionary notes because, while arousing at least some interest among a great many Burmans, they also generate a fair bit of at least disquiet and often censure. I wish to focus on what underlies many people's great interest in these cults and many other people's great disapproval of them. In both cases, much hinges on the matters of hierarchy, subordination, and autonomy.

I do not claim expertise in the study of either of these cults. I draw on the analyses of other researchers to cull material that casts light on issues of relevance to my own project. I make particularly extensive use of the invaluable work carried out by Bénédicte Brac de la Perrière on the *nat* cult (1989, 2005, 2009), and by Guillaume Rozenberg on the *wei'za* cult (2015), to suggest that ambivalences surrounding autonomy and attachment illuminate the controversies both cults generate.[20] In the case of the *nat* cult, we see that subordinating oneself to "lesser," because less distant and less detached, supernatural agents lays people open to charges of spiritual indiscretion. In the case of the *wei'za* cult, we see people trying to fend off charges of such misplaced and compromising allegiances without forswearing efforts to attach themselves to concentrations of great and effective power in pursuit of their ends, whether material or spiritual or both.

The *Nat* Cult

I review only the central points of Bénédicte Brac de la Perrière's thoroughgoing and illuminating accounts of the *nat* cult here. (Readers of Spiro's older report, *Burmese Supernaturalism* [1978], will find much here that is familiar, as well.) There is a practice of long standing among Burmans of venerating spirits, or *nats*,[21] who are believed to be in a position to intervene, to beneficent or malicious intent, in the affairs of humans. Such spirits' origins are traced back for the most part to historical figures who died prematurely in the course of Burman history, often at the hands of political authorities made anxious by their perceived powers and presumed ambitions. These "green deaths," as they are called, mean that the spirits remain bound to the world, rather than released to realms of greater remoteness and serenity. Humans can take advantage of their accessibility to enter into communication with them, through the good offices of mediums (*na' gado*), to obtain some boon. Most often the boon so sought is of a material nature, such as success in a business venture, and human supplicants vow that, should a *nat* help them succeed at whatever undertaking they embark on, they will hold a ritual celebration, a *nat pwe:*, in grateful return. These events were, up until the recent past, long (running a number of days and nights in succession), raucous, and, in the view of many, disreputable.[22]

One reason for the low opinion in which these events, and indeed the entire *nat* cult, are held by many is the nonnormative gender presentation of the mediums, most of whom cross-dress. When mediums contact spirits, they are possessed by them, and because mediums and spirits are joined together by "marriage," this means that the spirit is of the opposite gender from the medium. Many female mediums behave in a forthright manner, smoke cigarettes, and drink alcohol: their demeanor befits the masculine identity of the spirits who enter them. Male mediums, in contrast, comport themselves in an effeminate manner. It is not that they grow shy and self-effacing, as the model for young, modest women would encourage them to do, but rather that they affect graceful gestures and feminine pronouns to go with the extravagantly colorful outfits and elaborate makeup they put on. For the rest, though, in contrast to idealized feminine comportment, they speak with authority: like high-status, middle-aged women, they advise, instruct, and chide people freely.[23] Although female mediums are usually deemed mannish by Burmans but their sexuality not subject to much further concern, male mediums are usually thought of as *achau'*, that is, as being not only given to cross-dressing but also attracted sexually to masculine-gendered males, while themselves choosing to take the passive (anal-receptive) role in sex.

The exchanges people enter into with *nats* elicit further disdain because their frankly materialist nature is so little euphemized. Ritual events involving the *nats* and their mediums make no secret of, indeed, seem to glory in, displays of cold cash. The idiom of market exchange offends Burman sensibilities, as it does those of many people in lowland Southeast Asia, despite the fact that market exchange is a pervasive feature of everyone's lives. Money instantiates all that is thought unstable and disruptive in relationships, since it is predicated on the notion that exchange relations can be brief, unfeeling, and clearly self-interested.

How then not to react censoriously when the sponsors of a *nat pwe:* can be seen stuffing bills into a spirit medium's headdress when he or she is dancing as a *nat,* or attaching bills to articles of their clothing? *Nats* themselves are by no means above using their medium's voices to make outright demands for monetary gifts. At the same time, mediums arouse their audiences to some frenzy when they make dramatic displays of throwing money into the air for spectators to rush to grab for themselves. (The notes' denominations are small, but that does not dissuade people from making mad efforts to get them.) Money also attracts much attention because the musicians who keep a constant, loud background going throughout an event devoted to the *nats* are constantly receiving tips from the mediums. Indeed, in many instances, it is the musicians who stand first in line for the payments that sponsors and others provide. So not only are the sponsors of a *nat pwe:* presumed to be holding the event to fulfill a vow they made with a *nat* or *nats* in pursuit of material ends, such as by making a killing in business; the mediums themselves, the musicians accompanying them, and the spectators all appear to be much preoccupied with money. Nothing could appear further removed from—and indeed, it all takes on the atmosphere of a vulgar, transgressive, and perverse enterprise in dialogue with—Buddhism's distance toward worldly affairs, much the way that Las Vegas could be said to be in dialogue with the world's greatest art and architecture.

But the opprobrium that tends to surround the *nat* cult stems, first and foremost, I believe, from its critics' conviction that participants in it suffer from what we might call a status dysfunction disorder. As people invested in reformist Buddhist ideas point out ceaselessly, *nats* are of lower, not higher, status than humans. Thus we humans should spread loving compassion to them, to enable them to break free from the constraints that keep them from leaving this world behind. At the same time, we obviously gain nothing if we are so misguided as to subordinate ourselves to them, which we do when we strike deals with them. In effect, we lower ourselves to a status below our own by bowing down to *nats,* when we are obviously ontologically superior.

The mediums themselves, for their part, engage in the truly unworthy business of laying themselves open to possession. They insist (they have to insist) that they are unconscious of everything that transpires during the time they are possessed. Brac de la Perrière notes that the complete loss of autonomy that this implies at the start of a medium's career shifts through time, as the medium comes to assume greater control over the nature of their relations (1989, 119). Critics of the whole phenomenon, however, do not read this fine print about the changing nature of the relationships mediums enter into with spirits. They see only an individual's subjecting him- or herself to the control of an alien agent, and an agent of a status lower than humans, to boot. Nothing can redeem such a practice from the ignominy in which this self-abnegation, which is a form of self-erasure, places it. This is a society, after all, wherein self-making, which consists of consolidating claims to superior social standing, is of great and ongoing concern. A medium, by ceding control over his or her body to an outside agent, can only arouse contempt among the spiritually correct.

To many Burmans, it is obvious that women (and their transvestite friends and associates) are likely to interest themselves in this sort of activity, since women focus so much on material matters, on forging (dependent) connections with powerful others, and on finding opportunities to enter into exchanges by which to gain immediate profit. Indeed, women figure much more prominently in most of the events related to *nats* that I have observed. Men should not display any such interest. Or rather, they cannot do so without risk of injury to impressions of their own dignity. Males, as I discuss further in chapter 8, are usually careful to position themselves closer to the autonomy end of the spectrum that runs between it and attachment.[24]

Yet men know as well as women that there are clear disparities in the degree of spiritual power inhering in different individuals, objects, sites, and the like. This means that any given person, especially any given layperson, understands that if they look about they should be able to locate such concentrations of power, ones to which they may well wish to attach themselves in an effort to augment their own store of such power, or at least to benefit by the advantages proximity to such concentrations affords. This gives rise to a conundrum, especially for males. Subordinating oneself to others constitutes an obvious means of tapping into power, yet doing so compromises one's autonomy. And autonomy (as detachment) lies at the heart of strategies for obtaining as well as for displaying spiritual power. So the very means that any hierarchical system fosters as crucial in an individual's efforts to raise his standing—submitting to more powerful others by entering into relations predicated on mutual interdependence through difference—offers both a solution to the problem of how to get ahead and that solution's potential undoing. The *nat* cult may be all very well and good for women, whose access to both social standing and well-being hinges on their relations to other people (especially husbands, children, parents, and other kin) and to money, and so is quite compatible with fulsome (loud, often funny, sometimes risqué, in any case, intensely interactive) exchanges with spirits, and compatible, too, with a naked concern with what money can buy, including prestige. Men, or women with greater concern for their dignity than a fair number of their sisters, cannot engage so fecklessly with the rough and tumble world of the *nats,* their mediums, and their self-indulgent—boozey, raucous, appetite-driven—milieu.[25]

To an outsider, one more reason suggests itself as to why the *nat* cult should arouse such negative judgments in contemporary Burman Buddhist circles: it looks like a send-up of Buddhist exchanges between lay donors and the monks they support, a Rabelaisian look beneath the piety of monks and the pious euphemization of their relations with lay supporters. Monks claim the moral high ground by professing a lack of interest in worldly wealth. Many monks show a nevertheless real desire for such things as expensive photographic equipment, fancy cars, big and luxurious accommodations, and the like. Many of them may, as I have mentioned, refuse to indulge lay supporters by providing them with hints as to winning lottery numbers—but not all (Rozenberg 2005). And in any case, no matter how high-minded the monks may be, laypeople show themselves completely unpersuaded by Buddhism's core teachings about detachment when they pile on the gifts to powerful monks in the hopes of making out like bandits when it comes to maximizing merit. I infer that the frank and all-too-human fixation on bringing in lots of cash that *nats,* their mediums, and their supplicants all evince points up all too clearly the resemblance between maximizing cash and maximizing merit. This comes so close to giving the lie to much that goes on in the most proper lay-monastic circles that those people invested in proper exchange relations with monks must experience exposure to the *nat* cult as a kind of anxiety dream given ritual form.

The *Wei'za* Cult

The *wei'za* cult proffers alternative solutions, somewhat less tendentious ones, to this challenge as to how to submit to powerful others without besmirching one's good name. At least, so believe a certain number of Burman males. Much about the *wei'za* cult, too, arouses controversy; many are the Burman Buddhists who, while ready to admit that *wei'za* exist, find the claims made about those human figures said to be in contact with them, the *wei'za*s' mediums, unconvincing. Guillaume Rozenberg, in his immensely vivid and interesting account of one such cult centered in a village some way west of Mandalay, takes this matter of belief and skepticism as a central thread in his book, *The Immortals* (2015). I cannot do justice to the richness of Rozenberg's data and the acuity of his interpretations here. I highlight only those features of the cult he tells us about that illustrate the ambivalences that surround, especially for males, the matter of relating to power. If I nevertheless devote considerable space to reviewing Rozenberg's material, it is because his account illustrates so readily the conundrum concerning attachment (through subordination) and autonomy that I would offer as a complementary reading of the fascinating material his book contains.

Rozenberg tells us at the beginning of *The Immortals* that *wei'za* are beings who, though humans like others, have nevertheless succeeded in surpassing the span of an average human life, assuring themselves the capacity of remaining, in some conceptually vague but nevertheless real way, extant as they await the arrival of a future Buddha. (Anyone who is alive at that time will enjoy automatic access to nirvana.) In the cult that Rozenberg studied, four such *wei'za* began possessing a young, rather rowdy village man in the early 1950s, and continued to do so for decades thereafter. As the fame of the *wei'za* and their medium spread, increasing numbers of people flocked to the site where the medium lived. Surprisingly, the *wei'za* themselves, while often contenting themselves with speaking through their chosen medium, nevertheless sometimes chose to manifest themselves in the flesh, flying in upper-story windows of the building associated with their cult and performing impressive feats in demonstration of their great powers.

Rozenberg goes on to explain that these *wei'za* were ambiguous beings and aroused ambivalent reactions. For one thing, they achieved their extraordinary status, in most instances, by dint of alchemical and other practices never explicitly sanctioned by the Buddha.[26] Yet having attained that status, they are now believed to engage in intense meditation, the most highly valued activity one can undertake as a Buddhist, and they do so in a realm, Dragoness Mountain, removed from the known world (from not only the world visible to humans but also that which includes the various levels of heavens and hells known to Buddhist cosmology). At the same time, although apparently completely apart—detached—from this world, they also attend to the needs of supplicants, both through the offices of their medium, and sometimes in their own persons.

The astonishing feats the *wei'za* perform in the flesh are intended to demonstrate the reality of their existence to a skeptical public. As Rozenberg notes, in this respect they follow the Buddha's example, since he knew that he had to demonstrate supernatural abilities to win the attention and credence of his listeners (2015). But then, having won people's trust, the *wei'za* repeat the most conventional admonitions every Buddhist hears constantly: to take refuge in the Three Jewels, to avoid suffering by avoiding investments in the world, and so on. The *wei'za*, their medium, and the cult's adepts, we must infer, do not invest, at least not consciously, in any variant interpretation of Buddhist doctrine. On the contrary, they espouse its clearest, simplest, best-known notions with complete devotion. What they do that is remarkable is suggest that there might be more reassuring and effective methods than engaging in the usual forms of lay support of the sangha for obtaining perfectly familiar ends.

Burman males are reluctant, as I have noted, to subordinate themselves too obviously to anyone, since it risks making them appear dependent, unmanly, incompetent. It isn't so much that they want to *look* manly—this is not simply a matter of appearances, in the manner of young men the world over trying to develop big biceps—as that they want to avail themselves of the benefits of acting autonomously, since this is considered a means, the best means, of concentrating power in themselves. Thus most of them give *nat pwe*: a fairly wide berth, since everything about such events suggests subordinating oneself to other agents, and somewhat disreputable agents at that. The best course for males is that they imitate the Buddha: by becoming detached, which means, at the most obvious, by becoming monks. But Rozenberg shows that even lay males of considerable prestige can find it feasible, and not too compromising, to become adepts of—to subordinate themselves to—a medium who is (presumably *because* he is) male and linked to idealized male figures (*wei'za*) who are (in light of the fact that they reside in a distant and invisible realm) paragons of autonomy.

The men who decide to become supporters of a medium can use this second, somewhat less compromising, strategy in approaching concentrations of power by subordinating themselves to it, without too much loss of dignity because, at least in the case of the cult centered in Mebaygon that Rozenberg has reported on so engagingly, the medium himself works so hard to associate himself with (and to imitate) the autonomy of the *wei'za,* who themselves constitute so many imitators of the Gautama Buddha. At the same time, Rozenberg's data indicate that the closer one gets to the potent males who are *wei'za,* the greater the pull toward autonomy and withdrawal becomes.

Thus the *wei'za* cult makes available a range of options whereby males desirous of raising their karmic standing, and with it, their social standing, both in future lives and in the long-term pursuit of nirvana, can do so by means of a variety of relationships that they make intense efforts to enter into with these admirably remote yet paradoxically accessible figures. The *wei'za* are eminently orthodox, at least in their commitment, as proclaimed by their adepts, to fundamental Buddhist concepts. Yet they are also oddly interventionist in their willingness to mix in the affairs of their followers. They are, in sum, hugely powerful, Buddhist "saints," figures of immense spiritual power who are no longer present in this world; indeed they are highly remote, yet they are paradoxically still accessible to people's pleas for assistance and guidance.

This surprising and, to many people outside the cult, troubling, combination of features characteristic of *wei'za* and their cult actually reflects a more general point Rozenberg makes: that sources of supernatural potency are many and variable.

> An individual's supernatural potency can be the result, on the one hand, of his practice of concentration meditation, a contemplative technique consisting in focusing the mind on an object, an idea, or a sensation. Such a technique engenders a temporary state of absolute quietude, of indifference to the movements of the external world, and confers, after a certain degree of mental concentration (*thamadi*) has been attained, supernatural abilities.... These include the capacity to fly, to make oneself invisible, to multiply oneself, and so on.... An individual's supernatural potency can, on the other hand, be the result of a relationship he has established with an invisible entity endowed with extraordinary powers (a *weikza*, a tree spirit, a kind of ghost, etc.), or the result of the help brought by someone whose status grants him special capacities (a monk). (2015, 42)

Rearranging the points that Rozenberg makes in these passages to fit the organization of my own argument, I would note that the contrast between "the relationship [someone] has established with an invisible entity endowed with extraordinary powers ... or [with] someone whose status grants him special capacities," on the one hand, and the "practice of concentration meditation," on the other, parallels the contrast I have discussed between attachment and autonomy.

Controversy surrounds *wei'za* cults, in sum, because they use techniques, such as alchemy and cabalistic practices—techniques predicated on acting in the world in order to channel potency one's way, thereby implying at least some engagement with the world, some interaction in which one must depend on others or at least entities beyond one's self—in pursuit of nirvana, a state in which one's potency has reached such perfection that one surpasses all conditioned states, that is, a state in which one's autonomy is absolute. Those men, of whom Rozenberg describes a certain number, who find this paradoxical conflation of features compelling, undertake similarly paradoxical actions (including the practice of alchemy and the use of cabalistic figures) while submitting themselves to the ministrations of the *wei'za* themselves, or their medium. Yet they do this in pursuit of higher spiritual status in their next lives and, if things go well, attainment of the status of *wei'za* eventually, and so the guarantee of access to nirvana when the future Buddha appears.

A Martial Arts Troupe

To recap much of what I have covered in this chapter, I focus on one section of Rozenberg's book in which he writes about a number of prophylactic techniques made use of by a martial arts troupe linked to the *wei'za* cult of Mebaygon: cabalistic diagrams, often written on paper and then ingested, other tiny objects, powders, or liquids, put beneath the skin, and so on, all falling under the general rubric of invulnerability magic. Rozenberg's analysis of these data is largely Durkheimian: he sees young men getting transformed, usually at particularly precarious moments in their lives, in late adolescence and early adulthood, into mature members of their society, by means of their taking on (and often, taking in) such socially sanctioned symbols. Rozenberg sees in this process a message, one that subjects them to the power of the collectivity. I find Rozenberg's analysis convincing. I would simply complement it by pointing to the continuity his data shows with points I have made about alternative (or complementary) modes by which to enter into relations with nodes of power.

First, the relationship that young men in the troupe entered into with the older men who provided them with invulnerability magic (and this was characteristic of all such relationships, no matter what form that magic took) provides another example of mutual interdependence through difference. The differences are of course arranged hierarchically.

> Only [individuals accorded the status of] masters have the privilege of reproducing the diagram designs put forth by [the leader] Aung Thaung. Ordinary members must depend on those masters to get diagrams to ingest. The hierarchy within the group, with its three levels (leader, masters, members), corresponds to a one-way nutritional chain, one that makes someone who gets fed incapable of giving back what he has been given. Money that his disciples, both members and masters, give Aung Thaung as gifts, like the money given as gifts by disciples to the masters who have initiated them, can hardly be thought to equal in value the diagrams which have been bestowed upon them. Such gifts are more a way of paying tribute, to acknowledge one's subjection. (Rozenberg 2015, 213)

Gaining Access to Power 179

At the same time, superiors can be distinguished from subordinates—in this instance of the martial arts troupe, but the principle pertains to all manifestations of the *wei'za* cult Rozenberg studied—by their greater inclination toward practices that suggest autonomy. Let us start at the lower end of the continuum. Here is Rozenberg's description of an encounter between an ascetic and a young man taken to him by his teacher for treatment:

> The next morning, at about seven o'clock, the teacher takes his students to the Site of Success. He wishes to consult with U Sanda Thuriya, a disciple of the *weikza* path whose specialty is to treat (*hsay ku-*)—in other words, to lift—spells. The man, whose face sports a long, fine white beard, says he is ninety years old. A retired army captain, he has been an ascetic (*yathay*) since the death of his wife about ten years ago. He is an ascetic rather than a monk, because, in his view, treating people could not be, at least not as obviously in any case, the principal activity of a monk. Monastic discipline forbids it. Now having resided for six months at the Site of Success, he treats those who come seeking his assistance. The rest of the time he practices meditation in order to increase his power of mental concentration (*thamadi*). U Sanda Thuriya confirms the teacher's suspicions in diagnosing a spell. The person responsible for it would be an individual of Arakanese origin. (Arakan is the westernmost region of the country.) As a matter of fact, the boy's family has an Arakanese friend who is suspected of envying the family's wealth and the academic success of their children. With the help of a tattooing needle, the ascetic pricks the boy's shoulders and back in order to inject a powder mixed with a liquid. He does not make up the substances he uses himself. They are provided to him by his *weikza* masters, among them U Kawwida [one of the four *wei'za* associated with the Mebaygon cult]. A few hours later, he has his patient drink a powder mixed into coconut juice, a medicine whose power he has activated by murmuring a verse. Then he puts his hand on the boy's head and recites a long list of names, thirty-seven altogether (names of the five Buddhas of this world cycle along with those of *weikza*), beings whose support he requests to break the spell of which the boy is a victim. He taps the boy's head three times before concluding by proclaiming: "Success!" (*aung byi*). The treatment is finished. The four *weikza*, Tayza Htun explains, are of much too high a station to cure people in this way. They delegate the job to others, the ascetic among

them, while transmitting to them the energy (*dat*) necessary for the success of the operation. (2015, 40–41)

Note in how many ways this ascetic locates himself on ground midway between autonomy and attachment. Chronologically, he has shifted from being an obviously active authority in the world, as an army captain, to becoming someone to a considerable degree withdrawn from it, the change apparently occasioned by the death of his wife. As an ascetic, he has clearly distinguished himself from laypeople. Yet he has not become a monk, on the grounds that monastic discipline rules out the kind of involvement in laypeople's affairs that he engages in. He shores up his claims to effectiveness in treating people by undertaking meditation, in imitation of all potent beings. Yet he treats people: he deals with them, he acts in the world. He does so by injecting a liquid into their bodies—he could be said in this respect to penetrate them—and by reciting the names of powerful beings, using potent sound to release the liquid's force.[27] Neither of these means, neither injecting magical liquid nor what might be called detonating sound, originates with him. The sound is potent, presumably, because of the potency of the figures it names. The potent liquid is "provided to him" by his masters, by those *wei'za* to whom he subordinates himself.

Particularly notable is this man's remark that the *wei'za*'s status is such as to rule out their direct intervention in people's lives for the latter's benefit. High status implies remoteness, withdrawal, disengagement. The one way in which the truly potent affect the world is by "transmitting energy," radiating the effect of their own inward concentration. (Recall the lights flashing around the Buddha image's head at the Shweigyin Monastery evening recitation.) Whether they actively direct such energy toward the ascetic or it simply comes his way by dint of his own efforts is not clear from Rozenberg's phrasing. The distinction may not matter, actually, to his informants: Burmans, as noted above, often seem less concerned with how things work than with how effective they are.

Indeed, neither is it ever clear quite how the Gautama Buddha's potency benefits his devotees. Ideologically, the Buddha, having attained nirvana, is absent from the world and so is not in a position to address individuals in any way. Hence the claim, constantly repeated, that Buddhism has no supreme god. How people think about the matter in practice is less clear-cut. Do benevolent consequences believed to follow from reciting phrases in honor of the Three Jewels suggest an agent's conscious response? Praising the Buddha's virtues, a mainstay of recitation, does not mean addressing him as a supplicant addresses a personalized agent but rather invoking his powers. I use the English verb "to invoke" (in Burmese one simply says, "to recite") because it suggests the multiple meanings of the action very well, implying both "naming" and "calling forth."

The two options are, once again, key: someone who wishes to gain the benefits that access to stores of power affords people can do so through subordinating him or herself to persons, words, objects, spirits, or places imbued with potency, or through themselves acting like potent individuals, which is to say, disengaging from the world, withdrawing, and breaking their attachments. The hierarchical arrangement of participants in the *wei'za* cult can be plotted along the line that moves between those two ends of the spectrum.

Conclusion

Da'do, tattoos, cabalistic diagrams: these are all efforts to materialize charisma, to give it sufficient material reality to be able to hold on to it, as well as to feel secure in one's faith in its presence, and in the person from whom one has received it. In his book, Rozenberg emphasizes the question of belief, on the grounds that this preoccupies his informants, not just him. I, as suggested above, would tend rather to emphasize people's concern for the matter of effectiveness. In any case, physical control of some material realization of charisma grants people greater reassurance than the abstractions of a relationship, especially when the bond is with a being who is invisible.

> Only certain people or beings are capable of charging the procedure [of drawing powerful diagrams for others to ingest] with power, whether because, people in this world, they are responsible for its realization or because, invisible beings, they support it from afar. These people or beings are monks, ascetics, *weikza* and those aspiring to become *weikza*, or masters (*hsaya,* lay specialists of the techniques of invulnerability or healing gravitating toward the sphere of the *weikza* path). Their remarkable activating capacity stems from their status, which corresponds to a certain degree of spiritual achievement obtained through moral behavior and meditation, the latter alone allowing someone to attain a superior knowledge, inaccessible to ordinary people. (Rozenberg 2015, 217)

No matter how vividly its medium represents it, a bond with an invisible being is open to question—although if those beings can be seen to fly in the window, as Rozenberg reports, questions may fall away. In any case, he makes it clear that we should see in the whole matter of the four *wei'za* possessing their one medium in Mebaygon, as well as their occasional attendance at séances in their own persons, further responses to the fervent desire to be sure: to have clear proof that supernatural potency is not only (as everyone knows) abroad in the world, as well as beyond it, but actually present here, in this instance, in these objects, or in these figures. Yet, as that last sentence in the above quote also makes clear, the principle stands firm that the real path to "superior knowledge," to which "superior potency" must be assimilated, consists in meditation.

In the astonishing welter of stories Rozenberg relates (stories about the vagaries of his own ethnographic adventures complementing the profusion of stories that adepts of the cult recounted to him), this contradiction reappears constantly. People want to tap in to power but a pervasive assumption is that the best means for doing so consists in becoming monks and in doing meditation, which means generating one's own power, through concentration, rather than relying on that of others. Rozenberg suggests that the cult offers laypeople validation of their own path toward spiritual advancement distinct from that pursued by monks.

> Without denying the fundamental place and superior value of meditation in the Buddhist path of deliverance, the four *wei'za* make an effort through their sermons to sketch an image of the layperson that is not the negative obverse of that of a monk. Attention is shifted away from the spiritual virtuosity of the world-renouncer toward the ethical virtuosity of the man or woman in the world, with the creation of a distinctive lay ideal. Gratitude toward one's parents, donations, loving-kindness toward one's own people and toward others, in sum, moral virtue and its benefits, both immediate and eventual, in contrast to the agonies to be undergone by those who do not evince this attitude, are at the heart of their teaching, which is for that matter both accessible and expressive. (2015, 117–118)

Nevertheless, the question of whether people involved in the cult, in whatever respect, are acting in compliance with Buddhist tenets, as they themselves claim, or are diverging dangerously far from orthodox understandings and practice, haunts what they say about what they do and think. The ideological and rhetorical pull toward autonomy as the properly Buddhist goal for people's endeavors, and the means by which to enhance one's spiritual status (bringing one's standing in the world along in that process's wake), always tilts, in contemporary Burma, toward autonomy, whereas seeking out means of any other sort, such as turning to *nat* or *wei'za,* always arouses some degree of disquiet.

I have proceeded in this chapter to analyze the complicated ways in which Burmans try to face down the risks that they sense entering into relations with the world necessarily entails. I have set out various techniques by means of which risks are minimized and power is drawn upon on an individual's behalf, such that one can remain or become "cool." To the extent that individuals try to take advantage of concentrations of power that lie outside themselves, they must try to attach themselves in some way to those entities or beings. But such attachments necessarily imply some degree of subordination. The truest, or at least most prestigious, means of protecting oneself and amassing power is to do the opposite, to withdraw, to avoid attachments, to concentrate power by enacting the minimizing of one's presence in the world, indeed, the minimizing of one's self, that the most revered religious figures, and ultimately Gautama Buddha himself, implemented. The logic of the system, therefore, leads us inevitably to meditation.

Chapter Seven

MEDITATION

What then are we to make of meditation? Since the 1950s, Burma has witnessed an enormous growth in people's participation in meditation practice, and in public discourse surrounding that practice. History matters to any analysis of meditation in Burma, of course, since the phenomenon has undergone such extraordinary fluorescence over the course of the past hundred or so years. Yet I must defer to other scholars to trace the history of those developments.[1] My own focus falls on how laypeople and monks talk about it now.[2]

Almost no one I met in Burma ever contested the general view that meditating was the best and most effective, as well as the most challenging way to act on one's Buddhist commitments and to make headway in pursuit of one's goals, especially the most laudable goal of all, which is to reach nirvana. When pressed to explain why meditation constituted such a significant means to making spiritual progress, people offered a number of reasons. One, a reason that I at first tended to discount but which I heard repeated by enough people to realize that it actually deserved consideration, was that when meditating you were not engaged in any action, thus you were not generating any demerit. Since living, in a Buddhist view, entails ceaselessly generating both merit and demerit, any way to stop, however temporarily, increasing one's store of demerit brings benefits—even if only in the form of not causing yourself any further disadvantage.

When I asked people to compare meditation to other means at the disposal of laypeople for acquiring merit, such as donating to the sangha or engaging in charitable works, they always responded that those other activities were certainly meritorious. Yet meditation generated more merit and was to be preferred, particularly if one's goal was, as it should be, not simply to seek a good rebirth in one's next life but rather to make progress on one's path toward nirvana. The serious practice of meditation was the surest way to pursue that, the noblest of aims.

One well-educated monk I met said that monks tended to devote themselves either to textual study or to meditation, not both. He said this without prejudice toward textualists, and I have the impression that, until quite recently, many people would have agreed with his assertion. Indeed, I have the impression that his statement holds true to this day: I would hazard that relatively few monks who busy themselves with studying the canon and making their way, or at least trying, through the series of examinations leading to the Dhammasariya title or beyond, devote much if any time to meditation. Nevertheless, most monks I put the question to claimed to spend at least some time meditating each day. I am not in a position to say whether such statements were true in any given case. The point is that few monks feel themselves in a position to say that they do not meditate: it has become so much a part of people's expectations of a monk's practice as to make statements (or admissions) to the contrary ill-advised.

As Erik Braun's excellent account of Ledi Sayadaw's public career demonstrates, much of the emphasis contemporary Burmans place on meditation derives from that charismatic monk's lecturing and writing on the subject in the first years of the twentieth century (2013). Ledi Sayadaw set out in clear Burmese prose the basic justifications for meditative practice, and he capitalized on the methods for widespread dissemination that print-capitalism made available to him to address a literate public made deeply anxious by the effects of British colonialism on Burmese society and on the Buddhist religion.

A lay friend in Mandalay, a highly educated, very smart, and very experienced meditator, provided an interesting explanation for why there was little historical evidence for meditation practice in Burma prior to Ledi Sayadaw's endeavors. He said that Burmese monks had practiced meditation for centuries. What they hadn't done, but Ledi Sayadaw did, was to take pen and paper with them into the forest. Ledi Sayadaw realized that if he was going to instruct others in the practice, he would have to explain, in terms laypeople could understand, what it entailed. He took writing supplies but no books with him: he wanted to make sure he wrote only about what he himself experienced, without obscuring his report with the complexities of the commentarial tradition. The result was that Ledi Sayadaw's efforts made accessible to laypeople, not just monks, the great benefits of meditation for all Buddhists, and it has been gaining in popularity ever since. I am not sure that my friend's claim that Burmese monks had been doing meditation all along is true, or at least, verifiable. What is interesting is that to him, as to many contemporary Burmans, it was unthinkable that meditation was not widely practiced among monks in the past, even though he recognized that its widespread practice among laypeople was recent.

How much store the sangha has come to set by the practice of meditation was made clear to me by obligations imposed on monks hoping to obtain degrees from the state-sponsored University of Buddhism in Mandalay. One day I stopped by the school and sat talking to a few of the monks who were enrolled as students there. We were joined after a while by a few more students who, it turned out, were taking a short break from the ten-day meditation course they were doing elsewhere on the campus in order to complete requirements to obtain their undergraduate degree. Students who were in line to receive a master's degree were obliged to go to a meditation center in another part of the city and complete a forty-five day course to get their degree. This, especially, seems like an extraordinary requirement to impose on monks whose endeavors are primarily textual. Yet so crucial has meditation come to seem to many authorities in the sangha, as well as outside it, that imposing this discipline on monks has apparently come to appear justified in all cases.

Laypeople put great store in the importance and efficacy of meditation for themselves, not just for monks. Many men, especially, held forth at great length on the topic when I spoke with them. I eventually learned to ask people who launched into disquisitions on the topic whether they themselves had any experience of doing meditation. A surprising number admitted that they did not. But in making the admission, they felt constrained to provide excuses for why they had not yet had a chance to do so, usually by referring to their many other duties.

U Dhammananda himself, who was distinguished early in his career for his outstanding achievements in Pali study, and who was at the time of my stay at the Shweigyin Monastery widely renowned for his public sermons, nevertheless never tired of assuring me that meditation was the activity that most mattered for a true understanding of Buddhist teachings and a true implementation of its practice. He had done long meditation courses in the Mahasi method in the past. He told me he no longer felt the need to undertake such retreats but that he tried to make sure he sat in meditation about three times a day, for about an hour each time. He did this in the privacy of his own quarters so I never observed him doing it. I am certainly prepared to believe that he did indeed engage seriously in the practice. In any case, he believed firmly in meditation's many and varied benefits. Noting my penchant for daily physical exercise, he once expressed admiration for it but explained that monks were expressly forbidden to engage in physical exercise. The Buddha did recommend walking, however: here he counted off the five benefits, using his fingers to recall, first, the Pali terms the Buddha used to label these benefits, then their Burmese equivalents. The fifth benefit he mentioned was that it enables a person better to meditate: in U Dhammananda's telling, this is its greatest virtue. He went on to say that running enabled me to remain trim, but he controlled his own weight through meditation. To explain, he sat on the floor, placing his feet on either thigh, and demonstrated how he took a big breath, held it, and engaged in various physical movements. This, he noted, enabled him to develop the muscles of his chest and strengthen his lats; each such breath also reduced his weight, which he could reduce still more, with a lot of breaths, were he so inclined.[3]

Since U Dhammananda had first acquired fame for his having command of so many Pali texts, I was especially interested to hear him speak about the relative benefits of meditation versus textual study. He was emphatic that meditation practice held greater value. One reason he adduced for this was simply that meditation practice was so much harder. Memorizing a text, he claimed, was easy: on many occasions, when we talked about this undertaking, he would make gestures suggesting reading through a book he pretended to hold in his hands, reading off the Pali words at great speed, and then putting the book down and reciting the material again, now committed to memory. In other words, he thought memorizing texts was all very easy and straightforward. Meditating, in contrast, was very hard. Your mind wandered, you got bored, you got tired. Many people noted how tiring meditating is. A student convalescing on the monastery grounds said that he used to meditate but that now he was in poor health, he had to stop, since it was so taxing. Keeping your mind from wandering was, people seemed to agree, very hard.

For that matter, meditating effectively obviated the need to study the canon at all. You could come to know everything in the canon without reading it, U Dhammananda assured me, provided you attained sufficient proficiency in meditation. He cited as an example U Goenka, the Indian-Burmese man (born and raised in Mandalay, although he and his kin left for India when Ne Win started fomenting ethnic animosity in the 1960s) whose training method for meditation enjoys great prestige in Burma. U Goenka never studied the canon but knew everything in it, U Dhammananda assured me. No, he didn't know the texts themselves, rather, his knowledge of Buddhism was so thorough, his understanding so great, that he grasped all the concepts conveyed in those texts without needing to read them. At the same time, whereas one obtained merit from studying texts, only through meditation could one hope to acquire *dagou:*, the spiritual potency that matters both to the impression you make on others in this life and that affects the form you will take in your next one.

As a matter of fact, U Dhammananda said, textual study could actually encumber rather than encourage a monk engaged in meditation practice. Monks often find it particularly difficult to meditate. They sit listening to a meditation teacher and ask themselves whether what he is saying accords with what they have read in the canon. They are likely to note inconsistencies or points with which they disagree; this makes it more difficult for them to make any headway in controlling their own thoughts. U Dhammananda made this observation in a conversation we had shortly before I was leaving the monastery to start my first meditation course. He looked at me and said, "You haven't read the canon. But you've read a lot of books. You're going to have a hard time, too." He was right.

A Meditation Retreat

I have written at length (but in a personal, rather than a strictly academic, idiom) about my own experience undertaking two meditation retreats in Burma (once as a student of meditation, once as a "*dhamma* worker," that is, a person who engages in fewer hours of meditation each day but is available to minister to the needs of the meditators), and I will not reiterate that account here (Keeler nd.a). I provide only a brief chronicle of my experience to indicate the form such a retreat takes at the several meditation centers established under the auspices of U Goenka and the Vipassana Meditation organization.[4]

I checked into the Dhamma Mahima Vipassana Center located in Pyin Oo Lwin (formerly Maymyo, the erstwhile British colonial capital during the hot months of March, April, and May) one afternoon in late April 2012. There were about 130 of us students; about one hundred were women. (The relative proportions were not atypical, a point I take up below.) We were all housed in spartan but clean rooms, with individual bathrooms. After being served dinner the first evening, we were invited to listen to a recorded lecture about the regulations that would guide our behavior over the following ten days. These were straightforward, if rigorous. We were to engage in no reading, writing, or talking. Indeed, we were enjoined not even to glance at other *yo:gi* (students). We were to get up every morning at 4:00, start meditating at 4:30, and continue meditating in a series of sessions for a total of ten and a half hours every day, ending at about 9:00 or 9:30 at night. We would do all our meditation sitting on the floor (or on raised platforms in the case of monks and nuns, of which there were only a few among us). Most of the sessions took place in one large hall, where we sat on cushions in rows. Students with prior experience in U Goenka's method were arranged in order of how many retreats they had attended; those of us new to his courses were seated behind them. At times, some students were permitted to sit in meditation either in their own rooms or in small, individual cells at a pagoda on the center's grounds.

We would be served a simple vegan meal at seven o'clock in the morning and another one at eleven; like monks, we would have only fruit juice and toddy palm sugar later in the day, at 5:00 p.m. At 7:30 every evening, we would listen to a recorded lecture, delivered by U Goenka in English, or by a Burmese woman who had worked with him, in Burmese. We were to leave the center's grounds at no point for the duration of the retreat. *Dhamma* volunteers—people who had attended retreats in the past as students but were providing for the needs of students for this course—would be able to respond to simple requests we might have. They were free to engage in brief conversation with any of us, but only for the purpose of addressing some specific need. One male teacher and one female teacher were available to answer questions we might have at midday and in the evening of each day. But actual instruction consisted in the recorded lectures we listened to, not in any communication on the part of the teachers present. The prohibition on speech would be lifted midday on the tenth day. We would leave after breakfast on the eleventh day. We were in no way obligated to pay anything. We were welcome to make a monetary contribution for the benefit of others who would attend later courses, but no pressure was placed on us to do so, and no suggested amount was named.

U Goenka delivered his recorded lectures in an avuncular, charming, and expansive manner. When I was able to watch the DVDs of his lectures (the equipment was not functioning during my first retreat, so we could hear the sound of his voice but see no images), I noticed that he used no notes. I do not know just when the recordings were made, but clearly he already had decades of teaching experience behind him when he delivered these lectures. He stressed at many points the fact that you need not be Buddhist to engage in and benefit from vipassana meditation. Echoing sentiments expressed by many Burmans, he stated that meditation is a technique based simply on the way things are, unaffected by any ideology or faith. In fact, it seemed to me at many points that he brought Buddhist concepts in, and that without them his instructions and explanations would have lost much of their rationale. But for most of the people present, almost all of them Burman Buddhists, this of course constituted no problem.

For the first few days, we were told to concentrate our attention on our breath as it entered and exited our nostrils. We were not to think about anything else, and when we did—as we certainly would—we were simply to bring our attention back to the area immediately around our nostrils. This preliminary period was intended to enable us to concentrate our thinking, and the technique is one of many grouped under the rubric of "concentration meditation." Another widely practiced method concerning breathing, the Mahasai Sayadaw's, promotes focusing on the breath as it causes one's belly to expand and contract. Still another has you concentrate on the area between your breasts as your chest rises and falls. These differences in technique struck me as fairly inconsequential, but to meditators they are thought to be very important.

U Goenka seemed to me to have a somewhat misplaced faith in the ease with which some of us, at least, would be able to gain the ability to calm our minds. He made it sound in his lectures as though by the fourth day we would be fairly accomplished at this and so ready to proceed to the properly vipassana technique of surveying the surface of our bodies for physical sensation. I was interested to learn from a participant in the second retreat I enrolled in, in the afternoon before the rule of silence was imposed, that he had taken a sixty-day course in Mandalay in which a full ten days were devoted only to calming the mind—concentration meditation—before going on to initiating the techniques of vipassana. Possessed of a mind I think of as squirrely, but which the Buddhist tradition likens to that of a monkey, I would probably need a similarly long period to gain mastery over my thinking. But whether I could exercise such discipline for so long is not clear to me.

In any case, in the lecture of U Goenka we heard on the third evening, we were introduced to the more important practice of vipassana or "insight" meditation. We were to start implementing this practice the following day. It consisted of slowly and carefully surveying the surface of one's body with one's mind, checking for any and all physical sensations. Any sensation we experienced was to be noted; then it was to be passed on by. U Goenka claimed—and I believe this claim is shared by other vipassana teachers—that the entire surface of our bodies is constantly registering its experience of contact with its environment. What insight meditation does is to train us into realizing this fact and enabling us to become conscious of how our bodies are responding to external stimuli.

The contrast between concentration meditation and insight meditation (between *samadhi* meditation and *vipassana* meditation) has occasioned a great deal of exegesis among Buddhist commentators over the centuries. Braun summarizes the contrast well:

> The meditator cultivates calming prior to insight because it stabilizes the mind and gives it a penetrating focus. . . . Once the meditator has finished cultivating a calm and concentrated mind, he or she uses it for insight practice. It is insight meditation that actually gives rise to a liberative understanding of the impermanent (*anicca*), suffering-filled (*dukkha*), and essenceless (*anattā*) nature of all life. Insight meditation, then, is not the effort simply to achieve a temporary state of consciousness, as in the case of calming. It is, instead, the mindful observation (*sati*) of reality that confirms the lessons of Buddhism at a transformative level. (2013, 7–8)

Most people I spoke to in Burma referred to concentration meditation with a certain condescension. It is thought of as an elementary form of meditation. It is said to lead, in the case of highly experienced practitioners, to miraculous powers—but these are downgraded as something akin to tricks with which to impress those of little faith, rather than a truly valuable Buddhist attainment. It eventually occurred to me that, since virtually everyone I spoke with stated that they focused their practice on vipassana, not *samadhi,* meditation, the contrast served the purpose to which reform movements always lend themselves: establishing an opposition between that which is correct and distinguished, with which the speaker identifies him or herself, and that which is disvalued, inferior, and compromising, characteristic of other people of lesser standing—although in this case, the word would have to be, of lesser "insight."

After we were introduced to the technique of surveying our bodies for sensation, we were given a few more specific refinements in the instructions as to how to do this. Yet there were actually few new developments over the remaining six days as to what we were supposed to be doing. U Goenka made it sound as though those students who were proceeding apace would find themselves experiencing sensations over steadily greater portions of their bodies. Many meditators, apparently, find in the course of this practice that they enjoy pleasurable sensations—it sounded in U Goenka's telling like a kind of tingling—over portions or even the entire surface of their bodies. By the last few days, U Goenka's remarks suggested that he assumed we were all undergoing this experience. I never did, and since his descriptions did not apply to me, I began to feel somewhat left out. I am probably not terribly well-suited to the practice of meditation.

I was in considerable physical pain, although I was surprised to find that the pain moved about. For the first few days, my legs caused me agony. (I am a runner, which may have produced even greater pain in my legs than other people would experience if they sat on the floor for long periods.) I was astonished on the fourth day when that pain simply went away. The pain in my lower back never went away, although I did become better at managing it, and even at sitting with my back somewhat straighter than was possible for me to do at first. The teacher told me when I asked about this that becoming able to sit with your back truly straight (as I could see some of my peers doing with apparent ease) was something I would be able to do if I took a twenty-day or forty-five-day course.

I also experienced considerable emotional travail. It was impossible for me to sit for ten and a half hours a day with my eyes closed without pondering unhappy incidents in my life. I later discussed this point with the middle-aged man who was assigned the cushion immediately next to mine. I conversed with him on the last day of the retreat and then arranged to meet him on a later trip I made to Rangoon, where he lived. When I mentioned during that meeting that virtually each day of the retreat tears would at some point roll down my cheeks, he remarked that this happened to some people—but that you simply had to put such thoughts aside.

The ten-day course I took as a student was much more difficult than the one I did sixteen months later, as a "*dhamma* volunteer." Indeed, that first course was the most difficult undertaking I have ever embarked on. It was certainly a fascinating experience. I did not feel, as many people who undertake such courses do feel, that it was personally transformative. I followed all the rules to the letter, even the one according to which we were enjoined at three points each day to sit without moving for a full hour.[5] Yet as an educated person much invested in analyzing my experience, I found myself resisting the project of meditation, much as U Dhammananda had predicted I would, even as I engaged in it with as much commitment as I could muster. The analytical remarks that follow should be understood in such terms. They reflect the ruminations of someone who is interested and sympathetic to the project of meditation, and impressed with the many benefits its practitioners claim for it. Yet I remain an outsider who insists on looking on it as a feature of people's social lives and so amenable to analysis with reference to those lives.

Thinking Analytically about Controlling One's Thinking

Meditating means controlling one's mind, keeping it from wandering, making sure—or trying to—that it never strays beyond the confines of one's own body and the present moment. Two phrases that are constantly repeated in Burmans' discussion of meditation are "to be mindful" (more literally, "to notice") and "to focus [your] attention." The point is to take charge of your own consciousness and to keep it resolutely focused on your own person in the present moment.

In the telling of practitioners, whether on the basis of what they have experienced themselves or of what they have learned from their teachers and peers, coming to have such control is challenging at many different stages in a meditator's progress. At the outset, of course, gaining enough mastery over one's thinking to keep it from wandering hither and yon already poses great difficulty for most people. Indeed, several people I spoke to said that young people were relatively good at this but that becoming an adult made it progressively harder. The more responsibilities you have, the more trouble you have not thinking about them, not becoming distracted by what you are likely to feel like you should be doing in light of them, whereas you should actually be thinking only of your breathing and of the present moment. Even if you get beyond this initial stage, further difficulties arise. U Dhammananda explained that you become subject to "disturbances." You start to hear voices informing you of what is about to happen. You become interested, especially when these predictions turn out to be true. But these are spirits' ruses, intended to prevent you from making further progress. If you let your attention be drawn to them, before long you are being misinformed, misled by false prognostications—and meanwhile your progress at meditation has been stymied. U Dhammananda experienced all this himself in the 1990s, when he did a great deal of meditation. He was privy, he said, to all sorts of amazing things. But he realized eventually that these were distractions and that he must ignore them.

Pleasurable sensations also constitute potential stumbling blocks. In U Goenka's method, after the first few days of focusing on the breath as it enters your nostrils, as mentioned above, you start vipassana meditation: you start surveying your body for physical sensations. This can lead to very pleasant bodily feelings. (U Goenka refers to these as "subtle" sensations, as opposed to the "gross" sensations that cause meditators pain.) Practitioners are likely, in light of the pleasure, to become attached to these feelings. They may try to experience and prolong them, something they must not do, since the whole point is not to react to sensations, whether pleasurable or painful. U Dhammananda, too, referred to pleasant experiences, such as rising up toward the ceiling, as moments when one had to guard against becoming distracted.

A paradox which I never found anyone able to resolve was the fact that what a meditator must do is clear the mind of all extraneous matters, to bring his or her attention constantly back to him- or herself. Yet the great benefit of meditation, according to many people, is that it enables practitioners to sharpen their memory to such a point that they remember enormous amounts of material in their lives, and eventually, like the Buddha sitting under the bodhi tree, their past lives. As one lay friend put it, most of us have a hard time recalling what we had for lunch yesterday. An accomplished meditator can recall what he had for lunch on such-and-such a date in 2007. A truly advanced practitioner can recall what he had for lunch in a past life!

I infer, although I cannot support this reading by reference to people's comments, that the memories one retrieves do not contravene the injunction to remain focused on one's own body and bodily experience, because all such recollections are centered on oneself. They may implicate others, but their instructive content focuses on the individual and are therefore not thought a form of distraction but rather a message one derives out of one's own, personal experience.

I think the two, to me quite different, types of mental activity—focusing one's thoughts exclusively on one's own present physical sensations, on the one hand, and recalling earlier experience, on the other—are so easily conflated among Burman Buddhists because what matters is the degree to which a meditator enjoys mastery over his or her thoughts. Directing one's attention rather than letting it be diverted or carried this way and that, controlling its objects rather than suffering its vagaries: this is what defines success in meditation. To bring to mind intentionally experiences that normally lie beyond cognitive access constitutes a stunning display of mental mastery. To suffer the uncontrolled arising of thoughts, whether painful or pleasurable, is, on the contrary, emblematic of the way that most of us are at the mercy of—vulnerable to—experience, whether occasioned by the actions of others or by the actions, which is to say, reactions, of our bodies, in the form of pleasurable or painful (U Goenka's subtle or gross) sensations, or of our minds, in the form of the phenomena, including desires, painful recollections, distractions, and so on, to which we find ourselves constantly subject. Or perhaps better, to which we find ourselves constantly subjected, since this phrasing emphasizes the passivity, verging on victimization, that characterizes such experience.

Why Does Meditation Appeal?

I take this ability to protect oneself even from one's own thoughts, and above all, the emotional charges such thoughts bring with them (as per the man who told me that distressing thoughts must be "put aside") as crucial to the allure of meditation for many Burman Buddhists. In stating this, I both second and diverge from more orthodox readings of the practice. I concur with these inasmuch as the truth to which Burmese Buddhists say that meditation makes them more open, the one of which they become more perfectly aware through long periods of intense reflection, is the foundational, existential truth that lies at the heart of all Buddhist teaching: that all conditioned beings are impermanent and that to be in any way bound to them, including to one's own self, since it, too, is impermanent (and does not, indeed, exist, according to the doctrine of *anatta* or "non-self") necessarily causes pain. To think of anything beyond the present moment and one's own body indicates, at least as long as such thinking takes place haphazardly, outside one's own control, that one is invested in whatever the content of one's thoughts may be. Were one not so invested, one would not think of them; one's attention would not be drawn to them. Equanimity depends on giving up all such connections, on becoming without investments, on becoming detached.

I believe that in interpreting meditation in this way, I paraphrase what meditation teachers suggest in their instructions. It is difficult to cite specific texts or comments to this effect. Still, to support this interpretation, I would allude to U Goenka's remarks as to how vipassana meditation rids the meditator of defilements. According to U Goenka, in the course of our lives, we react to all experience, accumulating both positive and negative responses. These constitute *sangkara*, of which we are unaware but which remain with us. Only by means of vipassana meditation, as we survey our bodies for sensations, do these *sangkara* rise to the surface, causing sensations of pleasure or pain, and then dissipate. (Listening to U Goenka speak about these in the recorded lectures we heard every evening during the retreats I attended, I found myself thinking of them as similar to the knots in muscles that physical therapists work out, or that we can work out ourselves by the practice of yoga.) To the degree that we can stop ourselves from reacting further to our experience (whether with attraction or avoidance, pleasure or negativity), we can diminish the *sangkara* within ourselves and become capable of what U Goenka so often names as a condition to which we should aspire: equanimity.

Where I diverge from meditation teachers' take on the practice, and from that of their many followers, lies in my reduction of cosmological and existential accounts—phrased with reference to karma and nirvana, and backed up by an extremely elaborate psychology of perception—to social psychological explanations. I take the desire to protect oneself from thought to reflect a wariness toward personal experience, experience whose traces take the forms of memories, images, impulses: the flotsam and jetsam of our minds. I take the personal experience that most matters (whether consciously or unconsciously) to anyone anywhere to be that of their interaction with others. I agree with Buddhist teaching that the investments we place in others lay us open to (among other things) disappointment, frustration, and loss. I contravene Buddhist teaching in reading injunctions to meditate and, indeed, to "break attachments," of which meditation is the clearest and most dramatic form that implementing that plan can take, as coded expressions of a desire to escape the intensity, unpredictability, and risks that personal relationships necessarily entail.

I should emphasize that in saying this, I do not mean to contest the claim that Burmese Buddhism makes, to the effect that personal relations are fraught. Nor do I wish to argue that Buddhists are wrong when deciding, on the basis of that fact, that opting out, that giving up attachments, is the most judicious policy, that the goal, at least, of doing so constitutes a sensible strategy, a justified effort at a kind of ontological damage control or risk-abatement. Drawing this conclusion is a logical and well-reasoned response to the human condition. At the same time, it fits in with a general Burman inclination, especially among (and as prescribed for) males, to take autonomy as preferable to bondedness, to take autonomy figured as a form of ultimate invulnerability as preferable to attachments, with all their vicissitudes.

Buddhists who reflect deeply about meditation and about Buddhist ideas more generally would certainly contest my reading of the practice. Specifically, they would emphasize that to break attachments does not mean to remove oneself from all interaction. Ideally, it means becoming able to engage with others but with perfect attentiveness to them. One becomes able to perceive other people without distortion because one's own investments, now dissipated, no longer interfere with one's perception of them. Thus one does not withdraw from others. On the contrary, one can approach them more fully and more appropriately because one is no longer in the thrall of one's own wants and aversions. It is as though positivist (rational, systematic, and purposive) methods could be applied to one's relations not just with the natural world but also with the social one.

In this idiom, what exegetes of Buddhist meditation suggest resonates with what psychotherapists trained in Western psychological traditions would likely explain by reference to projection. People who have plumbed the depths of their own minds sufficiently, probably with the aid of a trained therapist, should learn to see how their earlier experience inclines them to see in others traits actually foreign to them, but characteristic of the people who cared for them in their childhood. People who have made these excavations into their own pasts then come to respond more appropriately—with less distortion—to people they encounter in their adult lives. The ability to respond to other people without the burden of one's past interfering with interaction in the present sounds very much like what Buddhists cite as a benefit of meditation: the ability to act in the moment in accordance with the conditions of that moment, rather than as misperceived because of the interfering traces of one's past. Only then can one respond to others with equanimity.

A Buddhist critique of my analysis, then, a critique to the effect that I have misunderstood what breaking attachments really means, would assert that I have taken too literally a concept that must be understood to refer not to minimizing relations with others but rather to minimizing the interference occasioned by one's own passions. It might well be held that I have too hastily drawn an analogy between the exceptional conditions of meditation practice and the relations to others that obtain in everyday life, that I have taken an exceptional practice as a metaphor, as well as a model, for everyday interaction.

Yet I would counter such a critique of my analysis of meditation by citing two points. First, Buddhist meditation, or for that matter, Buddhist doctrine more generally, does not, in any form in which I have encountered it, urge reflection on the idiosyncrasies of a specific individual's past. It does not therefore urge reflection on one's own behavior and its irrational elements (let alone other people's) but rather pits against such reflection a set of universalizing statements. "Reflection," in this case, implies thinking about one's own, individual experience, if at all, only in order to see how it fits a predetermined analysis, a number of fixed conclusions about the nature of existence and events. In the immensely detailed, endlessly elaborating lists that make up the text of the *Abhidhamma* and the commentaries on it, writers describe a universal, invariant set of mechanisms by which an individual mind, *any* individual mind, encounters phenomena. The vagaries of individual lives matter inasmuch as these will determine the stores of merit and demerit the individual accrues, with defining consequences for later births. But how a particular person responds to a specific environment hardly matters in Buddhist literature, except insofar as stories about named characters illustrate certain fundamental Buddhist truths: impermanence, suffering, non-self, and their overcoming in nirvana. The "insight" to be obtained from insight meditation is universal, existential, and therefore general, not individuating, and indeed, despite the staggeringly complex and arcane psychology of perception detailed in the *Abhidhamma*, not terribly complicated.

A conversation I had with U Dhammananda about textual references to meditation was revealing in this respect. I asked one evening whether the Buddha had provided extensive instruction about the practice. In light of the considerable attention the topic receives in contemporary Burman Buddhist circles, I assumed the answer would be yes. No, U Dhammananda replied, only one short text in the canon actually focused on the topic. With that, he got up, walked over to his bookcase, in which whole sets of the canon in impressive leather-bound volumes were housed, and after only a little searching, found the relevant volume and page. He showed me that the one text he identified as addressing the topic was only about twenty pages long. He explained that the Buddha had not felt constrained to expound at length about meditation because the concept of it was actually very simple. It is the implementation of it that is so difficult, and for that, there is not a great deal to say.

U Dhammananda's comment struck me as telling. I had been surprised, at the two meditation retreats I had at that point already undertaken, at how little actual instruction was provided as to how to proceed. To me, the fact that so little of the Pali canon is devoted to the subject suggests that it mattered much less in earlier periods of Buddhist history than it matters now in Burman Buddhist history. But that is my own reading, not a Burman Buddhist one. U Goenka provided instruction, as noted, to students as to how to go about meditating. The technical aspects of it, in his method at least, were quite streamlined: U Goenka had much to say about meditation but relatively little to say about how to do it. The point is that even if the Standard Edition of Freud's works and the Pali canon take up about equal amounts of shelf space, their contents are actually incommensurate: Freud was fascinated by all the different changes that the accidents of people's lives and circumstances can bring about in how their minds function, whereas Buddhism assures us that such surface details come down in the end to rather little. The fundamental facts about human existence are simple, and those facts, which it is incumbent on meditation to make us come fully to comprehend, and the response they should elicit as to how to live our lives, may be difficult to embrace truly. But they are not cognitively very complex.

I infer from this point that Buddhist meditation is not actually intended to make us more alert to the complexities of human relationships, certainly not to the complexities of our own past and current relationships. On the contrary, it urges us to cope with the difficulties our relationships may cause us by distancing ourselves, intellectually and emotionally, from them. Of course, the social isolation in which a meditation retreat places us is purely temporary, a brief release from our usual lives. (U Goenka, in encouraging students to stick with his demanding ten-day course, remarks charmingly that we should think about what a tiny portion of our lives a period of ten days actually represents, no matter how long the time feels in the midst of it. Surely—U Goenka seems almost to be cajoling us—we can spare that much of our lives to give the technique, one that so many people have found immensely helpful, a fair try?) Still, I take that isolation as a model for the distance that should keep us always at a remove from social relations, in spirit if not in fact, and from our own pasts, as well.

I am too wedded to Western depth psychology's assumptions to believe that such generalized assertions about the nature of all social relations—as a subset within the larger set of all conditioned things—suffice to address the specific difficulties any one person has in his or her relations with others. Quashing rather than investigating the quirks of one's own character, and using an understanding of such quirks to diagnose the nature of the difficulties one has had in relating to others, does not look to me like an effective technique for achieving insight into one's own actions and, on the basis of that insight, coming to relate with greater suppleness to others and in this way deriving from one's relationships greater satisfaction. Needless to say, that evaluation on my part reflects my own conditioning. I lay claim to the possession of no objective truth; I state only my subjective inclination, one that is of course culturally informed.[6]

I also freely acknowledge that my analysis is reductive: I am no more religiously musical than Weber said he was himself or a great many other social scientists can claim to be. As a child of the American middle class, my own inclinations tend elsewhere: toward finding ways to gain as much comfort and solace in my attachments as possible, this as a means to steel myself against the shocks that impermanence inevitably causes. Yet I reiterate that I am in no position to assign greater value to my approach to the conundrum of attachment than to the Burman Buddhist one, only to note and reflect on the difference. My Burmese colleague in meditation was not wrong to tell me that the appropriate response to emotionally painful moments that came to mind as I sat in meditation was to put them aside. Experienced in a number of meditation schools, he was speaking both conventionally and correctly about what Buddhist doctrine tells us is the appropriate way to handle emotional charges. I have simply been trained in a different doctrine.

More to the point, I see in this Burman Buddhist understanding of how to approach self and other a manifestation of a more general preference, particularly among males, to withdraw from interaction rather than struggle with it, to prize autonomy over the difficult business of coping with attachments that may very well go awry and, in any case, always entail risk.

The second point I would make against claims that I have misunderstood the nature of Buddhist teachings about meditation and social relationships is that the ideal that meditators are told to keep in mind is indeed that of an individual totally alone. In the instructions students receive at the beginning of the ten-day course in U Goenka's method, they are told not only that they must not speak among themselves until the prohibition on speaking is lifted on the tenth day of the course; they are told also they should make every effort to avoid so much as looking at one another. Indeed, they should imagine themselves imitating monks meditating alone in the forest.[7]

I propose that meditation appeals profoundly to Burman Buddhist sensibilities because it provides a template, and in the romanticized image of the monk in the forest, a model, for an impossible but alluring solution to the existential conundrum I have alluded to at several points, what might be called the dilemma of attachment's risk-laden allure. On the spectrum that runs from attachment to autonomy, meditation provides a model for existing entirely at the end marked autonomy, in complete emotional and social isolation. It models a mastery over one's body and one's mind such that one is only minimally subject to the indignities, frustrations, and above all, the vulnerabilities, that social life necessarily implies. It models being alive while remaining motionless, with one's eyes closed, and one's mind focused entirely inward.

The pull of this ideal was made particularly clear to me, touchingly so, in a series of conversations I had with a lay man who came irregularly but fairly often to visit the older monk who lived in a tiny cabin next to the quarters I had been assigned at the Shweigyin Monastery in 2011 and 2012. The monk, U Uttama, was in his later seventies. He was a cousin of the abbot and had become a monk only at the age of sixty, having been married for many years and having had three children. One of those children was a monk living at this same monastery. The other son lived in Rangoon with his family, while a daughter lived with her family elsewhere. U Uttama's wife still lived in the village where she, her husband, and the abbot all hailed from. She came by occasionally when travelling between the village and Rangoon. U Uttama intimated that she had not been pleased when he decided to take on the robe, but she had not blocked him from doing so. (A married man who wishes to become a monk must get signed permission from his wife to do so.) The lay man, Ko Than Aung, who came to visit from time to time was another relative of both U Uttama and the abbot. He worked as a driver for a local business. He stopped by to do odd jobs for U Uttama when he had a bit of spare time. If he saw that I was in my quarters, he would stop in for a chat and a cup of tea. I always enjoyed his visits, because he was both chatty and personable.

When we first met, he explained that he would turn forty-five the following April, and he hoped at that time to be able, like his older kinsman, to give up lay life and become a monk. He was not sure he would be able to do so, particularly because his wife did not seem amenable to the plan. However, he had tried to ready himself for the change. He had told his wife to cook only the simplest foods, without looking for variety. He wore only simple, old clothes, no longer trying to make himself look good. He slept next to his wife but they did not engage in sexual relations. (He explained that you can gain some measure of control over sexual impulses by controlling your diet. If you reduce how much you eat, you can reduce how much sexual desire you feel.) He had become a temporary monk during Buddhist New Year several times, and when he had done so, he had encouraged his wife to become a nun. He hoped that she would find the experience to her liking, so that he could become a monk and she a nun at the same time.[8]

I asked Ko Than Aung whether he felt like he had undergone much hardship in his life. No, he didn't feel that way, he said. He had experienced a very serious accident in his childhood, when he had suffered very bad burns. He had often wondered, thereafter, why that had happened to him. Obviously, as a boy of only three or four, he was not guilty of any serious actions that would warrant such severe, karmically induced punishment. He came to realize that it had to have been caused by demerits he had accrued in earlier lives. He wanted to become a monk because he wanted to feel "cool." Did he and his wife have any children? No, they did not. His wife had been sad about that for quite a while. But she had come to accept the fact.

Ko Than Aung was not sure that his plans would work out. If they did, however, he did not intend to take up residence in an urban monastery like his relative U Uttama had. He wanted instead to go to a monastery far from town, in the Shan Hills. He knew an old monk there he greatly admired, and he would ask permission to stay there. This monk won Ko Than Aung's respect because he meditated virtually all the time. He ate almost nothing. He hardly slept. He was a model of what Ko Than Aung believed a Buddhist should be.

Ko Than Aung's desire to follow the model of a monk who spent all his time in meditation startled me, especially in light of the pleasure he clearly took in conversing with people. Yet I do not wish in any way to pathologize Ko Than Aung. Although I found him particularly warm and friendly, his description of the monk he wished to emulate, and of his desires to become a monk, were actually highly conventional. The retired military officer I met with after we both did a meditation course in Pyin Oo Lwin expressed almost precisely the same sentiments. He was fifty-eight at the time of our conversation: at the age of sixty he hoped to become a monk. He and his wife had three children, then in their thirties and late twenties, none of them married (although he assumed they would marry eventually). His wife had no interest in meditation, although he had tried to encourage her to develop such an interest. Once he became a monk, he would no longer concern himself with any of these members of his family. His wife would stay with their children. Yes, he would be sorry not to spend time with any grandchildren he might eventually have. But such attachments were what you must learn to overcome. He, too, wanted to go to a forest monastery and model himself after a monk he particularly admired, a monk who slept at most four hours a night, spending all the rest of his time in meditation.

This former soldier had devoted much of the previous ten years to meditation. He had not been able to pursue his interest before that time. As a military officer, he had been too busy: he had taken part in some of Burma's ethnic wars, and had five gunshot wounds to prove it. (He showed me a scar left by one of them on his neck.) Every Sunday, he and a friend from the neighborhood where he lived spent the day alternating meditating for an hour and watching DVDs of Buddhist sermons. (A huge number of such DVDs are available for sale.) They did this from morning till evening, only taking a break for lunch. He had taken courses in a few different methods; he was particularly partial to that of the Mogok Sayadaw. In conversation with me, he was diplomatic, but he seemed to me somewhat lukewarm about U Goenka's method. The Mogok Sayadaw's method is famous for its elaborate chart, which introduces a good deal more Buddhist terminology into the proceedings than other methods. U Dhammananda, by way of contrast, found this method too intellectualized, commenting that it taught you *about* meditation, rather than teaching you *to meditate*.

When I returned to the Shweigyin Monastery in September 2013 and met with Ko Than Aung, he had not become a monk on his forty-fifth birthday after all. He did not blame his wife for this. Instead, he intimated that he himself had found it too daunting a prospect. He did not express great regret, giving the impression simply that he, like many other people, found giving up lay life in the world hard to do.

What stands out in these accounts is the image of the monk whose example summons a lay man to a life of almost constant meditation in the forest. My intuitive response to this image is to ask, why bother being alive if you are so removed from social relations as to be, in effect, dead? The question—mine admittedly, not that of people I knew in Burma—leads me to suggest that the real point is precisely to obscure the distinction between the two states.[9] A meditating monk is biologically alive, although largely insensate, and socially dead. The vulnerability of the physical body to the experience of pain is said always to be overcome in truly accomplished meditators: the cold, rain, wind, and the like of the elements are said to register in no way on a meditator's consciousness. By the same token, emotional experience holds no purchase over him. Snakes and other wild beasts approach him, but he remains impervious and they are calmed. Since he enters into no exchange with other individuals, he suffers none of the difficulties to which interaction gives rise. The competition for relative standing, the tensions about knowing one's place, acting on that knowledge, and demonstrating through that action that one is mindful of it fall away. The travails, disappointments, and sorrows of human relationships—as well as the passing pleasures and excitements that only intensify the losses we feel at their transience, or their frustration—no longer obtain.

James Siegel writes, with his characteristic combination of brilliant insight and oracular crypticness, about Javanese practices surrounding photographs and death (1986, 257–276). His discussion, only portions of which I follow (by which I mean not accept but rather grasp), invokes both hierarchy and the Javanese use of an Arabic loan-word, *iklas,* which Siegel translates (accurately, and for my purposes, highly pertinently) as "detached" (1986, 259). He starts his argument by noting a remarkable ability on the part of many Javanese (an ability I and other observers have also been deeply impressed by) to face the death of people dear to them with complete calm.[10] He then goes on to note,

> The corpse itself is a model of appropriate facial expression. . . . If one examines the photo albums of funerals, one finds pictures of family and neighbors gathered around the open coffin. In such photographs the similarity of the corpse's expression to those of the spectators is evident. The expression, however, is the same one Solonese put on whenever they expect their photographs to be taken. (1986, 264)

I invoke Siegel's insight into Javanese society not simply because it happens to be another Southeast Asian society in which I have spent considerable time but because his comment, to the effect that when people in Java have their pictures taken the expression they take on resembles that of the dead, is so telling. Siegel ties the ideal that such a resemblance implies to matters of language:

> Posing for one's picture, presenting one's best face, one pretends to a certain perfection whose model is the person freed from speech. What is imagined is not silence, which might, perhaps, be the place where speech would originate. It is, rather, freedom from the pressure that would dislocate one from one's social position. The attractiveness of the corpse is precisely that he or she cannot speak. Deceased persons are freed from the pressures that result in slips of good speech, marring perfect behavior. (1986, 265)

I would emend this analysis somewhat. Siegel's phrasing suggests that people fear making "slips of good speech." That is true as far as it goes, and it is true that the Javanese language, with its elaborate speech registers, makes the matter of good speech extraordinarily salient and thorny (Errington 1988; Keeler 1984). But I think the freedom that death suggests appeals not simply because it promises release from mishaps one might make, but also release from all the other risks that social relations entail. It is not the person freed from speech so much as the person freed from all interaction that constitutes the ideal.

The face of someone who is perfectly immune to the effects of social relations would be perfectly speechless, impassive, motionless—not dead, or not necessarily so, but rather, impervious, or, what is the same thing, meditative. The attractiveness of the corpse is not that it "cannot" speak but rather that it is beyond the need or reach of speech, beyond impulses of any kind, its own or others'. So it is like a *wei'za,* who is in some distant domain, neither here nor not here, in a condition that is neither dead nor in any obvious way living. Or, if we confine our imaginings to this world, but at its margins, like a monk meditating alone in the forest.

Who Meditates in Burma Today?

Two questions remain: Why should meditation have become so popular not simply among monks but also (and perhaps more so) among laypeople? And why, among laypeople, has meditation become salient to both men and women, yet much, much more widely practiced by women than men?

My hypothesis as to why meditation has become so much more widely practiced in Burma since, say, the 1950s, does not turn on the vagaries of Burma's political history, even if such an explanation is, on the surface, appealing. People have not taken up meditation, or taken up thinking and talking about it, as a response to a bleak, despair-inducing run of stubborn and autocratic military leaders quite prepared to run the economy and indeed the entire society into the ground out of a combination of narrow-minded xenophobia and personal venality. Such was in fact Burma's political history starting from Ne Win's coup in 1962 at least until 2011. (To what extent the situation has truly changed remains unclear, despite a considerable change in atmosphere since former general Thein Sein took over as president in March 2011.) But meditation's appeal started growing earlier, and a political explanation for its popularity would be unduly facile.

I have sought to analyze the compelling attractions of meditation with reference not to national politics but rather to the immediate politics, and affective experience, of everyday life. That its allure has come to resonate so much among laypeople reflects the kind of individuation of religious activity associated with religious reform in many traditions. In the past, meditation constituted an activity thought appropriate to monks, much more than laypeople (Braun 2013). Laypeople, as I have noted repeatedly, supported monks by making donations; monks sustained their own spiritual practice by means of study and/or meditation, while in accepting donations from the laity they granted the latter the opportunity to make merit—and increase their chances of being reborn as monks in later lives. Monks also supported the laity, and sustained the Buddhist dispensation, by studying the canon, chanting excerpts from it, and delivering sermons about it to laypeople. In other words, monks and laypeople formed relationships based on mutual interdependence through difference, and one of their primary differences concerned the kinds of religious activities they undertook. Laypeople would not be expected to undertake meditation, in these circumstances, because the whole model of detachment did not apply to them, certainly not in the form of social isolation as linked to the ascetic model.

The whole contrast between layperson and monk begins to blur once laypeople start undertaking meditation in large numbers. Even if Theravada Buddhism includes no tradition of confession such as characterizes Roman Catholicism (and I have noted above that when monks enact something like confession, they do so in such a conventional manner as to convey no actual information), it did long implicate the interdependence of laypeople and religious in a manner similar to lay Catholics' reliance on monks and priests. Meditation practices suggest an alternative: a direct implementation of Buddhist injunctions on the part of the laity themselves. Indeed, as observers have noted about the history of Buddhism since the nineteenth century, we might point to a "Protestant" reformation wherein monks no longer stand between lay individuals and the canon, or nirvana (Gombrich and Obeyesekere 1988). Hierarchical arrangements that place monks above laypeople still obtain. They simply lose some of their relevance, since laypeople can participate in some of the activity that grants monks so much prestige. Laypeople are not challenging monks, therefore, or their subordination to monks when they meditate; they are imitating them, and thereby coming to enjoy some of the prestige, and indeed, some of the autonomy, even if only in brief periods (of ten days, perhaps, or of an hour each morning), that monks enjoy as an ongoing privilege.

Buddhism edged Brahmins out of their paramount importance to religious activity in ancient India without challenging their role in Vedic sacrifice (Gombrich 1988). Lay Burman Buddhists edge monks out of their paramount importance for making progress toward nirvana in contemporary Burma without challenging the superordinate status monks continue to enjoy.

Much the same could be said about women vis-à-vis men in the practice of meditation. It is middle-class women who sign up for meditation classes in the greatest numbers. As noted, out of the 130 people signed up for the first meditation course I attended, one hundred were women. A similar proportion held true of the second course I did in Rangoon. Many men say, when asked why so few men do meditation courses, that it is because men are too busy making money to support their families, whereas women can take off for ten days without any difficulty. And men are too tired at the end of the day to practice meditation at home, whereas women have lots of free time and energy. I am little impressed by these arguments, since Burmese women can be observed working very hard a great deal of the time, while the men they are related to can often be observed spending a great deal of time in tea shops. True, middle-class women can sometimes rely on cooks and servants to take care of many household chores. Yet the rigors of meditation certainly challenge them just as much as they challenge any man. Men who explain women's affinity for meditation by denigrating their commitment to contributing to the running of a household disparage women unfairly.

As a matter of fact, these same men, if pressed, may very well cite an opposite point, repeating a remark, attributed to the Buddha himself, to the effect that for every male found in heaven, there are five hundred females—in other words, that women find it much easier than men to follow the precepts of Buddhism, thereby increasing their store of merit and enjoying a fortunate rebirth. Yet even this view can be turned against women: they find it easy to behave themselves because their impulses are so weak. Their lack of appetites explains their moral integrity, perhaps, but by the same token lessens impressions of that integrity's significance.

When asked, women say, as everybody in Burma who practices meditation in any form always says, that they do it to make their minds "peaceful" or "quiet," to make themselves "cool." One reason that meditation has this effect is that for the time they are enrolled in a course, they are relieved (as their male detractors note) of their household responsibilities. Janice Radway wrote, famously, in *Reading the Romance*, that women she spoke with in Ohio who consumed great numbers of Harlequin romances were reading idealizing versions of women's subordination: the inevitable happy endings saw the heroine swept up in the arms of an impossibly perfect Prince Charming (1984). Yet in telling all the people who were used to presuming on their time and energy that they were not available during their reading time, these women, in Radway's view, were standing up for themselves in meaningful ways. Similarly, women meditating are engaged in a socially admirable practice—and need concern themselves in no way whatsoever with all the domestic duties that usually fill their waking hours. An older woman in Mandalay told me that she went off to the local *dhamma* meeting hall in their neighborhood to meditate whenever it got too "noisy" at home. She meant, when the three generations of family living in the house were bickering too much.

Women are placed explicitly in an inferior position relative to men in Burmese society (a point I take up in chapter 9). Yet meditation offers something of a shortcut to greater prestige. It is status-enhancing in this life, inasmuch as it garners so much respect to say one has done a meditation course. More importantly, it promises a considerable reward in merit to take to the next life, and a good shot at being reborn a man. It does not grant women any escape from the hierarchical system that denigrates them. It does not challenge hierarchical understandings whereby simply being a woman denotes inferior standing. But it does promise a fast-track method for moving up within it. And precisely because they come out lower down in the prestige structure, women are particularly motivated to take up any option they may find to move up.

Finally, the radical autonomy that meditation models for them presents women a foretaste of what greatly higher status would afford them: a chance to be beyond reach, the ability to win the kind of autonomy usually reserved for men. Like a woman in Ohio "reading the romance," a meditating woman is collaborating wholeheartedly in an idealized version of arrangements that disadvantage her. Inasmuch as women are deemed less capable by nature of breaking attachments, validating efforts to maximize autonomy means assenting to values that place a handicap on women. Indeed, to the extent that meditating means subjecting oneself to the sorts of controls that are imposed on women at all times—controls over their comportment, their sexuality, and any individualized personal wants—they simply exaggerate their daily subjection to discipline. Nevertheless, when a woman chooses to do so, she can indulge herself in the fantasy that the system will turn out to fulfill some, at least, of her fondest aspirations, by granting her prestige, serenity, and autonomy.

One other consideration may come into play. Buddhist principles hold out the hope that if people in positions of weakness can learn to respond to their oppressors with loving-kindness and compassion, rather than with anger and hurt, then they will win out in the end. Women in Burma do often suffer at the hands of their husbands, particularly if the latter drink, womanize, and/or gamble on the lottery or at cards, as a fair number of Burmese men do. How can women best respond? Divorce is by no means difficult in Burmese society, but it is a difficult option for women to act on if they are not financially secure. It is also looked on as compromising to one's social standing. Better if a way can be found to make a husband "remember" and return to the straight and proper path. One frequently endorsed way to do so is to radiate loving-kindness and hope it somehow gets through to him.

Meditation and Attention

The last point I wish to make about meditation concerns attention. A contradiction that runs through the entire institution of a meditation course is that the goal is to restrict one's attention entirely to the confines of one's own body, but efforts at making the attempt draw great support from the fact that one is doing so in the presence of many fellows. Attachment theory suggests that shared attention on the part of a young child and a primary caregiver matters crucially for their coming to feel connected. Attention of each person to the other of course means a great deal to each. Any parent knows that a baby's smile is endlessly beguiling. But paying attention together to some other focal point also generates deep feelings of connection and resonance.

The conventional image of a monk meditating alone in the forest removes this last element of sociability from how meditation is conceptualized, and this must explain why the image holds its place as the ultimate ideal. Yet an unacknowledged part of a meditation course's effectiveness, and its allure, certainly turns on the fact that one is a member of a cohort, that even in the silence and the absence of interaction in any usual fashion, one is undergoing a highly unconventional experience in the company of others. Paradoxically, individuals get to experience the strange and much-longed-for world of autonomy while drawing comfort and encouragement from the presence of like-minded seekers after autonomy. With their eyes closed, they cannot together focus their attention, in any obvious way, on a single, shared object. They can, however, share the experience of trying (and often failing) to gain control over their own attention with a group of others trying (and often failing, presumably) to do the same thing.

I do not cite this fact to belittle the whole endeavor. I adduce it, rather, in support of my claim that we humans are fundamentally, and irrevocably, social beings, and that that element of our being shows even in the most concerted efforts we make to overcome it. Even attention is a form of attachment. Focusing on the surface of your own body still reminds you, if subliminally, that others have bodies like yours. In contrast to what Buddhism tells us, I, for one, believe that we can take some solace in that knowledge.

Chapter Eight

MASCULINITY

In chapter 3 I described how a monk in his late twenties, whom I had known in the monastery where I lived in 1987 and 1988, told me that his mother wept when he took on the robe and would do so again if he gave it up. As a monk *or* as a lay head of household, this man would be fulfilling conventional Burman notions of an appropriate masculine role, and a certain prestige accrues to fulfilling either role well. At the same time, since choosing one role means giving up the benefits of the other, neither role comes without costs—hence the monk's mother's tears. Still, in the opinion of most Burman Buddhists, becoming a monk wins a man the greater respect: the monk fulfills a more highly idealized masculine role than becoming a male head of household.

If the prestige that a monk enjoys in a Buddhist society seems obvious, there is nonetheless something quite unusual at play here. After all, the two things a Buddhist monk in Burma must never do if he is to fulfill the major obligations that his status imposes on him are engage in sex or earn money—especially engage in sex. In most societies, and indeed in Burman society outside religious contexts, having sex and making money are looked on as defining features of masculine identity. We must ask, therefore, how it is that masculinity can be idealized, without apparent inconsistency, in two contradictory ways: by maximizing or by minimizing both sex and productivity.

Something of a founding text for the study of masculinity is Raewyn Connell's book, *Masculinities* (1995). Much-cited particularly for the concept of a "hegemonic" masculinity as one among a number of available forms that masculinity can take in any given milieu, the book mounts effective arguments against essentializing treatments of the subject of sex and gender, and in favor of noting how great the costs to most men a hegemonic masculinity can be. Yet the Burmese idealization of both the monk and the householder, while still holding the former in higher esteem than the latter, encourages us to ask whether reference to a hegemonic masculinity might not prove misleading or, at least, might not narrow our thinking unduly.

Specifically, the presence of both a monk's and a lay man's version of how to fulfill idealized masculinity suggests that Connell's notion of "hegemonic" masculinity runs two risks: (1) inclining us to think that even if masculinity can be conceived as taking a number of different forms in any given society or at any given time, still there will be one preferred version that enjoys the greatest prestige and so constitutes a single measure against which all males can be judged; and (2) assuming that there can be alternative versions of masculinity (if there is a "hegemonic" one then "nonhegemonic" ones necessarily follow) inclines us to think that "masculinity" exists as a conceptual category to which people everywhere can be seen to subscribe, however they choose to think about what defines or characterizes it. My intention is not really to dismiss such implications in Connell's conceptualization of masculinities so much as to bring them to light and to see how, in doing so, we might be able to raise still more questions.[1]

I draw on Burmese material as well as a few widely read texts in the social sciences to suggest that, without, as I say, overturning Connell's analysis, which has proven itself both stimulating and useful, we can still find ways to reconceive our understanding of masculinity, or challenge assumptions we may take to its study. To do so, we should be particularly alert, as per Dumont's admonitions, to the ways that egalitarian proclivities among many observers may color the ways they think about conditions that prevail among the people they study. Specifically, if we thought about differences, including anatomical differences (biological sex) and conceptual ones (gender), in hierarchical terms, that is, in terms that come closer to how many people in the world think about difference, that might alter our understanding of how individuals relate to each other, including how men and women are expected to comport themselves in any given social context. If, furthermore, we asked how progressive commitments on the part of contemporary social scientists conveyed, perhaps covertly, ideological assumptions that once again established a standard against which people were judged, we might see that, even with the normalizing discourse of sex and gender stripped away, we can still find ourselves operating within a domain of judgments, and so of power, that the critique of that discourse was supposed to undermine.

What I propose to do, if only as an analytic experiment, is to substitute for the binary of male and female—which for obvious reasons makes intuitive sense to people everywhere and enjoys great cognitive and affective resonance—the spectrum of attachment and autonomy, a much more abstract and so less immediately compelling but also more plastic notion. The heuristic advantage gained by making this substitution is to introduce flexibility to our approach to sex and gender, a topic too easily reduced to binary oppositions. The primary use I make of this added flexibility is to understand better phenomena I observed in Burma, where contrasts between male and female are assumed but never thought absolute or unmalleable. I go on to widen my perspective, in chapter 9, by bringing in masculinity's others: women and cross-dressing males. I also allude to other areas of Southeast Asia by drawing on my own ethnographic material from Indonesia and Burma, as well as that reported by anthropologists working on both normative and nonnormative sexuality and gender presentation elsewhere in the region.

Performing Masculinity

Commentators have noted that for a long time few social scientists thought to query the topic of masculinity, even for many years after feminism had uncovered a rich mine in the study of women, and of sex and gender. Overlooking the study of masculinity stemmed from an impression that, however constructed a category the feminine might be, the masculine was not. Not constructed but rather obvious, not amenable to study because not elaborated culturally, masculinity, at least in its normative forms, became the ground against which such marked categories as femininity or homosexuality could be seen and thought about.

It is not only social scientists, however, who evince such little concern for the question as to what characterizes masculinity. People I spoke with in Burma were also little given to curiosity, or comment, about what the category entailed. A strategy I found useful to approach the topic was to look to representations of men in the performing arts to ask what traits figured in idealized images of males. Here, reflection on the topic was afforded because, on stage, males came literally into the limelight.

In earlier publications on the subject of performing arts genres in Mandalay, I described the presentation in performance of "princes," refined male leads in the *za' pwe:* theatrical tradition (Keeler 2005), and of rappers (Keeler 2009), often performed by the same players taking on different personas. A troupe's male stars present themselves, in certain portions of a performance, in the persona of a nineteenth-century Burman aristocrat, although, what with the elaborate makeup, jewelry, clothes, and the like, the effect is somewhat exaggerated.[2] As rappers, meanwhile, they do as good an imitation as they can muster (often quite an effective one, at least to these unpracticed eyes) of their American models.

These performers, princes and rappers, constitute two stylistically quite distinctive versions of idealized masculinity. The prince epitomizes the ideal of aristocratic grace and elegance, everything that distances him from the boorishness of the servants who attend him. Figures of masculine refinement are familiar from many Southeast Asian performing arts genres. The Burmese "prince" is clearly cognate with the "refined knight" (*satriya alus*) in the Javanese dance-drama (*wayang wong*) tradition, to name only one. Similarly familiar are the clown-figures—in Burma only male, in Javanese and Balinese performing arts genres both male and female—whose humble origins and earthy manners serve to emphasize by contrast what it means to be of a more elevated sort. Refinement in these Southeast Asian traditions does not mean weakness: courage and a warrior's fighting skills matter to the aura of the prince, as he demonstrates in athletic dance performances and well-choreographed fights. Sexual magnetism also matters. Indeed, recent developments in the *za' pwe:* genre make a prince less of an actor and dancer and more of a crooner, singing ballads and pop tunes to an admiring chorus of female dancers.

Women performing in this genre, meanwhile, enjoy less and less attention and become relegated to supporting roles. Even the "duets" that take place late in the all-night *za' pwe:* performances focus attention on male dancers who dance a few moments with one female partner, then soon turn to another one to dance a few steps with her. Males, the genre makes increasingly clear, are the people who matter; females are lovely props. Princes exert their power over their rivals by dint of physical prowess; over their servants by dint of occasional, and condescending, attention; and over women by brief, and once again condescending, interaction in the form of song and dance. The princes' power is discreet but indisputable.

Rappers, whether in *za' pwe:* or at rock concerts, have no truck with refinement, grace, or restraint. Particularly when portrayed in *za' pwe:* performances, so by a troupe's star now taking on a different persona from the prince, they are angry, assertive, and self-aggrandizing.[3] They show off their wealth by means of constant changes of costume and accessories. Their snarly self-presentation and harsh verbal delivery mark a clear break from any vestigial notion that prestige accrues to males with aristocratic manners. Very much in an international style that Burmese see in movies, these guys are tough.[4]

Rather than review the material and interpretations I set out concerning these two public representations of males whom spectators are meant to look on with admiration and respect, I highlight here the point that, despite the evident contrasts, in both genres we find attention focused on males, and these males interact very little with women. In the case of rap, women occasionally (but rarely) take on the role of rapper in Burma, but, as is the case elsewhere in the world, they are much more likely to appear as singers performing a few lines of pop music between the raps performed by a male. For the rest, women's part in rap is to serve as topic, intended listener, and/or trouble-causing antagonist, cause of the rapper's distress, dismay, and/or rage.

The princely tradition in *za' pwe:* displays less misogyny than often shows up in rap. Nevertheless, it also diminishes the significance of women. Indeed, changes in the *za' pwe:* tradition over the course of the past hundred years has increasingly been to make a single male star the focus of interest, to the detriment of secondary male performers and of female performers, that is, of virtually anyone else on stage. I was told that a troupe used to include male performers specializing in different kinds of roles, as well as female stars who might become famous in their own right.[5] Now, the troupe's principal male star must take on all important roles,[6] that of actor in a morality play, of dancing prince in the "duets," of pop singer and of rapper in the rock concert portion, and of the male lead in the soap opera included in most performances.

I attribute the diminution of women's prominence in performing arts traditions to two causes. First, Burmese have trouble (as do many people in the contemporary world) deciding what it would mean to represent a woman as both idealized, or idealizable, and modern. Second, and this helps explain the first point, performing modernity is usually construed as favoring autonomy over attachment, and autonomy is gendered masculine. I put this matter of women aside for the moment: I will return to it to consider the particular problems surrounding women (and nuns) in the following chapter.

Productivity and Exchange

I have relatively little to say about expectations that men will provide materially for their families. That expectation is real and it explains both why many Burman males express immense frustration at the lack of work in contemporary Burma and why so many of them are starting to leave the country to look for work elsewhere. It is only relatively recently that the government has made it easier for average citizens to obtain passports. It is still very difficult for Burmese to get working permits in other countries. If they are Shan speakers, living and working in Thailand is a bit easier than for other Burmese citizens. But the Thai government is inconsistent in its treatment of foreign (largely Burmese and Cambodian) nationals taking on low-paid work in the country. Furthermore, I met several men who had tried their hands at working in Malaysia and found it so dissatisfying, what with long hours, social isolation, and poor pay, that they decided to give it up and return to Burma after all. Since the political thaw that began in March 2011 with the establishment of a newly elected government, the economic as well as political mood in Burma has improved, although work is still extremely hard to find. As elsewhere in Southeast Asia, women often fare better at finding ways to get money to keep a household running, whether by cooking and selling food, working in petty trade at a market, or finding other, often poorly paid but still remunerative, work.

Nevertheless, the expectation that men will be productive and thereby provide for their families materially fits the model of complementary responsibilities and obligations that hierarchical understandings assume. It is unsurprising that in Burma, as elsewhere, fulfilling a masculine ideal so often requires that a man be able and ready to engage in productive activity, using his powers to the material benefit of his dependents. Particularly ideal is if he can do so with apparent ease and without appearing to be selfish or grasping.

Monks are not expected to be productive in any obvious, material sense. They must not, as noted, engage in productive labor such as working the land, and they must be particularly careful to avoid impressions of cupidity. At present, they may actually find ways to earn quite a bit of money, such as by giving public sermons, or even by renting out a car whose use they have been granted. This generates ambivalent feelings among many lay supporters, who recognize the fact that a monetized society makes it difficult to conform to Buddhist strictures against monks handling money but are still sometimes wary of monks who appear to be openly wheeling and dealing.

Indeed, contradictions with reference to the rules abound. It sometimes appears that monks have no qualms about handling money—provided no laypeople see them doing so, or only laypeople they know and trust. When I attended a ceremony an abbot presided over in a lay family's home, the abbot was assisted by a lay student residing at his monastery. (He hailed from a village near the abbot's natal village where the ritual was taking place.) When we got into the minivan put at the abbot's disposal after the conclusion of the event, the abbot immediately turned to the student and asked, "How much was in the envelope?" The donors had given the student the customary envelope containing their donation to the sangha, aware that the abbot himself did not handle money and that the student was invited along specifically for this purpose. So the rule against a monk handling money had been observed in public, but the abbot was by no means uninterested in the event's financial benefit.

In their own monasteries, monks habitually handle money freely. They receive it, and they dispense it, without hesitation. Indeed, U Dhammananda pointed out that sticking closely to the rules against monks handling money could actually disadvantage laypeople. If a distinguished monk scrupulously avoids handling money, a layperson has to accompany him when he is invited to travel about the country. This means that laypeople have not only to pay for his transport and incidental expenses but also to bear expenses for a second person. If that means a second airplane ticket, the added expense is real.

The somewhat heterodox relations between monks and money constitute so many compromises between a doctrine drawn up in an economically very different context and a modern, monetized economy wherein insulating any group of individuals from monetary exchange must of necessity prove difficult. More interesting, however, for my purposes, are two points. First, to the degree that monks are expected to eschew handling money, they protect themselves from a form of exchange. Exchange is essential to the relations they enter into with laypeople, since laypeople feed them and honor them with their respect, in return for the merit that those laypeople receive in turn. Yet exchange—reflecting investment in the goods or services one can obtain in return for goods or services rendered—is also what attachment is predicated on and so what monks must avoid. The contradictory relations monks have with the whole matter of exchange affects both their productivity and their sexuality: that is, they are obligated to enter into certain types of exchange for their material welfare, but these are highly euphemized. And they must absolutely avoid the exchange of touch—feelings both physical and emotional—that are implicit in sex.

Perhaps the best way to understand the way monks do and do not enter into exchange relations with their lay supporters, relations I have alluded to at several points, is to see how the situation constitutes a process of dematerialization. Laypeople give food, money, and sometimes labor to the monks they support, as well as signs of their obeisance and respect. In return, monks, by receiving those donations, grant lay supporters merit, while also maximizing their own spiritual authority, their *hpoun:* (see chapter 6). Neither karmic merit nor *hpoun:* takes material form. In fact, neither can in any way be seen, handled, or measured. As a return on a layperson's investment, therefore, what members of the sangha give back shifts from a material to an immaterial realm. The exchange is real but at the same time euphemized; it might be thought of as an alternative way in which all that is solid melts into air. What monks produce is both essential to Buddhist understandings of laypeople's and monks' spiritual advancement and very hard to pin down. It seems in this way fitting as a form of bond—attachment—between laypeople who depend on monks for their spiritual well-being and monks who depend for their spiritual well-being, in principle at least, on breaking all bonds, on becoming detached.

Masculinity and Sex

Any discussion of masculinity must address the topic of sex as an area of particular salience. U Dhammananda was both funny and frank about what place sexual desire plays in monks' lives. Speaking generally, U Dhammananda commented, on a few occasions, that what makes being a monk difficult shifts over the course of a man's lifetime. Between about the ages of fifteen to twenty-five or thirty, but especially around the age of eighteen to twenty-five, he said, sex constitutes a real struggle. After that, when a man is in his thirties and forties, sex still represents a problem but, added to it, and perhaps more challenging, is the desire for material goods and prestige. Once a monk turns fifty, as he himself had, however, all he really cares about is enjoying good health.

As I recounted earlier, one evening as U Dhammananda went through this list, U Kumara happened to walk through the room where we were sitting. Smilingly, U Dhammananda told me to ask him—he was about forty at the time—whether sex was still a problem for him. Smilingly, U Kumara said nothing, turned, and continued on his way.

In another conversation we had on the subject, U Dhammananda noted that if you lived with a woman, yes, there was a little bit of pleasure. But only a little. And there was a lot of trouble. (He used the Pali term, *dukkha,* for "suffering," but the Burmese rendering of the word is used frequently in colloquial speech). The Buddha said this, too. You work hard having sex, it's tiring, you sweat a lot. (Here he gestured as though wiping sweat off his forehead). And then you have to go wash (he gestured to his crotch, as if splashing water over it). And there's all the responsibility of taking care of children and supporting a family. It's much easier being alone. And all of this (he pointed to the hall in which we were sitting), you get for free (that is, if you're a monk, you get to live off donations).

Once I asked U Dhammananda whether he found it hard to stay away from women when he was younger. He said once again that from seventeen or eighteen to twenty-five, it was rough. He had a lot of sexual thoughts. But he spent fourteen years memorizing texts, from the age of fourteen to twenty-eight. When he was done, he had lost his looks, and (here he smiled and gestured to his crotch) there was no power left. I asked whether he had been sorry about that. No, it was a good thing. Sexual desire just gives rise to anger, envy, and greed. Memorizing all those texts kept all other thoughts out of mind. In that respect, it's like meditation. But learning texts only keeps you behaving well for a little while; the effect isn't as great as if you meditate. With meditation, you can reduce your desires a lot more.

Why Does Sex Matter So Much?

It may seem obvious that sex generates intense feelings everywhere and so hardly stands in need of further commentary. After all, it implicates so many significant issues in a man's life (as, too, in a woman's, but

Masculinity 221

in somewhat disparate ways), whether at the level of physical sensation, emotional experience, self-representation, kinship ties, relations with peers, and so on, that it has to figure prominently in a man's own thoughts and in others' thoughts about him. Yet it warrants pausing briefly to ask why impressions of a man's "virility," that is, his readiness to engage in sexual activity, matters so much to his own and others' estimation of him, if only because doing so may help us understand why a man's decision to forswear it, in ascetic traditions, carries such powerful messages.

That sexual acts necessarily and inevitably take on immense metaphorical resonance is reflected in the frequency with which men everywhere talk about sex among themselves.[7] Very familiar is the way that males look on their own sexual activity as a measure of their ability to fulfill an ideal role. The American idiom of "scoring" to refer to the number of sexual partners a man has summarizes the attitude perfectly: sex becomes a competition, played out among males, in which women become something ambiguously positioned between supporting players and equipment used in the game. Such discourse, of course, is familiar in all reported corners of the world; Southeast Asia is no exception. Indeed, in the past, at least, the higher a man's social standing, the more likely it was that he was permitted and expected to have a great number of sexual partners. The greater impressions of his potency, furthermore, the more his couplings were expected to generate children. One consequence of such reasoning was that a man who wished to impress others with the magnitude of his potency tried to sire a great many offspring. Nineteenth-century rulers of Thailand and Burma adopted that strategy with evident relish, although some of them actually failed to generate enough progeny to assure a smooth succession to the throne. Thailand's Chakri dynasty shows evidence of both: Mongkut, fourth ruler in the dynasty, had sired eighty-two children by the time of his death in 1868, his son Chulalangkorn after him seventy-seven, but then the latter's son, Vajirarudh (about whose virility doubts are indeed rife), only one daughter.

Clearly, men who draw on the idiom of sex to compete among themselves take sexual activity as a diagnostic for power. They can do so because male orgasm, and sexual intercourse as the locus classicus for its staging, provides a ready metaphor for power's exercise. The act of penetration is easily read as imposing oneself on another, perhaps aggressively, perhaps not, but in any case assertively. Ejaculation expresses a generative power: its consequences for a woman's body (should a man's partner be a fertile female), for a man's position in his community, for the continuation and productivity of his kin group (however formulated), are many and highly consequential.

It is important to recognize, however, that a great deal of the discourse surrounding masculine sexuality is expressed, however obliquely and often contradictorily, in the idiom of attachment and autonomy. Sexual activity can be construed as expressing deep feelings of commitment. Or not. The altogether conventional view of males as seeking momentary sexual pleasure and then pulling away as well as out emphasizes the ambiguity of masculine attitudes toward sex on just these grounds. A psychotherapeutic rendering of the conflicts to which males are given in their relationships with sexual partners turns on the difficulties men have when they worry that their autonomy is at risk. Such, certainly, is the tenor of Nancy Chodorow's famous critique of the Freudian view of women as insufficiently mature: pace Freud, women, according to Chodorow, can bond more effectively with others because they have not had to break the primary attachment they had with their mothers, whereas men, having had to make that traumatizing break, never stop worrying that they will fail to keep themselves distinct, self-possessed, and self-determining—in a word, autonomous (1978).

Discourse that celebrates a man's ability to ejaculate with great frequency, with a great many different partners, and without falling subject to any partner's emotional claims on him, idealizes a man's sexuality when it can be taken as an expression of autonomy, a game of emotional daring he plays and wins with his genitals, while leaving his heart out of it. But why should this view of men's sexuality ever be positive, rather than (as it of course often is) pejorative? And how, if such renderings of a man's sexual athleticism can stand so much to his credit, can the opposite—not conjugal fidelity but rather an ascetic's renunciation of sex—win such widespread admiration in so many religious traditions?

I have suggested that autonomy stands at one end of a spectrum that runs between it and attachment, and that this links it to the end of another spectrum that runs between superordination and subordination. In other words, engaging in sex without becoming personally entangled with someone looks like the behavior, or privilege, of the person who enjoys what might be termed, aptly if perhaps coyly, the upper hand: the agent endowed with greater power and superior standing, with greater freedom to maneuver, and so, autonomy. This brings us back to masculine sexuality as a metaphor for the exercise of power. But sexual intercourse, by presuming the participation of two parties, does not allow for complete autonomy: the introduction of a partner, although a subordinate one, still implicates a measure of dependence. Here is yet another, particularly affecting, instance of interdependence through difference. As per Dumont, one party to this relationship encompasses—both represents and takes precedence over—the other. Yet the superior party remains bound to that relationship, one that many societies try to make sure forms, at least in the instances that matter, part of a long-term pattern of exchange. Even Southeast Asian aristocrats, for however much they felt themselves above the petty constraints of a commoner's morality, had to have at least one officially recognized wife. Their marriage, like marriages elsewhere, bound together not just these two individuals (sexually and socially—emotionally or not was beside the point) but also their kin.[8]

Yet if taking the dominant role in sex grants the active, which is to say, masculine, party superior standing, and so is taken to express his power over his partner,[9] the diminution of autonomy evident in his need for a partner at all, even if only to display his superordinate status (but also, not incidentally, to enjoy sexual pleasure), necessarily compromises impressions of that power.[10] I assume that a great deal of misogyny follows from this fact: males may well be made uneasy at the degree to which they depend on women to attain their own desired ends. The putatively straightforward links between being male, being powerful, and being in a position to act as one pleases turn out to be subject to this unwanted complication, and this fact can generate deep-seated ambivalences. That so many representations of sex look like one party's forceful, or even violent, domination of another, rather than collaboration in pursuit of their respective and mutual pleasure, appears to be an effort to counter the irregularity that interdependence introduces in what many men think should be the proper alignment of masculinity, power, and autonomy. Hierarchical arrangements, in sex as in anything else, grant greater autonomy to one party in any dyad. Yet they still presume interdependence, which means that they deny the possibility of absolute autonomy even to the superior party.

If allowing a man to have many wives and concubines presents one means for countering impressions of his unseemly dependence on women, or any specific woman, renouncing sex resolves that tension still more effectively. I believe this explains why, in the case of a Buddhist monk, sex figures as the most important of the prohibitions on which his status hinges. Of all the 227 rules of the *vinaya* code regulating a monk's behavior, the rule that everyone, whether lay or religious, most emphasized in conversation with me was the prohibition on sexual activity of any sort. (The prohibition on murder applies just as forcefully, but it does not come in for mention in the way that the prohibition on sex does.) A novice must never, even when completely alone, remove all of his clothes at the same time.[11] I take it this reflects a view that adolescent males are particularly untrustworthy when it comes to resisting sexual impulses. U Dhammananda explained that a novice is still new to the rules constraining his behavior. A monk is assumed to have assimilated the rules more thoroughly and may, therefore, remove all of his clothes to bathe if he is assuredly alone. If a monk engages in any sexual activity, however, its discovery means that he is expelled immediately from the sangha and has no chance of taking on the robe again in his lifetime.[12]

Unlike in South Asia, where there is an elaborate sense of how much a man's loss of semen through ejaculation diminishes his powers (Alter 1992),[13] such concerns do not seem to be prevalent among Burmans. We must look elsewhere, therefore, for an explanation as to why Buddhists in Burma look on sexual activity as so completely incompatible with a monk's spiritual condition and prestige.[14] Buddhism is not, for that matter, the only religious tradition that urges celibacy on its adherents who are seeking exceptional status. Why should this be the case?

Why Not Fall Back on Oneself for Pleasure and Sustenance?

I suggest that sex figures so prominently in constructing, by prohibition, a monk's status because its pursuit would imply, as per my discussion above, that he must rely on someone else for his own satisfaction—in other words, that it would contradict the personal autonomy that is the foundation on which his prestige is based. If I am right, then two questions arise. First, masturbation would appear to allow for his sexual pleasure in the absence of any compromise to his autonomy. Why should it nevertheless be forbidden, as it were, out of hand? Second, if autonomy was what really mattered, then it should apply to all areas of a monk's life, and instead of enjoining monks to collect alms from laypeople, Buddhist doctrine could be expected to encourage monks to grow and cook their own food, as monks in the Christian tradition do.

Masturbation is very hard to talk about pretty much anywhere. Oddly, it seems to be harder to talk about seriously than other forms of sexual activity.[15] I assume the topic's discursive volatility, which the great avoidance of discussing it attests to, stems from the implication, as in incest, that one could withdraw completely from exchange, that the most powerful incentive groups have at their disposal for binding people together, sexual desire, could simply lose its effectiveness. Functionalist reasoning (which I do not think anthropologists any more than other social scientists are really ready to forswear) inclines me to think that people are aware at some level of this implication, and work hard to keep it from conscious recognition, their own or anyone else's.

Nevertheless, I knew a very few Burman men, lay and religious, well enough that I could broach the subject with them. Their response to my question of why monks must avoid masturbation as much as they avoided any other kind of sexual activity was, effectively, that it was a slippery slope: enjoying the pleasure of solitary sex could only lead a monk to look for still greater pleasure in sex with another person. In other words, it would lead him inevitably to feel and act on his desires and, as a consequence, make him prey to a need for others.

At the same time, renouncing sex represents a particularly stunning demonstration of an individual's power because it represents a particularly dramatic triumph of discipline over desire. Only such discipline assures an individual true autonomy. So to the extent that autonomy constitutes the solution to the dilemma of attachment, and autonomy enjoys a privileged place in hierarchical views of the world, giving up sex has to arouse maximal respect.

A man who shows himself capable of great virility by bedding a great many people, and who does so without entering into relationships that would bind him to those people, demonstrates one version of masculine power. He plays on the metaphorical capacity of male sexuality to promote impressions of his power over others. A man who shows himself capable of great self-possession by bedding no one, and who therefore can hold himself especially and demonstrably aloof from bonding deeply with others, demonstrates a still greater version of masculine power. Most impressive of all is a man who can resist his sexual urges so completely as to avoid even the solitary release of sexual pressure. In that case, he plays on the metaphorical effectiveness of resistance to male sexual desire's supposedly implacable force to represent his power even over himself. Among Burman Buddhists, at least, this ascetic display trumps in both prestige and persuasiveness any exuberant display of sexual potency a man might make.

But if a male does not engage in sexual behavior of any kind, mightn't it suggest that, rather than being a paragon, he might be in some way deficient, something less than a man? The question nagged sufficiently at ancient Buddhist commentators, we learn from John Powers' book, *A Bull of a Man,* that they felt obliged to make much of the Gautama Buddha's virility (2009). The impressive size of his penis received much emphasis, although, in light of South Asia's long-standing prudishness, it took fairly elaborate machinations to explain how that fact became known. For that matter, Gautama Buddha was married and had a son before he reached enlightenment. These facts help stave off questions about his sexual capacity.

If monks' prestige follows from their ability to avoid entangling themselves with others because of sexual desire, they are nevertheless *required* to rely on laypeople to satisfy their need for food. At least, they are required to do so if they are going to eat. Here the point at issue seems to be the investment of time and attention: if a monk grew food and/or cooked his own food, I was told, he would be devoting himself too much to this undertaking, rather than fixing his attention on spiritual matters, which is what, people agreed, his true responsibility must be. He would also, of course, deprive laypeople of what has long been taken to be their most important means for increasing their store of merit.

Sex must be completely avoided, then, because it too easily leads to wanting to enter into entangling and emotionally charged social relations. Eating cannot be completely avoided if a monk is going to remain alive, so monks should assure themselves a supply of food, but in such a way that involves them with laypeople, and with their own gustatory pleasure, as little as possible. Relations with lay donors of cooked food should be minimal; in the collection of alms that is the doctrinally favored manner for a monk to obtain his daily nutrition, as mentioned in chapter 3, food is offered and received in silence, usually outside the donors' homes, and (in principle) without attending to what ends up mixed with what. So the giving and receiving of alms between laypeople and monks represents another instance of mutual interdependence through difference, but in a highly depersonalized manner. It is as though individuals enact the relationship, but that relationship binds not specific people but rather two *types* of individuals, lay and religious, together. Of course, in actual practice monks obtain a good bit of their food in pleasanter circumstances, served a meal at the monastery or in laypeople's homes. But the ideal is clear and communicates the impression that eating is a concession to physical necessity, a physical obligation that should sit lightly on a monk and his daily routine, compromising impressions of his autonomy as little as possible.

The ideological pull toward autonomy appears even more clearly in the invariable mention made, when describing powerful monks meditating in the forest, of how little they ate, and/or how they ate only food that they could find on their own, such as fruit and nuts growing wild in the forest. Personal autonomy in this image approaches asymptotically a logical end point: zero exchange between the monk and the world. Eating almost nothing and ignoring everything about their surroundings, including the terrifying beasts that confront them, they show themselves to be without connection to the world, completely on their own. Breath becomes the only point of interaction between them and their environment.

Autonomy and the Right to Respect

Bourdieu describes in *Distinction* the highly interested misunderstanding that aesthetic preferences lend themselves to (1984). Individuals who display, as if by some natural or innate affinity, the "best" taste are easily if unthinkingly looked on as having not only a special discernment in the realm of aesthetics, but also a more generalized charisma, suggesting that they have a natural or innate right to rule. Bourdieu sees in this stealthy and little noticed slide from aesthetics to power, from the rules of art to the arts of rule, an unacknowledged (and therefore effective, unchallenged because unremarked on) consequence of material wealth. People who have grown up in unquestioned material security live surrounded by evidence of the most prestigious, "disinterested" approach to art. They can do so because disinterestedness is a class privilege, a reflection of the "freedom from necessity" that the wealthiest members of a society enjoy.

Bourdieu's analysis of aesthetic distinction suggests a model for analyzing monks' moral distinction. Their self-control, their ability to deny the intensely felt pressures of their own physical wants, suggests "freedom from desire," which is to say, a "natural" affinity with autonomy. To say that this might appear to give them the "right to rule" would be inappropriate, since ruling is precisely what monks, like other spiritual leaders in South Asia's tradition of diarchy, eschew.[16] It gives them instead the "right to respect," as well as the right to live off the material support of the laity. Whereas in Bourdieu's account, a spectrum calibrating degrees of aesthetic discernment links up with a spectrum calibrating degrees of fitness to rule, in Burmese Buddhism, the end of a spectrum calibrating degrees of autonomy links up with the end of a spectrum calibrating degrees of prestige.

To be in a position to exert one's authority over others has appealed to Burman males for a very long time, as the society's tumultuous history amply demonstrates. In this respect, Burma looks no different from a great many other places. Yet for many people, the impressiveness of power over others pales in comparison with power over the self, inasmuch as this implies that one might thereby escape all consequences of action, whether one's own or others'. It suggests, in the promise of such complete mastery, absolute invulnerability, and so a distinctive understanding of what it might mean to be "free."

I suggested at the beginning of this chapter that Connell's influential writing about "hegemonic masculinity" risks making us assume that, in any given society, a specific definition of masculinity will hold unquestioned dominance, and that other forms of masculinity, although recognized, will be disparaged relative to that most prized one. What I have reported about Burman notions of an idealized masculinity falls, ironically, on both sides of Connell's hegemonic masculinity. In the dual images of an active, assertive, sexually athletic and productive male, on the one hand, and a remote and sexually ascetic monk, on the other, we find two apparently radically different representations of idealized masculinity. To the extent that the ascetic option enjoys greater honor, it might be deemed the "hegemonic" view. Indeed, Dumont points out that hierarchical arrangements always imply a calibration in prestige, and that ordering certainly obtains here. Yet failing to sign on to the ascetic version of masculinity hardly discredits a lay male in any real way. Someone who does not manage to become a monk in this life can hope to do so in a future one. Little opprobrium, for that matter, falls on a man who has been a monk but chooses to disrobe. Burman Buddhists seem capable of entertaining very different ideas about how males can fulfill either of two idealized roles, according one greater honor but without evincing real prejudice against either one.

At the same time, what links these two different roles is that in each case, masculinity is defined by the exercise of power: over others, in the case of a lay male; over oneself in the case of a religious one. One might, therefore, say that exercising power is the hegemonic form that masculinity takes in Burman thinking. That, however, seems generalized to such a degree as to be not terribly helpful. It distracts us furthermore from the point that autonomy, as a condition in which ultimately all interaction falls away, constitutes an ideal in which even the exercise of power becomes irrelevant.

I have said that Burmans conceive of all social relations as hierarchical in nature, and that the (idealized) logic of hierarchy is understood to bind all participants together in mutual interdependence through difference. Neither a lay man nor a monk escapes that logic. Both occupy superordinate rather than subordinate positions vis-à-vis many other individuals, but they remain bound to those others. Only in the extreme case of a monk meditating alone in the forest (or still more extreme, a *wei'za* meditating for centuries in some other realm) do we find the image of an individual male able to transcend the principles of hierarchy. Inasmuch as these figures arouse the greatest respect among so many Burman Buddhists, we must conclude that autonomy constitutes an unrealizable but incontestable goal to which all males should strive, that it enjoys hegemonic authority.

Idealized Masculinities and Idealizing Subalterns

As noted above, Connell does not rule out, in fact she makes much of, the possibility of competing versions of masculinity obtaining in a particular place. She is scrupulous about insisting that no hegemony is ever perfectly effective, that any given "norm" will coexist with alternative and oppositional views. Such emphasis on Connell's part, however, is highly orthodox at this point. To see, following Gramsci, that ideology has real effects over people's thinking, even over people it disadvantages, is a somewhat grudging concession social scientists make to the evident fact that the people we want to idealize, the unjustly oppressed, often fail to fight against their oppression. To see that they do actually resist, only in ways subtler and more ingenious than we (and their oppressors) may at first grasp, such as in the "hidden transcripts" that Scott posits (1990), saves them from ignominy. That is, it enables us to sustain our idealizing treatment of them, and in that way avoid questioning our own assumptions about the appropriate and obvious, which is to say, honorable, response to disparities in the distribution of power in the world, which is to fight it.

Bourdieu and Dumont between them help us understand the nature of what we are doing when we make this move. Comfortable in our own freedom from necessity as well as our egalitarian commitments, we fantasize what it would be like to remain the same in our take on the world but in circumstances wherein such a perspective was impossible for us to maintain—or could be maintained only under duress, giving rise to heroic acts on the part of the dispossessed. Once when I was a child I remarked that I wished I were a duck, so that I could fly, swim, or walk on the ground, as I chose. An adult pointed out to me (a little unkindly, I felt) that no, what I wished was that I could be myself, but in the body of a duck: not the same thing. As progressive social scientists, we sometimes appear to wish that we could be ourselves in the bodies of the people with whom we sympathize, those who fight, or in any case, who we think should be fighting, the good fight against oppression. In identifying with the people we show a concern for, we too easily confuse fantasies of ourselves as subalterns with the subalterns we wish to idealize. Just as a Hollywood (or Bollywood) film enjoins us to do, we identify with the oppressed and take vicarious pleasure in fantasies wherein they fight back and win against their oppressors.[17] But idealizing people does them a disservice:[18] it establishes yet another standard by which they can be judged.

In Connell's writing—and in this respect Connell writes particularly lucidly along lines that many writers on masculinity pursue—there is an underlying suggestion that engaging in gender studies, particularly when focusing on masculinity, rightly implies that one is joining the fight against men's unjust hold on power, particularly when exercised by those possessed of whatever version of masculinity is "hegemonic." The ironic consequence of this worthy effort to eliminate discrimination against people of all gender presentations and/or sexual preferences is that it sets up a different but still real standard by which people, in this case scholars, can be judged. That is, people in possession of power in any form, and the privileges enjoyed by academics certainly qualify as one form power can take, must take on a responsibility to fight the unequal distribution of power from which they benefit. It is a responsibility they must not shirk.

Egalitarian ideology actually combines here with admiration for power and its exercise to set up criteria against which people can be measured. Gender performance falls away as the tool with which to judge people, and rightly so. Yet that does not obviate the more fundamental power move, which is to demand a certain type of performance (or at least, expressions of assent to the validity of the project), especially, of course, from males. No doubt Connell would say that such a demand is justified because males are the ones in possession of the power that both oppresses others (males who fail to measure up, as well as women) and with which their privilege could be effectively reduced. Yet a call to action, inasmuch as it valorizes activity (agency) and disvalues its opposite (passivity? collusion? any contrasting term carries with it a negative valence) sustains a masculinist perspective. It is masculinist because it praises action, struggle, resistance, speaking truth to power: all of the conventional labels people deeply invested in egalitarian ideology use to express what is good and righteous, but which celebrate, however covertly, the use of power to fight power.

I risk being accused of mounting a conservative critique, of failing to see that justice and morality oblige us to deconstruct masculine privilege if we are going to make the world a better place for all the people who cannot pass the test of masculinity, at least not in its hegemonic form. It is clearly true that a critique of activist calls for action could be used to phrase an attack on action in pursuit of justice. Such an attack is not my purpose at all. I applaud the many efforts on the part of feminists, gay rights activists, and other people committed to egalitarian ideals in politics and social movements everywhere. Nonetheless, we must see that admirable agendas may very well contain unrecognized affinities with the very assumptions or agendas they contest. Such, I believe, is the tenor of Bourdieu's comments on the risks inherent in the strategies of gay rights activists who chose to essentialize the categories of sexuality rather than contest the very existence of a field wherein such categories are set out (Bourdieu 2001, 118–124).

There is a curious antinomy at work here. As I discuss in chapter 9, Chie Ikeya points out that women in Southeast Asia have long enjoyed considerable room to maneuver as economic actors, leading Western observers to believe that they possessed real power. These Westerners did so without realizing that in the view of Southeast Asian Buddhists, such activity was spiritually polluting. Outsiders might suffer a similar block in their vision when observing how much more easily women are permitted, indeed encouraged, to form strong attachments with others, leading observers to think that they enjoy emotional benefits denied males, but without realizing that such attachments, as the opposite of autonomy, are looked upon by Southeast Asian Buddhists as a kind of weakness.

Yet if we celebrate academics who fight against gender discrimination and criticize those among our own ranks who remain invested in conventional ideas about the distribution of gender roles, then we join in the masculinist celebration of action, and the condemnation of whatever we might label its opposite. In deconstructing "hegemonic" masculinity, and praising those people who seek to undermine it by setting themselves up against it, as per Connell, we must watch out for falling into familiar and unfortunate habits of judging people for the degree of their conformity to a different standard—calibrated in this case according to the degree of their commitment to equality—that we have set them. This risk is one Dumont tried to warn us against but one that it is very difficult for us to assimilate. Yet failing to note that not everyone shares our egalitarian commitments, or interprets them as we do, will make it difficult for us to communicate effectively with scholars, or anyone else, from regions such as Southeast Asia who do not look upon gender and sexuality in the same way we do. We will then once again consider ourselves to be enlightened—and other people benighted.[19]

I make these remarks not to condemn efforts to promote justice for people whose inclinations are non- or counterhegemonic or nonnormative, whether with respect to gender or any other trait or activity. I wish only to point out that we must be wary of complacency about our own *partis pris,* a point that any regard for tolerance should make us take seriously and that we should be ready to take seriously, especially with respect to ourselves.

Chapter Nine

MASCULINITY'S OTHERS
Women, Nuns, and Trans Women

Gender, as mentioned in my discussion of Dumont in chapter 4, provides an obvious instance of difference pressed into use to bind people to each other in hierarchical relationships over the long term. In my account of masculinity up to this point, I have focused on two ways that some men's superior position vis-à-vis others can be justified. For lay males, superordinate status is achieved by reference to their productive and generative capacities. This is taken to imply their right to rule over others, that is, to justify their superordinate position in the long-term relationships they enter into with women and, for that matter, with males who are their subordinates. For monks, the difference that really matters, ideologically, is not gender difference at all but rather that between lay status and religious, since this is the basis on which relations of exchange are elaborated between the sangha and its supporters. Ostensibly, in the case of monks, male versus female does not matter as much as does lay versus religious as the difference on which mutual interdependence can be formulated.

Still, the status of monk is available only to males, and laywomen actually show themselves much readier than most lay males to support the sangha. Gender difference, in other words, brings an ideologically less emphasized but still obvious and, in practice, highly consequential, difference into play. Furthermore, since monks are, to put the paradox pointedly, especially invested in having no investments, which translates in practice into their concern to maintain their autonomy rather than affirming their attachments and bonds, the interdependence of sangha and laypeople is in many respects depersonalized, minimized, and/or at least euphemized.

Whether in the case of lay man or monk, idealized masculinity grants males prima facie superior standing vis-à-vis those who do not enjoy that privilege. What about individuals who do not qualify for superior standing? That deficiency applies, first of all, to women, both lay and religious. But it also applies to males who fail to measure up: to those who fulfill neither the lay nor the religious ideal of masculine roles. This question brings us to the nonnormatively gendered, both male and female, and the positions they enjoy, or suffer, in Burman society.

In this chapter, I draw on two different kinds of material to illustrate connections among Burman understandings of sex and gender, on the one hand, and my overarching concern, which is how hierarchical thinking inflects all areas of social life in Burma, on the other.[1] I treat first of women, and nuns, and then of trans women, looking on all of them through the lens of what it means to be either males manqués or what might be called "candidate males": individuals who are women or trans women in this existence, although not necessarily believed to have been so in previous or destined to be so in future ones. I describe the ways assumptions about women's inclinations, capacities, and roles conform to hierarchical understandings. These assumptions retain their resiliency even though they may well contradict observable experience. I then discuss the ambiguous place of nuns in Burma today as following from these same notions about how women compare to, and are thought in many respects to fall short of, but should indeed remain different from, men.

The Status of Women in Question

Chie Ikeya and Tharaphi Than have both written sustained studies in recent years of women's circumstances in Burma, and both challenge the oft-repeated claim that women have "traditionally" enjoyed high status in Burma (Ikeya 2005, 2011; Tharaphi Than 2104).[2] Both authors take a very dim view of this claim about women in Southeast Asia. Ikeya notes that people in both Burma and India used the supposed "high status" of women to a variety of different purposes during the British imperium. She suggests that claims for such high status were based not on actual circumstances but rather on specific political agendas. Tharaphi Than bewails the inclination of elite Burmese women to write in the same vein, presenting an idealized rather than a realistic account of women's usually subordinate, and often truly oppressed, condition.[3]

The evidence that Ikeya and Tharaphi Than muster to demonstrate how much Burmese women suffer under long-standing prejudices concerning women's capacities, their proper roles, and their appropriate relations with masculine authority is both impressive and incontestable. I do not wish to argue against the positions they take. I wish simply to show that we can better understand the basis for such prejudices if we ask why they make sense to so many men and even a fair number of women in Burma.

That Western observers might refer to what they have often perceived as Burman women's "equality," or near-equality, with men indicates Westerners' lack of insight into how Burmese thought, and continue to think, about gender. But neither Ikeya, who occasionally uses the word "equality" somewhat casually, nor Tharaphi Than seems to see that the point at issue is not really whether women enjoy equality with men—they certainly do not—but rather whether they might still enjoy a degree of autonomy in specific spheres that their sisters in other regions of Asia, and the West, for that matter, do not. I would note that "equality" and "subordination" may be mutually exclusive (although peers can be equal while still subordinated to others), but "autonomy" and "subordination" can coexist easily. It is a matter of degree and of contexts. Women in Burma may well enjoy autonomy in certain contexts, provided they understand that that autonomy is context-specific, precisely, and not to be taken to undermine encompassing hierarchical arrangements. I do not intend to justify, let alone support, such views insofar as they serve to deny women opportunities available to men. They do, however, need to be appreciated, if only in order better to counter them in the name of improving women's life chances in contemporary Burmese society.

Equality between the sexes has no place in any hierarchical conceptions. As I have sought to demonstrate, Burmese conceive of social relations in hierarchical terms, and I assume that this was as true in early twentieth-century Burma as now. People in India also thought in these terms, and so did Christian missionaries in Burma. The implications of women's subordinate status in Burma, however, differed from those that obtained in India, and those that Christian missionaries thought, at least, should obtain everywhere. In Burma, women were allowed a freedom of movement and of action, and a degree of legal privilege, that were not characteristic of many societies in India, or of many societies, until recently, in the West. This autonomy should not be confused with equality. But it explains why so many foreign observers were impressed with how women in Burma (and elsewhere in Southeast Asia) fared compared with women in other societies in which their autonomy was subject to greater restriction.

The nationalist movement in Burma illustrates the point. Ikeya provides a careful account of the ways women entered into nationalist agitation in the early twentieth century (2011), and Tharaphi Than recounts the experiences of women who joined the armed forces during World War II (2014). As seems characteristic of many such nationalist movements, Burmese women actively pursued a role in the fight for Burma's independence—but a supporting one. They contested British colonial rule, but they did not contest their position as subordinate partners to men. Many men encouraged them to become educated and active, but there seems little evidence that either these men or the women themselves sought to win women "equality" with men. This fact arouses Tharaphi Than's ire, particularly, as she decries "the tragedy of Burmese women denied a place in history" (2014, 108).

Both Ikeya and Tharaphi Than also dwell on how fears of miscegenation—but only if practiced by Burmese women, not men—haunted popular thinking and featured so prominently in nationalist agitation. Yet hierarchical conceptions of social relations, once again, are predicated on the idea that everyone is in it for the long term. If subordinates start opting out, not in sudden bursts of egalitarian expectation or assertion but rather in strategic decisions about to whom they think it best to subordinate themselves, they can only arouse consternation among the superiors who counted on them and expected to be counted on, and obeyed, in turn. Thus when Burmese Buddhist men railed against Burmese women marrying Indian/Muslim men (Ikeya 2005; Tharaphi Than 2014, 123–130), the vehemence of their condemnations of the women, and the anxiety the whole issue generated, followed from the fear that "their" subordinates would break out of the relationships within which they were properly contained.[4] What Buddhist men's fears of Buddhist women marrying Muslim men reflects is a concern—it has frighteningly paranoid as well as ethnonationalist features—on the part of men that "their" subordinates will find alternative superordinates with whom to cast their lot.

Neither nationalist feeling nor fears of miscegenation in Burma, I repeat, had to do with "equality." Rather both implicated the distribution of power and of relative standing. "The figure of the intermarrying and miscegenating Burmese female who racially and culturally degraded her people by getting into bed (literally) with the 'minions' of the British colonizers served to edify a singular conceptualization of the Burmese nation-state" (Ikeya 2005, 75).

I suspect that what Burmese women did when they got into bed with Indian males was to suggest that such males were of similar or even superior standing relative to Burmese males, an unforgivable affront to Burmese males' sense of their precedence over Indians. That considerations of relative prestige were at issue, and not the national versus the colonial and foreign, is supported by another point Ikeya makes: that "the Burmese public regarded relations with European men as means of accessing power, status, and socio-economic advancement and tended to find a Euro-Burmese union far less objectionable than an Indo-Burmese one" (2005, 67, fn. 14).[5]

I am not ready, therefore, despite the objections raised by Ikeya, Tharaphi Than, and others to too-optimistic estimations of women's circumstances in Southeast Asia, to renounce all claims that women in Burma have often enjoyed quite remarkable autonomy, and I am willing to say this autonomy has granted them a kind of "high status." Women were (and for the most part remain) subordinates who are obliged to know their place. But within the system, they still have specific privileges, as do all parties to hierarchical relationships, and those privileges include—at specific times, within specific limits—freedom of movement, and access to money, knowledge, and prestige, that many women in other parts of the world cannot legitimately lay claim to and would probably envy.

Women's Nature, Pro and Con

Women's relatively better fate in Southeast Asia certainly does not spare them being made subject to disparaging comment, whether in Burma or elsewhere. After I published an account of Javanese discourse surrounding gender, whereby men considered themselves (and some women shared this view) reasonable and self-controlled, and so able to control their emotions and their impulses better than women (Keeler 1990), Suzanne Brenner pointed out in an illuminating rejoinder (1995) that the representation I provided presented only half the story, that Javanese women had a counter-discourse (and many men shared this view), wherein men were described as little able to control their sensuous appetites, and were therefore incompetent and unreliable. Brenner was quite right in pointing out the partial nature of my account. Both takes on the differences between men and women coexisted in Javanese discourse, and I erred in failing to take the second of the two into consideration.

Interestingly, much the same set of contradictory views of men and women are prevalent in Mandalay. There, much as in Java, contrary representations of men's and women's inherent nature, representations that would appear to be mutually exclusive, nevertheless enjoy great currency, and may well be repeated by the same individual, apparently unmindful of the obvious incompatibility of their views. Chie Ikeya provides a succinct summary of these contrary views of women:

> It has to be said that although the female sex, more than the male counterpart, is associated with attachment to desire within Theravada Buddhism, qualities such as chastity, self-sacrifice, and suffering, epitomized by the devoted female followers of the Buddha, donors, and renunciants who figure in Buddhist literature, are at the same time identified as feminine virtues. (2011, 195–196, fn. 28)

The question arises how such glaring contradictions can be sustained. What logic makes the tolerance for such irreconcilable views possible?[6] I suggest that two sets of generalizing, indeed stereotyping, representations of both men and women can coexist easily because each set corresponds to inferences people make not so much on the basis of experience as on the basis of ideological assumptions.[7] In one view, males are able to control their impulses, to act judiciously, and to take charge of things because males are better able to remain uninvested in the world, and they are better able to establish and safeguard their autonomy as a result. That autonomy both explains and demonstrates their power. That is, autonomy—to take on a fashionable idiom that in this case seems useful rather than merely fashionable—is performative: it is taken to reveal what only its *enactment* establishes, or at least implies, namely, a man's control over himself, and his sole control over himself. As much as a Burman man can manage, he shows himself to be subject to no one other than himself. (This point does not preclude his choosing to subject himself to specific others when he is obliged or it suits his purposes to do so.)

By the same token, females, in this view, are too invested in their relationships, especially with their children and other kin, but also in material comfort and other immediate pleasures, to be able to act in the world with an appropriate and laudable reserve: their attachments prevent them, in most cases (it is said), from maintaining the autonomy that would both enable and demonstrate their control. People are always ready to concede that some women turn out to be exceptions to the rule, that some women show a considerable capacity to restrain their impulses. Still, to abjure their ties to their close kin is usually thought highly unlikely for women and, as Kawanami makes clear especially in the case of nuns (see below), somewhat suspect.

This flexibility in perspectives on women, that they are "mostly" one way but "often" not, especially that they are capable of self-restraint with respect to things and actions but less so with respect to personal relationships, actually enables both men and women to maintain pejorative stereotypes of women all the more easily. But then, to say that women are more concerned with their attachments—more caring toward their children and their other kin, especially their parents—is pejorative only in the strictest Buddhist reading. The negative judgment that follows from women's "inability" to break their attachments is countered by the sense that women's caring for others is also valuable, and that women who do not devote themselves to the people that matter to them are behaving in ways that are surprising and a bit odd, or even morally questionable.[8]

The welter of ideas, to some degree inconsistent and at times simply contradictory, about the differences between men and women admits of greater clarity when we note that, overall, autonomy is gendered masculine and attachment is gendered feminine in Burma.[9] And autonomy enjoys greater value than attachment, at least in the abstract, while at the same time attachment is understood to be important for people's well-being and happiness. Women are not considered fundamentally incapable of, or uninterested in, autonomy, any more than men are considered incapable of, or undesiring of, attachments. Exceptions are always allowed in specific instances. Yet the assumption remains that men incline toward, and are praised for, breaking attachments in favor of their autonomy, whereas women are inclined toward, and are for the most part held to, fostering their attachments, to the diminution of their autonomy.

Two kinds of discourse reveal assumptions about women, their abilities and their weaknesses, in telling ways. One concerns sexual impulses and impulsivity: a sense that women are given over to their sexual desires in ways men are not. The other concerns their relations with Buddhism, and especially public attitudes toward nuns, who are treated with ambivalence by some Burmans and outright disdain by others. Neither discourse, whether about sex or religion, is internally consistent. Nor is either applied dogmatically to every actual woman or nun. Individual women, and individual nuns, may be exempted completely from pejorative generalizations about "most" members of their sex. Yet unsurprisingly, if unfortunately, in each case discourse tends not to work in women's favor, no matter what role women take on.

Women's Sexuality

With reference to sexuality, I venture beyond explicit comments made by people I spoke with in Mandalay and suggest what looks to me like the logic that informs various understandings they have concerning gender, sex, and relative standing. In doing so, I commit what some people now condemn as analytic hubris. I find such assertions, or accusations, about outsiders' analyses unconvincing because I am ready to believe that Burmans, like everyone else, can well be unaware of ideas that motivate what they do and say, much as speakers of a language can be unaware of the patterns that inform the ways they speak. I am also ready to believe that I, as an outsider, may have insights that many people in situ do not share, whether because I ask questions to which their attention is not drawn, or because I apply analytic techniques that to them are foreign. I am not claiming intellectual superiority on my part but rather intellectual and cultural difference, difference that entails both informational deficits on my part and, for addressing questions of interest to social scientists, analytic advantages that follow from contrasting perspectives.

The gendering of the distinction between autonomy and attachment helps account for a claim, widespread in Southeast Asia (and elsewhere), to the effect that women are given over to their own sexual impulses to a degree that men are not. Mere empirical evidence, of which I am quite certain an immense preponderance would indicate that the reverse is true, that men are more likely to find it difficult to control their sexual desires, fails to undermine the complacency with which many men (and even some women) make this assertion. As per Stephen Colbert's brilliant concept of "truthiness," the assertion is patently false but it *ought* to be true, since it accords so well with so much else of what people think. Therefore, to many, it is, and it stands in need of no experiential data for confirmation.

Sexuality gives rise to such contradictory impressions because it can be construed in such various and inconsistent ways. As mentioned in the preceding chapter, sexual intercourse can be thought of as a man's assertion of power over the person he penetrates (presumed to be female although, as material I will report below on trans women shows, not necessarily so biologically). It need not be construed as indicating any further engagement with, that is, investment in, the person or the relationship that joins them. Public standards of morality, whether phrased in Buddhist or other terms, exhort men to treat the people with whom they have sex as partners in long-term relationships, in accordance with hierarchical understandings. Yet there is nothing about sexual acts that necessarily imposes such attitudes, or necessarily entails their linkage to anything beyond momentary encounter.

To continue to review points made in the preceding chapter, the equivocation on exercising power over oneself and exercising power over others enables people to represent men's sexuality as an expression of autonomy both when a man gives it up, as monks do, and when he gives himself over to it, as men who claim great sexual potency do. What matters, given the positive valence accorded to autonomy, at least when demonstrated by males, is that he not become entangled. In this way, he remains superordinate in a relationship, whether it is with a sexual partner (which means he must be in charge and little invested) or with himself (in which case he must be so in charge of himself as to deny his own desires).

No matter what principles should inform men's behavior, people in Mandalay know perfectly well (and here I attend to the counterdiscourse that I failed to note in the Javanese case) that it is men who are sexually promiscuous, men who gamble, men who get into fights, men who respond impulsively and unreasonably to many events. In sum, that men tend to have greater difficulty controlling themselves. Yet these facts fit another, different, and yet still positive representation of men: as powerful and assertive, as individuals ready to impress themselves on the world, to possess and act on their power. Women's relatively weaker sexual desire, which was alluded to in conversation with me by many men and women, could then be, if not held against them, at least used as an argument with which to diminish the significance of any self-control they evince. After all, if you don't feel tempted by something, how impressive is it that you have no trouble resisting it?

Yet this discourse exists alongside one of an opposite tenor, to the effect that women cannot resist the force of their own sexuality. I believe this rhetoric follows from the fact that women are subordinates relative to men. Subordinates must enter into relations with others, relations that often mix material and emotional elements without distinction, in order to sustain themselves. They must, therefore, be open to others, just as women's bodies are open to others. This accounts for both their vulnerability and their productiveness, as well as men's pleasure. They must be ready to bond, even to cling, as they invest in others: in sum, to attach. Sexual union looks like physical attachment, and one of particular intensity, so it *stands to reason* that women would be particularly ready for it, drawn to it, enthusiastic about it. They are, in a word, open to it. That they tend not to be so preoccupied with it as men are does not suffice to counter the persuasiveness, the "truthiness," of the proposition.

Since women cannot in most instances, and in the thinking of many should not, try to take superordinate roles vis-à-vis men, then they are free neither to treat sexual relations casually nor, at least until later in their lives, to give them up. It is an easy step further to believe not only that they are not in a position to exempt themselves from the exchanges, including sex, that characterize all of their relations with others in the world, but also that women are ill-equipped to do so, and indeed, moving still further along the same line of argument, that they are unwilling or unable to do so, that they cannot control the inordinate expression of what is, after all, their fundamental way of being in the world, which we might label "exchange" or, more suggestively, "intercourse." Despite what may happen in day-to-day life, the logic of these assumptions triumphs over mere data, and women are said, generally speaking, to be sexually irrepressible. So women are damned if they do and damned even though they do not, because the logic of the system would have it they do and therefore they must. QED.

Women and Buddhism

But not all women. Women have means to gainsay negative assumptions about their inclinations, and Burmans are usually ready to see individual women as exceptions to the rule. As in many parts of the world, one way for Burman women to counter negative assumptions and win respect is to engage in religious activity. In the vast majority of cases, this means supporting the sangha, whether by giving daily food offerings to monks and novices as they pass outside their homes in the morning or by going to monasteries and performing whatever sort of helpful service they can. Women are considered monks' obvious source of support. Interactions among monks and women are presumed to be appropriately asexual, hierarchically ordered, and therefore beyond question.

Randall Collins has written, in a collection of essays inspired by Bourdieu's *Distinction,* that women in the United States take responsibility for a family's cultural capital, while their husbands take responsibility for their economic capital (1992). A fair bit of male contempt is expressed, especially among working-class males in the United States, for women's concern with "appearances" and their off-putting preoccupation with cleanliness and propriety. These latter concerns are particularly evident, Collins notes, among working-class housewives, who can demonstrate or seek to augment their cultural capital only within the limits of their own households. Upper-class women can undertake the same project of augmenting the family's cultural capital outside the home, rather than in it. They can leave housework to people they hire, while pursuing cultural capital through charitable and socially sanctioned activity (e.g., by participating in arts organizations). But the nature of the endeavor, whether on the part of working-class or upper-class women, is fundamentally similar: to gain not wealth and clout but rather prominence and respect. If Buddhist women use wealth brought into the household by their husbands' productive activities to support the sangha, they are making a clear conversion, as Bourdieu would put it, of economic into cultural capital.

When men in Mandalay say that they cannot engage in religious good works or meditate because they have to bring in money for the family, they may not be representing what actually happens with any accuracy. But they are representing how they and others think things should happen. Many women, who may spend a great deal of energy and time engaging in moneymaking activities, nevertheless try hard to engage in activity in support of the sangha, and they may undertake meditation retreats. These activities are what they themselves as well as others consider worthy of notice, because in these activities they fulfill positive expectations, ones that win them prestige and respect.

Such prestige redounds to the credit of their families, and it may have certain economic benefits in the long run. A "good reputation" never hurts in the business world. Yet it would be inappropriately cynical to see commercial ends as the real motivation for women's religious activities. Instead, they are engaging in behavior that increases their own and their family's prestige, and they are doing so in a way that accords with hierarchical expectations that they will subordinate themselves to individuals, the members of the sangha, whose sanctity outstrips their own yet at the same time requires their service for its maintenance.

Where Burman ideas diverge from those Collins discerns in the United States stems from the fact that males in Burma are believed to be endowed with greater ability to gain wealth, status, and power than women, that their advantage as males always trumps women's capacities. Yet men must make a choice. Men who choose a religious path are opting for prestige rather than wealth or power, or are believed to be doing so by most Burmans. An outsider may see a good deal of power-seeking maneuvering taking place among Burman monks, and/or efforts to maximize their wealth. Burmans seem for the most part to find this an ever-present possibility, but still exceptional. As a result, the close connection between laywomen and monks constitutes a collaboration wherein maximizing not only merit but also prestige, the cultural capital that deep involvement in Buddhist matters wins women, matters importantly.

The hierarchical differentiation between women and monks depends on the propensity of women to form attachments (as they do when they subordinate themselves to monks), and of monks to forgo them in favor of their autonomy. A paradox inheres in the point that monks do, indeed, depend on women for their basic needs. But this dependency is effaced, conceptually at least, in light of monks' lack of investment in the relations they have with laypeople. Their autonomy remains unimpeachable, and the prestige it wins them trickles down to the women who make their claims to it possible.

Suspect Detachment and the Ambiguous Status of Nuns

Burmans, as mentioned above, always allow for individual variation, such that even if women as a group are deemed unlikely to be able to give up their attachments, especially the affective bonds that tie them to those they feel close to, still people readily admit that some women do manage to accomplish this feat. Indeed, some individual women become noted for their great religious convictions and can, as nuns, attract very powerful donors. At the same time, Burman attitudes toward nuns remain highly ambivalent.

A nun to whom I was introduced by U Dhammananda provided striking evidence of how important and powerful a nun may become. The abbess of a large nunnery in Mandalay is an old friend of U Dhammananda, and she was happy to receive us both one day in her quarters, along with the second in charge of the establishment, who is her long-time companion. The nunnery she heads lies near but not in the newly developed part of Mandalay, the "New City" (*myou. thi'*). At the time of our visit, an enormous new building on the nunnery's grounds was nearing completion: it would house a large number of nuns, as well as providing a large space in which to hold classes or allow laypeople to hold weddings and other events. The dedication ceremony was to take place two months later.

The abbess grew up in a village near Monywa. She moved to a nunnery in the town of Monywa at the age of ten, with her parents' blessing. But in a common pattern, as Kawanami also reports on the basis of nuns she spoke with (2013), they later tried to persuade her to give up her religious calling and return to lay life. She always resisted their pressure on her to do so. She moved at the age of twelve to a nunnery in Sagaing, where her grandfather's sister was a nun: many girls who become interested in pursuing a nun's path join a female relative (or sometimes a male one) who has already taken on the robe at a monastery or nunnery (Kawanami 2013). She made the move in order to get access to better instruction in Pali, and while staying there, she proved her skills by passing the whole set of Dhammasariya examinations. She and the nunnery's second-in-charge had met in the nunnery they both lived in in Monywa. This friend did not move with her to Sagaing, but did then move to this nunnery once the abbess moved here, thirty years prior to our meeting in 2011.[10]

The nunnery was, at the time of our visit, clearly flourishing. It counted 255 nuns in residence, about a hundred of them from the Shan States. The abbess is willing to accept girls as young as ten years of age, but most come at about the age of twelve, thirteen, or fourteen. She requires that, once they take up residence at the nunnery, they continue to wear lay clothes for two Sabbaths. If they are able to observe all the precepts during that period, they are allowed to become nuns and remain.

The building under construction was by any standard very impressive. The abbess gave us a tour. The lower floor was being used as temporary living quarters for the many construction workers working on the project. In another section of the ground floor were an enormous number of wrapped bundles: these were one thousand monks' robes and one thousand nuns' robes, which were to be donated at the time of the building's inauguration. The very large hall on the second floor had an elaborate plaster mural at the eastern end, where a Buddha image was placed on a raised platform. Along the walls of the hall a great many pictures of nuns were hung: many of these nuns had figured among the abbess's teachers. One hundred and twenty nuns were already living on the third floor. More would move in once the building was completed. We reached the roof by means of the elevator (still a rarity in buildings other than hotels in Mandalay), where a copy of the pagoda in Bodhgaya, the site of the Buddha's enlightenment, stood. It contained a twelve-foot-high wooden statue of the Buddha, made from a single piece of teak. The view of the surrounding city and the Shan Hills to the east was magnificent.

How was the abbess able to marshal the immense resources required to build such an imposing structure? U Dhammananda had explained to me before our visit, and the abbess reiterated to me, that when she was a young girl she lived near a very important, highly respected monk, the Botataung Sayadaw. (When she started speaking of him, her companion turned on the light that shone on a very large portrait of him hanging in her quarters.) He took an interest in her, sending her loving compassion and also giving her gifts, as did another monk, a student of the Botataung Sayadaw who was himself a very prominent abbot. The beneficial influence of these two monks explained the great fame and power she came to acquire—although on occasion U Dhammananda also used a more properly Buddhist idiom by stating that she had such a considerable store of merit that she had gotten to live near them and to attract their avuncular attention. In any case, she eventually came to enjoy the support of the very powerful General Khin Nyunt before his fall from power, and another, still powerful general continued to support her. He and the head of Mandalay Division would be coming to the new building's dedication ceremony.

U Dhammananda said unequivocally that although the abbess had passed far fewer Pali exams than he had, and therefore fell short of him with respect to Buddhist learning, she clearly possessed much greater spiritual potency (*dagou:*) than he.[11] The very fact that she had such powerful connections to the national regime, as well as the magnificence of the ceremony she held to inaugurate the new building, and for that matter the impressive dimensions of that building, all attested to her stunning concentration of spiritual power. U Dhammananda was proud of the pagoda he had built in his native village. But it was a very modest structure in comparison to the one the abbess showed off to us.

Yet at the same time, like any other nun in Burma, the abbess's status was diminished relative to his, or any other monk's, in structural terms.[12] Not only does the status of nuns equal that only of novices, rather than that of fully ordained monks, but public attitudes toward nuns are dogged by ambivalence about the very notion of a woman taking up a spiritual path rather than participating in normal lay life. Kawanami provides ample evidence of that ambivalence toward Buddhist nuns in Burma.[13] In fact, a reader of her book is likely to experience a certain confusion. Kawanami notes at several points the fact that nuns enjoy increasing respect: she writes, for example, of "a positive shift in people's perceptions that is becoming much more accepting of them" (2013, 110). She also notes at several points the fact that nuns are looked on with considerable suspicion by the Burmese public, and often by their own kin. She writes, for example, that "there is a marked difference in traditional attitudes towards male and female renunciation in Myanmar; becoming a monk is openly celebrated and praised, whereas becoming a nun is generally disparaged by society" (2013, 51). A reader's confusion stems not from inconsistencies in Kawanami's analysis but rather from conflicting and shifting attitudes among Burman Buddhists toward nuns as a class, evidenced most pointedly by Kawanami's frequent use of the word "ambiguous" to describe their current situation.[14]

The very terms with which nuns are addressed reflect Burmans' ambivalent, often disparaging, inclinations with respect to nuns. A monk is addressed as *hpaya:* (literally, "lord"). A nun is addressed *hsaya lei:* (literally, "little teacher"). If she is the head of a nunnery, she is addressed *hsaya kyi:* (literally, "big" or "great" teacher). The term *hsaya*, meaning "teacher," implies considerable respect, yet in this usage the term still falls short of the term *sayado* (literally, "royal" or "venerable" teacher), reserved for Buddhist abbots. As mentioned earlier, although monks and novices are given cooked food by lay donors when they go on alms rounds, nuns are given raw food, mostly in the form of small quantities of uncooked rice. The underlying message seems clear: they're women; they can cook for themselves.

I take the ambivalence characteristic of Burman attitudes toward nuns as reflecting a deep-seated, if little explicit, sense that women, as subordinates, should be closely bound to others. It is precisely those bonds that nuns choose to avoid, to the confusion, and at times consternation, of lay Burmans.[15] Kawanami writes that women who choose to become nuns "have voluntarily opted out of their socially prescribed womanhood" (2013, 54). She continues, "There is a general understanding that they are going against the dominant social mores expected of women, but some could not articulate what exactly they were going against. Nonetheless, the desire for independence and self-determination is quite evident when talking to them" (2013, 54).

As the last sentence makes clear, women who choose to become nuns are favoring autonomy over bonds, and by doing so, posing something of a conundrum for other members of Burman society. Autonomy, once again, is gendered masculine for most Burmans. Men are enjoined to maximize their autonomy: in a Buddhist idiom, they are urged to break their attachments. What is one to make of women and girls who engage in such behavior? Is it just as laudable for women to fulfill Buddhist ideals by renouncing life in the world, by breaking their attachments?

A great many parents of women who wish to become nuns think not and do everything in their power to prevent them from doing so. Indeed, Kawanami reports incidents evocative of a conservative American family's reaction to a son who announces that he is gay:

> Many nuns spoke of the trauma they encountered when their families came to know of their decision to renounce. In most cases, the initial response of family members is outright opposition, fury, and exasperation. They do not comprehend what has gotten into her head and do not believe that their daughter has decided to do it entirely of her own accord. They respond with anger and grief as if their precious child has been "lured away." Heartbreaking episodes are common. (2013, 77)

The resonance with American coming-out stories must stem from an impression, in both instances, that individuals are contravening the order on which social relations are based, that fundamental ordering principles of people's ties to others are being challenged at a fundamental level.[16]

Ironically, much about nuns' deportment and self-presentation affirm their submission to traditional constraints on female conduct, emphasizing their shyness, their modesty, as well as their moral purity (Kawanami 2013, 91–95). Yet such self-restraint does not, in the eyes of many, including often their kin, win them the right to exist outside the relationships women are normally expected to enter into. Sexual abstinence is deemed inappropriate for women (Kawanami 2013, 95), and even nuns who have long taken up a religious life are often called on to go home and tend to sick relatives. In sum, they are constantly pressured to revert to the role of individuals attached (and subordinated) to others, rather than garnering respect as individuals pursuing religious improvement by establishing and safeguarding their autonomy.

The very relationship that enables a nun to pursue her religious vocation may turn out to cause her not a sought-for autonomy but rather a compromising dependence.

> Once established, a regular relationship between a nun beneficiary and a non-relation benefactor tends to become morally taxing on the nun recipient. In many cases, a nun ends up confined to an exclusive relationship of "reciprocal dependence," perhaps with one or two non-relation sponsors. In such a relationship, she becomes obliged often morally, to serve and look after her patrons. Such dependence is not a situation that a nun initially set out to achieve in her monastic life, but the social implications of an "unreciprocated gift" eventually appear to catch up. (Kawanami 2013, 134)

Why should this relationship between lay donor and nun prove onerous in a way that monks do not experience it, or, if they do, to a lesser degree? I suggest that women are thought suited to engaging in exchange in its obvious and immediate forms. The exchange that binds a lay donor to a monk, granting the latter material sustenance and the former spiritual merit, euphemizes the monk's dependence on the layperson. Even if U Dhammananda still finds it compromising to rely on lay supporters, as I recounted in chapter 3, neither he nor other monks appear to feel obligated to such people in the way that Kawanami describes in the case of nuns. For many Burmans, the power to effect such a conversion, between material and spiritual spheres, does not lie within the capacities of a nun. Even when nuns take on a role for which they are uniquely well-positioned, such as when providing information about monks to laypeople (Kawanami 2013, 155), they are confirming the role of women as intermediaries:

they are fostering ties in such a way as to enable monks to minimize them.

Perhaps most pointedly and sadly, tensions between a nun's commitments to a partner, and/or to her own kin, can lead to the undoing of whatever institution-building she has accomplished as an abbess: "There is no guarantee that [a nunnery's] senior nuns in positions of authority can keep their family interests at bay, even after having lived communally together all their lives" (Kawanami 2013, 231). Kawanami documents how conflict occurs particularly at the time of an abbess's passing. Unlike in the case of monasteries, a nunnery consists only of privately held property, much of it held by the abbess. Upon her death, her kin often reclaim control of that property. Or they insist on the right to determine who will replace her as abbess, often another one of their kinswomen, and not necessarily a well-qualified one. This can put them at odds with the abbess's partner, or even the partner's kin. It may also alter the character of the nunnery itself. Kawanami notes, "Many nunnery schools have disintegrated into something like a boarding house for rural relatives of resident nuns" (2013, 220).

Nuns, in sum, seem always to struggle with both public ambivalence toward their desire to pursue their own spiritual betterment at the expense of their bonds to others, and with the pressures exerted on them by their kin. We can read both forms this tension takes as following from the expectations that hierarchical considerations place on them as women. Mutual interdependence through difference is taken by most Burmans to imply that, as women, they differ from men in their greater capacity, need, and inclination to invest in their relationships with others, that is, to form strong and lasting attachments. To try instead to maintain their autonomy—by choosing to remain celibate, to live apart from kin, and to pursue religious study and practice—wins the respect of a certain number of others, both monks and laypeople. But most Burmans remain skeptical at best, and often simply dismissive of the whole notion, or indeed hostile to it.

Trans Women

I turn now to another category of individuals who fail to measure up to normative notions of masculinity in Burma. Like other regions of Southeast Asia, Burma has a long-documented tradition of cross-dressing individuals, both male and female.[17] And as in any society in which hierarchical understandings hold sway, the differences attributed to such individuals affect the places they can take up in the social relations they enter into. Unlike some other societies, in which nonnormative gender and sexuality enjoy no public toleration whatever, Burmans are generally ready to accord transgender people places in their society. Individuals who take up those places are often looked on with condescension or even contempt. Yet they are not *excluded* from relations with others. Provided they know their place, they have a place. "Nonnormative" does not mean "unnatural" or "intolerable," just "not normal," and so, "different—with consequences."

A considerable literature now exists on nonnormative gender presentation and sexual preference in Southeast Asia.[18] Interesting, diverse, and often illuminating, this literature is too large and complex to take fully into account here. Somewhat opportunistically, I make only a few general observations to link that literature to my own project.

With reference specifically to Burma, much of the ethnographic literature has focused on the role of transvestite ritual practitioners, *na' ga̲do,* who participate in spirit possession cults. As mentioned in chapter 6, Melford Spiro and Bénédicte Brac de la Perrière have both reported extensively on these individuals and the cults in which they take leading roles (Spiro 1978; Brac de la Perrière 1989). During my stays in the city, many trans women in Mandalay combined the role of spirit medium with that of cosmetician, or confined their activities exclusively to the latter. The shift in where they are likely to seek a professional niche appears to stem from two facts: local authorities are placing increasing constraints on spirit medium cults, restricting the places and times when troupes can hold public ceremonies; and more and more women are turning to experts to get themselves dressed for big public events in which they are going to participate, such as weddings, university graduations, novices' ordinations, and the like. Most spirit mediums are still nonnormative in their gender presentation: males are almost invariably effeminate and cross-dressed; females tend to be masculine in their gender presentation and often, if less consistently, cross-dress as well. Yet many trans women (by which I mean biological males who present themselves as women) I met remarked how they had no interest in spirit mediumship. Indeed, the role had come to be seen by many of them as inappropriate to a modern, middle-class social standing, which could be much more effectively sustained by specializing in the beauty business.[19]

Many outsiders have remarked, for centuries, on how frequently they observed nonnormatively gendered individuals out and about in

Southeast Asian societies (Reid 1988). I myself was surprised in 1987 and 1988 that trans women and men could be received at middle-class social events with complete equanimity. Public tolerance of gender presentation that failed to align with presumed biological sex could be counted on much more readily in Mandalay than in the United States. I have sensed a certain tightening up of attitudes since that time. Some trans women acquaintances have told me that they feel no less well-respected, or at least tolerated, now than they did ten or twenty years ago. Others say they feel like the authorities are causing trans people more trouble now than they did in the past.

In Mandalay, the focal point for nonnormative gender presentation and sexual preference is located in an area in front of the city's one large, expensive hotel. Every evening groups of males and trans women gather there, talking, strolling, and passing time. The spot, along the large moat surrounding the site of the royal palace built in the mid-nineteenth century (and sadly, destroyed by fire shortly before the end of World War II), attracts strollers throughout the day, from people walking, jogging, and doing calisthenics before dawn to people taking a bit of the evening air shortly before dark. But after dark, most people who stay there for more than a few moments are trans or their friends (virtually all male), or interested observers.

It is the hotel across the way that makes the spot of such great interest both to its habitués and to the police who, unpredictably, hassle or ignore them. Foreigners, particularly but not solely Western ones, appear to many Burmese to be uniformly rich, worldly, and modern. (Asians who can afford to stay at the hotel may come in for similar, stereotyping idealization, although less consistently so.) Many queer people in Mandalay dream of getting to know such a paragon of everything they yearn for, and spending time in front of the hotel offers the best means of, if not precisely working toward that goal, at least trying one's luck. A few stories circulate about Westerners coming across the street and finding partners among the people hanging about. A tourism boom was clearly coming by the time I left Mandalay in July 2012, but numbers were not yet very large. I assume that more stories circulate by now.

Precisely because this spot is where the wealthiest, therefore presumably most important and highest-status, foreigners congregate in the city, as well as the highest members of the Burmese military and civil service, the local authorities are particularly concerned with how it makes the city and its inhabitants appear. In May 2011, police raided the area, hauling a number of people into police trucks and taking them off to jail. They were released soon after, but the point seemed to be to scare people away from meeting there by threatening them with public humiliation. This continues to happen on an irregular basis.[20] Acquaintances assured me that people whose gender presentation was nonnormative would risk no such treatment elsewhere in the city. It was because foreigners would see them acting rowdy, making too much noise, and generally misbehaving that the police become impatient. But months can go by without the police implementing such intimidation tactics. People assume that everything depends on the whim of the local authorities and how they feel about any particular guests—both important foreigners and important Burmese officials—staying at the hotel at any given time.[21]

Official inclinations to ignore trans people most of the time, and to harass and humiliate them at other times, exemplifies Burman attitudes toward them more generally. As a category of individuals, trans women are subject to mockery and sometime contempt. In *za' pwe:* performances and in films, they are invariably subjects of derisive fun. It is not always hostile fun; indeed it can be quite affectionate. Yet it is condescending at best. Individually, however, such people are often treated cordially.

Ms. Ruby was a middle-aged cosmetician in Mandalay who had been the long-time, and openly acknowledged, mistress of a middle-class man, himself married with children. She had broken off her ties with him when he took another younger, biologically female, mistress. (He had tried to prevent the break, in Ms. Ruby's telling, but she rebuffed his attempts at reconciliation.) Ms. Ruby invited me one evening to visit friends of hers, a dentist and his family, eminently respectable people. They told me they had all been friends for many years. Similarly, a family very prominent in Mandalay's social circles—because its patriarch was the head of a nationally known charitable organization that gathered donations of rice from all over the country on behalf of monks and nuns in the region of Mandalay—are long-time friends of a trans woman I have known for several years, Miss Bling. Granted, her role in their household stood somewhat ambiguously in the boundary zone between friend and domestic helper. But that did not prevent us all from chatting together amiably sitting on the plush chairs in their front room: this is not something Miss Bling could have done had she been of truly subordinate standing. One evening when I went to visit Ms. Bling and her husband at her beauty parlor, I learned that they had both gone to the hospital. Their neighbor's daughter had been in a minor accident of some sort and Miss Bling and Ko Maung Kyi, as long-time neighbors and friends, had gone along out of interest and concern for the young girl. Miss Bling and her husband, that is, could participate in the social life of their neighborhood like any other couple.

Noteworthy, in fact, is the readiness with which trans women are accorded respect if they distinguish themselves at a role, particularly that of cosmetician or wedding planner, to which they are thought to be particularly qualified. Indeed, they are often said by gender-normative people in Mandalay, both male and female, to be better at making women beautiful than women are.[22]

This issue of respect is, for trans people as much as everyone else in Mandalay, a matter of great concern. A couple I met through Miss Bling, whom I will call Mother Kyaw and Ko Thet, had been together for forty-five years in 2011.[23] Mother Kyaw was now ninety-one years old (Ko Thet was sixty-one), and had taught most of the trans beauticians in the city their trade. She was highly revered: she was the oldest of sixteen cosmeticians honored by the trans community in Mandalay in 2010. (Such an event, a *ga̲do bwe:,* takes the form of a meal in a public venue, with speeches, entertainment, and much photo-taking. People hold them in honor of their teachers, whether of an academic subject, occupational skills, the arts, or the like.) She told me proudly that the others so honored had been in their seventies and eighties but she alone was in her nineties. Photographs she and Ko Thet showed me, taken of her when she was teaching dance in her youth, made it clear that she had been very attractive. In response to my questions, Mother Kyaw said that trans women had previously enjoyed public respect in Mandalay but no longer did. She attributed the change to their own inappropriate behavior: noisy, dissolute, and often outrageous. And then the HIV-AIDS epidemic had further sullied their image. She estimated that one hundred trans cosmeticians in Mandalay had died of the disease.

If in Mother Kyaw's view it was trans women themselves who had caused their decline in standing, public impressions of the men with whom they form long-term relationships are prejudicial but for very different reasons. Men such as Ko Thet, and Miss Bling's husband, Ko Maung Kyi, are referred to by their spouses and by others as "real men" (*jau'kja: a̲si'*). This means they are masculine-presenting and assumed to be the penetrating party in sex. Such males do not suffer any public disdain on the basis of the biological sex of their partners. They do, however, suffer disrespect as a class on the grounds that they are motivated to live with a trans woman for financial reasons. Since many trans women are able to earn money as spirit mediums or as cosmeticians—this in a society where earning even a meager living has often been difficult—men who choose to live with them stand accused of opportunism and laziness. They are assumed to prefer to let their spouses work hard while they take it easy. My own observations do not bear this out in the cases I have just mentioned. Ko Thet worked hard at creating bouquets and corsages for the events he and Mother Kyaw were contracted to help decorate. Ko Maung Kyi worked long hours as a motorbike taxi driver. Still, mutual friends casually disparaged Ko Maung Kyi as living off his wife's earnings.[24] Conventional ideas seemed in this case to trump behavior people could have taken note of but did not.

I should not misrepresent matters by suggesting that trans women form long-term unions with "real men" just as easily as biological females do. Neither of these couples was thought exceptional, but it would not be true to say that they represented a norm. Most of the trans women I met had had relationships with "real men" of greater or lesser duration at points in their lives, but for the most part they now live alone. Indeed, a good friend of Ms. Ruby, who, like her, had once been a pupil of Mother Kyaw and was now in her fifties or sixties, told me with some bitterness that when they were young, men paid them good money to have sex with them. Now, on the contrary, they had to pay younger guys to have sex with them, even though these "real men" were going to have their own pleasure (since they would do the penetrating).

When people in Mandalay talk about males who have sex with males, they tend to use one of three labels: *mein:masha* or *achau'*, for feminine-presenting, usually cross-dressing trans women, who are assumed always to be, and always to want to be, penetrated in sex; "real men," who, as noted above, are masculine-presenting and assumed always to penetrate in sex—such people are not thought in any way distinct from other males, so outsiders might label them "gay" but most Burmans would not; and *apoun:*, from *poun:*, "to hide," which refers to males who are masculine-presenting but who prefer to be penetrated in sex.[25] A man who falls into the last category is assumed by others to want to cross-dress or at least to behave in an effeminate manner, but to feel too inhibited by social disapproval to do so.[26]

The category that many outsiders would think missing from the above list would name masculine-presenting males who choose to have sex with other masculine-presenting males: the set of males most outsiders (or at least most Westerners) would group together and call "gay." That sex among similarly gendered males happens is by no means unknown, at least to some Burmans. In prison, in military camps, on crowded buses, many men, especially young ones, are thought always ready to seize on opportunities for sexual play and, although discretion is necessary, little meaning is attached to any given instance of it. But masculine-presenting men who are attracted to similarly masculine-presenting men have no distinct label, because most Burmans do not think that an encounter between two such individuals would constitute anything more than a passing occurrence. Nor, as noted above, do they think that the biological sex of one's partner matters as much as who penetrates and who is penetrated. Although a slang term exists for males who take both positions in sex (the word, hilariously, is a homonym for the Burmese pronunciation of "England," punning on Burmese words for "member" and "reversal"), most people assume any given male chooses one role or the other, not both. And as noted above, a man who appears masculine but wishes to be penetrated is assumed, like trans women, to have a "woman's mind" and to want to present himself in a feminine manner. He simply feels too inhibited to do so.

Rosalind Morris suggested in a famous analysis that Thais conceived of gender and sexuality according to two different systems. One was a three-part system of male, female, and *kathoey* (cross-dressing individuals, previously referring to both males and females, more recently applied only to males), based on gender presentation. The other was a four-part system based on sexuality, with individuals of one of two sexes, male and female, having two possible object-choices, male or female, this system corresponding to Western understandings (Morris 1994). Burmans in Mandalay seem primarily committed to the first system, stressing gender presentation, except that the category of *apoun:* introduces something like a subcategory. Still, such individuals, apparently members of one category (males) but secretly wishing to be members of a different one (trans women), could certainly still be understood within a tripartite conceptual scheme.

Peter Jackson and Gerard Sullivan, however, have countered Morris's analysis on the grounds that Thais do not separate out gender and sexuality: gender presentation is assumed to imply sexual preference, as well (1999). Jackson and Sullivan's point is well taken, since, as I have indicated, Burmans do indeed think that "real men" penetrate, whereas females and trans women are penetrated. (I address the topic of trans men below.)

Making sense of data I have reported above for Mandalay, and that Morris, Jackson, and others have reported about nonnormative gender and sexuality elsewhere in Southeast Asia, becomes easier in light of the view that long-term relations are predicated on mutual interdependence through difference. Gender difference provides an extremely effective form of difference with which to bind people together. Gender similarity, obviously, does not. How could it? Individuals who contravene the usual association of a specific sex with a specific gender presentation and the sexual position it usually implies can do so if they so choose. But they must still observe the expectation that they will bond to others through difference. As Michael Peletz, among others, has emphasized (2009), in Southeast Asia, gender binarism, which governs publicly performed roles, has long taken precedence over private acts, about which people may make assumptions but which do not matter a lot to what Jackson calls a "régime of appearances" (2004).

Furthermore, since every difference implies, as Dumont says, a difference in value, individuals who give up a higher position for a lower one must accept the loss of standing that that move implies. Masculine presentation—and the masculine penetrating role in sex it is assumed to imply—enjoy greater prestige than feminine presentation and the feminine, penetrated, role in sex. A biological male who chooses to step down the prestige ladder by giving up the superior roles to which he has clear access suffers derision because it is so clearly an ill-advised, indeed laughable, move. But if he chooses to do so, he can. His father may well beat him for engaging in effeminate behavior, since a person who diminishes his own standing in this way diminishes that of his kin at the same time. But even fathers eventually give up, or so several of my acquaintances told me in relating their own experiences at home. Indeed, if the trans woman manages to do well by her own profession, her father may happily come around. A highly educated and elegant trans woman I met in Lashio received me at her home, with her father sitting nearby. He contributed occasionally to our conversation with evident goodwill. Another trans woman in the town told me later that the father had strenuously opposed his child's first moves away from a masculine presentation: only once she had become rich and successful did his attitude soften.

I observed fewer trans men than trans women in Mandalay, and I cannot claim to have become personally acquainted with any, although they can be seen in public in Mandalay just as trans women can. However, a number of people told me that people whose daughters started to exhibit masculine behavior usually felt no unhappiness about it. Indeed, some people told me, they might well be pleased. A daughter who takes on a masculine demeanor sets her parents' minds at ease because she is assumed to have no interest in having sex with a man, assuaging parents' constant fear that she will become pregnant before she marries and so bring shame down on the family. She will not, it is true, obtain the superior standing that accrues to a man on the basis of his biological sex. Obtaining male privilege is not that easy. But while parents often express consternation at a son whose behavior at puberty (or even before) suggests that a "woman's mind has popped out," as people put it in Burmese (*mein:ma. sei' pau'te*), they may express no such dismay at a man's mind popping out in a daughter.

A conversation I had with a middle-aged couple at their home north of Mandalay was illuminating in this respect. In response to my questions about *mein:masha,* they expressed amusement and casual disdain for males who dressed and acted like women, saying that parents whose son turned out to be a transvestite felt "downhearted, dejected" (*a:ngeya.de*). A male, after all, can become a monk, bringing prestige and merit to his parents. A transvestite could never do such a thing. More generally, they said, females are of lower status than males, so it was a step down to give up being a male in favor of being a female. Their remarks suggested that a male who gave up his masculinity disgraced himself and his relatives because he foolishly and inexplicably gives up an advantage he would otherwise bring to the social competition that preoccupies pretty much all adult Burmans.

This couple's two children, a son and a daughter, were both in their early twenties when I spoke with their parents in 2007. I did not meet their children, but as we talked, and when they showed me a photo, it became evident that their daughter dressed and acted in a manly way, that she was a *jau'kjasha*. This, they assured me, was of no consequence. Would she marry? She seemed to have no interest in doing so, they told me. They were not concerned about this: she would just go on living with them, which would be fine. It is common in much of Southeast Asia for one among a family's daughters to continue to live with and eventually care for her parents, even if she marries, so there was nothing unusual in their expectation that she would remain living with them. Less typical was the parents' unconcern that their daughter might never marry and have children.[27] But the fact that a woman acting and dressing as though she were a man aroused so little reaction implies that the gesture was not scandalous, at least not for these parents, and I infer that it was not scandalous because it would not mean gratuitously forswearing a privilege one already enjoyed, which is what is so egregious about a man choosing to present himself as gendered female.

Mutual interdependence through difference grants everyone a place, provided they know their place. Nonnormatively gendered people play on difference but they do not, in most circumstances, undermine the fundamental view that difference matters, and that it always matters. This explains a phenomenon a number of outsiders have remarked on—that gender "deviance" elicits attitudes ranging from condescension to contempt but little or no violence (Jackson 1997, 1999; Boellstorff 2007) in Southeast Asia. Giving up male privilege is a wrong move, in the view of most people, laying those males who do so open to mockery. But foolishness does not provoke violence.

A discourse, however, that promotes the "rights" of the nonnormatively gendered makes little sense to many people in Burma (as elsewhere). If it implies that an individual who differs in important ways (e.g., in gender presentation and presumably, sexual preference) from those with similar bodies should be treated, or would expect to be treated, no differently from them, then it flies in the face of fundamental assumptions about the nature of social relations. Of course males who fail to perform a masculine role are found curious and will be treated accordingly. How could they assume that their public behavior would not be subject to public comment and reaction? Jackson (1997) and Boellstorff (2005, 2007) report that even if effeminacy is relatively tolerated in Thailand and Indonesia, respectively, sexual relations among similarly gendered individuals are not. So Thai academics urge tolerance toward trans women (*kathoey*) but inveigh against masculine-presenting males who have sex with similar males. Within the terms of hierarchical thinking, this stands to reason. The scandal of masculine-presenting men forming long-term relationships with similarly masculine-presenting men is above all a *logical* one. To a great many people in Burma and elsewhere in the region, it simply makes no sense.

Conclusion: The Great Chain of Burman Buddhist Being

By way of conclusion, I review in a few pages my argument not just in this chapter but in all of the preceding ones. I do so by reiterating in summary fashion the downward progression from revered and idealized renderings of autonomy to ordinary, unprestigious figures of secular life caught up in their attachments and relationships.

I have referred at several points in the preceding pages to binary oppositions, such as masculine and feminine, religious and lay, autonomous and attached, that stand in relation to each other not as simple antonyms but rather as poles at either end of a continuum. To think in terms of a spectrum is likely to bring to mind a horizontal line. But much as Dumont instructs us, oppositions in hierarchical arrangements necessarily bring with them differences in value. So the continuum that each of those oppositions, or better, ranges, implies should be pictured as a vertical line, not a horizontal one. Or better yet, it should be represented by the sort of diagram Dumont provides of "encompassment," wherein one term lies embedded within a larger, more encompassing one, which is also a more prestigious one, much as Adam represents both "Man," and "man (as opposed to woman)," with woman, a dependent and less prestigious being, originating in his rib (Dumont 1980, 239–245).

Buddhism, at least as conceived of and acted on by Burmans, posits as the ultimate goal a condition of absolute autonomy, nirvana. Doctrinally, neither goals nor conditions pertain to nirvana, so this statement is no doubt conceptually flawed. But neither I nor most Burmans, it's safe to say, understand the concept of nirvana in all its theological complexity. And I myself, parting ways with both scholars of Buddhist doctrine and with practicing Burman Buddhists, opt to read nirvana as a statement about social relations: I am proposing a "vulgar" reading of nirvana after the fashion of Bourdieu's self-labeled vulgar reading of Kantian aesthetics (Bourdieu 1984). In this light, nirvana stands as an ideal, but a social one, unattainable but compelling (although more compelling to some than to others) wherein all the travails and vulnerabilities implicit in social relations fall away.

Seeking nirvana, which I am taking to mean absolute autonomy, stands as the most valuable and most highly validated endeavor any Buddhist can undertake. Monks stand the best chance of reaching it, or in any case are best prepared to go about seeking it, among beings in this world. By the same token, monks best personify individuals who, in their detachment from all worldly goals and all normal social relations, act autonomously. In other words, soteriological preoccupations and sociological orientations complement each other well. Of course, monks' autonomy is highly paradoxical, since the rules that prevent them from producing and processing their own food mean that they are forever dependent on others simply to remain alive. But the exchange relationships in which they participate, whereby they receive material sustenance in exchange for providing instruction, ritual assistance, and above all, opportunities for laypeople to acquire merit, euphemize the exchange, or etherealize it, and (albeit to varying degrees) depersonalize it. So although monks are themselves still caught up in exchange relations and so remain vulnerable to the vagaries of social relations, they are less deeply entangled in such relations than laypeople.

A monk's role positions him best to seek nirvana among categories of humans, and his relative marginality to worldly affairs makes him a model of what withdrawal into autonomy would look like. Meditation is the *activity* that best instantiates in this world what the condition of being in nirvana would look like. It best instantiates an existence apart from social relations, without attachments, without investments. By virtue of my own sociological focus, I would underline the fact that this version of autonomy means without attachments to other humans, since these are the attachments, I would claim, that matter most to people, even if they might appear to be more invested in rubies or SUVs (in the case of laypeople) or Buddhist learning (in the case of monks).

As I have noted repeatedly, the apogee of Burman Buddhist ideals is figured in the monk meditating alone in the forest, obtaining the minimal requirements for life in what foodstuffs he finds for himself in the natural environment. To what extent any actual individuals have pursued this path in Burmese history is impossible to know. But that is, for me, immaterial: it is the power of the image that matters, since it provides the logical endpoint, or rather, summit, of Burman Buddhist understandings of life in this world.

Even though he is the ultimate ideal among living humans, the lone monk meditating in the forest stands below the *wei'za* meditating in the distinct domain inhabited by those beings, who were once human but have transcended that status. As Rozenberg demonstrates (2015), some Burman Buddhists believe that *wei'za,* although they have surpassed biological processes of growth and decay and spend their time in meditation while awaiting the advent of the next Buddha, can still be appealed to to intervene benevolently in human affairs. That claim does not persuade all Burman Buddhists by any means. Yet the desire to find in *wei'za* means to worthy or desired ends (however conventional—and the more material those ends, the less worthy they appear) is telling: it points up the felt need of many individuals whose capacity to establish and maintain their own autonomy falls short to compensate for that lack by gaining access to other, more highly autonomous beings' concentrations of power. Paradoxically, the greater such others' displays of autonomy, the more resolutely some people try to connect themselves, which is to say, subordinate themselves, to them.

As one moves down the scale, among living beings, from most autonomous to less so, which is a movement from an encompassing ideal to a less-impressive deflection from that ideal, autonomy becomes compromised in ever-greater degrees of attachment. This is true cognitively, emotionally, and socially. Laypeople invest in the passing matters of everyday life as though unmindful of the transient and unreliable nature of all conditioned things. Meditation assures, or seeks to assure, absolute control over one's own thinking, absolute insulation from emotional variability, and absolute removal from social experience. But meditation is agreed by most practitioners to be very hard. In each field, obstacles to achieving the goal signals vestigial attachments, investments that still stand in need of expunging. With concentration and, still better (in contemporary Burman meditation traditions), with insight, individuals rid themselves of such investments and become released from them—into greater autonomy.

Males are deemed more capable of breaking their attachments than females. Or at least, certain lines of argument represent males in this way, even if a counter-discourse, as mentioned, makes an opposing claim. What seems clear is that males are readier to reduce or break affective ties, particularly with kin, than females usually are, even if males are generally thought less able to overcome the investments they have in sexual and other pleasures. (But here, too, there is a contradictory discourse in play, to the effect that women endure frustration of their wants less well than men.) Males, therefore, are deemed more capable of resisting, or removing themselves from, long-term relationships of exchange. Since, in marriage, they take the superordinate role, breaking the relationship in order to become a monk means giving up the responsibilities that come with that role, as well as the privileges. A woman has the right to refuse her husband that option: she can insist on remaining dependent on him. She will win praise, however, should she agree to let him pursue his spiritual advancement.

Even if men do not leave the world of lay affairs behind and become monks, or do so only briefly, such as for ten days or so at the time of the Buddhist New Year in April, as has become popular in recent years, they are still mindful of the many ways in which their relations with the world pose threats to their safety and well-being. To shore up the resistance to external influence they believe important to their own health and welfare, they can take up a number of practices, such as assimilating powerful texts (through memorizing them or ingesting them), inscribing their bodies with powerful tattoos, and/or taking on other forms of invulnerability magic. These cognitive and physical gestures, by indicating how important strengthening the mind and body against external attack is, point to how vulnerable men feel to attack, that is, to how much interaction for them appears to entail risk.

Men try to protect themselves; many do so quite assiduously. Depending on temperament and position, however, they may find it necessary to complement the measures they take, or to substitute for them, by forging relationships with others. They may turn to powerful monks, powerful secular figures, and/or objects in which great concentrations of power are thought to reside in pursuit of safety from threats both material and immaterial. In each case, they must subordinate themselves. But if the concentration of power to which they turn offers sufficient return on that investment, or the promise of such, then they may well feel that the diminution of their own autonomy is well justified.

Women seek protection and, aside from protection, material and emotional well-being, by attaching themselves to powerful others, most notably their husbands and monks. They also form attachments to beings, particularly children, still weaker than themselves. In centering their lives on their relations with others, they minimize all chances of attaining autonomy for themselves, to the diminution, necessarily, of their prestige and standing. But that is in the order of things. It is women's place, a subordinate one, to be invested in this world, and especially, to be invested in their relationships. In assuming a subordinate position, they should win the indulgent consideration of their betters—and make it possible for those individuals, lay males and monks, to sustain the superior standing that they enjoy. Women's engagement with the world, with the messiness of money, of child-rearing, of relations with spirits, provides a base on which the prestige of males can be founded. They suffer condescending remarks about their inability to control themselves: their desires, their emotions, and their speech. And their bodies, particularly before they reach menopause, provide vivid evidence of their implication in bodily processes, in flux,[28] that are the antithesis of Buddhist detachment and integrity. But those very elements that compromise their integrity constitute the reasons why they are essential participants in human society. The exchanges they enter into with others—in commerce, in sex, in tending to children's needs, in providing for monks' sustenance—allow human lives to proceed appropriately, affording men the chance to pursue greater autonomy and standing, even as those same exchanges consign women to lower standing.

Burman social arrangements are not so rigid as to rule out the possibility for individuals, female as well as male, to forge alternate paths, to pursue less-obvious options, in how they live their lives. In this respect, Burma's society does look "loosely structured." Yet contrarian life-courses arouse ambivalent responses. Women who become nuns make a good deal of sense as Buddhists pursuing a laudable goal, a religious life ostensibly removed from secular entanglements. Yet as women they make very little sense, since women's rightful place lies in the thick of such entanglements, that is, enmeshed in attachments and exchanges. Thus nuns arouse great ambivalence, and they find themselves constantly pulled back into relationships, with their kin and/or with monks, that their religious vocation should enable them to put aside. Trans women, too, arouse ambivalence, or worse, outright contempt, because they so egregiously undermine the dignity and autonomy they could enjoy as males. They do so by entering into relationships with spirits and with "real men" who penetrate them. Trans men garner far less pejorative comment. They do not acquire the prestige that comes to males. They make themselves irrelevant by giving up standard female roles, but they are likely to continue to participate as members of their natal families and they lay no claim to the special status of nuns. Believed by most people to be asexual, they make of their bodies self-enclosed units, a move that wins a certain respect, while challenging nothing about the prestige of autonomy, so sought after by males, or about the compromising nature of women's normal, exchange-based roles.

The above paragraphs summarize the broad lines of the analysis I have proffered in chapter 5 through chapter 9, of relations among monks and laypeople, and among men, women, and trans men and women, in contemporary Burma. This summary recaps my argument not in the order in which I have set it out but rather by moving from the top of the Burman prestige ladder to its base. In chapter 10 I suggest how some of the points I have made with reference to Burma might prove relevant to other societies.

Chapter Ten

TAKING AUTONOMY AND ATTACHMENT FURTHER AFIELD

At various points in the preceding chapters I have made fleeting reference to my research in Indonesia, and to other scholars' work in other societies outside Burma. For the most part, I have restricted such references. I have also resisted any pull I might feel to generalizing broadly about the human condition. After all, universalizing statements do not fare well in anthropological circles anymore. Gone are the days when late nineteenth-century Westerners could pronounce upon the nature of all civilizational progress and plot every society, or (when it better suited their purposes) any one feature of a society, along a line that led, inexorably and comfortingly, to the world's apotheosis, which happened to be exemplified in those very scholars themselves working calmly in their study. Anthropologists' habit of irresponsibly picking and choosing among data culled from hither and yon, and complacent scholars' ex cathedra pronouncements on the nature of "man," or "society," or any other too-general topic, should make us all chary of such inclinations to pontificate.

Unfortunately, the reaction against such arrogant complacency, and worse, on the part of our forebears has led to a crisis in anthropological writing. Do we consider anthropology so sullied by its practical and ideological association with Western colonialism, with all its cruelty and smugness, as to be unethical when pursued outside our own societies? Such is what Richard Handler suggested in an engaging series of interviews he undertook with David Schneider (Schneider 1995).[1] Or if we pursue our studies outside our own societies of origin, do we simply describe, with no pretension to world-historical significance, data from a specific place and time? If we do formulate abstract statements, must they be highly qualified, and warily proffered, generalizations that might apply to a certain number of people (safer if, as per Handler, they concern people much like the writer) in a certain number of places, perhaps? Even if some people continue to conduct ethnographic research, and to do so among people much *un*like themselves, still anthropologists' loss of nerve has reached such a point that it becomes tendentious to engage in cross-cultural comparison of any kind. How can we claim to respect the integrity and uniqueness of other people's ways and notions if we extract from their full context specific elements that capture our interest for one reason or another, but in any case, for *our* reasons, not theirs?

Whether undertaking cultural comparison has any intellectual validity concerns me because I am frequently struck by affinities in what I have observed in the three societies, Burma, Java, and Bali, where I have lived periods of anywhere from one to several years. In addition, I find further affinities, often striking, in reading ethnographic, historical, and fictional materials from other Southeast Asian societies. When I read about South or East Asia, by contrast, I am more often struck by the many ways in which societies of those regions contrast with those I am familiar with in Southeast Asia. Yet whenever I make remarks about "Southeast Asia," even among sympathetic listeners, I am often told that such generalizations are overdrawn, that it ill-suits an anthropologist, or any scholar, to speak in such broadly generalizing ways.[2] I take heart in reading the work of a scholar such as Tony Day, who shows great interest in finding affinities across times and regions of Southeast Asian history (2002). Such comparativists, however, are rare.

A still more censorious reaction often greets any contrast I might want to draw between Southeast Asians, on the one hand, and "Westerners," on the other. Surely, people tell me, I cannot seriously claim that there exists such an animal as a "Westerner"! I am guilty, it seems, of Orientalism and Occidentalism both, and come in for some of the impatience that Dumont's distinction between hierarchical and egalitarian (or "modern") ideology aroused.

I would like to put forth two different justifications for cultural comparison, one substantive, the other methodological. With respect to substance, I would stake a claim for the validity of identifying, or at least suggesting, commonalities among specific societies for the simple reason that the resemblances are there, they are real, they are not perforce or invariably constructed out of an analyst's artful (or suspect) handling of cherry-picked data. Like any scientific claim, such suggestions have to be supported with evidence, and they stand open to rejection or revision. But they should not be ruled out of order prima facie. When I read the works of other scholars who work in lowland Southeast Asian societies, whether on the mainland or on the islands, I am interested, and often enlightened, to see commonalities with what is familiar to me from my own fieldwork.[3] It seems to me a needless impoverishment of anthropological study to pass over such resemblances in silence on the grounds that noting them suggests stereotyping, which is what accusations of "overgeneralizing" imply.

Two examples of such commonalities in Southeast Asia can illustrate the point. The three Southeast Asian languages of Burmese, Javanese, and Balinese distinguish speech registers to quite elaborate degrees. The rules for their use varies in each case, and those contrasts are enlightening, since they link to important features of each society's organization and values. But in all three cases, their use illustrates the obligation of certain individuals to address and refer to other individuals in a way that underlines the differences—differences in standing—between the speaker and his or her interlocutor. Such differences underpin all of their relations, but the focus on speech makes face-to-face interaction an area of particularly intense concern. Indonesian (derived primarily from Malay) does not have formally distinguished speech registers, although, as Anderson pointed out (1990b), its speakers are inclined to introduce similar considerations in their use of pronouns and other particularly ticklish vocabulary items. (These include those that draw attention to the connections between speaker and interlocutor, e.g., "to give," "to say," "to accompany.") Pali, I am told, lacks such speech registers. Thus lowland Southeast Asians share, at least in some cases, reflexes about language use that their neighbors care little about, even those neighbors (in the case of the Indian subcontinent) from whom they have borrowed immense amounts of cultural material. Surely we can take these facts as license to venture some comparative thoughts about the interplay of language, hierarchy, and encounter in Southeast Asia, in contrast to South Asia.[4]

To consider a second example, feminist scholars of Southeast Asia are sometimes at pains, as I discussed in chapter 9, to counter long-held claims as to the relatively "high" status of women in the region. No doubt such scholars are right to evaluate skeptically any too-sanguine representations of how women fare in societies where males still control most resources. Yet women's greater freedom of movement, greater legal standing, and greater participation in public life, relative certainly to South Asia and East Asia, remain well-attested. It seems both justifiable and potentially very fruitful to consider how women's roles in many Southeast Asian societies may resemble one another, and how their roles link to other features of the societies in which they live.

Cross-cultural comparison across the region can prove as illuminating when highlighting contrasts as affinities. Shelly Errington's much-cited contribution to the volume *Power and Difference* demonstrates the effectiveness of both moves, since Errington elaborates two different models of social organization with which to understand the workings of many societies of island Southeast Asia (Errington 1990). My point is not to deny variation—clearly among Southeast Asian societies we see much of it—but rather to quash objections to seeking out affinities and contrasts in the data we gather from our own fieldwork and from those reported by others. Once again, cross-cultural comparison should not fall prey to an excess of anthropological correctness.

If looking for affinities and contrasts among geographically proximate societies may seem relatively admissible, on the grounds that all societies have long been in contact with their neighbors and the notion of a society existing in pristine isolation is a fantasy, we must still address the question of whether comparison on a broader scale, and in a more conceptual or theoretical fashion, can be entertained. Charges of overgeneralizing, and so of stereotyping, come thick and fast as soon as anthropologists venture onto this terrain.

Bonded yet Unbound

To resolve this dilemma, I propose to replace universal statements with a universal question, or conundrum, one that I have raised at a number of points and that admits of varying answers. To wit: people everywhere experience a contradiction between a desire to feel closely connected to other individuals, on the one hand, and a desire to feel free to act as they wish, without constraint, on the other. They wish to feel bonded but not bound. How then to mediate between these conflicting wants, which I have treated as desires for "attachment" and for "autonomy," respectively? The problem is existential: it admits of no solution. What is interesting is to consider how people in specific times and places address the question, argue about it, act on it, while necessarily failing to resolve it.[5]

In Burma, I have tried to show that this conundrum underlies much about people's behavior and is implicit in people's comments about their own and others' lives. The tension between the desire for autonomy and the desire for attachment encompasses the Dumontian opposition between hierarchy and individualism as discernible in Burman social relations. Of particular interest to me, as summarized in chapters 8 and 9, is how the spectrum running from attachment to autonomy maps onto gender expectations, giving understandings of masculinity and its others their overall shape. It helps explain the widespread, contrasting idealizations of Buddhist monks and of women householders, and, too, the widespread (if inconsistent) denigration of trans women and nuns. It also helps explain, as I hope to have made clear, a great preoccupation in contemporary Burman public discourse with meditation.

Autonomy and Attachment in Sociology's Founding Texts

It is worth pausing to review ways that a few of our predecessors' works implicate this existential conundrum, the conflicting desires to feel bonded yet not bound. Western thinking about the issue has certainly generated a great deal of discourse: the intractable nature of the problem helps explain some of the antinomies that arise. Dumont found much of value in Tocqueville's remarks on hierarchical versus egalitarian understandings. I would complement that reading with a glance at how Marx, Durkheim, and Weber all attend, if only implicitly, to this matter of autonomy and attachment.

Marx saw how industrialization was imposing terrible constraints on people's actions, in effect binding them to machines and at the same time stripping away their bonds to one another. The depersonalization of social relations in capitalism meant that personal connections either dissolved or became forms of servitude, rather than consisting of lasting, fulfilling ties. With a curiously diabolical optimism, Marx thought the dénouement would be people coming to recognize how much their mutual relations mattered, an awareness that industrial capitalism would foster by dint of its inhuman exploitativeness. That is, the very force of capitalism's attack on people's social relations would enable them to become aware of its true nature, while at the same time capitalism's capacity to generate material plenty, through industrialization, would enable them to act on that awareness and get beyond capitalist arrangements. At a certain point, as a result of the scales falling from workers' eyes and new wealth at the same time filling their bellies, everyone would become "free." But Marx did not specify what might then bind them to one another. Perhaps he felt no need to do so out of a fundamental conviction that we are indeed all social beings by nature and will therefore bond together by virtue of our "species-being."

Considering the range of possible mediations between connectedness (attachment) and dispersion (autonomy), Durkheim realized that "freedom" might be just another word for no bonds left to rely on. Anomie labels much of the territory at the unconstrained end of the spectrum, or at the far end of what might be called freedom's rainbow. He, like Tocqueville, worried about what might serve to glue us together, about what would assure our mutual attachment when the cohesiveness religion fostered no longer seemed persuasive. Durkheim's remarks, in the conclusion of the *Elementary Forms of the Religious Life,* are at once touching and pallid, or rather, touching because they are so pallid.[6]

One way of reading the religions of the world with Weber (rather than reading Weber's often brilliant but now outdated analyses, driven as they are, and so sometimes distorted, by his overriding concern to understand what happened in northern European history) (Weber 1958a) would be to consider what solutions different traditions propose to the question of how to reconcile felt needs for attachment, on the one hand, and autonomy, on the other. Indeed, I have attempted just that with reference to Buddhism as commented and acted on by Burman monks and laypeople, although in doing so I put aside Weber's own often insightful but no longer adequate take on Buddhism (Weber 1958b).

A great many religions, for all their diverse forms, turn out on closer examination to share one fundamental assumption: that the world (or better, the cosmos, with our world included in it) is hierarchical in nature. Beings or entities both seen and unseen can be ordered serially, as is clear in Buddhism's thirty-one planes of existence or medieval Europe's great chain of being (Lovejoy 1964). Religions deal with the extensions of hierarchical ordering beyond the immediately apprehensible, ordinary realm of everyday life (in which social relations are of primary significance). Getting beyond the limits of the perceivable world at its upper and lower reaches, to the realms of gods, demons, and territorial spirits, religions provide instruction as to how humans should try to enter into relations with those beings or entities: how to make sure that they and we are all bound together in hierarchically ordered relationships.

Durkheim cautioned us in the *Elementary Forms* that religions need not presume the existence of anthropomorphic beings (Durkheim 1915, 44–50). But concentrations of power, whether or not they take on human, animal, or any other recognizable form, are prominent in religious thinking and procedures, and I would insist that how to enter into relations with such concentrations of power drives the religious enterprise pretty much everywhere. Furthermore, how people enter into relations with each other will predispose them to try to enter into relations with everything else in similar ways. If hierarchical considerations pervade social relations in this world, they are likely to pervade approaches to relations outside or beyond it, as well. Such certainly is the case for the various forms of religious activity, that is, efforts to enter into appropriately ordered relations with beings of all sorts, that I have observed in Burma, Java, and Bali.

The inclination to subordinate oneself in entering into relations with nonhuman concentrations of great power is not only commonly found in societies where hierarchical thinking enjoys largely unchallenged sway. Even a brief listen to fundamentalist American preachers reveals how much hierarchical thinking pervades their understanding of how both social life in this world and the workings of the cosmos operate (Harding 2000). Tanya Luhrmann's sympathetic account of American Protestants who assert confidently that God is their best buddy demonstrates, moreover, the ironies of people with deeply egalitarian commitments forging a relationship with an immensely powerful entity on whom they still wish to rely (2012). When God turns out to be at once omnipotent, omniscient, and the sort of guy you'd like to have a beer with on Saturday night, all your needs—those that both hierarchical and egalitarian arrangements are designed to address—have been taken care of. Pretty neat.

The irresolvable contradiction between the needs for attachment and for autonomy spans whatever boundaries we might try to establish between sociology and psychology. Burma is not a place where people speak in terms informed by depth psychology, and I am not trained (other than in my own experience as a patient of psychotherapy) to listen to what they say in light of that interpretive stream. Still, I find it interesting to reflect on what people in Burma tell me about their lives, and how they think about them, and to do so with reference to what I consider the endlessly thorny but also endlessly compelling question I have set out, one that we all face, concerning efforts people make to mediate among their own irreconcilable wants.

In doing so, I follow in Weber's footsteps once again inasmuch as, like him, I think it worthwhile to ask what psychological corollaries there might be to cosmological and sociological notions. I say "corollaries," not "consequences," because, unlike Weber, I am not confident about drawing direct causal links. Weber thought that the idea of predestination as formulated by John Calvin had to have generated intense psychological tension (Weber 1958a, 104). In his analysis he then made predestination the starting point, and that tension (and resultant behavior) its effect: a religious concept turned out to have unintended but extraordinarily significant consequences.

I am not ready to pronounce on what idea or behavior came first and what followed therefrom in Burman Buddhist society. If obliged to name any starting point, I would incline toward sociological determinism: I take after Durkheim in thinking that an individual's experience of social life is formative to a degree surpassing all other factors. So the tenor of social relations he or she experiences is likely to shape responses to ideas and practices of any sort. In this respect, I side with Mary Douglas rather than Lévi-Strauss, when she proclaimed her belief that sociological concerns really mattered more to people than did logical relations, rendered in any possible idiom (sociological, astronomical, culinary, or the like), *pace* the position taken by structural anthropology's more rigorous master (Douglas 1966).

Some readers will be made uneasy by my raising issues that might be more appropriately, not to say more competently, addressed by psychologists than by anthropologists. But anthropology's allure, as well as its explanatory power, stems in large part from the fact that it concerns itself with specific individuals, rather than only or primarily with the aggregated masses of people that draw the attention of many sociologists, or the culture-free individuals postulated by many psychologists. If anthropologists are going to interpret actual individuals' experience, they are obliged to take up issues of a psychological nature while attending to the matter of culture's implication in those issues. Since individuals everywhere must confront the issue of how they enter into relations with others, I must track the ways they are inclined (by culture, among other things) to act on the issue if I am going to get any sense of how they live their lives.[7]

I should note in this regard a contemporary tendency among Western psychologists, and probably most Westerners who reflect on these matters, to value attachment over any possible antonym. My use of the word "attachment" necessarily, and deliberately, alludes to a body of literature in psychology, attachment theory, that has assumed great importance in recent decades.[8] This theory, as developed by John Bowlby and many researchers following up on his original insights for decades after him (Karen 1994), is intended to identify difficulties people have experienced in their earliest relationships, difficulties that help explain problems they encounter later in life. The goal is to help such people identify the roots of their present difficulties and to address them so that they can form deeper, more satisfying, less troubled, and so more lasting attachments.

I should say that for myself, I find what I know of this psychological literature both enlightening and welcome. Indeed, I regret not having become acquainted with it much earlier in my own life, since it might have helped me better handle emotional difficulties I have faced. Nonetheless, it is important to see that taking attachment as an ultimate goal, to assume that forming deep and lasting attachments determines the degree of satisfaction obtainable in one's life, means making a value judgment, one that has no necessary, "objective" justification. Intuitively obvious to me though it may seem that deep and secure attachments are, however elusive, of unique value, they do not constitute a, let alone *the*, uncontested good to everyone everywhere. I can, as per Weber (2004), decide what commitments I wish to make about values in my own life. I must be careful not to assume that others share those commitments. Nor can I judge people lacking or in error for failing to do so. Many Burmans simply do not appear to share Western psychologists' view, one shared by many laypeople in the West, that attachment is the true key to personal satisfaction.

The antonym of attachment, as I have suggested repeatedly, is "autonomy." Autonomy implies that one can act on one's own, that one is not constrained by others to act in determined ways. No one's autonomy is total: humans are so helpless for so long after birth that much by way of autonomy is out of the question for years, and at no point in the average life is living alone, for most people (except the relatively wealthy), easily practicable.[9] Living with others requires at least some degree of deference to or accommodation of others' wants. Indeed, simply to use language is already to subject oneself to constraint, a subjection one accepts in order to be understood more effectively than would otherwise be possible. And language is a crucial tool for the development and maintenance of attachments.[10] But how much autonomy matters, how willing one is to trade away connection to others in favor of the assurance of one's own autonomy, varies from individual to individual—and evokes varying evaluations in diverse cultural milieux. Again, there is no correct or best view. There are only variable suggestions, each one entailing its own trade-offs: advantages, losses, goals, compromises, and attendant regrets.

I suggest that in Buddhist Burma (and I would make a similar claim for much of lowland Southeast Asia), people do not focus their attention on, or romanticize, matters of attachment as much as many contemporary Westerners (especially of the middle class) do. I emphasize that individuals make their own way in the endeavor to balance these contrasting wants; I do not want to promote psychologizing stereotypes. Nor, however, do I want to rule out the evidence, to be found in work by other researchers in Southeast Asia as well as in my own, that interaction and social relations do often demonstrate patterns different there from those likely to occur elsewhere, certainly in many Western societies. To deny, out of a fear of unwarranted generalizing, that societies differ, and that what people want out of their social relations within those societies might constitute an important, and recognizably patterned, part of the difference, would be to fall into a straitened form of analytic caution, one both irreproachable and intellectually confining.

Autonomy, Attachment, and Popular Culture

To support my claim that the conflicting desires for autonomy and attachment provide a way to engage in fruitful cultural comparison beyond the confines of my own regional specialization in Southeast Asia, let me make a final excursus, this time into the realm of international popular culture.[11] Three films, one made in Bollywood, one made in the United Kingdom by a cosmopolitan but originally South Asian director, and one made in Thailand, point out by virtue of their affinities and their differences how salient the existential problem surrounding needs to feel bonded but not bound turn out to be for many audiences in many places. Indeed, all three films enjoyed considerable international success. I believe their popularity stems from the various ways each addresses matters of attachment and autonomy, and does so in ways that implicate much of what I have already noted about the allure as well as the burden of hierarchical arrangements.

The Bollywood film I press into service is *Dilwale Dulhania Le Jayange,* abbreviated for convenience here (and everywhere) to *DDLJ.* (Its English title is *The Brave-Hearted Will Take Away the Bride,* but it is rarely referred to by that name.) As of 2015 the longest-running film in Indian film history, it follows the adventures of nonresident Indian families in the United Kingdom, focusing particularly on a feckless youth who at the start of the film is irresponsible, disrespectful, and deceitful, and on a young woman, a demure and obedient paragon of young South Asian womanhood who eventually falls in love with him.

The plot turns on the issue of how Indian values that promote respect for one's parents, especially for paternal authority, can be maintained even among Indians living in the West, and how those values can be reconciled with a Western or modern celebration of romantic love and autonomy. Resolution of the dilemma follows from the young man's eventual determination to win the woman's father's consent before marrying her (rather than eloping with her), and the father's eventual realization that everyone's happiness is better assured by his granting that consent.

Much about the film is likely to put off observers who hold progressive and egalitarian, especially feminist, values. Bollywood filmmakers must always confront the problem of how to make a virtuous token of idealized womanhood interesting, rather than just admirable. *DDLJ* solves this challenge in what is in Bollywood a highly conventional fashion: as soon as Simran, the heroine, takes a drop of alcohol, presumably her first ever, she becomes instantly intoxicated, and in this way becomes susceptible to the young man's, Raj's, charms. In a scene in which she expresses the fear that she has, unwittingly, suffered some compromise (perhaps irrevocable) of her virginal honor, Raj teases her in a way we are intended to find funny, whereas it is hard not to find it both distasteful and cruel. When he then says, sententiously, that as an Indian male he would never take advantage of a woman to the detriment of her honor, we are, apparently, supposed to take him at his word. Overall, the film falls back on a conservative celebration of masculine authority and feminine submissiveness: Simran, we see at the film's end, has been passed on, honorably, from father to future husband. Yet the film conveys this message while simultaneously celebrating the happy-go-lucky adventures of a young, unmarried couple enjoying themselves, often unchaperoned, in Switzerland, London, and India.

Lévi-Strauss suggested in his famous essay, "The Structural Study of Myth," that "the purpose of myth is to provide a logical model capable of overcoming a contradiction (an impossible achievement if, as it happens, the contradiction is real)" (1955, 443). Many readers have found his suggestion that the Oedipal myth addresses the contradiction between belief in people's autochthonous origins and knowledge of their actually resulting from the union of man and woman unconvincing (1955, 434–435).[12] Nevertheless, his general point strikes me as both true and illuminating: any apparent resolution of an existential dilemma holds great appeal, even if that resolution is necessarily "impossible."

DDLJ achieves just such a fantasized resolution of the contradiction between attachment and autonomy that I have posited as a pervasive preoccupation among humans. The contradiction between authority remaining vested in patriarchal figures—and Simran's father, Baldev, plays the role with all the impatience and imperiousness of the conventional, indeed stock-character, Indian patriarch—and young people's desires to indulge their desires without concern for their parents, kin, or larger social context, is easily mapped on to the contrast between Western and Indian ways. But that device, of course, is an obvious rendering of a much more pervasive tension, one that the modern West's ideological tilt toward egalitarianism may highlight but that certainly existed long before the West's Enlightenment thought gained such widespread acceptance, and in places other than the West. When a young woman can honor her father *and* choose her lover—or more precisely, allow herself to be chosen by a man she finds on her own—then patriarchal authority (a particularly widespread version of hierarchical arrangements) and individual autonomy, even for women, appear to be reconcilable.

Bend It Like Beckham (BILB) was released in 2002, seven years after *DDLJ*. As in the earlier film, a South Asian family living in London provides the story's focus, and once again, the frictions that arise between Indian parents with conservative notions of a young woman's proper behavior, and their daughters who, having grown up in England, have other ideas, motivate much of the action. In this case, one daughter engages in the timeless maneuver of pretending to fulfill her parents' expectations while sneaking around, and making out, with her boyfriend. She urges the same behavior on her younger sister, Jess, who, however, wishes to pursue her interest in soccer (and the team's male Irish coach) in the open. Engagingly, the filmmakers pair this family drama against another one, in which a young Englishwoman's mother urges conventional feminine behavior on her: she suggests, among other things, that her daughter consider wearing falsies. To parallel a South Asian mother's dismay at a daughter's wearing skimpy clothing and engaging in physical activity with males in public (i.e., playing soccer), the script arranges for the English girl's mother to think, mistakenly, that her daughter is having a lesbian affair. In light of how hard it would be to find anything in a child's behavior to dismay English parents as much as any number of activities their daughters might get up to would outrage conservative South Asian ones, this attribution of homophobic panic to the English girl's mother is a brilliant move.[13]

The problem that arises between Jess and her parents—but really, what matters is the opinion of her father—hinges not on the choice of a fiancé but rather on whether or not she should pursue her interest in soccer, specifically by taking up a scholarship at an American university. Once again, the dilemma is resolved when the father comes finally to see that he should agree to her doing so: she can "pursue her dream" (a notion that rarely fits well with hierarchical arrangements) without needing to defy patriarchal authority, although the physical distance about to separate them will no doubt diminish his control.

Simran's father in *DDLJ* is something of a caricature (and Raj's, a bit of a clown), whereas Jess's father, in *BILB*, is more complex, and the English girl's father, apparently working class, is both likable and more sympathetic to his daughter's wishes. Yet if *BILB* trades less obviously in stock types in the case of fathers, mothers become figures of fun: affectionate fun, but fun nonetheless, little capable of getting or seeing beyond conventional gender roles.

Overall, the two films resemble each other inasmuch as, in both, resolution comes when the father finally approves his daughter's choice as to what comes next in her life. *BILB* shows greater sophistication with respect to what Western viewers would want to see in a film about intergenerational conflict. Yet it still makes paternal authority what matters, since Jess's father's consent to her departure allows the dramatic tension's release. As a matter of fact, paternal authority is defining even in the case of the Irish soccer coach, who recounts the loss of his ties to his cold and misogynist father as an important, and determining, event in his own life.

That forging one's own way, in the tradition of an English celebration of individual autonomy over bonds to one's kin, nonetheless entails trade-offs is something the makers of *BILB* point out in one very telling shot. In preparation for a big, South Asian wedding, we see crowds of Indian women gathered together, talking and enjoying themselves while cooking up a feast. As the scene ends, the camera pans back to show immediately next to that lively and crowded scene, behind a wall separating the Indian family's home from the neighbor's yard, a lone, middle-aged white Englishwoman hanging up laundry on a clothesline. For a moment, the film allows that the contradiction between autonomy and attachment is not so easily overcome, and *pace* pop culture's conventional validation of individual autonomy, that the latter does not come without cost.

That the romantic and sexual relationship between a young man and a young woman should provide the plot's focus in so much cultural expression the world over, in ancient times as well as in all times since, may make further comment appear otiose: whether highbrow or lowbrow, classical or contemporary, pop or esoteric, representation in any genre can count on people's interest in young people and their desires. Nevertheless, I would point out that the bond of romantic love between two individuals (usually one of each sex, or at least one of each gender presentation) suggests an evident effort at resolution between the wishes for feeling bonded and for feeling unbound, that is, unconstrained. After all, romantic and sexual desires are often thought of as particularly powerful incentives to attachment. At the same time, when someone is connected to only one other individual, or at least, takes that one bond as important above all others, then he or she is only one degree away, as it were, from complete autonomy.

The third film I use to illustrate fantasized resolutions to the desires for bonds and freedom, the Thai martial arts film *Ong-Bak*,[14] does not, indeed, feature a pair of young lovers as central to its plot. The male protagonist represents all the "best" in idealized Thai masculinity without the complications of sexual desire. He is a village youth, named Ting, who trains in Thai boxing with a monk and turns out to have remarkable skills. The theft by evil city types of the head of the village's Buddha statue sets the plot in motion. Villagers make what small contributions they can to fund the young man's trip to

Bangkok, where he will not only trace the stolen artifact, but also look for his cousin, long since disappeared, and as it turns out, lost to all dignity, honor, and concern for his kin. (He has changed his name to "George," and at first denies even knowing the village youth, Ting, when the latter tracks down and greets him.) The film consists largely of a series of hostile encounters between the effortlessly graceful and powerful Ting and his opponents. These are ruffians and foreigners of various sorts, whose ways—dishonorable, vicious, and ineffective—only point up the virtues of Ting's consummately fair play.[15] The film leads, unsurprisingly, to the retrieval of the Buddha head when the evil cabal who stole it is defeated. It leads at the same time to the depraved cousin's final realization of his errors, made clear by his dying request that Ting convey to his parents his apologies for having failed to ordain as a monk, as would have brought them great merit.

Dangerously nativist elements in the film make it disturbing when examined at all closely. The evil instigator of the holy Buddha head may well be Sino-Thai; Ting's last boxing opponent is from Thailand's long-time enemy, Burma, and he cheats; young Westerners are underhanded, drunken brutes. Women, meanwhile, are purely secondary to the proceedings. One young woman, sympathetically portrayed, has however been led so far astray as to come to depend on the drug-dealing, gambling cousin, George, causing her to neglect her university studies and risk the sort of corruption that causes another woman's death from a drug overdose. Virtue, in this simple if exhaustingly testosterone-driven tale, resides in the village, in traditional practices, in submission to rightful authority, whether in the person of the village headman or a Buddhist monk—in sum, in all the romanticized images of solidarity ordered through hierarchy that modern Thai urbanites hold of rural life. Of course, this nativist message is communicated by means of sophisticated film techniques and a purely "international," that is, rock and hip-hop based, score.

The fact that the handsome, virile young Ting exhibits no romantic or sexual urges points up, by omission, the difficulties that such urges always pose to idealizing representations of harmonious social relations, especially if such representations are to include young males.[16] I mentioned in chapter 8 that women's allure threatens to grant them power in their relations with males, a threat many males find disturbing. The film's makers could, certainly, have tossed in a fair and modest young village woman as a love interest without putting their overall schema at risk. Still, the film's focus is on young masculine power put at the service of righteous elders, and in conflict with unrighteous others. Solidarity—attachment—comes in the form of relations we are to assume pervade village life, and, more immediately, in the male bonding that is forged, or reforged, between Ting and his cousin. Easier, then, just to leave women out of it.

Romanticizing a rural existence few or none of its spectators would consider taking up or returning to, while representing violence as both elegant and invariably just in its outcomes, *Ong-Bak* plays on people's desires—young men's desires perhaps most acutely—to feel both connected and free, attached and autonomous, righteous and honorable in one's willingness to show respect where it is due and at the same time to be the object of others' respect. In other words, it finds ways, to borrow once again Clifford Geertz's memorable phrase, to make "inequality enchant" (1980, 123). The bulk of the film, however, glorifies the assertion of autonomy that comes with the violent defeat of one's opponents. The latter are representatives of kinds of others who must be put in their place by means of their utter defeat and perhaps extinction.

Expressions of nativism of this sort are dangerous precisely because, as Dumont said of American racism (1980, 247–266), they treat difference as radical, a difference so profound as to preclude the possibility of bonds, rather than the foundation on which to elaborate ongoing relationships. Tragically, communitarian violence in a great many places today, whether in Burma, Thailand, Indonesia, or beyond Southeast Asia, in Africa, the Middle East, or US cities, suggests that this renunciation of the possibility of forging bonds across difference grows increasingly common the world over.

Supporting claims about social life by reference to representations of social life in popular culture is the latter-day equivalent to the nineteenth-century anthropological habit, a bad one, that I alluded to in this chapter's opening of culling evidence from hither and yon to support a preconceived idea. I noted that such selective use of data has brought cultural comparison into disrepute. It has certainly vitiated the persuasiveness of much analysis in cultural studies. I would defend my embarking on the above excursus, or at least beg my readers' indulgence for having done so, by suggesting that an enormous number of films, particularly those from Hollywood and Bollywood that attract the greatest number of spectators all over the world, are susceptible to fruitful analysis with reference to the contradiction between attachment and autonomy that I have applied as an analytic approach to the three films discussed above—but with the note that popular culture tends to incline toward celebration of autonomy rather more than attachment.[17] Even if three films seems a meager number of ingredients for pudding, I would invite readers to consider any films they have seen recently and ask whether they might not provide further proof.

Autonomy, Attachment, and Market Exchange

I conclude by citing one more, pervasive and familiar, element of contemporary life everywhere to shore up my contention that analyzing social relations from the perspective of conflicting desires for autonomy and attachment is illuminating. Or I return to it, since I invoked it—market exchange—in concluding my remarks about tea shops at the end of chapter 1. I suggested then that the allure of market exchange lay in its making it possible for people of means to satisfy their desires by dint of others' service without suffering the burdens and constraints of ongoing relationships. This much is clear from the writings of Marx, Mauss, and Polanyi.[18] I would tie this point to Dumont's analysis of hierarchy by noting that market exchange constitutes an excellent meeting ground for those people whose fundamental convictions are of a hierarchical sort as well as for those people who profess egalitarian ideas. It does so by appealing so compellingly—and in this it is quite in line with popular culture—to people's desire for autonomy, while dissembling the consequences that celebrating autonomy might have for their attachments, and at the same time dissembling the severe challenges that the market poses toward any egalitarian commitments people might lay claim to.

If hierarchical convictions justify difference as in the order of things, then the way that market exchange grants greater autonomy to some parties—those who enter the market with greater stores of power (money or marketable goods or services or skills)—than others holds nothing anomalous or scandalous. Power on the market translates into greater autonomy inasmuch as it assures someone the privilege of participating more "freely" than would be the case for someone who, in the classical Marxist case, has only his or her labor to sell. The latter individual is clearly more constrained, and more dependent, having no choice but to put his or her labor up for daily sale. Thus powerful actors in the marketplace can choose when, to what degree, and with whom to enter into exchange; weaker actors have much less room for maneuver. Yet even the powerful will still be obliged to enter into exchange with some others at some times. What happens on the market, therefore, the exchanges that take place, still appears to fulfill the fundamental hierarchical principle of mutual interdependence through difference.

At the same time, everyone participating in market exchange gets to try their hand at getting ahead. They can enter into the fray and try to raise themselves above others through their artful and alert surveying of the field for any opportunities that might arise. All of this looks familiar to anyone experienced in the competition for status and power pervasive in hierarchical circumstances. The marketplace looks like one more arena in which the traffic in hierarchy takes place: exchange, alliances, dispersals, and betrayals all feature prominently in relationships among economic actors, just as they do among political and other actors. Indeed, as observers of corrupt governments the world over well know, the analytic distinction between economic and political actors is often conceptual rather than real.

For those people who hold egalitarian convictions, market exchange can easily be represented as just because it posits the existence of one sphere of activity, the economic, standing apart from all others and therefore positing nothing about different kinds of selves or individual actors' rights or privileges. It asserts that every market is level ground on which, like the flat surface of a football field, individuals given equal chances contest their talents and come eventually to an uneven but fair resolution. Equality of rights at the outset, we are told, need imply nothing about equality of outcomes. It is this radical, and altogether nonsensical, differentiation of the economic from all other elements of social relations that Dumont congratulates Polanyi for having revealed to be the distinctive feature of modern, Western ideology, and that he, Dumont, condemns as both wrong and dangerous (Dumont 1983).

Of course, this claim that differences in wealth do not constitute a fundamental and distorting inequality in all areas of life, one that incontestably disadvantages some among any market's participants (indeed, the vast majority, but to varying degrees) from the start, is the glaring untruth on which all defenses of market mechanisms must rest. Proponents of "free markets" draw on this reasoning to convince people who subscribe (however casually) to egalitarian values that the market is defensibly fair, rewarding effort and inventiveness and discouraging sloth. Astonishingly, a great many people the world over are ready to believe this. Many such people even proclaim that they stand for egalitarian values and see the market economy as the only possible way for resources to be distributed fairly and "efficiently."[19]

The claim, once again, is that the market works justly because it apportions rewards according to the contributions individual actors, enjoying equal rights, make. It is therefore consonant with egalitarian values. Some people's readiness to accept this self-evidently false claim reflects simple cynicism. Rich people protect their privileges while hypocritically espousing loftily democratic principles. Yet the effectiveness of conservative rhetoric in winning over not only members of the dominant class but also a great many far humbler citizens even of societies in which egalitarian rhetoric appears to hold sway requires further explanation. I suggest that the key lies at least in part in the pull we all feel toward individual autonomy, a willingness to believe that we might be able to escape constraints on our freedom of action without suffering unwanted consequences.

The simple flaw in this belief, or wish, lies in the fact that when we act as individuals, our sense of freedom only disguises the powerlessness that acting alone, for most people, entails. We enjoy the ability to change jobs, or to buy what we wish, or to act on whatever turn our sexual desires might take, or to express our personal political beliefs. These are real and valuable attainments, and I do not in any way wish to gainsay their significance or worth. Yet in choosing individual autonomy in all of these domains, we risk minimizing any impact any one of us might have upon our social context, or even any sense of our own place therein. We are remarkably and often commendably free. We are also free to become unemployed, consumer-driven, lonely, and/or a voter whose vote matters very little. The more thoroughly we are persuaded that our individual satisfaction comes from our acting individually, the more we risk finding ourselves reduced to being individual consumers rather than social actors—or beings.

Autonomy, I repeat, is not by any means an evil. Seeking to maximize it, whether as a Buddhist monk in Burma or as a first-generation college student in the United States who leaves home (and the community of support for which it stands) in pursuit of a degree, often makes excellent sense. Social mobility may motivate both actors, and opportunities to enhance social mobility are a good that any progressive citizen must applaud. But there are always trade-offs, and it is by occluding that fact that public discourse can mislead. Taking one's own freedom of action as the primary criterion by which to decide one's course has to implicate the tenor of one's relationships with others, and so, one's attachments.

I do not wish to appear to be an apologist for hierarchical arrangements. Since these rarely provide any means of assuring that superordinates fulfill their responsibilities, they always open on to the possibility of exploitation, a possibility amply illustrated the world over and quite dramatically in Burma's recent history. I am not seeking to promote hierarchical understandings but rather to grasp their logic and note their consequences for people's social relations. At the same time, I want to show that acting in favor of hierarchical or egalitarian commitments necessarily entails trade-offs.

Trade-offs apply at the level of individuals and at the level of much larger collectivities. Losing sight of the common good, which the loss of an effective socialist discourse in Western societies both signals and exacerbates, in favor of an ideological individualism applied to all areas of social life, can only increase inequality and misery, as the history of the United States since 1970, with its ever-increasing degree of inequalities in wealth, certainly demonstrates. The work of Robert Bellah et al., as recorded in the series of editions of *Habits of the Heart,* demonstrates how difficult it is even for progressive Americans to formulate any statement with reference to groups—even a group as tiny as the conjugal family (2008).

The ideology of the free market and popular culture link up most obviously, and particularly corrosively, in advertising. Advertising sustains the illusion that total satisfaction is attainable in the absence, indeed, avoidance of long-term relations of exchange, by inducing us to associate anomic action in the marketplace, as consumers, with highly idealized social relations. We engage in the exchange of goods and services on the market, where trades are made impersonally. ("Click Submit" represents only a logical extreme of such depersonalized exchange.) We do this by means of the trace-effacing medium of money. (Again, numbers read off a small piece of plastic constitute only the latest instantiation of an ancient concept, the storing of power over others in a perfectly liquid form.) The benefits of clear-cut, brief, unentangling exchange are real: I am not alone in finding it easier to go to one of the few supermarkets in Mandalay rather than the more familiar, time-consuming open-air markets.

Yet such short-term interaction, multiplied in a great many such exchanges to constitute the consumerist lifestyle, is represented in advertising as being able to bring us all the joys of close, personal relationships with people we care about and who care about us. Buying cigarettes "means" fulfilling the fantasy of the powerful, lone man in the American West, and yet also enjoying outings with other, energetic, happy, and attractive young people with whom we happily, if unconsciously, identify. Shampoo (probably the most pervasive television advertising content in Southeast Asia) will grant a woman immense sexual attractiveness, the sine qua non for her entering into a richly satisfying relationship (and eventual marriage) with a desirable, which is to say reliably loving and materially supportive, male. Fine Italian tailoring will assure aging males similar, or rather, complementary, satisfactions (minus any reference to marriage). Families will be made harmonious and joyful by their shared consumption of potato chips.

The fact that these highly clichéd images nevertheless remain effective—or so I assume, since so much money continues to flow into advertisers' coffers—demonstrates how vulnerable people are to these messages. I take this somewhat worrisome and saddening fact as evidence that the existential contradiction between desires for autonomy and attachment remains potent and irresolvable. I say worrisome because our consumption patterns are clearly driving us all to our doom, if not as individuals then certainly as a species. And I say saddening because the message that satisfying social relations are to be obtained through material consumption is so clearly wrong.

Notes

Introduction

1. I choose not to substitute the new names of the nation-state of "Burma" and its capital city of "Rangoon" when I write in English, despite the Burmese government's instructions that people do so. Official justification for changing the name of the country (in the early 1990s) from "Burma" to "Myanmar" was based on the claim that the former made it appear that the dominant ethnic group, the Burmans, who make up about two-thirds of the population of the country, enjoyed precedence over the nation's other ethnic groups. Changing the name was supposed to counter such unwanted implications (Dittmer 2008). However, the two names for the country both derive from the language of the Burmans; they differ only in that one (Burma) is from the informal or colloquial register, whereas the other (Myanmar) is from the formal one. It is hard to convey the difference between the two names in English. But if there was a country named "the United States of White America," and many of its citizens found the name, with good reason, exclusionary, it would do little good to substitute the name "the United States of Caucasian America." Such a change would effect a change in register but not in meaning. The final *r* in the official "Myanmar," meanwhile, is supposed to indicate a lengthened *ah* sound, as in the Queen's English. There is no *r* sound in contemporary Burmese, so pronouncing the name as written, for those of us who do not belong to England's upper class, means introducing a further distortion. Daw Aung San Suu Kyi, incidentally, uses "Myanma" when she speaks in Burmese but "Burma" when she speaks in English, despite the government having publicly chastised her for using the latter label when she travelled abroad in 2012. Changing "Rangoon" to "Yangon," another substitution promoted by the military regime, brings English pronunciation marginally closer to Burmese pronunciation, in that most contemporary speakers of Burmese use a *y* sound when they name the city. (Residents of the area probably pronounced it with a flapped *r*, however, when Westerners started showing up there, which explains the English rendering of the name. The name translates as "the end of strife.") But I am not inclined to change the way I speak English out of deference to Burmese officialdom, any more than I would show such deference to French officials were they

to inform me I should start saying "Paree" when I speak in English of their capital city.

2. But no motorcycles. Remarkably, motorcycles are not permitted in the city of Rangoon. Deeply contrary to the interests of the millions of ordinary inhabitants who could afford to buy a motorcycle smuggled into the country from China, as people in the rest of the country do, this policy could at the same time be said to serve a public good, since it makes Rangoon's streets far less congested and dangerous than those of Mandalay, Bangkok, or Jakarta.

3. I use the term "Buddhist" without further qualifiers despite the existence of many different strands in "the" Buddhist tradition. I do so because virtually all the Burman Buddhists with whom I came in contact called themselves "Buddhist" and, if asked for further details, would have (but only if they enjoyed a certain degree of education) used the term "Theravada." Scholars of Buddhism point out that this label is actually of recent vintage: Perreira claims its use derives from the work of a Burmese Buddhist monk of Irish origin (!) (Perreira 2012). But while among historians of Buddhism the provenance and application of names for Buddhism's many schools matter importantly (Skilling et al. 2012), they are not of great salience to most Burman Buddhists, who are confident that their version of Buddhism is the most orthodox and valid.

4. Dumont tried to explain to hierarchy's detractors, whom he referred to as those holding an egalitarian ideology, why they should develop a subtler understanding of how hierarchical social systems work (1980). I introduce some of his basic points, which he made in reference to India, at the conclusion of my discussion of traffic in chapter 1 and at the beginning of the account of Buddhist sermons that follows.

5. Marx did so most notably in his *Manuscripts of 1844*, especially in his pointed remarks about how a man who wished to enjoy a woman's romantic favor in the absence of the market economy would be forced to rely on his charms rather than his money to win her over (Tucker 1978, 105). Polanyi expanded on the point in his magisterial book, *The Great Transformation* ([1944] 1957), a French edition of which is graced with an introduction by Dumont (1983).

Chapter 1: Everyday Forms of Hierarchical Observance

1. And, in the larger context, because of the destruction of the forests in Upper Burma, which explains much of the terrible flooding that now afflicts the country with ever greater ferocity.

2. In his underappreciated book about male moviegoers in India, Steve Derné shows how young men will cheer on the romantic leads who defy parental authority in pursuit of what might be called marital self-determination, while stating without hesitation that they of course intend to let their parents arrange their own marriages, since everyone knows that love marriages fail (2000).

3. Even though I want to show that Burmese traffic exhibits its own coherence, at the same time it is worth noting the ways that the vagaries of history have

given Burmese traffic some singularly loony features. Like most of the rest of Asia, traffic in Burma drove on the left until General Ne Win, the army general who seized power in 1962 from the civilian government of Prime Minister Nu, decided, suddenly, in 1970 that it should shift to the right. Ne Win's governing ideology was simple: never explain, never apologize. So there is no clear account of why he made the change, although most Burmese assume he did so on the advice of his always influential astrologers. In any case, he forced the change, and suddenly buses that had opened their doors for passengers to step down onto the sidewalk now opened their doors to let people down into the middle of traffic.

As the Burmese economy slowly, and then, by the 1980s, more quickly, collapsed, and traffic on the roads diminished, the ill-effects of the change perhaps paled compared with other facets of Burma's economic, political, educational, and social stagnation. But once Ne Win was replaced, in 1988, by a new set of generals, ones interested in bringing about greater economic growth (even if they did so, as it appeared, primarily for their own enrichment), the number of vehicles on the roads increased. The economy grew fairly rapidly in the early 1990s, then less so once it became clear that the generals insisted on retaining an iron grip on both politics and markets, but then more quickly again, especially after about 2000, as Chinese and Southeast Asian investment picked up despite Western and (somewhat halfhearted) Japanese strictures against supporting an illegitimate regime. This meant more and more used vehicles were imported from overseas, especially from Japan. In Japan, traffic drives on the left. Steering wheels in Japanese vehicles are therefore on the right. Burma's roads are now filled with cars driving in the right lane but with their drivers seated on the right and so unable to see around traffic ahead of them. The military keeps itself funded well enough that some of the vehicles they buy for themselves, although only some, are new, and those vehicles have the steering wheel on the left. Almost no other vehicles in Burma do. Even the tiny segment of very wealthy civilian elite who can afford to buy SUVs almost invariably buy used ones, as is made evident by the fact that the steering wheel is on the right. Some of the fanciest buses plying long-distance routes, for example, between Rangoon and Mandalay, have the steering wheel on the left, but by no means all.

The Burmese press suddenly developed an astonishing degree of license during my most recent long stay in the country, from mid-2011 to mid-2012. For decades, newspapers printed only official "news," consisting of dutiful reports of what important government officials had recently done. No actual political or social news was reported, and very few people bothered to read these stultifyingly dull pages printed by government mouthpieces. But then, with the new civilian regime in place, as of March 2011, it became possible for weekly newspapers to cover other topics. A great many articles about what needed to be done to reform Burmese society started to appear.

Yet to my knowledge, no one ever suggested that traffic revert to driving on the left. Certain difficulties would have to be addressed: traffic lights and signs, and traffic circles, have now all been set up in accordance with the practice of driving on the right. But the inconvenience to which changing all this would give rise for authorities charged with overseeing the roads would seem more than outweighed by the greater convenience and safety afforded drivers, almost all of whom drive vehicles in which the steering wheel is on the right. Perhaps the Burmese authorities avoid such a change in light of what they no doubt expect to be increasing traffic between Burma and China: Chinese drive on the right. But in Burma's other adjacent neighbors, India, Thailand, and Malaysia, driving is on the left. Shifting back to driving on the left would make road links with China more difficult but with India and other neighbors easier—and it would mean that as long as Burmese continue to import used cars from Japan in large numbers, as it seems clear they will, the convenience and safety of drivers would be greatly enhanced. Unsurprisingly, Burmese government officials appear inclined to do the opposite: to impose (or talk about imposing) stricter controls, such that only vehicles with steering wheels on the left be permitted on the roads. Such a policy would drive the vast proportion of vehicles off the roads—or at least, out of legality, making drivers vulnerable to yet another set of fines.

People I spoke with about which side of the road to drive on, when I brought it up, never seemed to find the topic interesting. Nor did they seem to think it likely that any government official would entertain such an idea. To think so would require revising one's understanding of the relationship between the government and the citizenry in profound ways. It would imply that it was incumbent on officials to find ways to make life safer and more convenient for an anonymous but deserving citizenry. This does not correspond to Burmese understandings of how individuals relate to power, which is always personalized and opportunistic. Political relationships are, like most relationships, dyadic, hierarchical, and contingent: there is little notion of a public good. For the record, let me note that such a notion seems to be suffering ever greater eclipse in the West, as well. Privatization does not serve the interests of a public good, as the word itself should make clear.

4. My impression is that Australians have fared a bit better at figuring this matter of egalitarianism out, but Bruce Kapferer has demonstrated that their egalitarianism, too, has its limits (2012).

5. To many readers, the Sanskrit word, *dharma,* will be more familiar than the Pali word, *dhamma,* I use here. Both languages are sacred languages of Buddhism, but Pali is much more widely studied and known in Burma than Sanskrit. I use the Pali words throughout what follows because that is what Burmese Buddhists invariably use.

6. That many Burman Buddhists feel a desire for such personal connection calls to mind Howe's analysis of why some Balinese find the Sai Baba version of Hinduism so compelling. Howe points out that the usual form of religious activity in Bali is communal, rich in ritual activity but lacking much by way of emotional resonance, and he notes how much more emotionally engaging Sai Baba's

followers found activities in the cult as compared with traditional forms of Balinese worship (2001, 180–181).

7. Alicia Turner reports on the great popularity of what she calls "preaching events" in early twentieth-century Burma in her fine study of Buddhist reform movements in the colonial era (2014, 96–100). She shows how the preference for events intended to induce discipline and devoutness rather than fun responded to a moral anxiety occasioned at least in part by colonialism. The colonial enterprise is long gone, but efforts to make Buddhist morality stick continue unabated, as do of course the behaviors they are meant to stop.

8. I find it useful, when I am puzzled by some behavior, to try to think of analogous practices in my own life that may correspond to the apparently strange behavior of others. In the case of audiences taking such pleasure in hearing familiar statements about Buddhist teachings, I realize that I am equally enthralled to read articles in the American press about how to assure one's good health. When I come upon an article about how important it is to get regular exercise, or to limit one's intake of deep-fried foods, or to assure oneself adequate sleep, I, who pride myself on conforming to these recommendations quite strictly, read every word of such articles with relish. Since all of these points have been known to members of the American middle class at least since the 1960s, nothing in these articles is surprising or new—which in no way diminishes my self-congratulatory pleasure in reading them through to the very end. "How many times a week at minimum should one get twenty minutes of exercise?" "Three times a week, Venerable Health Editor of the *New York Times*!"

9. Monks do not attend their colleagues' sermons in large numbers. Even when the Sitagu Sayadaw—who might be deemed the Luciano Pavarotti of sermon-givers in Burma—came to the Shweigyin monastery where I was staying in Mandalay to give a sermon to a huge crowd, monks resident at the monastery did not attend it. I do not know whether Placido Domingo attended Pavarotti's performances at the Met. But the way they performed together as peers (in the lamentable "Three Tenors" concerts) would be unimaginable in the case of Burman sermon-givers.

10. I develop this point at greater length in chapter 9.

11. I develop this point at greater length in chapter 8.

12. Guillaume Rozenberg provides vivid accounts of how deeply involved laypeople become in the affairs of those monks they look on with special reverence (2010, 2011).

13. I use the masculine pronoun advisedly: the vast majority of customers are male.

14. A frequent gesture of sociability is to prepare a cup in this way for each of one's companions at a table and then fill each one with green tea. Better and slightly more expensive tea shops have recently started placing freshly washed little cups on a table as customers sit down, reflecting a growing concern for health and respectability.

15. On more recent trips to Burma, I have noticed young women taking on the role of waiter in some upscale tea shops. This remains, as of 2016, quite exceptional, however.

16. Kirsch makes passing reference to this point in his contribution to the collection of essays (1969, 57).

17. Recent efforts on the part of anthropologists to undermine stereotypical representations of Japanese as group-oriented and rigidly conformist are no doubt worthy. At the same time, ethnographic data reported by those same anthropologists often vitiates the point they wish to make, as in Dorinne Kondo's vivid report of workers at a Tokyo sweets factory (1990).

18. Joel Robbins, who has made innovative use of Dumont's work, makes some progress along such lines in his analysis of what converting to charismatic Christianity has brought about among the Urapmin in Papua New Guinea (2009). Lucien Pye makes bolder, if more tendentious because less fine-grained, characterizations in the field of comparative politics among societies organized hierarchically (1985).

19. The color of the license plate on cars, minivans, and trucks, whether black or red, carries some weight, because red indicates that the vehicle's owner is in the military. But many drivers are not the vehicles' owners, who may have leased it to others, so granting such drivers the deference the military usually expects of others may well be uncalled for.

20. An American ethic of "service with a smile," by way of contrast, encourages just such a euphemization of inequality to assuage egalitarian consciences. Remarkably, service people in the United States are so little sensitized to the status implications of their interactions with customers that they can often provide service with a smile without feeling demeaned.

21. Much that is reported about private life in many parts of the world today suggests that a similar inclination is coming increasingly to apply to intimate and kin-based relations, as well.

Chapter 2: A Description of the Shweigyin Monastery

1. As per standard anthropological practice, I use a pseudonym to name this monastery, just as I do to allude to other individuals and institutions throughout this book. The only exceptions are in cases of well-known individuals whose public profile is such as to make the use of pseudonyms beside the point.

The Shweigyin is a smaller, stricter sect within Burman Buddhist circles, compared with the more populous "Thudamma" sect. The identification of the monastery where I have stayed as "Shweigyin" contributes to the relatively high esteem in which it is held. The distinction has lost much of its significance in the past few decades, however, so much so that a number of monks who label themselves Thudamma reside at this Shweigyin monastery. For information about the history and significance of such sects in Burmese history, see Mendelson (1975), and for the Shweigyin sect in particular, Ferguson (1978) and Carbine (2011).

2. I lived in what I am calling the "Shweigyin Monastery" a total of seven months in 2011 and 2012, five weeks in 2013, and three weeks in 2014, as compared with two and a half months at the Buddhist academy (which was also a monastery) where I first lived in Mandalay in 2011, and about three months in another monastery in Mandalay in 1988.

3. It has become common practice in Anglophone writing to label as "lent" or "lenten season" the three lunar months out of every year during which monks are enjoined to engage in particularly intensive study and ascetic practice, while moving about and engaging with laypeople relatively little.

4. The Palaung make up one of Burma's many ethnic minorities. Like many Palaung, this monk hails originally from Shan State in eastern Burma.

5. To speak of "names" here is something of a misnomer. When a boy becomes a novice, his lay name is suppressed in favor of a "title," two or more Pali syllables that he now takes on as his name. Often, that title is changed when he becomes ordained as a monk in his twentieth year.

6. Similar to Sunday for Christians and Friday for Muslims, the Buddhist Sabbath gives rise to greater religious activity, and less commercial activity, than other days of the week. However, the fact that it falls at slightly irregular intervals gives rise to a certain confusion. In Rangoon, it is observed much less widely than in Mandalay; in the latter city, the markets are closed on the Sabbath, although schools and other government institutions are instead closed on Saturday and Sunday.

7. Relatively few urban-dwelling Burmese males now smoke cheroots, the cigars made from Burmese tobacco leaves. These come in both "strong" and "light" or "weak" varieties. Their use was still pervasive when I was in Burma in 1987 and 1988 but has fallen precipitously since then. Western-style cigarettes have become much more common, especially among younger men, but they are expensive. Most men buy them singly or in small numbers, often at tea shops, rather than in packs. One simple way to track the ups and downs of the Burmese economy is to note how many cigarettes are being consumed among men sitting in tea shops.

8. Gustaaf Houtman presents an extensive account of the difficulties the Burmese military leaders had coping with the fact that the great nationalist leader who both founded the Burmese army and won Burma independence from British colonial rule, General Aung San, who was assassinated in 1947, could no longer be the object of public veneration, or even mentioned, once his daughter, Daw Aung San Suu Kyi, became the public face of opposition to their autocratic rule in 1988 (Houtman 1999). The conundrum was only resolved when the photograph of President Thein Sein and Daw Aung Suu Kyi standing below Aung San's portrait was permitted widespread circulation in August 2011. See preface.

9. This building was completely refurbished during my absence between July 2012 and September 2013. The corrugated metal roof was replaced with ceramic tiles, a much cooler alternative but an unusual luxury anywhere in Burma, and the exterior was repainted.

10. Nuns who go on alms rounds two days before each Sabbath day, on the contrary, are given uncooked food, particularly uncooked grains of rice. As discussed in chapter 9, their status is comparable to that of novices, not monks, and they do not enjoy the prestige of monks.

11. Turner reports that Ledi Sayadaw, among others, urged Buddhists to commit themselves to a vegetarian diet early in the twentieth century (2014, 96–99). I came across no such campaigns during my stays in Burma.

12. When I returned in 2013, he had moved out of that structure and into one of the other, larger halls where a number of monks resided. I did not hear an explanation for the move, but it was probably because the abbot had chosen to house another, visiting monk in private quarters, and to do so had granted him the use of the small building where the abbot's cousin had been living until that time. A structure a monk could consider his own, even an insubstantial one, would be more appropriate in such circumstances than assigning him to stay with other monks with less privacy. A layman who takes on the robe at an advanced age enjoys much less respect than does a monk who has never married. This probably explains why the abbot's cousin had had to give up his quarters.

13. Even after I bought and had the step-up transformer installed, the power supply remained inadequate to make the air conditioner work effectively. When I returned in September 2013, the power supply at the monastery was much improved and the people occupying the quarters I had stayed in previously were enjoying the use of the equipment I had donated. In September the weather in Mandalay is still warm but not unbearably so, and I lived in a hall with monks and novices, a more advantageous site for learning about their lives, although the bedbugs in the floorboards obliged me to move my mat and mosquito net out onto the stone-floored verandah at night when I wanted to sleep.

14. This is, as a matter of fact, the name a Buddhist abbot gave me, through a Burman friend (the late, much-lamented Daw May Kyi Win), who asked for one on my behalf when I first arrived in Rangoon in 1987. The name suits me inasmuch as I was born on a Friday: Burmans' names are chosen according to the fit between certain initial syllables and the day of the week on which someone was born.

15. He often asked me to repeat, as a contrasting pair, the English words "fashion" and "passion," which he heard on TV, so that he could learn to hear the difference. I'm not sure he ever did really get the difference down. Burmese phonology includes an initial aspirated sound similar to English *p* but it lacks anything resembling an *f*.

16. I lack information as to the first language of an additional seven novices.

17. I have never met a Burman, a member of the nation's dominant ethnic group (making up about 65 percent of the population) who speaks Shan. Such people must exist, but the order of languages is such that Burmans do not often feel motivated to learn the language well.

18. People speaking Burmese talk of "going down" to a village, in precisely

the same way as Indonesian speakers do. Hierarchical understandings permeate both societies and deeply color representations of the relations between cities and villages.

19. Hayashi reports that a "forest monastery" was built very close to a "village monastery" in a village where he did fieldwork in northeast Thailand. They differed primarily in the nature of the relationships that lay villagers entered into with monks in the two establishments. I am not aware of such a phenomenon, wherein conceptual distinctions between monasteries take precedence over physical location, in this way in Burma (cf. Hayashi 2003).

CHAPTER 3: DISCRETIONARY ATTACHMENTS

1. I could not, as a layperson, be seated near them for the meal and indeed usually chose to find my own food outside. Monks and laypeople often expressed surprise that I did so, assuring me that there is always a surplus of food at a monastery and I should feel free to avail myself of it. But I did not think that laypeople's donations should be going to support a foreign anthropologist's research on anything more than an occasional basis, and I sensed that U Dhammananda approved of this choice on my part, although he never said anything explicitly on the topic.

2. As an aging male with increasingly truculent guts, I knew exactly what U Dhammananda meant. Nevertheless, his remark surprised me a little, since Burmans generally show greater tolerance for the wayward inclinations of the human body than middle-class Westerners often do.

3. I have to rely on my observations of monks' relations among themselves, rather than on comments I could elicit, because monks clearly found my questions discomfiting. If I asked, for example, who their closest friends were among their peers, they usually denied having any, saying that they got along well with all of them.

4. The warmth of these relationships resembles what Jeffrey Samuels reports among Sri Lankan monks in his engaging book, *Attracting the Heart* (2010).

5. One day Ko Kyaw stopped by my quarters and insisted on moving a calendar I had suspended from one of the posts used for hanging a mosquito net above my sleeping platform. He noted that the calendar featured the images of a number of famous abbots. I had known to suspend it high above my head, but he objected to the fact that it hung at the foot of the bed, whereas it needed to be hung at the head. He took it upon himself to make this change. Unfortunately, this placement meant that the calendar was too far away for me to consult when I sat at my desk. But practical considerations are trumped by matters of respect whenever it comes to abbots, even in the case of small cameo images of them.

6. One evening all three of us went to hear the Sitagu Sayadaw give a *dhamma* talk in the business district of Mandalay: whole blocks of the downtown

streets had been blocked off to accommodate the huge crowd that came to hear the famous monk speak.

7. U Dhammananda assured me that young monks, in their twenties and perhaps into their early thirties, moved from monastery to monastery often. Provided someone known to the abbot of a monastery to which they wished to move could vouch for them, they were unlikely to be denied permission to enter one. Petitions for permission to move in this way on the part of older monks, however, would be looked on with some suspicion. What was it that was driving a monk to seek to make such a move? A whiff of impropriety accompanied such intentions in the case of older monks, who were expected to be well settled in a monastery. No eyebrows were raised when younger monks expressed such a desire: they were assumed to be restless by nature.

8. I was sometimes surprised at how public this lower floor of the building in which U Dhammananda had his private quarters actually was. One day I visited U Dhammananda and found a large group of Sino-Burmese women in the room, many of them going in and out of the area in which the bath and toilet were located. When I questioned U Dhammananda about who these women were, he assured me he had no idea. He added simply that the abbot had told them to come use the facilities here.

9. I, on the other hand, could only be struck at the irony of the situation, wherein newlyweds were being told what they might give someone else in a monk's unbridled registry of wants.

Chapter 4: Taking Dumont to Southeast Asia

1. Ruth Benedict's remarkable book, *The Chrysanthemum and the Sword*, however, sheds fascinating light on Japanese understandings of hierarchy (1946).

2. Rio and Smedal provide a good summary of the critiques Dumont's work on India elicited from Indianists (2009a, 12–20). Dumont himself took on many of his first critics in the "Preface to the Complete English Edition" that appeared in 1980 (1980, xi–xliii).

3. I am not alone in believing that it behooves anthropologists to pay renewed attention to Dumont's work, as indicated by a number of relatively recent publications that draw on his contributions to the field. These include Bruce Kapferer's comparative study of Sri Lanka and Australia (2012) and his article devoted to Dumont's legacy (2010), Rio and Smedal's edited volume of essays on the topic of hierarchy (2009b), and an issue of *Anthropology Theory*, edited by Joel Robbins and Jukka Siikala, titled "Special Issue on Dumont, Values, and Contemporary Cultural Change" (2014).

4. Dumont writes, "Power exists in the society, and the Brahman who thinks in terms of hierarchy knows this perfectly well; yet hierarchy cannot give a place to power as such, without contradicting its own principle. Therefore it must give a place to power without saying so, and it is obliged to close its eyes to this point on pain of destroying itself" (1980, 77).

5. Thatcher made this statement in an interview on September 23, 1987. The interview as a whole (http://www.margaretthatcher.org/ document/106689) presents in an engaging manner all of the commonsense assumptions about social relations that made Thatcher, her friend Ronald Reagan, and many other conservatives so persuasive, even appealing, in their heartless denial of interdependence.

6. Even a scholar who expresses explicit appreciation for Dumont's work admits that "there is in Dumont a bit of a 'West and the rest' tinge to the individualist'/holist opposition" (Robbins 2009, 79).

7. Anderson names as one of the "three fundamental cultural conceptions . . . [that] lost their axiomatic grip on men's minds" around the time of the eighteenth century "the belief that society was naturally organized around and under high centres—monarchs who were persons apart from other human beings and who ruled by some form of cosmological (divine) dispensation. Human societies were necessarily hierarchical and centripetal" (1991, 36).

8. In later reflections on his essay about power in Java, Anderson enjoys himself catching Weber out in moments where he appears to lose sight of his own argument that charisma consists only in supernatural powers people *attribute to* some figure, moments at which Weber appears to suggest that there could actually *be* such a thing as charisma. In other words, even the all-seeing Weber has moments in which he falls back upon this "traditional" conception of Power (Anderson 1990a, 90).

9. Indeed, perhaps this need to feel "empowered" despite the loss of hierarchy's safety net helps explain the current fashion for "agency" in the writings of social scientists who are themselves subject to the neoliberal onslaught on their (as well as everyone else's) well-being.

10. That radicalization only went so far, of course. They looked on each other, similarly privileged members of the colonial elite, as equals, but as is well-known, they did not extend that recognition to people who were not male, white, and propertied.

11. Dumont sometimes uses the label "value-idea" (1986, 252).

12. Much of how Kapferer accounts for ethnic violence in Sri Lanka resonates, sadly, with the recent surge of anti-Muslim violence in Burma. Irrational paranoia about a Muslim conspiracy to take control of the country, and claims that Muslims are by nature violent and intolerant, in contrast to Buddhists' universal tolerance, suggest that Burmese Buddhists fear Muslims are trying to break out of their subordinate position in Burmese society and need therefore to be chastened and/or expelled. However, the roots of contemporary Buddhist violence against Muslims in Burma remain difficult to determine. (Jacques Leider 2013 traces the long history of tension among Muslims and other residents of Arakan.) Rather than speculate on a topic—the current violence being perpetrated by Burman Buddhists against Muslims—that remains confusing and fast-changing, I wish to look here at the broader context of Burman Buddhist assumptions about hierarchy and its workings.

13. Tellingly, when a prominent Burmese essayist gave a lecture titled "On Love" to an audience of university students in Mandalay in 2011, he spoke at length of parental love and the enormous debt of gratitude everyone must bear toward their parents as a result, and passed over the subject of conjugal love in just a few quick phrases.

14. In doing so, I follow Joel Robbins's example when he discusses a shift in the "paramount value" of the society in PNG, that of the Urapmin, which he has studied (2009).

15. So it is said about him, on the website of the organization he founded, that "between the years 1975–78, he lived in seclusion and practised meditation at the forest monastery of Thabaik Aing Taw-ya in Mon State Lower Myanmar." http://sitagu.org/austin/About/Nyanissara/Nyanissara.html.

16. Commenting on another instance of a society that prizes autonomy, Dumont cites appreciatively an article by Francis Hsu naming "self-reliance" as the "American core value." But Dumont goes on to say, "Now self-reliance implies contradiction in its application, for men are social beings and depend heavily on each other in actual fact" (1986, 238). I share Dumont's impression that "self-reliance" combines very uneasily with humans' fundamentally social nature. But I believe that tension applies much more pervasively among societies the world over than only those Dumont would label "modern."

Chapter 5: Hierarchical Habits

1. Indeed, it is so intuitively convincing that it remains an important undercurrent, little recognized but deeply influential, in contemporary American public discourse. That it is both present and unrecognized, an ideological id that distorts our politics greatly, is a point I intend to pursue in future projects.

2. I cite again Dumont's remark in passing that the ideal of equality "runs counter to the general tendencies of societies" (1980, 20).

3. For a vivid account of how binding the insistence on good form is in Bali, see Wikan (1990). For my concern that Wikan has neglected important contextual features, stemming from hierarchical considerations, in that account, see Keeler (1993).

4. See, for Javanese, J. Joseph Errington (1988, 1998), and Keeler (1984); for Balinese, see Kersten (1984) and Keeler (1975).

5. The first-person pronoun of greatest formality has an alternate form for a female speaker, *kja̰ma.*, although women in Mandalay have at least until recently not used this term, preferring to use *kjundo* as a gender-neutral one. Recently, however, this holdout against general usage seems to be losing ground among Mandalay's female speakers.

6. The government dictionary would transliterate the word for such spirits *na'*. But in deference to long-standing practice among scholars, I will render it *nat*.

7. An odd but instructive parallel is in the remarkable increase in physical modesty evident among Westerners. When I was growing up in the United States,

men in locker rooms were uninhibited about their bodies. Recently, only men above the age of forty or so retain this nonchalance: younger men, whether fit or not, evince an insistence on privacy that would have laid them open to ridicule in my youth. The change must derive from a sense that their bodies are subject to constant evaluation, that at no time can they consider their bodies to be a matter of indifference to others, and so can never be casually exposed. In other words, their bodies are always "on stage," so exposure can never be casual, and vigilance must be constant. Southeast Asians' constant concern for how others estimate their standing might be thought to parallel young Westerners' concern for how others observe their bodies.

8. Robert Hinton makes the pointed remark that Westerners who lived in Cambodia prior to 1975 often described their Khmer acquaintances as gentle, peaceful, considerate, and so on, and expressed incomprehension at the tales of violence that came out following the fall of the Khmer Rouge in 1979 (2005, 253). What they failed to reflect on was the fact that the behavior those Khmer displayed toward them, their wealthy foreign employers, followed from their relative status: their behavior reflected not some intrinsic personal character but rather the nature of their position in specific, hierarchically inflected relationships. How they behaved toward superordinates upon whom they depended had no bearing on how they behaved toward people they perceived as their rivals or even, as the Khmer Rouge taught them, mortal threats.

9. Hierarchy's claims were coming into question but not yet outright challenge in early modern England. Shakespeare's low-status characters do not resist or criticize their betters but rather fall on their faces when trying to imitate them.

10. Conversation with Brooke Zorbist, who works with educational NGOs in Burma, brought my attention to this topic.

11. This suspicion conforms closely to long-held views that any teacher withholds the most crucial elements of his knowledge, such as of magic formulas, from everyone, lest anyone come to equal him in his powers. (I use the masculine pronoun advisedly, because teachers of occult knowledge are usually thought of as male, although exceptions are admitted.)

12. Leo Howe provides an excellent contemporary example of such strife in the case of a kin group trying to elicit deferential speech from their neighbors in light of documentary evidence of their "forgotten" noble ancestry. Unsurprisingly, many of their neighbors weren't buying it (2001, 36–42).

Chapter 6: Gaining Access to Power

1. English expressions that indicate positive evaluation by referring to someone or something as being "hot" cannot be translated directly into Burmese.

2. See my discussion of Anderson's essay in chapter 4.

3. I follow Weber's example, obviously, in trying to discern the psychological correlates of religious ideas (Weber 1958a) when I suggest that Burmans respond to the emphases and potential knots in their experience of social life when

they formulate their ideals, whether proximate or ultimate. Unlike Weber, I am not willing to take religious dogma as the starting point. I see it, rather, as part of a complex of ideas about social relations, as expressed through various, including religious, idioms.

4. Steve Collins makes a good case for why very little can be said about it. Since, according to what Collins calls the "Pali imaginaire," it is the nature of all conditioned things to generate suffering, then the only escape from suffering must lie in gaining access to what is unconditioned. But nirvana, which names this domain apart, cannot be described precisely because, if it could, it would be conditioned (1998, 135–190).

5. In drawing a line starting from making donations to the sangha through efforts to direct the flow of power toward oneself and, ultimately, to meditation, I am connecting two categories that Hayashi chooses to distinguish. He writes of the "Buddhism of rebirth," on the one hand, and the "Buddhism of power," on the other, in his very interesting and subtle analysis of "practical Buddhism," that is, Buddhism as actually practiced, in northeast Thailand (2003). The former, Buddhism of rebirth, in his analysis, focuses on accumulating an ever-greater store of merit, particularly with an eye to one's future rebirth, whereas the latter, Buddhism of power, addresses people's need, pressing especially in their current lives, to find ways to protect themselves from the forces of the world of spirits, usually with the assistance of lay specialists (who are often former monks). Hayashi's distinctions are helpful, and I do not wish to dispute them. I wish simply to point out that differences in these facets of Buddhist practice do not gainsay the continuities among them, and the ways they can be seen to articulate with meditation.

6. Another kind of gift many people seek from a powerful monk, one providing not protection but wealth, although only some monks are willing to engage in this activity, is the bestowal of hints (only hints) of what lottery numbers will be chosen in an upcoming drawing, whether in Burma or Thailand. Rozenberg has described this quest for winning numbers arrestingly, and I will not reiterate that material here (2005). No monks at the monasteries where I stayed were willing to indulge laypeople in this way, so I do not have any ethnographic data to add. I witnessed very similar sorts of activity in Java, where both intense enthusiasm for betting on lotteries and the conviction that spiritually potent individuals can provide clues about forthcoming numbers are widespread.

7. I translate the word for effeminate male transvestite, *achau'*, with the pejorative "faggot" because that was the tenor of how he said the word, one that tends to have a negative valence in Burmese, although not necessarily as strongly negative as the English term.

8. Rozenberg notes the same ubiquity of Shan individuals in Burman thinking about specialists in cabalistic figures and other forms of protective magic (2015, 185–241).

9. Rozenberg tells a fascinating story about a British colonial court of law responding to the presence of tattoos on a suspected anticolonial fighter by as-

suming that they indicated intent to rebel, and a Burmese judge intervening to tell the British prosecutor that all Burmese believed that tattoos were essential methods for staving off the threat of snake bites (2015, 219–220).

10. Guillaume Rozenberg writes about the role of relics in Burmese Buddhism (2011).

11. Schober notes that attitudes exhibited toward Buddha images have aroused a certain amount of debate among Buddhologists over the years (1997). But less so among Southeast Asian Buddhists themselves.

12. The most remarkable illustration I have encountered of how Buddha images relate to one another as distinct entities even though they represent a single referent came not in Burma but rather in Siem Reap, the city near the ancient Khmer temple complex of Angkor Wat in Cambodia. In that city, two Buddha images, both looked upon as something like the city's patron saints, are housed in a building off the city's main square. A Cambodian tour guide explained that the two images are thought of as "older brother and younger brother," and indeed, one is set somewhat higher than the other, as older brothers are granted greater deference than younger ones.

13. I was not aware of the fact when friends took me to the pagoda outside Pyin Oo Lwin but have read since that the image that is housed there was one of three being transported to China at the time. I assume that the other two communicated no such reluctance to abandon their native Burma and continued on their way to China.

14. Even a monk's robes may be likened to the various objects just named. Speaking of monks who reside at the monastery at Mebaygon, Guillaume Rozenberg makes it sound as though for them, donning the robe constituted one more form of invulnerability magic: "Furthermore, the monastic robe is potent: wearing it protects you. It attenuates the ravages of fate that befall some people, who, victims of an evil spell cast by some envious person, suffer personality disorders or repeated misfortune" (2015, 84).

15. Collins explains that this is "the third part of the canon, mostly scholastic matters of psychology and philosophy rather than narratives and sermons, and specifically the lists of psycho-physical elements in to which human persons are analyzed" (1998, 50 n. 63).

16. Braun writes about the philosophical texts making up the *Abhidhamma*, "Considered the most complex and demanding of all the Buddha's teachings, these works were held in great esteem among the [Burmese] populace, especially the teaching of the twenty-four conditional relations (*paṭṭhāna*) [*Paḥtan*: in Burmese] that explain the origination of all phenomena" (2013, 4).

17. The light show behind the Buddha image's head in the main hall of the Shweigyin Monastery commemorates that event.

18. Justin McDaniel pointed this fact out in a presentation he gave concerning Thai Buddhists' use of palm-leaf manuscripts, noting that when Thais say that a text in their possession is of the *Abhidhamma*, it usually turns out that it is not.

He contrasted Thai practice, wherein few people read the *Abhidhamma,* and Burmese, where people read it much more devoutly (2013).

19. U Dhammananda attributed Nargis's devastation to the delta-dwellers' reliance on shrimp and fish farming as a (relatively recent) way of earning a living. This highly demerit-producing activity, since it requires taking life constantly, could only invite disastrous retribution, in his view.

20. On the subject of *wei'za* I draw largely on the work of Rozenberg because his book (2015) is particularly rich and interesting. A number of scholars, including Rozenberg, have written shorter accounts, collected in Brac de la Perrière, Rozenberg, and Turner, eds. (2014).

21. Somewhat confusingly, the Burmese use the same word, *nat,* to refer both to spirits whose origins were usually human and who met early, often violent, deaths, and to the beings who inhabit the various Buddhist heavens, beings that English speakers more readily term "gods." Context makes clear which sort of being is invoked in any given instance.

22. I say until recently because, although I saw many all-night *nat pwe:* taking place in Mandalay in 1987 and 1988, in more recent years the authorities there have grown much more exacting about how the events can be staged. They have encouraged celebrants to hold the events at the foot of Mandalay Hill, rather than at other sites in the city. Not all *nat pwe:* have been banished to that one site, but as far as I have observed, the authorities' insistence that they take place only during the day, not at night, seems to be sticking.

23. Vivid illustration of these points can be found in Lindsey Merrison's compelling film, *Friends in High Places* (2001).

24. No Burman has ever drawn the analogy explicitly to me, but the similarity of having one's mind penetrated by a spirit and one's body penetrated physically (in sex) would appear to support associations of the *nat* cult with women and trans women.

25. Nu Nu Yi's novel, *Smile as They Bow* (Nu Nu Yi 2008), provides telling glimpses of this colorful, if often conflict-ridden, district of Burmese social life.

26. Rozenberg alludes to the dim view that many Burman Buddhists take of alchemical pursuits. The point was made vivid to me one day when U Dhammananda saw a copy of the French edition of Rozenberg's book on my table. The book sports on its cover a startling image of a monk wearing goggles while holding a large bellows in his hands: he must be trying to effect the transformation of a ball from some metal or metals into gold. U Dhammananda smiled and commented, "That can't have been taken here in Burma." I assured him it was and reminded him that I had introduced him to the book's author, Guillaume Rozenberg, when he had paid me a visit at the monastery. U Dhammananda was amazed to think that a Burmese monk would engage in such alchemical practices, but he had to admit that the monk was wearing a robe of a color seen in Burma, and not elsewhere in Southeast Asia.

27. The number thirty-seven in itself bespeaks power. It is the number of *nats* always invoked by spirit mediums, a number that has remained stable for centuries, although the content of the list varies both through time and from one master to another.

Chapter 7: Meditation

1. Three outsiders have written quite extensively on the subject. Gustaaf Houtman and Ingrid Jordt both spent time engaging very seriously in meditation at the Mahasi Meditation Center in Rangoon in the 1980s and have written books drawing on the experience (Houtman 1999; Jordt 2007). Erik Braun has published a biography of Ledi Sayadaw, born in the mid-nineteenth century, who more than anyone else promoted the "revival" of Buddhist meditational practice during a career of constant travel and preaching (2013). Other scholars working on religious topics in Burma—Spiro, Schober, Rozenberg, Gravers, Charney, and Brac de la Perrière, among others—have made more or less extensive reference to the topic. I approach the matter here to ask how it fits into ongoing preoccupations in Burmese thinking about social relations.

2. I should also note at the outset that my exposure to meditation in Burma is hardly extensive. There are many different schools of meditation within the Burmese Buddhist tradition. I have firsthand experience of only one; I have read accounts of a few others. There is no doubt a great deal more nuance and detail to fill in about the commonalities and contrasts among these various approaches. I can only hope that other scholars, and practitioners, will enlighten us as to these variations in coming years. The fact that so many outsiders are attracted to Burma because of the great richness of its meditation tradition provides grounds for optimism in this respect.

3. U Dhammananda was not as roly-poly as many monks, but he was still possessed of a fair girth, so it seemed clear that he was not so inclined.

4. U Goenka, as I learned listening to his taped lectures in the course of both retreats I undertook, was born to a prominent Indian-Burmese family in Mandalay. He received instruction in meditation, initially as a way to address the terrible migraine headaches he suffered, from U Ba Khin in Rangoon in the 1950s. He eventually moved to India, where he started passing along what he knew of the technique, first to his parents, eventually to other kin and friends, and finally to an ever-widening circle of students. Centers propagating his method can now be found throughout the world. U Goenka died in 2013.

5. Perhaps a little more detail will allow me to retain a sense of my own integrity. I was able during these "hours of resolve" to remain sitting with my legs crossed and my hands in my lap. Moving my head, neck, and back, which I tried to minimize but could not avoid completely, may have constituted a degree of malfeasance.

6. My conclusion accords with statements a famous proponent of Buddhist meditation in the United States, Jack Kornfield, has made about the relative

benefits to be obtained from meditation and psychotherapy (nd), comments rejected by Kearny (nd). My thanks to Steve Collins for drawing my attention to these references.

7. Just how powerful that image is, how much it fascinates and impresses people in Thailand (and this seems just as true in Burma), receives vivid illustration in Kamala Tiyavanich's book *Forest Recollections* (Kamala 1997), about Thai monks living in Northern and Northeast Thailand in the first part of the twentieth century. In this book, the romanticization of the lone ascetic confronting the dangers of the tropical wild finds vivid expression. Kamala herself clearly sympathizes with the monks who took on this role, while she finds fault with the arrogance, narrow-mindedness, and text-focused practices of Bangkok's powerful monks, their lives taken up with enjoying their proximity to worldly power. There is a certain Wild West element to her descriptions of ascetic monks, and her feelings—representative of many Burmese as well as Thai Buddhists' views of monks who meditate in the forest—call to mind an American fascination with a cowboy alone in the arid and dangerous West.

8. This would be by no means unprecedented. I met a family at a meditation center-cum-monastery on the flanks of Mandalay Hill where a grown daughter had become a nun, and was soon joined by both her parents, who had become a monk and a nun living there (in separate quarters) as well.

9. None of my informants expressed themselves in this way about meditation. Still, many people insist that meditation is especially appropriate for older people to undertake, since it is the best possible way to prepare oneself for death.

10. Clifford Geertz's account of a Javanese funeral is well-known: in it he relates what happened when a funeral's normal procedure went awry, but notes how very uncommon this was (1973, 142–169). I have written about a man whose son had just died in a traffic accident receiving guests at the funeral that same morning with unflappable equanimity (Keeler 1987). Many years later, I cannot tell this story about a man, the father of the deceased, whose life was marked by so much tragedy and for whom I felt such devotion (I lived in his household during my dissertation fieldwork and learned immense amounts from him) without choking up. Obviously, I lack the resources Javanese have for dealing with trauma so bravely.

Chapter 8: Masculinity

1. The topic of masculinity has given rise to a considerable literature in the wake of Connell's pioneering work. Connell and Messerschmidt formulated a more recent and more nuanced version of Connell's original ideas (2005). An excellent recent sampling of work on masculinity plus an extensive bibliography are to be found in a reader assembled by two sociologists who draw much inspiration from Connell (Pascoe and Bridges 2016).

2. Gorgeous images of such male stars are to be found in Dan Ehrlich's

book of photographs devoted to the theatre scene in Mandalay (2012). Music that was performed in such performances in the past can be heard on an AIMP set of two CDs (Keeler 2010).

3. Other performers identify solely as rappers, appearing in concerts in town, rather than as participants in all-night *za' pwe:* performances. Such rappers tend to have specific personas, which may be more or less rebarbative. But toughness tends to come with the territory.

4. In analyzing Burmese rappers' performances, I argued that scholars who wish to see progressive arguments against inequality and injustice in rap (wherever it is to be found) are projecting wishes to find organic intellectuals voicing opinions similar to their, the scholars', own on the material they observe. Such sentiments hardly figure in Burmese rap, I contend, or indeed in most rap, American or otherwise (cf. Keeler 2009).

5. A distinct theatrical tradition, *anyein.*, in which a woman dancer engages in banter with male comics and then sings and dances on her own, grants a woman more time in the limelight. The genre's fortunes have waxed and waned over the years: it appeared almost dead in the late 1980s but relatively vibrant in 2011. (Some people explained this renewed frequency of *anyein.* performances to the fact that it cost so much less to put on than a *za' pwe:*.) But it is in any case secondary to *za' pwe:* in its popularity and prominence.

6. I should perhaps say not "important" but rather "high-status." Male comics appear in groups at many points in a performance, cracking jokes and cutting up. (A troupe's princes do not take on a comic's role, although they may converse with them from time to time.) A few such comics have become nationally famous. But in most performances, they are a chorus, usually dressed in uniform (if outlandish) outfits, and do not take on individual identities. They stand for average, low-status, and insignificant males, people of no consequence, however great their entertainment value.

7. Much struggle for justice in the field of gender and sexuality would be abetted if only people could be persuaded to abandon some of those metaphorical readings. What if sexual acts of whatever sort referred to nothing other than themselves?

8. Kukrit Pramoj's serial novel, *Four Reigns,* illustrates the vagaries of aristocratic unions in Southeast Asia's past vividly (1998). The protagonist's marriage is highly idealized, but there are a great many unhappy marriages all about, starting from the bond between her father and his official wife, which at the start of the novel has already been broken by the wife's departure, and between her father and the protagonist's lower-status mother, as well as the marriages of her brother, her children, and so on.

9. For purposes of rhetorical simplicity, I am identifying the active (penetrating) role in sex with a male actor. Halberstam (1998) and others make it clear that no such easy assumption can be sustained: masculinity and roles associated with it are not the exclusive preserve of biological males. But such alternatives

are not widely recognized in Burma. In Southeast Asia, meanwhile, the biological sex of the passive (penetrated) party is less significant than in the West, as discussed with reference to nonnormative sexuality in the next chapter.

10. Simon Hardy argues along similar lines, in a very different context, in his book *The Reader, the Author, His Woman, and Her Lover* (1998).

11. Even when Burmans bathe in sex-segregated spaces, they always remain clothed, keeping a cylinder of cloth wrapped around their bodies as they pour water over themselves, and then letting it drop to the ground but only as they hold a dry cloth in place, ready to wrap it around themselves once they are done.

12. Because breaking the prohibition on sexual activity of any kind carries such heavy sanction, the topic of sexual activity taking place among monks or novices was one I could not discuss with residents of any of the monasteries where I have resided.

13. Western athletes often evince the same sense that sex is enfeebling (cf. Wacquant 2004).

14. Buddhism in other societies and other versions shares this monastic rule, but it is not necessarily observed so stringently. Tibetan Buddhist monks and Japanese Buddhist monks engage in sexual intercourse with women to much less public condemnation than would be the case in Burma (Gutschow 2004; Faure 1998).

15. That it is a secret we all know about and must never discuss was made particularly clear in President Clinton's cowardly dismissal of his surgeon general, Jocelyn Elders, in 1994, when she suggested masturbation constituted a physically and emotionally safer alternative to sexual intercourse for young people.

16. Matters are not actually as clear-cut as my statement—which applies to people's attitudes rather more than actual events—implies. During the civic uprising in 1988, the police and the military in Mandalay withdrew into their barracks, leaving a complete absence in the provision of security throughout the city for several weeks. As I have described elsewhere (Keeler 1997), young monks stepped into the breach, directing traffic, commandeering jeeps, and taking charge in a variety of ways. Although it seemed clear to me that they were enjoying themselves exercising power in lay environments, no one I spoke to at the time shared my view. Everyone insisted that monks have no interest in worldly power and claimed that my inference that some of them took pleasure in their new role as powerful agents in the city was misplaced.

17. A particularly stunning demonstration of how Americans, and not just the social scientists among them, enjoy identifying with the people who fight the people who go about exploiting the world and polluting the environment is the film *Avatar*. The fact that it is Americans who are polluting the world at a greater per capita rate than anyone else in the world does not undermine the pleasure American viewers took in identifying with the film's protagonists, who oppose what might be called a hyperpollutionist lifestyle as practiced by . . . Americans, such as those very viewers themselves.

18. Although by no means the first to make this point, Lutz and Collins make it well in their very useful *Reading National Geographic* (1993).

19. I pursued a similar point concerning egalitarian versus hierarchical thinking in a discussion of postmodern literature (Keeler 2002).

CHAPTER 9: MASCULINITY'S OTHERS

1. I have demonstrated my case here only for Burma. For the rest of Southeast Asia, I have made only passing references, but I have written an article to make the point more generally for Southeast Asia (Keeler nd.b).

2. Ikeya's work focuses on the colonial era, not the present, but much of what she relates remains relevant. Tharaphi Than draws on historical materials from the colonial period, from that of World War II, and from the early postwar years. But she goes on to discuss some more recent developments, including both Ne Win's dictatorship and the SLORC and SPDC years (1989 through 2011). A third recent book, Jessica Harriden's *The Authority of Influence: Women and Power in Burmese History* (2012), addresses the same topic of how women have fared in Burmese history. I do not make reference to this work in what follows because it is based on limited ethnographic engagement. It presents a useful compendium of historical evidence indicative of Burmese women's subordination without providing an analytic frame with which to deepen our understanding of it.

3. Tharaphi Than refers at many points, and not without traces of exasperation, to Daw Ni Ni Myint's completely uncritical and complacent rehearsal of the standard clichés about Burmese women's happy condition (Ni Ni Myint 2002). I would line these up with U Tin U's explanation of "*a:nade*" as reflecting a putatively innate and universal Burmese "delicacy of feeling," cited in chapter 5, for the ways that idealizing tropes drive all awareness of sociological factors, and everyday experience, out of mind (Tharaphi Than 2014, 1–4, 67–68).

4. Ikeya's article (2005) and Tharaphi Than's book (2014) both provide very useful reminders, in the context of appalling violence perpetrated against Muslims in Burma starting in May 2012, and of laws passed in 2015 to discourage Buddhist women from marrying non-Buddhist males, that the current controversy about Burmese women marrying outside their faith has deep historical roots.

5. In her book, Ikeya provides further information on this matter of the relative vehemence with which Burmese males condemned Burmese women's marriages with Indian versus British men. In the 1930s it appears that the latter unions came in for more sustained attack than previously. Still, even then it seems clear that it was marriage to Indian/Muslim men that aroused the greatest recriminations (cf. Ikeya 2011, 120–142).

6. Melford Spiro emphasizes the negative stereotypes with which Burmese men idealize themselves and denigrate women. He calls ideological claims along these lines the "'Ideology of the Superior Male,' [whereby] males are superior to females spiritually, intellectually, and morally," and the "Ideology of the Dangerous

Female," which he further parses as consisting of "the Ideology of the Morally Dangerous Female," and "the Ideology of the Sexually Dangerous Female" (1992, 223). He interprets these ideological stereotypes in a characteristically Freudian manner. I find much of his analysis convincing, but it lies at something of a remove from my concerns, which are more sociological, or social-psychological, than depth-psychological in nature. See also note 7.

7. Spiro attributes men's negative views of women to castration anxiety (1992, 223–246). I find his account persuasive, but I believe his psychological account should be supplemented with one of a more sociological nature, such as I suggest.

8. Keyes makes a similar point concerning women in Thailand (1984).

9. I owe this phrasing to Margaret Jolly, who attended a lecture I gave on the subject of gender in Burma at the ANU in July 2012.

10. Kawanami notes how frequently nuns form partnerships "to help each other and spread the load [of work and study]" (2013, 206–209).

11. Kawanami notes that a nun could, indeed, be seen to exert great charisma, that it was not monks alone who can attract a large following and win great financial support (2013, 139–140).

12. An incident at the first monastery I stayed at in 2011 made the point clear. Two young nuns knocked on my door one afternoon to ask whether I knew the whereabouts of the monk who lived in the quarters immediately next to mine. One of them had washed his robes for him: a nun, they told me, earned considerable merit by doing this for a monk. When I said I did not know where he was, they suggested I knock on his door. Doing so themselves, it seemed, would be inappropriately forward on their part. When I got no reply, I said he must be either out or having a nap. They urged me to knock again. This woke him up, which I realized was quite probably what they had intended. As a consequence, he was made aware of the service the nun had provided him, assuring her obtaining merit, and I was the person responsible for having disturbed his sleep.

13. I draw extensively on Kawanami's invaluable account (2013) of her research into the lives and conditions of nuns in Burma. I rephrase some of what she reports not to contest her conclusions but rather to complement her analysis with mine, which is informed by somewhat different analytic emphases.

14. Other scholars have noted the ambiguous status of nuns in Burmese Buddhism. Laure Carbonnel writes tellingly about the contrasting implications of nuns' alms-seeking and other activities, making them resemble monks in some contexts and laywomen in others (2009).

15. The same sentiments seem to characterize Thai attitudes toward those among their female kin who choose to pursue a religious vocation. See for a vivid illustration of such ambivalence Brown (2001).

16. Burman parents, especially fathers, may respond with hostility to a son who begins to appear effeminate. Yet they will eventually throw up their hands,

whereas a nun's parents, as Kawanami discusses, may continue to place demands on her time and attention throughout her life.

17. See Michael Peletz's article on this region-wide practice (2006).

18. Michael Peletz's *Gender Pluralism* provides an excellent overview of this literature (2009).

19. I have written elsewhere about the trans women I got to know in Mandalay over a number of years (Keeler 2015). Here, I simply summarize the points most relevant to my present argument.

20. A similar incident was reported in July 2013. See http://www.dvb.no/dvb-video/trans-women-assaulted-by-police/29938.

21. Peter Jackson notes in an arresting essay (2004) that in Thailand, what matters is not realities but rather appearances. Behavior and speech must be policed when they are public; the nature of that policing turns not on what is true but rather on what would be true in the best case and must therefore be publicly maintained. Much the same could be said of Burma. That people transgress gender and sexual norms is common knowledge; what must be policed is public *display* of such transgression, particularly before people whose standing is such that impressions they come away with are thought to matter.

22. I provide my take on why this opinion should be so widespread in Mandalay in Keeler 2015 and will not repeat it here.

23. I write "Mother Kyaw" because she used "Mami," a Burmese rendering of the American "Mommy" as her title. The diminishing effect of the American term is inordinate, so I have used "Mother" instead.

24. I have written of "marriage" and "spouses." Same-sex marriage enjoys no legal status in Burma. But official procedures surrounding marriage seem to be of little concern, and people speak of long-term same-sex relationships in the same way they do about other such ties. Like German, the Burmese language refers to spouses as "man" and "woman," so it is not possible to track whether speakers are conceiving of a couple specifically as married or only as a pair otherwise linked to each other.

25. More categories do exist in contemporary Burmese slang. Gilbert 2013 provides a full list. Some of these terms are also current in Mandalay, but there is less of a subculture there than in Rangoon, and knowledge of all these terms seemed to me to be less widely distributed.

26. In actual fact, my impression is that most gender- and sex-normative Burmans do not really think about the existence of masculine-presenting males who secretly prefer to be penetrated in sex. So the tripartite categorization of biological males is really salient only among men who have sex with men.

27. I was surprised in Burma that while parents brought some pressure on their children to have children in turn, this insistence seemed less inexorable than Boellstorff reports (2005), and I observed, in Indonesia.

28. The point was made about representations of women more broadly by

Sherry Ortner in her widely cited contribution in something of the founding text of feminist anthropology, Rosaldo and Lamphere's edited collection, *Woman, Culture and Society* (Ortner 1974).

Chapter 10: Taking Autonomy and Attachment Further Afield

1. Schneider, for the record, rejected Handler's position out of hand (1995).

2. Academic attacks on the concept of "Southeast Asia" as one imposed on the region in the context of the Cold War are many. A cogent one, although it is one I would dispute, was made by Craig Reynolds (1995).

3. I say "lowland" because I have no fieldwork experience in any "highland" Southeast Asian society. (The distinction between highly centralized societies of Southeast Asia and those with much more dispersed settlement and diffuse political arrangements can only rather casually be rendered by the terms "lowland" versus "highland." But the usage is of long standing and suits my purposes here.) Nevertheless, affinities with those regions often seem real enough. I must leave it to other scholars better versed in such areas to decide how fruitful comparison between highland and lowland societies is likely to be.

4. I am unaware of the degree to which the languages of China, or those of other areas of East Asia, do or do not include status markers. Japanese clearly does so to a considerable degree.

5. Jane Fajans anticipates some of the questions I wish to pose here when she points to autonomy and "relatedness" as two values people in societies negotiate variably. She fits her analysis into a Piagetian frame, contrasting "assimilation" with "accommodation" in an individual's engagement with the world (Fajans 2006). This gives her approach a somewhat different focus than mine, inspired as I am particularly by a Dumontian attention to matters of hierarchy. Nevertheless, her essay is fruitful and germane to the analysis I want to pursue for Burmese material, particularly with reference to the links between autonomy, attachment, and gender.

6. So he writes that "we are going through a stage of transition and moral mediocrity.... The great things of the past which filled our fathers with enthusiasm do not excite the same ardour in us ... but as yet there is nothing to replace them" (Durkheim 1915, 475). He holds out the hope that science will come to be our religion, but even he seems unsure of just how that will work (1915, 474–479).

7. Douglas Hollan muses cogently on the relevance of psychoanalysis to anthropology (2012).

8. Robert Karen provides an engaging and clear account of attachment theory's development in the latter half of the twentieth century in his book *Becoming Attached* (1994).

9. In his somewhat iconoclastic study, Eric Klinenberg suggests that people the world over prefer to live alone, provided they have the means, and access to sufficient social services, to do so without material fears (2012).

10. Much that frustrates about contemporary art stems from so many artists' impulse to emphasize their autonomy by minimizing the degree to which they use a shared language: of images, of a musical scale, of any code that enables the rest of us to grasp what they are "saying." (Lévi-Strauss pointed out the difficulties such avoidance of codes entailed in the case of "music of the concrete" in his "Overture" to *The Raw and the Cooked*, 1969, 23–26.) A music critic, unfortunately I can't recall who, wrote of classical music fans feeling "jilted" by twentieth-century composers, a comment that captures perfectly my sense, as a lover of classical music, of an attachment betrayed by dint of this refusal on the part of most contemporary composers to use a language I can apprehend.

11. I have written about my use of these (and other) films in undergraduate teaching in Keeler 2013.

12. His restatement of the matter, though, makes it more resonant: "born from one or born from two? born from different or born from same?" (Lévi-Strauss 1995, 434).

13. It is a mark of the filmmakers' egalitarian commitments that the film includes a sympathetic portrait of a gay male character. Unsurprisingly, however, he is a secondary figure in the plot, and the actor who plays him is less physically attractive than the principal characters. Degrees of physical attractiveness always indicate where a commercial film's makers want us to invest our attention and concern.

14. The film was released with various subtitles, and in various versions, in different countries. See https://en.wikipedia.org/wiki/Ong-Bak:_Muay_Thai_Warrior.

15. To anyone familiar with the Javanese shadow play tradition, or with Benedict Anderson's essay about it (Anderson 1965), the affinities between the fights in *Ong-Bak* and the fight between the refined Arjuna and the uncouth Buta Cakil, which appears in every performance of the genre, are obvious.

16. I examined these issues—conflicting desires to make use of youthful masculine power and fear of its deployment—in Keeler 2009.

17. Films targeted specifically at female audiences often diverge from this tendency to celebrate autonomy over attachment. Films intended to become blockbusters rarely do so.

18. Dumont discusses all three of these authors on the subject of market exchange in his preface to the French translation of Polanyi's *La Grande Transformation* (Dumont 1983).

19. Susan George shows how much the concept of efficiency has been used to justify neoliberalism's assault on fairness in the late twentieth century in her "Short History of Neoliberalism" (1999).

References

Alter, Joseph. 1992. *The Wrestler's Body: Identity and Ideology in North India.* Berkeley: University of California Press.
Anderson, Benedict. 1965. *Mythology and the Tolerance of the Javanese.* Ithaca, NY: Modern Indonesia Project, Southeast Asia Program, Cornell University Department of Asian Studies.
———. 1972. "The Idea of Power in Javanese Culture." In *Culture and Politics in Indonesia,* edited by Claire Holt with the assistance of Benedict Anderson and James Siegel, 1–69. Ithaca, NY: Cornell University Press.
———. 1990a. "Further Adventures of Charisma." In *Language and Power: Exploring Political Cultures in Indonesia,* 78–93. Ithaca: Cornell University Press.
———. 1990b. "The Languages of Indonesian Politics." In *Language and Power: Exploring Political Cultures in Indonesia,* 123–151. Ithaca: Cornell University Press.
———. 1991. *Imagined Communities: Reflections on the Rise and Spread of Nationalism.* 2nd ed. New York: Verso.
Appadurai, Arjun. 1984. "Is Homo Hierarchicus?" *American Ethnologist* 13 (4): 745–761.
———. 1988. "Putting Hierarchy in Its Place." *Cultural Anthropology* 3 (1): 36–49.
Aung-Thwin, Michael. 1985. *Pagan: The Origins of Modern Burma.* Honolulu: University of Hawai'i Press.
Bellah, Robert, Richard Madsen, William M. Sullivan, Ann Swidler, and Steven M. Tipton, eds. 2008. *Habits of the Heart: Individualism and Commitment in American Life.* With a new preface. Berkeley: University of California Press.
Benedict, Ruth. 1946. *The Chrysanthemum and the Sword: Patterns in Japanese Culture.* New York: New American Library.
Boellstorff, Tom. 2005. *The Gay Archipelago: Sexuality and Nation in Indonesia.* Princeton, NJ: Princeton University Press.
———. 2007. *A Coincidence of Desires: Anthropology, Queer Studies, Indonesia.* Durham, NC: Duke University Press.

Boon, James. 1977. *The Anthropological Romance of Bali: Dynamic Relations in Marriage and Caste, Politics, and Religion.* Cambridge: Cambridge University Press.
Bourdieu, Pierre. 1984. *Distinction: A Social Critique of the Judgement of Taste.* Translated by Richard Nice. Cambridge, MA: Harvard University Press.
———. 1990. *The Logic of Practice.* Translated by Richard Nice. Stanford, CA: Stanford University Press.
———. 2000. *Pascalian Meditations.* Translated by Richard Nice. Cambridge: Polity Press.
———. 2001. *Masculine Domination.* Translated by Richard Nice. Cambridge: Polity Press.
Brac de la Perrière, Bénédicte. 1989. *Les Rituels de Possession en Birmanie: du Culte d'Etat aux Cérémonies Privées.* Paris: Editions Recherches sur les civilisations.
———. 2005. "The Taungbyoun Festival: Locality and Nation-Confronting in the Cult of the 37 Lords." Translated by Annabelle Dolidon. In *Burma at the Turn of the 21st Century,* edited by Monique Skidmore, 65–89. Honolulu: University of Hawai'i Press.
———. 2009. *Sur les Rives de l'Irrawaddy. Essai d'Interprétation de la Possession d'Esprit dans la Religion Birmane.* Thèse d'habilitation à diriger des recherches. Paris: EHESS.
Brac de la Perrière, Bénédicte, Guillaume Rozenberg, and Alicia Turner, eds. 2014. *Champions of Buddhism: Weikza Cults in Contemporary Burma.* Singapore: NUS Press.
Braun, Erik. 2013. *The Birth of Insight: Meditation, Modern Buddhism, and the Burmese Monk Ledi Sayadaw.* Chicago: University of Chicago Press.
Brenner, Suzanne. 1995. "Why Women Rule the Roost: Rethinking Javanese Ideologies of Gender and Self-Control." In *Bewitching Women, Pious Men: Gender and the Body Politics in Southeast Asia,* edited by Aihwa Ong and Michael Peletz, 19–50. Berkeley: University of California Press.
Brown, Sid. 2001. *The Journey of One Buddhist Nun: Even Against the Wind.* Albany: State University of New York Press.
Bunnag, Jane. 1973. *Buddhist Monk, Buddhist Layman: A Study of Urban Monastic Organization in Central Thailand.* Cambridge: Cambridge University Press.
Cannell, Fenella. 1995. "The Power of Appearances: Beauty, Mimicry and Transformation in Bicol." In *Discrepant Histories: Translocal Essays on Filipino Culture,* edited by Vincente Rafael, 223–258. Philadelphia, PA: Temple University Press.
———. 1999. *Power and Intimacy in the Christian Philippines.* Cambridge: Cambridge University Press.
Carbine, Jason A. 2011. *Sons of the Buddha: Continuities and Ruptures in a Burmese Monastic Tradition.* Berlin: De Gruyter.

Carbonnel, Laure. 2009. "On the Ambivalence of Female Monasticism in Theravada Buddhism." *Asian Ethnology* 68 (2): 265–282.
de Certeau, Michel. 1984. *The Practice of Everyday Life*. Translated by Steven Rendall. Berkeley: University of California Press.
Chodorow, Nancy. 1978. *The Reproduction of Mothering: Psychoanalysis and the Sociology of Gender*. Berkeley: University of California Press.
Coedès, George. 1968. *The Indianized States of Southeast Asia*. Translated by Susan Brown Cowing. Honolulu: East-West Center Press.
Collins, Randall. 1992. "Women and the Production of Status Cultures." In *Cultivating Differences: Symbolic Boundaries and the Making of Inequality*, edited by Michèle Lamont and Marcel Fournier, 213–231. Chicago: University of Chicago Press.
Collins, Steven. 1998. *Nirvana and Other Buddhist Felicities*. Cambridge: Cambridge University Press.
Connell, Raewyn. 1995. *Masculinities*. Cambridge: Polity Press.
Connell, Raewyn, and James W. Messerschmidt. 2005. "Hegemonic Masculinity: Rethinking the Concept." *Gender and Society* 19 (6): 829–859.
Cook, Nerida, and Peter A. Jackson. 1999. "Introduction: Desiring Constructs: Transforming Sex/Gender Orders in Twentieth-Century Thailand." In *Genders and Sexualities in Modern Thailand*, edited by Nerida Cook and Peter A. Jackson, 1–27. Chiang Mai: Silkworm Books.
Day, Tony. 2002. *Fluid Iron: State Formation in Southeast Asia*. Honolulu: University of Hawai'i Press.
Derné, Steve. 2000. *Movies, Masculinity, and Modernity: An Ethnography of Men's Filmgoing in India*. Westport, CO: Greenwood Press.
Dirks, Nicholas. 1987. "Introduction: The Study of State and Society in India." In *The Hollow Crown: Ethnohistory of an Indian Kingdom*, 3–16. Cambridge: Cambridge University Press.
Dittmer, Lowell. 2008. "Burma vs. Myanmar: What's in a Name?" *Asian Survey* 48 (6): 885–888.
Douglas, Mary. 1966. *Purity and Danger: An Analysis of Concepts of Pollution and Taboo*. New York: Praeger.
Dumont, Louis. 1977. *From Mandeville to Marx: The Genesis and Triumph of Economic Ideology*. Chicago: University of Chicago Press.
———. 1980. *Homo Hierarchicus: The Caste System and Its Implications*. Translated by Mark Sainsbury, Louis Dumont, and Basia Gulati. Chicago: University of Chicago Press.
———. 1983. "Préface." In *La Grande Transformation: Aux Origines Politiques et Economiques de Notre Temps*, by Karl Polanyi. Translated by C. Malamoud and M. Angeno. Paris: Gallimard.
———. 1986. *Essays on Individualism: Modern Ideology in Anthropological Perspective*. Chicago: University of Chicago Press.

———. 1994. *German Ideology: From France to Germany and Back*. Chicago: University of Chicago Press.

Durkheim, Emile. 1915. *The Elementary Forms of Religious Life*. Translated by Joseph Ward Swain. New York: Free Press.

Eberhardt, Nancy. 2006. *Imagining the Course of Life: Self-Transformation in a Shan Buddhist Community*. Honolulu: University of Hawai'i Press.

Ehrlich, Daniel. 2012. *Backstage Mandalay: The Netherworld of Burmese Performing*. Bangkok: River Books.

Embree, John. 1939. *Suye Mura: A Japanese Village*. Chicago: University of Chicago Press.

———. 1950. "Thailand: A Loosely Structured Social System." *American Anthropologist* 52 (2): 181–193. Reprinted in Evers, ed. 1969, 3–15.

Errington, J. Joseph. 1988. *Structure and Style in Javanese: A Semiotic View of Linguistic Etiquette*. Philadelphia: University of Pennsylvania Press.

———. 1998. *Shifting Languages: Interaction and Identity in Javanese Indonesia*. Cambridge: Cambridge University Press.

Errington, Shelly. 1989. *Meaning and Power in a Southeast Asian Realm*. Princeton, NJ: Princeton University Press.

———. 1990. "Recasting Sex, Gender, and Power: A Theoretical and Regional Overview." In *Power and Difference: Gender in Island Southeast Asia*, edited by Jane Monnig Atkinson and Shelly Errington, 1–58. Stanford, CA: Stanford University Press.

Evers, Hans-Dieter. 1969a. "Introduction." In *Loosely Structured Social Systems: Thailand in Comparative Perspective*, edited by Hans-Dieter Evers, 1–2. Association for Asian Studies Cultural Report Series No. 17. New Haven, CT: Yale University Southeast Asia Studies.

———, ed. 1969b. *Loosely Structured Social Systems: Thailand in Comparative Perspective*. Association for Asian Studies Cultural Report Series No. 17. New Haven, CT: Yale University Southeast Asia Studies.

Ewing, Katherine P. 1990. "The Illusion of Wholeness: Culture, Self, and the Experience of Inconsistency." *Ethos* 18 (3): 251–278.

Fajans, Jane. 2006. "Autonomy and Relatedness: The Tension between Individuality and Sociality." *Critique of Anthropology* 26 (1): 103–119.

Ferguson, John. 1978. "The Quest for Legitimation by Burmese Monks and Kings: The Case of the Shwegyin Sect (19th–20th Centuries)." In *Religion and Legitimation of Power in Thailand, Laos, and Burma*, edited by Bardwell Smith, 66–86. Chambersburg, PA: Anima Books.

Faure, Bernard. 1998. *The Red Thread: Buddhist Approaches to Sexuality*. Princeton, NJ: Princeton University Press.

Geertz, Clifford. 1973. *The Interpretation of Cultures*. New York: Basic Books.

———. 1980. *Negara: The Theatre State in Nineteenth-Century Bali*. Princeton, NJ: Princeton University Press.

Geertz, Hildred. 1975. *Kinship in Bali*. Chicago: University of Chicago Press.

George, Susan. 1999. "A Short History of Neoliberalism." Presented at the Conference on Economic Sovereignty in a Globalising World, Bangkok, March 24–26, 1999. https://www.tni.org/en/article/short-history-neoliberalism.

Gibson, Thomas, and Kenneth Sillander, eds. 2011. *Anarchic Solidarity: Autonomy, Equality, and Fellowship in Southeast Asia*. New Haven, CT: Yale University Southeast Asia Studies.

Gilbert, David. 2013. "Categorizing Gender in Queer Yangon." *Sojourn: Journal of Social Issues in Southeast Asia* 28 (2): 241–271.

Gombrich, Richard. 1988. *Theravada Buddhism: A Social History from Ancient Benares to Modern Colombo*. New York: Routledge & Kegan Paul.

Gombrich, Richard, and Gananath Obeyesekere. 1988. *Buddhism Transformed: Religious Changes in Sri Lanka*. Princeton, NJ: Princeton University Press.

Gravers, Mikael. 2012. "Monks, Morality and Military: The Struggle for Moral Power in Burma—and Budddhism's Uneasy Relation with Lay Power." *Contemporary Buddhism* 13 (1): 1–33.

Gutschow, Kim. 2004. *Being a Buddhist Nun: The Struggle for Enlightenment in the Himalayas*. Cambridge, MA: Harvard University Press.

Halberstam, Judith. 1998. *Female Masculinity*. Durham, NC: Duke University Press.

Harding, Susan. 2000. *The Book of Jerry Falwell: Fundamentalist Language and Politics*. Princeton, NJ: Princeton University Press.

Hardy, Simon. 1998. *The Reader, the Author, His Woman, and Her Lover: Soft-Core Pornography and Heterosexual Men*. London: Cassell.

Harriden, Jessica. 2012. *The Authority of Influence: Women and Power in Burmese History*. Copenhagen: NIAS Press.

Harvey, G. E. 1967. *History of Burma*. New York: Octagon Books.

Hayashi, Yukio. 2003. *Practical Buddhism among the Thai-Lao: Religion in the Making of Region*. Kyoto: Kyoto University Press.

Heyes, Cressida. 1997. "Anti-Essentialism in Practice: Carol Gilligan and Feminist Philosophy." *Hypatia* 12 (3): 142–163.

Hinton, Alexander. 2005. *Why Did They Kill?: Cambodia in the Shadow of Genocide*. Berkeley: University of California Press.

Hollan, Douglas. 2012. "On the Varieties and Particularities of Cultural Experience." *Ethos* 40 (1): 37–53.

Houtman, Gustaaf. 1999. *Mental Culture in Burmese Crisis Politics: Aung San Suu Kyi and the National League for Democracy*. ILCAA Study of Languages and Cultures of Asia and Africa Monograph Series No. 33. Tokyo University of Foreign Studies, Institute for the Study of Languages and Cultures of Asia and Africa.

Howe, Leo. 2001. *Hinduism and Hierarchy in Bali*. Santa Fe, NM: School of American Research.

Ikeya, Chie. 2005. "The 'Traditional' High Status of Women in Burma: A Historical Reconsideration." *Journal of Burma Studies* 10:51–81.

———. 2011. *Refiguring Women, Colonialism, and Modernity in Burma.* Honolulu: University of Hawai'i Press.

Jackson, Peter A. 1997. "Thai Research on Male Homosexuality and Transgenderism and the Cultural Limits of Foucauldian Analysis." *Journal of the History of Sexuality* 8 (1): 52–85.

———. 1999. "Tolerant but Unaccepting: The Myth of a Thai 'Gay Paradise.'" In *Genders and Sexualities in Modern Thailand,* edited by Peter A. Jackson and Nerida M. Cook, 226–242. Chiang Mai: Silkworm Books.

———. 2004. "The Thai Regime of Images." *Sojourn: Journal of Social Issues in Southeast Asia* 19 (2): 181–218.

Jackson, Peter A., and Gerard Sullivan. 1999. "A Panoply of Roles: Sexual and Gender Diversity in Contemporary Thailand." *Journal of Gay and Lesbian Social Services* 9 (2–3): 1–27.

Johnson, Mark. 1997. *Beauty and Power: Transgendering and Cultural Transformation in the Southern Philippines.* New York: Berg.

Jordt, Ingrid. 2007. *Burma's Mass Lay Meditation Movement: Buddhism and the Cultural Construction of Power.* Athens: Ohio University Press.

Kamala Tiyavanich. 1997. *Forest Recollections: Wandering Monks in Twentieth-century Thailand.* Honolulu: University of Hawai'i Press.

Kapferer, Bruce. 2010. "Louis Dumont and a Holist Anthropology." In *Experiments in Holism: Theory and Practice in Contemporary Anthropology,* edited by Ton Otto and Nils Bubandt, 187–208. Malden, MA: Wiley-Blackwell.

———. 2012. *Legends of People, Myths of State: Violence, Intolerance, and Political Culture in Sri Lanka and Australia.* Revised edition. New York: Berghahn Books. First published 1988.

Karen, Robert. 1994. *Becoming Attached: Unfolding the Mystery of the Infant-Mother Bond and Its Impact on Later Life.* New York: Warner Books.

Kawanami, Hiroko. 2013. *Renunciation and Empowerment of Buddhist Nuns in Myanmar-Burma: Building a Community of Female Faithful.* Leiden: Brill.

Kearney, Patrick. nd. "Still Crazy After All These Years: Why Meditation Isn't Psychotherapy." http://www.buddhanet.net/crazy.htm.

Keeler, Ward. 1975. "Musical Encounter in Java and Bali." *Indonesia* 19:85–126.

———. 1983. "Shame and Stagefright in Java." *Ethos* 11 (3): 152–165.

———. 1984. *Javanese: A Cultural Approach.* Athens: Ohio University Center for International Studies, Monograph 69.

———. 1987. *Javanese Shadow Plays, Javanese Selves.* Princeton, NJ: Princeton University Press.

———. 1990. "Speaking of Gender in Java." In *Power and Difference: Gender in Island Southeast Asia,* edited by Jane Atkinson and Shelly Errington, 127–152. Stanford, CA: Stanford University Press.

———. 1993. "Book Review: *Managing Turbulent Hearts,* by Unni Wikan." *American Ethnologist* 21 (2): 434–435.

———. 1997. "Fighting for Democracy on a Heap of Jewels: Mandalay in 1988." Centre of Southeast Asian Studies Working Paper No. 102. Clayton, VIC: Monash University Centre of Southeast Asian Studies.

———. 2002. "Durga Umayi and the Postcolonialist Dilemma." In *Clearing a Space: Postcolonial Readings of Modern Indonesian Literature,* edited by Keith Foulcher and Tony Day, 349–369. Leiden: KITLV Press.

———. 2005. "'But Princes Jump!': Performing Masculinity in Mandalay." In *Burma at the Turn of the 21st Century,* edited by Monique Skidmore, 206–228. Honolulu: University of Hawai'i Press.

———. 2009. "What's Burmese about Burmese Rap?: Why Some Expressive Forms Go Global." *American Ethnologist* 36 (1): 2–19.

———. 2010. *Burma: Classical Theatre Music.* Two-CD set. Produced by Ward Keeler. Liner notes by Ward Keeler. Archives Internationales de Musique Populaire, Musée d'Ethnographie, Geneva. AIMP XCVI-XCVII (VDE CD-1317/1318).

———. 2013. "Engaging Students with Fiction, Memoirs, and Film." In *Novel Approaches to Anthropology: Contributions to Literary Anthropology,* edited by Marilyn Cohen, 227–244. Lanham, MD: Lexington Books.

———. 2015. "Shifting Transversals: Trans Women's Move from Spirit Mediumship to Beauty Work in Mandalay." *Ethnos: Journal of Anthropology.* doi:10.1080/00141844.2014.992930.

———. nd.a. *Becoming Detached.* Unpublished book manuscript.

———. nd.b. "Comparative Queer Southeast Asian Studies." Unpublished article.

Kersten, J. 1984. *Bahasa Bali.* Ende, Flores: Nusa Indah.

Keyes, Charles. 1984. "Mother or Mistress but Never a Monk: Buddhist Notions of Female Gender in Rural Thailand." *American Ethnologist* 11 (2): 223–241.

Kirsch, A. Thomas. 1969. "Loose Structure: Theory or Description?" In *Loosely Structured Social Systems: Thailand in Comparative Perspective,* edited by Hans-Dieter Evers, 39–60. Association for Asian Studies Cultural Report Series No. 17. New Haven, CT: Yale University Southeast Asia Studies.

Klinenberg, Eric. 2012. *Going Solo: The Extraordinary Rise and Surprising Appeal of Living Alone.* New York: Penguin Books.

Kondo, Dorinne. 1990. *Crafting Selves: Power, Gender, and Discourses of Identity in a Japanese Workplace.* Chicago: University of Chicago Press.

Kornfield, Jack. nd. "Even the Best Meditators Have Old Wounds to Heal." http://www.buddhanet.net/psymed1.htm.

Kukrit Pramoj. 1998. *Four Reigns.* Translated by Tulachandra. Chiang Mai: Silkworm Books.

Leach, Edmund. 1968. "Book Review: *Burmese Supernaturalism,* by Melford Spiro." *Pacific Affairs* 41 (2): 297–298.

Lehmann, F. K. 1998. "Book Review: *Burmese Supernaturalism,* by Melford Spiro." *Anthropos* 93 (4–6): 643–645.

Leider, Jacques. 2013. "Rohingya: The Name, the Movement, the Quest for Identity." In *Nation Building in Myanmar*, 204–255. Yangon: Myanmar EGRESS/Myanmar Peace Center.
Lévi-Strauss, Claude. 1955. "The Structural Study of Myth." *Journal of American Folklore* 68 (270): 428–444.
———. 1969. *The Raw and the Cooked*. Translated by John and Doreen Weightman. New York: Harper and Row.
Lintner, Bertil. 1990. *Outrage: Burma's Struggle for Democracy*. London: White Lotus.
Lovejoy, Arthur O. 1964. *The Great Chain of Being: A Study of the History of an Idea*. Cambridge, MA: Harvard University Press.
Lubeigt, Guy. 2012. *Nay Pyi Taw, une Résidence Royale pour l'Armée Birmane*. Bangkok: IRASEC-Les Indes Savantes.
Luhrmann, Tanya. 2012. *When God Talks Back: Understanding the American Evangelical Relationship with God*. New York: Alfred A. Knopf.
Lutz, Catherine A., and Jane L. Collins. 1993. *Reading National Geographic*. Chicago: University of Chicago Press.
Marshall, Andrew MacGregor. 2014. *A Kingdom in Crisis: Thailand's Struggle for Democracy in the Twenty-First Century*. London: Zed Books.
Mauss, Marcel. 1990. *The Gift: The Form and Reason for Exchange in Archaic Societies*. Translated by W. D. Halls. New York: Routledge.
McDaniel, Justin. 2011. *The Lovelorn Ghost and the Magical Monk: Practicing Buddhism in Modern Thailand*. New York: Columbia University Press.
———. 2013. "Manuscripts and Monastic Education: Textual Anthropology in Laos and Thailand." Oral presentation at the First Workshop in the Ateliers Anthropologie Comparée du Bouddhisme 2013–2014: le Champ Religieux, organized by Bénédicte Brac de la Perrière and Nicholas Sihlé, December 20, 2013.
Mendelson, E. Michael. 1975. *Sangha and State in Burma: A Study of Monastic Sectarianism and Leadership*. Edited by John Ferguson. Ithaca: Cornell University Press.
Merrison, Lindsey. 2001. *Friends in High Places*. DVD. Watertown, MA: Documentary Education Resources.
Morris, Rosalind. 1994. "Three Sexes and Four Sexualities: Redressing the Discourses on Gender and Sexuality in Contemporary Thailand." *positions* 2 (1): 15–43.
Mulder, Nils. 1969. "Origin, Development, and Use of the Concept of 'Loose Structure' in Literature about Thailand: An Evaluation." In *Loosely Structured Social Systems: Thailand in Comparative Perspective,* edited by Hans-Dieter Evers, 16–24. Association for Asian Studies Cultural Report Series No. 17. New Haven, CT: Yale University Southeast Asia Studies.

Myanmar Language Commission. 1998. *Myanmar–English Dictionary*. Fifth printing. Yangon: Department of the Myanmar Language Commission, Ministry of Education, Union of Myanmar.

Nash, Manning. 1965. *The Golden Road to Modernity: Village Life in Contemporary Burma*. New York: Wiley.

Ni Ni Myint. 2002. *The Status of Myanmar Women*. Myanmar: Universities Historical Research Centre.

Nu Nu Yi. 2008. *Smile as They Bow*. Translated by Alfred Birnaum and Thi Thi Aye. New York: Hyperion.

Ortner, Sherry. 1974. "Is Female to Male as Nature Is to Culture?" In *Woman, Culture and Society*, edited by Michelle Rosaldo and Louise Lamphere, 67–87. Stanford, CA: Stanford University Press.

Pascoe, C.J., and Tristan Bridges, eds. 2016. *Exploring Masculinities: Identity, Inequality, Continuity, and Change*. New York: Oxford University Press.

Pattana Kitiarsa. 2011. *Magic, Monks, and Amulets: Thai Popular Buddhism Today*. Seattle: University of Washington Press.

Peletz, Michael. 2006. "Transgenderism and Gender Pluralism in Southeast Asia since Early Modern Times." *Current Anthropology* 47 (2): 309–340.

———. 2009. *Gender Pluralism: Southeast Asia since Early Modern Times*. New York: Routledge.

Perreira, Todd LeRoy. 2012. "Whence Theravāda? The Modern Genealogy of an Ancient Term." In *How Theravāda is Theravāda? Exploring Buddhist Identities*, edited by Peter Skilling, Jason A. Carbine, Claudio Cicuzza, and Santi Pakdeekham, 443–571. Chiang Mai: Silkworm Books.

Phillips, Herbert P. 1965. *Thai Peasant Personality: The Patterning of Interpersonal Behavior in the Village of Bang Chan*. Berkeley: University of California Press.

———. 1969 "The Scope and Limits of the 'Loose Structure' Concept." In *Loosely Structured Social Systems: Thailand in Comparative Perspective*, edited by Hans-Dieter Evers, 25–38. Association for Asian Studies Cultural Report Series No. 17. New Haven, CT: Yale University Southeast Asia Studies.

Piker, Steven. 1969. "'Loose Structure' and the Analysis of Thai Social Organization." In *Loosely Structured Social Systems: Thailand in Comparative Perspective*, edited by Hans-Dieter Evers, 61–76. Association for Asian Studies Cultural Report Series No. 17. New Haven, CT: Yale University Southeast Asia Studies.

Piliavsky, Anastasia. 2014. "India's Demotic Democracy and Its Depravities." In *Patronage as Politics in South Asia*, edited by Anastasia Piliavsky, 154–175. Cambridge: Cambridge University Press.

Polanyi, Karl. 1944 (1957). *The Great Transformation: The Economic and Political Transformation of Our Time*. Boston: Beacon Press.

Powers, John. 2009. *A Bull of a Man: Images of Masculinity, Sex, and the Body in Indian Buddhism.* Cambridge, MA: Harvard University Press.

Pye, Lucian W. 1985. *Asian Power and Politics: The Cultural Dimensions of Authority.* Cambridge, MA: Harvard University Press.

Radway, Janice. 1984. *Reading the Romance: Women, Patriarchy, and Popular Literature.* Chapel Hill: University of North Carolina Press.

Reed, Betsy, and Katha Pollitt. 2015. "Spreading Feminism Far and Wide: Straight Talk About Essentialism, Sexism, Leaning In and Speaking Out." *The Nation,* April 6, 2015.

Reid, Anthony. 1988. *Southeast Asia in the Age of Commerce: 1450–1680. Volume 1: The Land Below the Winds.* New Haven, CT: Yale University Press.

Reynolds, Craig. 1995. "A New Look at Old Southeast Asia." *Journal of Asian Studies* 54 (2): 419–446.

Rio, Knut, and Olaf Smedal. 2009a. "Hierarchy and Its Alternatives: An Introduction of Movements of Totalization and Detotalization." In *Hierarchy: Persistence and Transformation in Social Formations,* edited by Knut Rio and Olaf Smedal, 1–63. New York: Berghahn Books.

———, eds. 2009b. *Hierarchy: Persistence and Transformation in Social Formations.* New York: Berghahn Books.

Robbins, Joel. 2009. "Conversion, Hierarchy, and Cultural Change: Value and Syncretism in the Globalization of Pentecostal and Charismatic Christianity." In *Hierarchy: Persistence and Transformation in Social Formations,* edited by Knut Rio and Olaf Smedal, 66–88. New York: Berghahn Books.

Robbins, Joel, and Jukka Siikala, eds. 2014. "Special Issue on Dumont, Values, and Contemporary Cultural Change." *Anthropological Theory* 14 (2).

Rozenberg, Guillaume. 2005. "The Cheaters: Journey to the Land of the Lottery." In *Burma at the Turn of the 21st Century,* edited by Monique Skidmore, 19–40. Honolulu: University of Hawai'i Press.

———. 2010 *Renunciation and Power: The Quest for Sainthood in Contemporary Burma.* Translated by Jessica Hackett. Monograph 59, Yale Southeast Asia Studies. New Haven, CT: Yale University Southeast Asia Studies.

———. 2011. "The Saint Who Did Not Want to Die: The Multiple Deaths of an Immortal Burmese Holy Man." Translated by Ward Keeler. *Journal of Burma Studies* 15 (1): 69–118.

———. 2015. *The Immortals: Faces of the Incredible in Burma.* Translated by Ward Keeler. Honolulu: University of Hawai'i Press.

Samuels, Jeffrey. 2010. *Attracting the Heart: Social Relations and the Aesthetics of Emotion in Sri Lankan Monastic Culture.* Honolulu: University of Hawai'i Press.

Schneider, David. 1995. *Schneider on Schneider: The Conversion of the Jews and Other Anthropological Stories. David M. Schneider as Told to Richard Handler, Edited, Transcribed, and with an Introduction by Richard Handler.* Durham, NC: Duke University Press.

Schober, Juliane. 1997. "Introduction." In *Sacred Biography in the Buddhist Tradition in South and Southeast Asia*, edited by Juliane Schober, 1–15. Honolulu: University of Hawai'i Press.

———. 2011. *Modern Buddhist Conjunctures in Myanmar: Cultural Narratives, Colonial Legacies, and Civil Society.* Honolulu: University of Hawai'i Press.

Scott, James C. 1990. *Domination and the Arts of Resistance: Hidden Transcripts.* New Haven, CT: Yale University Press.

———. 2009. *The Art of Not Being Governed: An Anarchist History of Upland Southeast Asia.* New Haven, CT: Yale University Press.

Scott, Joan. 1988. "Deconstructing Equality-versus-Difference: Or, the Uses of Poststructuralist Theory for Feminism." *Feminist Studies* 14 (1): 32–50.

Siegel, James. 1986. *Solo in the New Order: Language and Hierarchy in an Indonesian City.* Princeton, NJ: Princeton University Press.

Skilling, Peter, Jason A. Carbine, Claudio Cicuzza, and Santi Pakdeekham, eds. 2012. *How Theravāda Is Theravāda? Exploring Buddhist Identities.* Chiang Mai: Silkworm Books.

Smith, Bardwell, ed. 1978. *Religion and Legitimation of Power in Thailand, Laos, and Burma.* Chambersburg, PA: Anima Books.

Spiro, Melford. 1978. *Burmese Supernaturalism.* Philadelphia, PA: Institute for the Study of Human Issues.

———. 1982. *Buddhism and Society: A Great Tradition and Its Burmese Vicissitudes.* Berkeley: University of California Press.

———. 1992. *Anthropological Other or Burmese Brother: Studies in Cultural Analysis.* New Brunswick, NJ: Transaction Publishers.

Supiot, Alain. 2005. *Homo Juridicus: Essai sur la Fonction Anthropologique du Droit.* Paris: Éditions du Seuil.

Tambiah, Stanley. 1984. *The Buddhist Saints of the Forest and the Cult of Amulets: A Study in Charisma, Hagiography, Sectarianism, and Millennial Buddhism.* Cambridge: Cambridge University Press.

Tcherkézoff, Serge. 2009. "Hierarchy Is Not Inequality—in Polynesia, for Instance." In *Hierarchy: Persistence and Transformation in Social Formations*, edited by Knut Rio and Olaf Smedal, 299–329. New York: Berghahn Books.

Thant Myint-U. 2006. *The River of Lost Footsteps: Histories of Burma.* New York: Farrar, Straus, and Giroux.

Tharaphi Than. 2014. *Women in Modern Burma.* London: Routledge.

Tin U, U. 2011. "Some Endearing Aspects of Our Country." *Today*, July, 2011.

Tucker, Robert C., ed. 1978. *The Marx-Engels Reader.* Second edition. New York: W. W. Norton & Company.

Turner, Alicia. 2014. *Saving Buddhism: The Impermanence of Religion in Colonial Burma.* Honolulu: University of Hawai'i Press.

Wacquant, Loïc. 2004. *Body and Soul: Notebooks of an Apprentice Boxer.* New York: Oxford University Press.

Wagner, Peter. 2007. "Modernity: One or Many?" In *The Blackwell Companion to Sociology*, edited by Judith E. Blau, 30–42. Malden, MA: Blackwell Publishing.

Warner, Marina. 1995. *From the Beast to the Blonde: On Fairy Tales and Their Tellers*. New York: Farrar, Straus, and Giroux.

Weber, Max. 1947. *The Theory of Social and Economic Organization*. Edited by Talcott Parsons. Translated by A. M. Henderson and Talcott Parsons. New York: The Free Press.

———. 1958a. *The Protestant Ethic and the Spirit of Capitalism*. Translated by Talcott Parsons. New York: Charles Scribner's Sons.

———. 1958b. *The Religion of India: The Sociology of Hinduism and Buddhism*. Translated by Hans H. Gerth and Don Martindale. Glencoe, IL: Free Press.

———. 2004. "The 'Objectivity' of Knowledge in Social Science and Social Policy." Translated by Keith Tribe. In *The Essential Weber*, edited by S. Whimster, 359–404. London: Routledge.

Wikan, Unni. 1990. *Managing Turbulent Hearts: A Balinese Formula for Living*. Chicago: University of Chicago Press.

Wilson, Liz. 1996. *Charming Cadavers: Horrific Figurations of the Feminine in Indian Buddhist Hagiographic Literature*. Chicago: University of Chicago Press.

Wilson, William A. 1973. "Herder, Folklore and Romantic Nationalism." *Journal of Popular Culture* 6:819–835.

Index

abbess, 95, 245. *See also* Buddhist nuns
abbot, 36, 38–40, 82–83, 89. *See also* Buddhist monks
Abhidhamma texts, 71, 74, 164–165, 198, 301nn.15–16, 301n.18
advertising, 285–286
alchemy, 175, 177, 302n.26
alms-seeking: by monks and novices, 53, 55–58, 65, 86, 97, 104–105, 226; by nuns, 247, 294n.10
amulets, 159–160
a:nade, 145–146, 307n.3
Anderson, Benedict, 4, 118–121, 153, 297nn.7–8
anthropological work, history of comparisons in, 266–269
anyein. performance, 305n.5
apoun:, 255, 256
Appadurai, Arjun, 110
asceticism, 88–89, 201–204, 227, 261–262, 304n.7. *See also* Buddhist monks; sex and sexuality
attachments: *vs.* autonomy, 94, 128, 274–275; films on, 275–282, 311nn.14–15; gender and, 238–240, 262–263; market exchange and, 282–286; marriage as, 93, 294n.12; nuns and, 244–250; power from detachment, 152, 154–158; sociological texts on, 270–275. *See also* autonomy; relationships
attachment theory, 274
Attracting the Heart (Samuels), 295n.4
Aung Kyi, x–xi, xiii, 46, 293n.8
Aung San, ix–x
Aung San Suu Kyi, Daw, xi–xiii, 46, 287n.1, 293n.8
Australia, 26, 116, 122, 290n.4, 296n.3

authenticity, 120
The Authority of Influence (Harriden), 307n.2
autonomy: *vs.* attachments, 94, 128, 274–275; *vs.* equality, 235–236; films on, 275–282, 311nn.14–15; market exchange and, 282–286; masculinity and, 227–229; meditation and, 209–211; men and, 19–20, 26; recitations and, 40–43; renouncement as, 130–131; respect and, 227–229; sex and, 221–226; sociological texts on, 270–275; Tocqueville on, 129–130. *See also* attachments; nirvana; power

Bali, 150, 290n.6
Bama, as name, 287n.1
Bangkok, street traffic in, 60, 288n.2. *See also* Thailand
bathing, 43–44, 52, 63, 66, 306n.11
Bellah, Robert, 285
Bend It Like Beckham (BILB, film), 277–279
Benedict, Ruth, 296n.1
betel chewing and betel leaf stands, 45, 49
Bhumipol IX, King of Thailand, 115
bicycles, 5–6
black tea, 23–24. *See also* tea shops
Boellstorff, Tom, 147
Bourdieu, Pierre, 43, 120, 136, 141, 227–228, 231, 243
boys: distractions of, 79; initiation ritual for, 91–92; language study by, 65–66, 69–70; tea shops and, 24, 26. *See also* Buddhist novices; men
Brac de la Perrière, Bénédicte, 169, 170, 251
Braun, Erik, 128, 185, 191, 301n.16, 303n.1

The Brave-Hearted Will Take Away the Bride. See *Dilwale Dulhania Le Jayange* (DDLJ, film)
Brenner, Suzanne, 237–238
Buddha: diet of, 58; images of, 20, 36–37, 162, 163, 301nn.11–13; as one of Three Jewels, 17, 18; predictions of impermanence, 166; recitations for, 35, 40; sex and, 226
Buddhism: Burmese schools of, 288n.3; continuum in, 155, 159, 179, 260–265; daily recitations, 35–43; in India, 207; lent (or lenten season), 53, 293n.3; material artifacts in, 159–162, 301n.14; Pali exams, 77–81; Pali study, 65, 68–77, 92, 163; Sabbath, 39, 63, 72, 293n.6; sects of, 292n.1; on sexual activity, 224–226, 306n.14; women and, 242–244. See also Shweigyin Monastery; *vinaya*
Buddhist laypeople: cooking by, 52–53; donations by, 62, 83–84; hierarchy and, 12, 21–22; meditation by, 185–186, 207; merit and, 13, 15–16, 57; relationship with monks, 17–21, 85, 100–109, 127, 219. See also men; women
Buddhist monks: abbot of Shweigyin Monastery, 36, 38–40, 82, 89; alms-seeking by, 53, 55–58, 65, 86, 97, 104–105, 226; bathing of, 43–44, 52, 63, 66; currency and, 61, 89, 178, 217–219; donations for, 13–14, 16, 20, 67; hierarchy and, 12, 21–22; interactions and deference towards, 135–141; lottery hints by, 173–174, 300n.6; maintenance tasks of, 67–68; masculinity and role of, 212–213; motivation for advancement as, 86–92; movement of, 100–101, 296n.7; naming practice of, 293n.5; protests by, xii, 43, 57; rank and prestige of, 81–84, 91; recitations of, 35–43, 63, 163–168; relationships of, 17–21, 85, 93–109, 125–127, 219, 295nn.3–4; relative standing and, 82; residences of, 39, 51, 59–67, 294n.13; robes of, 36, 52, 66, 71, 101, 156, 301n.14; self-control of, 20, 57; sex and, 93–94, 171, 219n.9, 306n.12; social relations of, 93–109; terms for, 247. See also *dhamma* talks; Pali texts and language; *vinaya*

Buddhist novices: alms-seeking by, 53, 55–58, 65, 86, 97, 104–105, 226; housing and study of, 65–66; initiation ritual of, 91–92; recitations by, 35–39; relationships of, 97–100. See also Pali texts and language
Buddhist nuns: alms-seeking by, 247, 294n.10; ambiguous status of, 247–248, 264, 308n.14; attachment and, 244–246; charisma and support of, 308n.12; kinship ties of, 95, 248–250, 308n.16; partnerships of, 308n.10; support of, 246–247, 249, 308n.11; terms for, 247; U Dhammananda on power of abbess, 108, 153, 245, 246. See also women
A Bull of a Man (Powers), 226
Burma *vs.* Myanmar, as name, 287n.1
Burmese as ethnicity, xi
Burmese language and writing system, 65, 69, 71, 85, 287n.1. See also *other languages*
Burmese Supernaturalism (Spiro), 170

cabalistic practices, 175, 177, 178, 181, 300n.8
cafes. See tea shops
Cambodia, 109, 217, 299n.8, 301n.12
Cannell, Fenella, 147
Carbonnel, Laure, 308n.14
caste system, 110, 112, 116, 125. See also hierarchy; racial classification
Catholicism, 106, 207
celibacy. See sex and sexuality
censorship of press, xiii, 45–46, 289n.3
Chakri dynasty, 115, 221
chanting. See recitations
charisma, 118–119, 120, 181, 227, 297n.8, 308n.11
China, viii, 44, 290n.3
Chin ethnic group, ix
Chodorow, Nancy, 222
Christianity, 85, 272
Chrysanthemum and the Sword, The (Benedict), 296n.1
coffee, 47. See also tea shops
Collins, Randall, 243
Collins, Steve, 154, 300n.4, 301n.15
concentration meditation technique, 190–191
condensed milk, sweetened, 23–24

Connell, Raewyn, 212–213, 228–229, 304n.1
cooking, 46–47, 52–59, 226–227. *See also* diet
"coolness," 152, 164, 165, 167
cosmeticians, 251, 253, 254
cross-cultural comparisons, 266–269
cross-dressing. *See* trans men; trans women
cults. *See* nat cult; wei'za cult
currency: demonetization of, viii, x; exchange in tea shops, 25–26; for laundry services, 49; monks and, 61, 89, 178, 217–218, 217–219; *nat* cult and, 171. *See also* market exchange
Cyclone Nargis, xii, 165, 302n.19

da'do, 161–162
dagou:, 101, 153, 188, 246. See also *hpoun:*
Danu dialect, 85
Day, Tony, 267
death and merit, 101–102. *See also* nirvana
deferential gestures and language, 101, 135–141. *See also* relative standing
Democracy in America (Tocqueville), 129
demonetization, viii, x
Derné, Steve, 288n.2 (chap. 1)
detachment. *See* attachments; autonomy
Dhammananda, U: on abbess' power, 108, 153, 245, 246; on author's residence, 54, 58, 68; *dhamma* talks by, 18, 108; display by, 19, 48; on eating, 58, 59; gestures of deference towards, 101–102, 138; on meditation, 186–188, 194, 199, 204; money and, 84, 218; natal village and monastery of, 89–90; on natural disasters, 165, 302n.19; on *Pahtan:* recitation, 165; on Pali study, 74, 75–76, 78–79, 186–188; physical description of, 303n.3; on recitations, 39–40, 41; relationships of, 82, 96–97, 98–99, 101, 107–109; residence of, 63, 296n.8; on restless young monks, 296n.7; on sex, 219, 220; on succeeding abbot, 61, 82
Dhammasariya exams. *See* Pali texts and language
dhamma talks, 12–22; *dhamma* defined, 17, 290n.5; gender and, 19–20, 30–31, 149; merit and, 15–17; monks attending other, 291n.9; prestige through, 91; ritual protocol of, 13–15; styles and content of sermons, 17–19; summary of hierarchy in, 12, 21–22, 30–31. *See also* Buddhist monks; *specific monks*
dhamma volunteers, 164, 189, 193
dharma vs. dhamma, 290n.5
diet, 47, 57–59, 58, 202, 226, 294n.11. *See also* cooking
difference and inclusion, 114–117
Dilwale Dulhania Le Jayange (DDLJ, film), 276–278
Dirks, Nicholas, 110
Distinction (Bourdieu), 227–228
divorce, 210
donations: of food, 55–56, 104–105, 247; for monastic event, 83–84; for monks, 13–14, 16, 20; for nuns, 294n.10; to Shweigyin Monastery, 62; of technological devices, 67, 79, 103–104
Douglas, Mary, 273
Dumont, Louis: criticism against, 110, 113, 296n.2; on difference and inclusion, 114–117; on hierarchical relationships, 21, 22; *Homo Hierarchicus*, 22, 113, 114, 116, 117, 129, 130; on negative view of hierarchy, 29; on power *vs.* prestige, 110–111, 296n.4; summary of theories by, 3–4, 110–114, 131–133, 260, 288nn.4–5
Durkheim, Emile, 111–112, 130, 271, 272, 273, 310n.6

eating. *See* cooking; diet
education system: in Burma, 59, 88–89, 147–149; in US, 11–12. *See also* Pali texts and language
egalitarianism, 7–12, 26, 111–113, 117, 290n.4. *See also* hierarchy 8/8/88, xi
Elders, Jocelyn, 306n.15
Elementary Forms of the Religious Life (Durkheim), 271, 272
Embree, John, 27–28, 29
English language, 76, 287n.1, 294n.15
equality *vs.* autonomy, 235–236
Errington, Shelly, 33, 269
ethnographic style, 33–35
Evers, Hans-Dieter, 27

fairy tales, 121–122
Fajans, Jane, 310n.5
fathers, 96

feminine presentation, 214, 256–257. *See also* masculinity; trans women; women
films on autonomy and attachment, 275–282, 311nn.14–15
flooding, 7, 288n.1
food. *See* cooking; diet
food stalls, 46–47. *See also* tea shops
forest monastery, 88–89, 295n.19
Forest Recollections (Tiyavanich), 304n.7
Four Eights. *See* 8/8/88
Four Reigns (Pramoj), 305n.8
free market. *See* market exchange
From the Beast to the Blonde (Warner), 121
fundamental rights, 7–12, 290n.3. *See also* egalitarianism; hierarchy

gado bwe:, 254
"gay" men, 256, 309nn.24–26. *See also* trans women
Geertz, Clifford, 141, 144, 145, 150, 281, 304n.10
gender and gender ideology, 212–265; *dhamma* talks and, 19–20, 30–31; Dumont on, 116–117; feminine presentation, 214, 256–257; idealized stereotypes of, 237–240, 262–264; performing arts and, 214–217, 304n.2, 305nn.5–6; tea shops and, 23, 24, 291n.13, 292n.15; trans men and trans women, 250–260, 264, 309nn.24–26; Warner on fairy tales and, 121–122. *See also* masculinity; men; women
George, Susan, 311n.19
gestures and relative standing, 101, 135–141
girls, 91, 245. *See also* women
Goenka, U: about, 188, 303n.4; meditation technique and retreats by, 188–192, 194, 199–200, 201; on *sangkara*, 196; on temporality of retreats, 200
Greenblatt, Stephen, 147
green tea, 23–24, 291n.14. *See also* tea shops

Habits of the Heart (Bellah), 285
Handler, Richard, 266
Harriden, Jessica, 307n.2
Hayashi, Yukio, 295n.19, 300n.5
hegemonic masculinity, 212–213, 228–232. *See also* masculinity
hierarchy: caste system, 110, 112, 116, 125; of *dhamma* talks, 12–22, 21–22,
30–31; Dumont on (*See* Dumont, Louis); *vs.* egalitarianism, 7–8, 9–10; fundamental rights and, 7–12, 290n.3; interdependence and, 111–113, 226–229, 297n.5; racial classification, 116, 281; in religions, 271–272; sex and, 222–224; of street traffic, 5–7, 29–30; summary of, 1–4, 29–32, 124–127, 288nn.4–5; in tea shops, 2, 3, 25–26, 31; in Thai society, 29; in *wei'za* cult, 178–181. *See also* autonomy; relationships; relative standing
Hinton, Robert, 299n.8
HIV-AIDS epidemic, 254
holism. *See* individualism *vs.* holism
Homo Hierarchicus (Dumont), 22, 113, 114, 116, 117, 129, 130. *See also* Dumont, Louis
"hot" feeling, 152, 299n.1
housing. *See* residences
Houtman, Gustaaf, 293n.8, 303n.1
Howe, Leo, 290n.6, 299n.12
hpoun:, 153, 219. *See also dagou: hsayado*. *See* abbot
Htun Hmat Win, U Saw, 75–76

"The Idea of Power in Javanese Culture" (Anderson), 118
Ikeya, Chie, 231, 234–235, 238, 307n.2, 307nn.4–5
Imagined Communities (Anderson), 118, 119
The Immortals (Rozenberg), 174–182
impermanence, 195–196
inclusion and difference, 114–117
independence of Burma (1948), ix–x
India: Bollywood film on autonomy and attachment, 276–278; Buddhism in, 207; Burmese marriage with men from, 236–237, 307nn.4–5; marriage arrangements in, 288n.2 (chap. 1); tea in, 23; women's status in, 235–236. *See also* Dumont, Louis
indifference, 114–115, 130
individualism *vs.* holism, 112–113, 129–131, 297n.6. *See also* autonomy; hierarchy
Indonesia. *See* Bali; Jakarta; Java
inequality. *See* hierarchy
insight meditation technique, 190–191

interactions: language and gestures in, 101, 135–141; shame and vulnerability in, 141–146
interdependence, 111–113, 226–229, 297n.5. *See also* autonomy; kinship ties; relationships
Internet access, 48, 67
invulnerability magic, 178–181

Jackson, Peter, 256–257, 309n.21
Jakarta, 60, 288n.2
Japan: language of, 310n.4; social system in, 28, 29, 292n.17; street traffic and vehicle trade from, 289n.3
Java: filial piety in, 126; gender differences in, 215, 237–238; language in, 136; photographs and death in, 204–205; power in, 4, 118, 129, 153, 162, 166; shame in, 141
Johnson, Mark, 147
Jordt, Ingrid, 303n.1

Kachin ethnic group, ix
Kalyana, U, 87
Kapferer, Bruce, 122–124, 296n.3, 297n.12
Karen ethnic group, ix, x
kathoey, 256, 259. *See also* trans women
Kawanami, Hiroko: on ambiguous status of nuns, 247; on charisma of nuns, 308n.11; on interactions, 145–146; on kinship ties, 95, 245, 248–250, 308n.16; on partnerships of nuns, 308n.10
Keyes, Charles, 96, 308n.8
Khin Nyunt, 246
Khmer Rouge, 299n.8
kinship ties: in monasteries and monks, 86, 91, 94–97; monastic transition and, 201–202, 304n.8; of nuns, 95, 248–250, 308n.16; social organization and, 125–126; in Thailand, 27; trans women and, 257–258. *See also* interdependence; relationships
Kirsch, A. Thomas, 28, 292n.16
Kitiarsa, Pattana, 160
Klinenberg, Eric, 310n.9
Ko Htut Htun, 164
Ko Kyaw, 51, 100, 295nn.5–6
Ko Maung Kyi, 254, 255
Ko Min, 93, 102–103
Kondo, Dorinne, 292n.17

Kornfield, Jack, 303n.6
Ko Than Aung, 202–203
Ko Thet, 254, 255
Kumara, U, 74, 98–99, 106–107, 220

language: attachment and, 275; of Burma, ix, 287n.1; cultural comparisons of, 268; *dhamma* vs. *dharma*, 290n.5; and gestures in relative standing, 101, 135–141, 298n.5; hierarchy and, 294nn.17–18; monastic motivation and, 87; study of, 65–66, 69–70. See also *specific languages*
laypeople. See Buddhist laypeople
Leach, Edmund, 169
Ledi Sayadaw, 128, 185–186, 294n.11, 303n.1. *See also* meditation
Legends of People, Myths of State (Kapferer), 123
Lehmann, F. K., 169
lent (or lenten season), 53, 293n.3
Lévi-Strauss, Claude, 273, 277, 311n.10, 311n.12
lottery, 174, 300.6
lu. ahkwin. ayei:, 11
Luhrmann, Tanya, 272

magic, 159–162, 178–181
maintenance tasks, monastery, 67–68
Malaysia, 103, 217, 290n.3
Mandalay: mosquitoes in, 37; street traffic in, 5–6, 44, 288n.2; tea shops in, 23; *za'pwe:* in, 15. *See also* Shweigyin Monastery
market exchange: autonomy *vs.* attachment and, 282–286; *nats* and, 171; Sabbath and, 293n.6; tea shops and, 3, 26; Western values of, 31. *See also* currency
marriage: as attachment, 93, 294n.12; divorce, 210; in elite class, 223, 305n.8; in India, 236–237, 288n.2 (chap. 1), 307nn.4–5; *nat* cult and, 170; restrictions on women, 236, 307nn.4–5; in trans community, 309n.24
Marshall, Andrew MacGregor, 115
Marx, Karl, 3, 270–271, 288n.5
Masculinities (Connell), 212–213
masculinity, 212–232; autonomy and, 227–229; Connell on, 212–213, 304n.1; cults and, 175–176; nonnormative forms

masculinity (cont.)
of, 233–234, 250–251; *Ong-Bak* film on, 279–281; as performance, 214–217, 304n.2, 305n.6; representation of, 212–214, 229–232; sex and sexuality, 93–94, 219–227, 305n.9; Spiro on ideological stereotypes of, 307n.6; trans women and, 254–255; work and, 212, 217–219. *See also* gender and gender ideology; men; nonnormative masculinity; trans women

Ma Soe Yein Tai' monasteries, 80

masturbation, 224–225, 306n.15. *See also* sex and sexuality

material exchange, 13–14, 16, 21. *See also* market exchange

McDaniel, Justin, 160, 169

Mebaygon cult, 178–181, 182. See also *wei'za* cult

meditation, 184–211; attention and, 210–211; autonomy and, 209–211; Burmese practitioners of, 206–210, 303n.2; in continuum of power, 159, 300n.5; history of, 184, 303n.1; by laypeople, 185–186, 207; as mind-control, 193–195, 220; motivation for, 184–185, 195–206; *vs.* Pali study, 185, 187; physical fitness and, 187; retreats of, 188–193; summary of, 184–188, 261–262; techniques of, 190–192; by women, 208–209. *See also* Ledi Sayadaw; Pali texts and language

memory and meditation, 192, 194–195

men: betel chewing by, 45; cults and, 170–171, 172–173, 175–176; *dhamma* talks and, 19–20, 30, 149; "gay" men, 256, 259–260, 309nn.24–26; tea shops and, 23, 24, 26, 291n.13; trans men and trans women, 250–260, 309nn.24–26. *See also* masculinity; women

merit: access to power through, 154–155, 219; Buddhist laypeople and, 13, 15–17, 57, 101–102; Buddhist monks and, 15–17, 108–109; women and, 242–244

Messerschmidt, James W., 304n.1

methodological cultural comparisons, 267–269

military rule, x–xi, xii

military service, women in, 236

Ministry for Religious Affairs, 75, 77

miscegenation, 236–237, 307nn.4–5

modesty, physical, 298n.7

monasteries. See *specific names and types*

monastery schools, 88–89

money. *See* currency; market exchange

monks. *See* Buddhist monks

Morris, Rosalind, 256

Mother Kyaw, 254, 309n.23

mothers, 96–97, 222

motorcycles, 5–6, 288n.2

Ms. Bling, 253–254

Ms. Ruby, 253

Mulder, Niels, 28

Muslim communities, 80, 122–124, 236, 293n.6, 297n.12, 307nn.4–5

Myanmar *vs.* Burma, as name, 287n.1

na', 302n.21

na' gado, 251

naming practices, 293n.5, 294n.14

nat cult, 159, 166–174, 251, 302n.22, 302n.24, 303n.27

National League for Democracy, xii, xiii. *See also* Aung San Suu Kyi, Daw

nat pwe:, 170–171, 176, 302n.22

natural disasters, xii, 165, 302n.19

Naypyidaw, 43

Ne Win, viii–xi, 153, 206, 288n.3 (chap. 1)

New Light of Myanmar, 45

New Ma Soe Yein Monastery, 80

Ni Ni Myint, 307n.3

nirvana, 101–102, 154–155, 184–185, 260–261, 300n.4

nonnormative masculinity, 233–234, 250–251. *See also* masculinity; trans women

non-self, 147–151

Nu, U, ix, x

nunnery, 245–246

nuns. *See* Buddhist nuns

Ong-Bak (film), 279–281, 311nn.14–15

opportunity, 9, 11–12, 30

organic *vs.* mechanical solidarity, 111

Pahtan: recitation, 41, 164–168, 301n.16

Palaung ethnic group and language, 65, 85, 87, 293n.4

Pali texts and language: exams on, 77–81; *vs.* meditation, 185, 187–188; nuns' study of, 245; *Pahtan:* recitation, 164–168, 301nn.15–16; recitation and power of,

37, 163–168; study of, 65, 68–77, 92, 163; use of, 290n.5. *See also* recitations
Papua New Guinea, 292n.18, 298n.14
Pascalian Meditations (Bordieu), 141
paṭṭhāna recitation, 164–168
pedestrians, 1–2, 6–7. *See also* street traffic
Peletz, Michael, 257
performing arts and gender, 214–217, 304n.2, 305nn.5–6
Phillips, Herbert, 28–29, 135
Piker, Steven, 28
Polanyi, Karl, 3, 283, 288n.5
popular culture, 275–282
power: Anderson on, 118, 297n.8; Dumont on prestige *vs.*, 110–111, 296n.4; elective subordination and, 156–159; idealizing subalterns and, 229–231; sex and, 221–223, 225; terms for, 152–153; through Pali study, 37, 163–168; vulnerability to, 154–159. *See also* autonomy; hierarchy; relative standing
Power and Difference (Errington), 269
Powers, John, 226
Pramoj, Kukrit, 305n.8
predestination, 273
press censorship, 45–46, 289n.3, xiii
prince, masculine performance as, 215–216, 305n.6
privatization, 290n.3
prostration, 13, 21, 139, 140
protests, xii, 43, 57
public good as ideal, 290n.3
Pye Lucien, 292n.18

racial classification, 116, 281
Radway, Janice, 208–209
Rangoon: 8/8/88 violence in, xi; name of, 287n.1; traffic in, 1–2, 6, 288n.2
rapper, masculine performance of, 215, 216, 305nn.3–4
Reading the Romance (Radway), 208–209
recitations, 35–43, 63, 163–168. *See also* Pali texts and language
redistributive systems, 12–13
relationships: interdependence and, 111–113, 226–227, 297n.3; meditation and, 196–200; of monks, 16, 17–21, 93–109, 127, 219, 295nn.3–4; resistance and, 8–9; at tea shops, 25–26. *See also* attachments; hierarchy; kinship ties

relative standing: abbot succession and, 61, 82–83; deferential language and gestures, 101, 135–141, 298n.5; elective subordination, 156–159; public display and, 48; relationships and, 8–9; results of, 10–11; shame and vulnerability in, 141–146; traffic rights *vs.*, 5, 7–12. *See also* hierarchy; power
religions, hierarchy in, 271–272. *See also* Buddhism; hierarchy
renouncement, 130, 248
Renunciation and Power (Rozenberg), 159
residences, 39, 51, 59–67, 294n.13
respect, 227–229, 253–254. *See also* merit; power
rights. *See* fundamental rights
Rio, Knut, 296nn.2–3
The River of Lost Footsteps (Thant), 50
road rage, 10
Robbins, Joel, 292n.18, 298n.14
robes of monks, 36, 52, 66, 71, 101, 156, 301n.14
romantic love, 276, 279, 288n.2, 298n.13. *See also* marriage; relationships
Rozenberg, Guillaume, 149, 159, 169, 174–182, 300nn.8–9

Sabbath, Buddhist, 39, 63, 72, 293n.6
Saffron Revolution (2007), 43, 57
Sai Baba, 290n.6
samadhi meditation, 190–192
Samoa, 12
Samuels, Jeffrey, 295n.4
sangha, defined, 17. *See also* Buddhist monks
sangkara, 196
Sanskrit language, 73, 290n.5
Saw Maung, xii
Schneider, David, 266
schools. *See* education system
Scott, James, 9, 120
Sein Lwin, xi
self-fashioning, 147–151
September 18, 1988 violence, xii
sermon-preaching. *See dhamma* talks
sex and sexuality: masculinity and, 93–94, 171, 219–227, 305n.9; masturbation, 224–225, 306n.15; in trans community, 250–260, 309nn.24–26; *vinaya* on, 103, 224, 306n.12; of women, 240–242. *See also* asceticism

shame in interactions, 141–146
Shan State and ethnic group: Buddhist novices from, 85–86, 87; independence and, ix; language of, 65, 85, 217, 294n.17; protective magic and, 161, 300n.8; religion of, 85
shin byu ritual, 91–92
Shweigyin Monastery, 33–92; abbot succession at, 61, 82–83; cooking and eating at, 46, 52–59; inside compound of, 50–52; kinship ties at, 86, 91, 95, 125–126; maintenance of, 67–68; P<u>a</u>htan: recitation at, 163–168, 301n.17; Pali exams at, 77–81; Pali study at, 68–77; periphery grounds of, 43–49; recitations at, 35–43; residences in, 39, 51, 59–67, 294n.13; as sect, 292n.1; sociological analysis of, 84–86
sidewalks, 7
Siegel, James, 204–205
Sinhalese Buddhist communities, 122–124
sisters, 97
Sitagu Sayadaw, 15, 18, 128, 291n.9, 295n.6
Smedal, Olaf, 296nn.2–3
Smile as They Bow (Nu Nu Yi), 302n.25
snakes, protective tattoos against, 161, 300n.9
soccer, 23, 48, 51, 52, 67
social relationships. *See* relationships
sociological texts on autonomy and attachments, 270–275
solidarity, 41–42, 111, 117, 119, 280–281
"Some Endearing Aspects of Our Country" (Tin U), 142–144
Spiro, Melford, 169, 170, 307n.6, 308n.7
Sri Lanka, 122–124, 295n.4, 297n.12
State Law and Order Council, 124–125
street traffic: about, 1–2; horns and, 6; motorcycles, 288n.2; opportunity and, 9, 11–12, 30; policy changes in, 288n.3 (chap. 1); relative standing *vs.* rights in, 7–12; road rage, 10; summary of hierarchy in, 5–7, 29–30
"The Structural Study of Myth" (Lévi-Strauss), 277
subalterns, representation of, 229–232, 306n.17
subordination, elective, 156–159
substantive cultural comparisons, 267–269

Sullivan, Gerard, 256–257
Suye Mura: A Japanese Village (Embree), 28

tai'kya', 36
tai'ou', 36, 61
Tambiah, Stanley, 29, 159, 169
Tamil Hindu communities, 122–124
tattoos, 160–161, 300n.9
Tcherkézoff, Serge, 12
tea shops, 2–3, 23–26, 31, 46–49, 291n.13, 292n.15
Thailand: amulets in, 159–160; Burmese work permits in, 217; Chakri dynasty, 115, 221; gender presentation in, 256–257, 259; hierarchy of monasteries in, 295n.19; kinship in, 27; martial arts film from, 279–281; practicing Buddhism in, 300n.5, 301n.18, 308n.15; recitations in, 41; social system of, 27–29; street traffic of, 60, 288n.2; unofficial trade with, viii
"Thailand: A Loosely Structured Social System" (Embree), 27–28
Than, Tharaphi, 234–235, 236, 307nn.2–4
Than Shwe, xii
Thant Myint-U, 50
Tharana, U: about, 64; Pali study and, 73–74, 77, 79–80; relationships of, 100, 103, 105–106
Thatcher, Margaret, 113, 297n.5
Thein Sein, xii–xiii, 46, 206
Theravada Buddhism, 288n.3. *See also* Buddhism
Thibaw, King of Burma, 115, 149
Three Jewels, 17, 18, 37. *See also* Buddha; *dhamma* talks; sangha
Thudamma Buddhism, 292n.1
Time in Asia (magazine), 80
Tin U, U, 142–144, 307n.3
tipping waiters, 25, 26
Tiyavanich, Kamala, 304n.7
tobacco use, 45
Tocqueville, Alexis de, 115, 116, 117, 129–130, 270, 271
Today (magazine), 142
Tonle Sap, Cambodia, 109
tourism, x, 252–253
trade, unofficial networks of, viii, 44, 290n.3
traffic. *See* street traffic

Index

trans men, 258–259
trans women, 250–258, 264, 309nn.24–26. *See also* women
Turner, Alicia, 291n.7

Union of Burma, proposed, ix–x
United States: customer service in, 292n.20; egalitarianism ideals and, 11–12; masturbation in, 306n.15; pedestrian rights in, 8, 10; physical modesty in, 298n.7; trans community in, 252
urbanization, 87–88, 90
Uttama, U, 201–202

vegetarian diet, 58, 294n.11
vehicles, 1–2, 59–60, 288n.2, 289n.3, 292n.19. *See also* street traffic; *specific types*
village monasteries, 88–89, 295n.19
vinaya: on food, 47, 58, 226; on material ownership, 61; merit and, 127; reading event at Shweigyin Monastery, 167; on sexual activity, 103, 224, 306n.12; on sports, 52; study of, 74
violent incidents: in Bali, 150; in Burma, ix, xi, xii, 115, 150; in Sri Lanka, 122–124, 297n.12
vipassana mediation, 188–192
vulnerability in interactions, 141–146

Wa Kye' Sayadaw, 89
Wa language, 85

Warner, Marina, 4, 121–122
Weber, Max, 119–120, 271, 273, 297n.8
wei'za cult, 159, 168–170, 174–182, 302n.20. *See also* asceticism
Winnie, Daw, 140
Wirathu, U, 80
women, 233–265; *anyein.* performance, 305n.5; attachments and, 238–240; autonomy and, 210, 231–232, 235–236; Buddhism and, 242–244; cross-cultural comparisons on, 268–269; *dhamma* talks and, 19, 30–31, 149; films on popular values of, 276–279; ideological stereotypes of, 237–240, 262–264, 307n.6; kinship ties and, 96–97; marriage restrictions on, 236, 307nn.4–5; meditation by, 208–209; *nat* cult and, 170–171, 172, 173, 302n.24; performing arts and, 215–217, 304n.2, 305nn.5–6; recitations by, 63; sexuality of, 240–242; status of, 234–235, 307n.3; tea shops and, 292n.15; trans men and trans women, 250–260, 309nn.24–26; Warner on fairy tales and, 121–122. *See also* Buddhist nuns; men
work and masculinity, 212, 217–219

Yangon, as name, 287n.1. *See also* Rangoon

za'pwe:, 15, 18, 215–216, 253, 291n.7, 305n.3, 305n.5. See also *dhamma* talks

About the Author

Ward Keeler is associate professor of anthropology at the University of Texas at Austin. He has conducted fieldwork in Java and Bali (Indonesia) and in Burma, focusing on the performing arts, gender, and language. His earlier publications include *Javanese Shadow Plays, Javanese Selves,* which was awarded the Harry S. Benda Prize by the Association for Asian Studies; *Javanese: A Cultural Approach*; and an annotated translation of an Indonesian novel, *Durga/Umayi*, by Y. Mangunwijaya; as well as a number of articles. In addition, he has produced CDs of Burmese music: *Mahagita* (with Rick Heizman, issued by the Smithsonian) and *Burma: Classical Theatre Music* (Musée d'Ethnographie Genève). He has received fellowships from, among others, the Institute for Advanced Study (Princeton), the National Endowment for the Humanities, the Asian Cultural Council, the Asia Research Institute at the National University of Singapore, the International Institute for Asian Studies (Leiden), and the Institut d'Études Avancées de Nantes, as well as from the University of Texas. He is currently preparing textbooks for foreign learners of Burmese (with coauthor Allen Lyan) and a collection of essays on the performing arts in Southeast Asia, as well as a memoir based on his long experience in Southeast Asia.